To Sara,
Love, Mom
Christmas 2002

A Century of Mormon Cookery

Hermine B. Horman & Connie Fairbanks

Published by Distinctive Publishers
14 Sunwood Lane
Sandy, Utah 84092

1st printing	1985
2nd printing	1986
3rd printing	1987
4th & 5th printing	1988
6th printing	1989
7th & 8th printing	1990
9th printing	1991
10th printing	1992
11th printing	1994
12th printing	1995
13th printing	1996
14th printing	1997
15th printing	1998
16th printing	1999
17th printing	2000

ISBN No. 1-880328-23-2

PRINTED IN USA

DEDICATION

A CENTURY OF MORMON COOKERY is the culmination of the dreams of many magnificent cooks. However, it is especially dedicated to two very special women, Joan Ririe and Ruth Glick. They influenced the compilers to take on a project that otherwise might not have seen fruition had they not done much of the mental research it required.

Joan Harker Ririe, a native of Magrath, Alberta, Canada, was a victim of polymyasitis, a disease that partially confined her to home for many years, and to a wheel chair for three. Joan loved to cook, and poured over cookbooks like some women do novels. She enjoyed entertaining, and even though eventually confined to her chair, Hermine's children learned to "cook-at-her-knees" as it were, with her giving animated direction, criticism or approval. Though her body was restricted, her spirit could not be confined. She brought the world within her walls through notes and gifts of love. She influenced countless lives because of her strength of character. Each of us has a little more empathy for one another, love more freely, give more readily, and stand a bit taller because of her. The world and we are better because of Joan. Joan and Hermine shared life on a daily basis the last three years she lived in Salt Lake City. They planned to publish a cook book, but Joan died in 1980 before fulfilling that dream.

Ruth Adams Glick, known and loved by so many in the Salt Lake Valley for her way with foods, as well as her talent in art, tested, tried, and shared many years of cooking experience with Connie, who conveniently lived just across the street. They collaborated on many large and small catering projects and attended and taught gourmet cooking classes. Connie credits Ruth, more than any one person, for having a profound effect upon her life. She was a positive personality, and could always find the good qualities in people. She had abundant energy and directed it in the service of others.

Her family describe her in one word: majestic. Her husband, Harry, writing Ruth's life story, ended with the comment: "If food is any part of life in the world hereafter, Ruth will be preparing gourmet meals to celebrate the arrival of those she loves." Ruth died of cancer in 1983. Her daughter, Barbara Mason, illustrated this book.

Connie and Hermine have been closely associated for many years. They shared mutual friends through belonging to the same ward in Salt Lake City. Connie frequently gave food demonstrations in Relief Society and is dubbed a "gourmet." Hermine heard Connie had begun catering, so hired her to cater her daughter's wedding. It was a smashing success from the kitchen, so Hermine decided she and Connie "had bigger fish to fry." Approached on the cookbook idea, it took about a minute to secure her enthusiastic response!

Both are married and each has seven children--hence much of their happy time has been spent in the kitchen. Their recipes are a collection from "hither and yon" and represent a cross-section of the best of many tried and tested. They have endeavored to add a fresh, new approach to food through the addition of some great gourmet recipes, as well as including many of the timeless favorites.

Granted, their pioneer grandmothers knew little of many of the combinations afforded in today's kitchens, but they were knowledgeable in matters of nutrition, even with limited resources, and served delicious food for their time. They pay tribute to them for making their kitchens places of hospitality and love. If Hermine and Connie can do as well in their time, the compilation of this book will be most worthwhile.

* * * *

Connie Fairbanks   Hermine Horman

Hermine Briggs Horman was born in Magrath, Alberta, Canada. She is married to Phares T. Horman, Jr., a civil engineer from Salt Lake City.

Her talents and accomplishments are many and varied. She filled a mission to the Southern States and served on the Y.W.M.I.A. General Board. Her decided literary tendency led her into editing church publications, editing and typing countless private manuscripts, and writing articles and stories for publication. Her business career took her from the Yukon, where she worked for the U. S. Army, to Brigham Young University, where she was office manager of the Church Department of Education in charge of Seminaries and Institutes. She has also been a substitute teacher in the Salt Lake City schools, as well as in the LDS Seminaries.

Even though marriage and family came later for Hermine and Phares, they were not long in acquiring a brood of seven, including two sets of twins! A talented family, they produced and performed musical-magic programs throughout the Intermountain West. She has traveled extensively abroad, and has collected recipes along the way.

Hermine's love of people has given others occasion to speak of the "Horman-Halfway-House." Many from near and far have found a welcome there on a brief or extended visit. This same love of people has made it necessary to dispense countless meals. Her delicious preparations are always a source of satisfying delight.

Constance Edwards Fairbanks (Connie) was born in Washington, D. C., and she grew up an only child. She married R. Frank Fairbanks while he was a pre-dental student, and spent the first seven years of her marriage as a student wife. Upon graduating, they returned to Salt Lake City where he is currently in practice. They are the parents of six sons and a daughter.

Connie has been extremely active in community volunteer positions, working with unwed mothers, delinquents, welfare services for the LDS Church, president of the PTA, and president of the Salt Lake District Dental Auxiliary. She has had countless young people besides her own, live in her home. Because of her rich background working with people, it was natural that she had a latent desire to return to college. This she did in 1978. She has two bachelor degrees, and in 1984 earned the Master of Social Work degree from the University of Utah. Her professional interest is in Marriage and Family Therapy, but her hobby will always be doing the thing she enjoys most, entertaining and preparing delicious food.

TABLE OF CONTENTS

Appetizers 1

Breads 19

Salads 45

Soups 69

Vegetables 101

Pasta 137

Meats 157

Fish 201

Poultry 225

Eggs and Cheese 245

Desserts 265

Cakes 297

Cookies 325

Pies 349

Candy 373

Sauces 401

Preserves 417

Pot Pourri 433

Index 465

Notes

appetizers

Notes

ELEGANT LAST MINUTE HORS D'OEUVRE

Stem 12 firm med. size mushrooms. Stuff with 1 pkg Boursin cheese (garlic herb flavored) and dip tops in chopped parsley.

HOT STUFF

Keep a mixture of 1 c grated Parmesan cheese and 1 c mayonnaise in covered container in the frig. Just add 2 Tb frozen chopped onion to each cup of mix. Spread on melba toast or crustless bread triangles and broil till bubbly brown. Nice with lemonade.

CHEESE OLIVE SNACK

For easy hors d'oeuvres, chop 4½ oz can pitted black olives. Mix with one 3-oz pkg cream cheese and 1 oz blue cheese. Add salt and pepper to taste. Spread on crackers.

BACON WRAPPED DATES

Cut thinly sliced bacon in thirds. Wrap a third of a slice around a date and secure with a toothpick. Put under broiler until brown and crisp.

BACON & MUSHROOMS

Wrap ½ slice bacon around whole fresh mushrooms. Hold with toothpick. Place on cookie sheet and broil 5 min. Serve hot.

WARM CRAB DIP

Combine 8 oz pkg cream cheese, softened and 1 Tb milk. Add 6½ oz can flaked crab meat, 2 Tb finely chopped onions, ½ ts cream style horseradish, ¼ ts salt, dash of pepper. Blend well. Spoon into ovenproof dish sprinkle with sliced almonds. Bake 375° for 15 min.

DEVILED CHEESE FILLING

(for hor d'oeuvre size cream puffs)

1 c grated American cheese
½ ts worcestershire sauce
5-6 drops Tobasco sauce
3 Tb mayonnaise
¼ ts prepared mustard
1 ts grated onion
¼ ts celery seeds

Mix well. Makes 1 c.

BLUE CHEESE BITES

1 8-oz can buttermilk biscuits. Cut each biscuit in quarters. Grease two 8" round cake or pie pans. Put biscuits in pan touching each other. Melt ¼ c butter and 3 Tb blue cheese. Pour over biscuits. Coat well. Bake 400° for 12-15 min or until golden. Serve hot.

SHRIMP COCKTAIL

1 lg can tomato juice
1 small bottle catsup
1 c finely chopped celery
3 Tb worcestershire sauce
½ ts garlic salt
2 cans shrimp broken in small pcs
4 Tb (or less) horseradish
½ ts salt
3 Tb sugar
juice of 1 lemon

Mix and chill overnight. Makes 10 glasses.

CHEESE PUFFS

½ lb cheddar cheese grated
1 c sifted flour
¼ lb butter or margarine
1/8 ts salt

Mix together then roll into balls about size of marble. Roll each ball in sesame seeds. Place on cookie sheet and bake at 350° for 10 min. These may be made ahead and the balls frozen and baked just before you want to use them. Make them extra special by hiding a green olive inside. You could also use shrimp, bacon or other surprise.

ONION-CEREAL-NUT CRUNCH

Quick and Easy--A party Pleaser

1 envelope Lipton onion or beefy onion soup mix
6 c bite size shredded wheat, rice, or corn cereals
3/4 c dry roasted mixed nuts
6 Tb butter or margarine melted
Preheat oven to 300°
In saucepan, combine soup mix, cereals and nuts. Add butter and mix thoroughly. Turn into shallow baking pan and bake 10 min. Cool.

GLAZED ALMONDS

1 c whole blanched almonds	½ c sugar
2 Tb butter or margarine	½ ts vanilla

In heavy skillet combine whole almonds, sugar and butter. Cook stirring constantly over med. low heat till almonds are well coated and the sugar is golden brown. (About 15 min.) Stir in vanilla. Spread nuts on a large sheet of aluminum foil. Immediately separate the almonds. Sprinkle the glazed nuts lightly with the salt. Cool. Store in tightly covered container in cool dry place.

CHILI CON QUESO

Saute 1 c chopped onion in butter. Add 4 small cans green chilies (chopped), remove seeds.
Add 2 c canned tomatoes (pulp only)
Simmer 10 min. Add 2 lb cheese (1 lb Old English, 1 lb Velveeta.) Heat till cheese melts. Dip with tortilla chips.

FRUIT DIP

1 pkg (3 oz) instant vanilla pudding
1 c sour cream
¼ c frozen orange juice concentrate
Make pudding according to directions and add sour cream and orange juice. Dip fresh fruits such as strawberries, canteloupe, bananas, etc.

SOMBRERO BREAD

½ lb ground beef
½ c chopped onion
¼ c extra hot catsup
1½ ts chili powder
½ c chopped stuffed gr. olives
½ ts salt
1 8-oz can red kidney beans
½ c shredded sharp cheddar cheese
corn chips or Mexican tostados

Brown meat and ¼ c onion in skillet. Stir in catsup, chili powder and salt. Mash in beans (with liquid) Heat. Garnish with cheese, ¼ c onion and olives. Makes 1½ c. Serve hot in chafing dish as spread for corn chips or tostados.

TACO CHICKEN WINGS

½ c flour
1 1¼ oz taco seasoning mix
3 lb (about 16) chicken wings (tips removed and cut at joints)
6 Tb butter or margarine
1 c crushed corn chips

Combine flour and taco seasoning. Mix in paper or plastic bag. Add 2-3 pieces at a time and shake to coat. Melt butter in 15½ x 10½ x 1" baking dish. Place chicken in pan turning once to butter surfaces. Roll in corn chips and return to pan. Bake 350° for 40-45 min. Makes about 32 pieces.

HONEYDEW BALLS

Mix honeydew balls, blueberries and tiny snippetts of candied ginger. Pour icy gingerale over all.

CREAM PUFFS

4 eggs
1 c flour
½ ts salt
1 c boiling water
½ c butter

Combine butter, salt, water. Heat to boiling. Add flour all at once to boiling mixture. Beat vigorously till it leaves the side of pan. Remove from heat. Cool slightly. Add unbeaten eggs one at a time. Beat thoroughly after each egg. Drop by tablespoon full on cookie sheet. Bake at 400° for 30 min and 350° for 10 min. Cool. Cut off tops, fill with chicken salad or tuna salad.

CHEESE BOARD

Few foods are as popular as cheese and an attractively arranged cheese board is a special pleasure.

Keep these pointers in mind. When planning a cheese board serve a variety of cheeses. Your guests' tastes will differ, so offer one mild cheese like Jack or Edam-a Swiss type like Gruere, or Appenzell; one soft, ripened cheese, such as Brie or Camembert and one blue cheese such as Roquefort or domestic Blue. Other possibilities include cheddars spiced or flavored cheeses and cheese balls.

Avoid over-decorating the cheese board. Few things are more naturally beautiful than good cheese or plain wood. Don't crowd the board. Leave enough room between cheeses for cutting. Be sure you have enough knives. Offer 2-3 kinds of breads and crackers with the cheese. Add a bowl of grapes or pears or crisp apples as a welcome accompaniment.

MAGIC MUFFINS

Cut English muffins in half and toast. Spread each half with real butter. Sprinkle with Spice Island salad seasoning. Place under broiler until top has that bubbly-melt-in-mouth look. Cut in quarters. Serve hot.

CHEESE YUMMIES

1 lb soft butter / 1 lb grated sharp cheese
1 jar Old English cheese spread
2 Tb worcestershire sauce / 2 Tb prepared mustard

Beat well. Spread on crustless bread (triangle shape) making about 75-100 (3 loaves). Bake on cookie sheet 350-375° for 20 min.

CHINESE MEAT BALLS

2 c cubed bread
½ c milk
1 lb ground beef
½ ts onion powder
1 ts garlic salt
1 Tb soy sauce
½ ts Tobasco
½ ts Accent
1 5-oz can water chestnuts. chopped fine

Spread bread cubes with milk and press out as much milk as possible. Add bread to meat along with seasoning. Add water chestnuts. Mix well and shape into 48 tiny meat balls. Brown in 2 Tb shortening in skillet and serve warm with mustard sauce or chill sauce or in a sweet and sour sauce. A little bit of sausage added to ground beef adds nice flavor.

MARINATED MUSHROOMS

2/3 c vinegar
1 clove garlic
1 ts salt, dash pepper
1 med onion sliced
½ c oil
1 Tb sugar
2 Tb cold water
2 pts fresh mushrooms, med. size wash and stem

Mix all ingredients and refrigerate at least 8 hrs. Stir occasionally. Drain and serve.

CRAB GRAPEFRUIT

1 can crab meat, shredded
1 No. 2 can broken grapefruit and juice
3/4 bottle catsup
½ c lemon juice (about 3 lemons)
Combine well and chill. Marvelous as an appetizer!

* * * *

"Tell me what you eat, and I'll tell you what you are," said a lunch-counter philosopher.

Whereupon a meek little man, sitting a few stools away, called to the waitress: "Cancel my order for shrimp salad, please."

TOASTED MUSHROOM ROLLS

1 c chopped mushrooms
1 Tb butter
1 Tb flour
1/3 c milk
salt and pepper

Cook mushrooms in butter. Add the flour, salt and pepper and milk. Cook until thickened. Cool. Spread on thin slices of bread from which the crust has been removed. Roll up. Fasten with toothpick. Toast till light brown on both sides.

CHEESE & HAM ROLLUPS

2 3-oz cream cheese
1 ts horseradish
1 ts lemon juice
1 Tb minced dill pickle or more
1 3-oz blue cheese
2 Tb sour cream
8 thin slices boiled ham (Danish)

Mix together all ingredients but ham. Spread on ham. Roll up. Wrap in waxed paper. Chill 2 hrs or in freezer. Slice, secure with toothpicks.

CORN BEEF ROLL

12 slices Leo's or Carl Buddig Corn Beef pkgs.
1 8-oz cream cheese softened
stuffed green olives
dash worcestershire sauce
2 Tb horseradish or less
2 Tb Miracle Whip or mayonnaise

On wax paper lay beef slices three-across and 4 down overlapping edges. Beat rest of ingredients together. Spread over beef. Lay olives end to end and roll up jelly roll style. Chill thoroughly. Cut in slices. Serve alone or on small crackers.

TRISCUITS

Break triscuits in half lengthwise. Spread with peanut butter. Add a little chutney on top. Top with crumbled bacon. Bake in oven under broiler.

AVOCADO TUNA SPREAD

Stir together thoroughly 1 lg avocado (mashed)
1 can (6½ oz) chunk style tuna drained and mashed
1 c ricotta cheese
¼ c thinkly sliced green onions including green tops
1 med size sliced green pepper (seeded & chopped fine)
1½ ts garlic salt 2 ts mustard
1 ts prepared horseradish and dash of pepper
For appetizers, serve tuna mixture in a bowl with crackers and alfalfa sprouts alongside. Makes 2½ c spread. Can use for sandwiches. Makes 5.

TUNA CHEESE SPREAD

Beat 2 3-oz pkg cream cheese with 2 lb lemon juice until fluffy. Stir in 1 can (6½ oz) chunk style tuna, drained and mashed. Then add:
¼ c each pimiento, stuffed olives, sliced
¼ c chopped almonds
¼ c finely chopped sweet pickle
¼ c sliced green onions
Serve in celery sticks, wide green pepper strips or crackers. Good in sandwiches too! Makes 2½ c.

CHEESE LOAF

1 lg pkg cream cheese 1 jar blue cheese (3/4 c)
2 jars Old English sharp cheddar spread
½ ts worcestershire 1 sm grated onion
salt and pepper ½ c grated pecans
½ c parsley
Cream till blended. Make into ball. Wrap in wax paper. Put in frig. For serving roll in ½ c more parsley and ½ c more pecans. Can put half in freezer.

STUFFED DILL PICKLE

Remove ends of pickle. Hollow inside and drain dry. Fill with any cheese spread. Place in frig to set. Slice into one-half inch slices. A tasty, easy, low calorie snack for weight watchers.

HOT CLAM DIP

Hollow out a round loaf of pumpernickel bread. Arrange bite-size pieces around the following to dip:

8 oz. cream cheese
½ c sour cream
1 can drained clams
½ c grated cheese
½ ts onion salt
2 Tb mayonnaise
½ ts worcestershire sauce

Mix well and put in bake dish. Top with ¼ c grated cheese and bake 300° for 45 min.

FROZEN FRUIT COCKTAIL SLUSH
(Needs 2 qts ice)

Boil 2 c sugar and 2 c water for 5 min. Add 2 c more cold water and 3/4 c strained lemon juice. Place in freezer (stir and freeze solid).

Pour off most of juice and freeze 2 pts fruit cocktail. Half hour before serving remove from frig and place in mixing bowl. Then add 5 bananas that have been chilled and frozen blueberries. Stir in 1 qt lemon ice.

Variation: 2 qt lemon ice and 2 pkg frozen blueberries and 2 pkg frozen raspberries and 1 lg can pineapple tidbits and 6 sliced bananas. (Use any fruit, but blueberries and bananas are a must.)

RUBY GRAPEFRUIT

4 pink grapefruit
2 to 4 Tb sugar
1 pkg (10 oz) frozen raspberries with syrup

Peel and section grapefruit, saving all juice. Squeeze membrane for removing juice. Put sections and juice in bowl. Set aside. Heat raspberries until thawed. Add sugar if needed. Remove from heat and puree in blender. Strain. Pour strained juice over grapefruit. Makes 6-8 servings. Delightfully different!

* * * *

It is useless to put your best foot forward--and then drag the other.

ZIPPY PINEAPPLE SAUCE

Combine one 12 oz jar pineapple preserves (1 c)
¼ c prepared mustard and ¼ c prepared horseradish
Heat thoroughly. Makes 1½ c.

CURRANT-ORANGE SAUCE

½ c currant jelly
¼ c orange juice
1 Tb grated orange rind
3/4 ts dry mustard
½ ts ginger
1 Tb wine vinegar

Break up jelly with fork and add other ingredients. Heat thoroughly.

MUFFINS PLUS

2 Tb shredded carrots
2 Tb finely chopped celery
2 Tb finely chopped onion
1 Tb margarine or butter
1 (4½ oz) can deviled ham
2 c packaged biscuit mix
1 Tb sugar
½ c (2 oz) shredded sharp cheese
1 egg
2/3 c milk

In a small skillet cook carrot, celery and onion in butter until tender. Cool. Stir in deviled ham. Set aside. In medium bowl, combine remaining ingredients. Beat by hand for ½ min. Fill 1 3/4" greased muffin pans 2/3 full of batter. Make an indentation in center of each and fill with a little deviled ham mixture. Bake 400° for 16-18 min or till browned. Remove from pans while hot. Cool on rack. Makes 16.

* * * *

Why doesn't the Department of Internal Revenue offer us our money back if we're not satisfied?

Some people pay when due. Some pay when over-due. Some never do.

Experience is a wonderful thing, for it enables you to recognize a mistake when you make it again.

BARBECUED HAM BITES

1 c soft bread crumbs ½ c milk
1 egg 1 Tb chopped green onion
dash pepper 3 c ground cooked ham
1 (13¼ oz) can pineapple tidbits
¼ c packed brown sugar 2 Tb cornstarch
2 ts instant chicken bouillon granules
1 ts dry mustard ½ c honey
1/3 c vinegar

Combine crumbs, milk, egg, onion, and pepper in bowl. Add ham and mix thoroughly. Drain pineapple reserving syrup. Form meat mixture into tiny balls. Serve around pineapple tidbits. Place in 15½ x 10½ x 1" baking dish. Pour honey glaze over all. Bake in 375° oven for 30 min. Keep warm in chafing dish. Garnish with additional tidbits if desired. Makes about 80 meatballs. Honey glaze: Add enough water to reserved pineapple syrup to make 1½ c. In saucepan combine brown sugar, cornstarch, chicken bouillon granules and dry mustard. Stir in pineapple syrup mixture, honey and vinegar. Cook and stir till bubbly.

BLEACHED BLONDE RADISHES

2 bunches radishes, washed and trimmed
¼ ts salt ¼ c salad oil
2 c water 3/4 ts salt
1/3 c vinegar ¼ ts white pepper

Boil cleaned radishes in ¼ ts salt and 2 c water until they lose color. Do not boil more than 10 min. Drain and cool. Mix together balance of ingredients and marinate radishes overnight in frig.

* * * *

Getting an idea should be like sitting down on a pin. It should make you get up and do something about it.

Let's cross electric blankets with electric toasters and pop people out of bed.

GOT-LET CHICKEN WINGS

1 c soy sauce ½ c peanut oil
3/4 c white sugar 2 cloves garlic or garlic powder
4 lb chicken wings cut in half and tip discarded
(Push meat down to resemble little drumsticks)

1. Marinate 1 hr. Bake covered 1 to 1½ hrs until sauce sticks to chicken and chicken is tender. Make day ahead and warm slightly to serve. Can cook in electric frypan.

2. Deep Fry. Moisten Got-Let in milk and egg mixture. Dip in flour and fry in ¼ c oil or shortening over Med. heat for 12-15 min or until cooked. Serve with sauce.

3. Oven Fry. Moisten Got-Let in milk and egg mixture. Dip in a coating mix. Arrange on a greased cookie sheet in a single layer. Bake at 400° for 1 hr. Serve with sauce.

These are mainly used as hor d'oeuves but can be used as an entree with a Chinese dinner.

SAUCES FOR GOT-LET CHICKEN:

PLUM SAUCE

Heat 1 jar of plum preserves or jam to a sauce. Add white vinegar to taste. Blend in corn starch to thicken.

CHINESE SWEET & SOUR SAUCE

Have ready a paste of 2 Tb cornstarch, ½ c chicken broth and 2 Tb soy sauce. Melt in heavy pan 2 Tb butter, add 1 c chicken broth, 3/4 to 1 c diced green peppers, 6 slices canned pineapple diced. Cover and simmer for 5 min. Add cornstarch paste and the following:

½ c vinegar 1 ts salt
3/4 c pineapple juice ¼ ts ginger
½ c sugar

Simmer, stirring constantly until mixture thickens.

DILLY AVOCADO BOATS

1 med avocado halved, seeded and peeled
½ c cream style cottage cheese, drained
1 ts lemon juice ¼ ts salt
¼ ts dried dill weed few drops onion juice
3½ to 4 doz. cherry tomatoes
fresh dill sprigs
Place avocado in small mixer bowl. Beat at low speed of electric mixer till smooth. Add cottage cheese, lemon juice, salt, dill weed and onion juice. Beat till well blended. Make crosswise cut in top of tomatoes. Sprinkle inside lightly with salt. Fill with avocado mixture. Chill. Top with dill. Makes 3½-4 doz.

ARTICHOKE FRITTATA

2 jars marinated artichoke hearts (6 oz)
1 small onion finely chopped
1 clove garlic minced if desired
4 eggs
¼ c fine bread crumbs
½ ts salt
1/8 ts pepper, oregano, tobasco
½ lb sharp cheddar cheese grated
2 Tb minced parsley
Drain marinade from 1 jar. Saute marinade onion, garlic (if used) 5 min. Drain other jar. Chop artichokes fine. Beat eggs, add crumbs, salt, pepper, oregano and tobasco. Stir in cheese, parsley, chokes, onion saute. Pour into greased 7 x 11 pan. Bake 30 min. Cool. Cut into 1" squares. Can double recipe and put into 9 x 13 pan.

* * * *

The world is divided into people who do things and people who get the credit. Try, if you can, to belong to the first class. There's far less competition.

It used to be that a man who saved money was a miser; nowadays he's a wonder.

ITALIAN TUNA DIP

1 c dairy sour cream
1 (3¼ oz) can tuna drained and flaked
¼ c grated Parmesan cheese
1 hard cooked egg chopped
1 Tb lemon juice
2 ts dry Italian salad dressing mix
Sieved egg yolk
Paprika
Vegetable dippers
In small bowl combine sour cream, tuna, parmesan cheese, hard cooked egg, lemon juice and salad dressing mix. Cover and chill. Sprinkle with sieved egg yolk and paprika. Garnish with parsley sprig if desired. Serve with vegetable dippers. Makes 1½ c.

VEGETABLE DIP

1½ c sour cream
1 c finely chopped onion
½ ts tabasco
¼ ts garlic powder
½ ts pepper
2½ c mayonnaise
½ c pimento chopped fine
1 c finely chopped green pepper
1¼ ts salt
Blend well together and chill.

CHEESE CRAB DIP

3/4 lb butter
3 jars Kraft Old English Cheese
1½ lb crab meat
Heat together over hot water. Wheat crackers are good with this.

FRUIT DIP

1 8-oz pkg cream cheese
1 7-oz jar marshmallow creme
1/8 ts nutmeg
1/8 ts ginger
1 Tb lemon or orange rind
Mix till smooth. Serve with fresh fruit chunks.

CLAM-CHEESE DIP

2 pkg (3 oz) each cream cheese
1 ts onion powder
1 Tb mayonnaise
Garlic salt to taste
1 can (7½ oz) minced clams, drained
juice of 1 small lemon
1 ts worcestershire sauce

Mash cheese with fork; add onion powder, mayonnaise, garlic salt and worcestershire. Mix well. Add clams and lemon juice to cheese mixture and beat until ingredients are well blended. Makes 1 c. Serve with vegetables or chips. A family favorite for sure!

CHEESE FILLED TRIANGLES

1 8-oz pkg cream cheese
1 pt large curd cottage cheese
1 lb Fetta cheese, crumbled
½ c Parmesan cheese (grated)
4 eggs
1 lb Fillo
1 lb butter, melted

Mix all the cheese and eggs well with mixer. Cut Fillo into strips 2½" wide. Brush with melted butter. Place a ts of filling in center 1" from end. Fold one corner over in triangle. Fold in the edges about 1/3 then continue turning over the triangle to end of fillo strip. Place triangle on cookie sheet and bake at 350° for 25 min or until golden brown. Remove from pan immediately and serve hot. Makes 90 tarts.

To freeze, freeze on cookie sheet and then put in tupper ware layered. Variation: chop spinach and green onions in cheese.

* * * *

If you can't hear a pin drop, ten to one there's something wrong with your bowling.

Someone has said that the world's greatest undeveloped area lies under people's hats.

SPINACH STUFFED MUSHROOMS

40 med. fresh mushrooms
1 pkg frozen chopped spinach
3 Tb butter
½ ts salt
3 Tb Parmesan cheese
Wash mushrooms and remove stems. Stuff with cooked spinach to which has been added butter, salt & 2 Tb Parmesan cheese. Place in oven dish and sprinkle Parmesan cheese on top. Bake at 350° for 20 min.

TWIN CHEESE MOLD

2 pkg (3 oz) cream cheese) Beat together in small
1 can (4¼ oz) deviled ham)
1 ts prepared mustard) mixing bowl
Stir in:
2 c finely shredded Cheddar cheese
2 Tb chopped chives
If necessary, chill for ease in handling before shaping into ball and roll in:
3/4 c chopped macadamia nuts
Sprinkle with paprika and serve with assorted crackers. Makes about 2 c.

MEXICALI BEAN DIP

1 (1 lb) can red kidney beans
¼ c butter
¼ ts garlic powder
¼ ts cumin seeds, crushed
1 c shredded Cheddar cheese
Drain beans, reserving liquid. Mash beans and put in saucepan over med. heat. Add garlic and cumin seeds. Add bean liquid a tablespoon at a time to make desired consistency. Stir in cheese and serve warm. Dip with corn chips. Makes 1½ c.

TEX-MEX DIP

3 avocadoes)
2 Tb lemon juice) Mash and mix
pinch of salt)

1 c sour cream)
½ c mayonnaise) Mix together
1 pkg Lowry's taco seasoning)

2 11-oz cans refried beans OR
 1 can refried beans and 1 can Jalepeno bean dip mixed

1 lg bunch green onions and tops chopped fine
3 med. tomatoes, chopped
2 small cans sliced olives
2 c shredded sharp cheddar cheese
2 pkg chips (corn or potato)
Spread bean mixture on bottom of container; then spread avocado mix, sour cream and taco seasoning mix. Sprinkle with onions, tomatoes and olives. Cover with cheese. Serve chilled. A great favorite when serving either a small group or a large crowd.

* * * *

Chewing gum proves that motion doesn't always mean progress.

The nice thing about dictating letters is that you can use words you won't know how to spell.

There is no right way to do the wrong thing.

Inflation is like putting on weight; it's easier to start than to stop.

ELEGANT SPINACH DIP

2 c sour cream
1 c mayonnaise
1 box frozen chopped spinach, drained well
1 box Knorr vegetable soup
3 green onions, chopped
1 can water chestnuts, sliced.

Blend and serve with crackers or vegetables.

VEGETABLE DIAMONDS

1 frozen pkg Pillsbury Cresent rolls
1 8-oz pkg cream cheese
1/3 c mayonnaise

Roll out the crescent rolls and put in 9x13 pan. Cook in one piece as directed. Blend the cream cheese and mayonnaise until fluffy. Ice the roll base.

Grate very fine carrots, radishes, green onions, peppers and celery and sprinkle over crust. Cut in delicious triangles and serve. One pkg makes about 24 triangles.

STUFFED DATES

Carefully split dates and fill with smooth peanut butter. Roll in sugar and cinnamon (1/4 c sugar to 3/4 ts cinnamon).

SHRIMP COCKTAIL DIP

2 8-oz pkg. cream cheese
1 lb shrimp (fresh or frozen, cooked)
1 t lemon juice
dash garlic powder

Soften cream cheese and spread on large platter. Add lemon juice and garlic powder to shrimp. Spread on top of cream cheese. Pour cocktail sauce over it.

Notes

Notes

breads

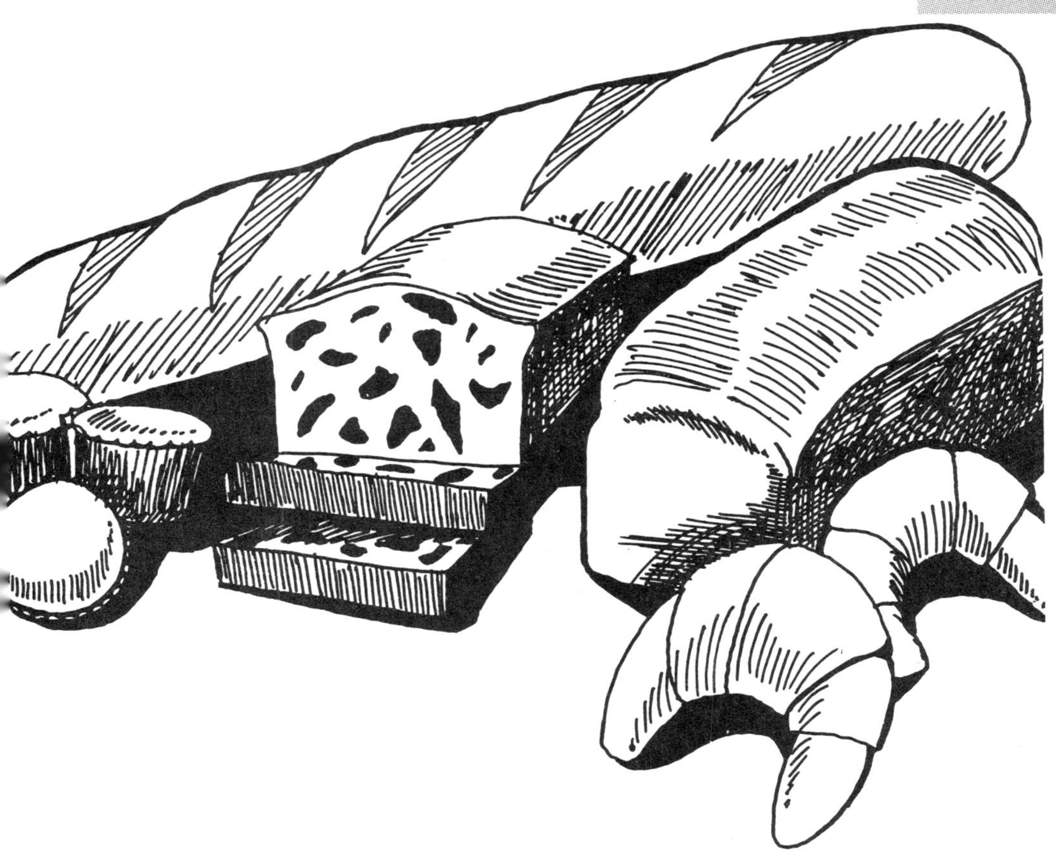

Notes

SAN FRANCISCO SOUR DOUGH BREAD

Friends won't believe you made it!

The Sponge:

1 c starter (directions follow)
2 c unsifted flour
1 c warm water

The Dough:

2 pkg dry yeast
1 c warm water
1 teaspoon honey
1 Tb salt, optional
4 c flour

For starter, combine 1 envelope yeast, 2 c water and 2 c white or whole wheat flour. Combine in glass, plastic or pottery container, not metal. Cover with cheesecloth and let stand at room temp. for 48 hrs stirring down several times. A clear, yellowish liquid often accumulates on top.

After removing starter to make bread, replenish the remaining starter by stirring in equal amounts of flour and water. Refrigerate when not in use, but bring to room temp before using to make bread. If you do not use the starter weekly, freshen it about every 10 days. To freshen, discard half the starter, add equal amounts of flour and water, keep at room temp until it bubbles, then refrigerate, lightly covered.

For sourdough bread, the night before you bake, mix 1 c starter with 2 c flour and 1 c warm water. Cover tightly and leave in a warm place. This is your sponge. Next morning, it should have risen in the bowl.

To make dough, mix sponge with yeast, warm water, honey and salt. Add flour a cup at a time. Knead for 1 or 2 min, returning to greased bowl and let rise again for about 45 mins. Knead 1 or 2 mins and then shape into 4 long loaves. Place in greased French-bread loaf pans and sprinkle with white cornmeal or on cornmeal-sprinkled cookie sheets. Cover; let rise until almost double, about 45 mins.

With sharp knife, slash tops of loaves diagonally about 2" apart. Spray with water; sprinkle with sesame seeds if desired. Bake 25 to 30 min at 425°. About 15 mins into baking, spray with water again for a superb crust. Makes 2-4 loaves.

ORANGE BOWKNOTS

(Start preparing 5 hrs before serving time)

1¼ c milk, scalded
1/3 c sugar
1 Tb or 1 pkg dried yeast
¼ c orange juice
4½ c flour
½ c shortening
1 ts salt
2 eggs, well beaten
2 Tb grated orange peel

Combine milk, shortening, sugar and salt; cool to lukewarm. Soften yeast in this mixture. Add eggs, orange juice and peel, beat thoroughly. Add flour and mix to soft dough. Cover. Let stand 10 min. Knead on lightly floured surface. Place in greased bowl and let rise for 3½ hrs. (Punch down twice during this time.) Roll out to ½" thickness. Cut in 8" strips ½ to 3/4" wide. Tie in knot. Melt butter on baking sheets and place knot on sheet (usually uses two sheets.) Let rise 1½ hrs. Bake at 400° 15 min. until golden brown. Spread with orange topping made by blending 2 Tb orange juice, 1 ts grated rind and 1 c sifted powdered sugar. Makes 36 rolls.

TWO-HOUR ROLLS

1 c scalded milk
1 ts salt
3 eggs, well beaten
4½ c flour
3 Tb sugar
3 heaping Tb shortening
2 yeast cakes dissolved in ½ c warm water

Let rise until bubbly. Add sufficient flour to handle and form on sheet. Let rise for 2 hrs. at room temp. or until double in bulk. Bake at 375° for 12-15 min.

* * * *

Those people who have no trouble separating the men from the boys are called women.

Never in the history of fashion has so little material been raised so high to reveal so much that needs to be covered so badly.

WHEAT BREAD

The Sponge:

½ c warm water
1½ Tb dry yeast
1 Tb sugar

The Dough:

5 c white flour
2 c cracked wheat
6 Tb instant dry milk
4 Tb oil
3 Tb salt & 4 Tb sugar
1 c raw wheat germ
12-14 c wheat flour
8 c hot tap water
2 Tb honey

Mix all dry ingredients adding oil and tapwater last. Add yeast mixture. Stir well. Add 8 c wheat flour. By then you may start using your hands. Gradually add the remaining flour. Knead for 10 min. Divide into 4 loaves. Place into greased pans. If using new yeast, rise in warm oven for 20 min. If yeast is old, will require 1-1½ hrs. Turn heat up to 350° and bake for 1 hr.

Any of the bread recipes are short-cut and simplified if you have a bread mixer. Results are usually more consistently light. However, if you don't have one, nothing is lost in quality by the old-fashioned kneading process. And nothing is as satisfying as the smell and taste of homemade bread!

POPPY SEED ROLLS

Open one package of Pillsbury biscuits and dip one side of each roll into poppy seeds (1 pkg). Roll each biscuit with your hands into a 5" rope. Tie in a knot and tuck the ends under. Place in a baking dish and brush lightly with 2 Tb melted butter or margarine and bake according to package directions for the biscuits. (Makes approximately 10 servings.)

ORANGE ROLLS

2 pkg yeast dissolved in ¼ c warm water
½ c sugar — ¼ lb butter or margarine
1½ ts salt — 3 beaten eggs
1 c warm water — 4½ c flour

Glaze: orange juice from orange and powdered sugar.

Filling: Grated rind of 1 orange
½ c sugar
1/3 c melted butter

Combine sugar, butter, beaten eggs and water. Add 3 c flour and beat well with electric mixer 2 min. Add rest of flour. Cover and let rise 1½ hr. Pour on board and cut dough in half and roll to 18 x 6. Pour on half of filling and roll up as jelly roll. Cut into 18 1" rolls. Put in greased muffin tins and let rise 1½ hrs. Bake 400° for 12-15 min. Remove from oven and put on glaze.

CRESCENT ROLLS

1 1/3 c milk, scalded — 2 Tb margarine
4 Tb sugar — 1 ts salt
2 pkg yeast — ½ c warm water
2 eggs, well beaten — 4½ c flour

Scald milk; add margarine, sugar and salt. Cool to room temperature.

Dissolve yeast in warm water. Add cooled milk mixture to yeast. Pour into mixer. Beat eggs and add to liquid mixture. Add 2½ c flour and beat at low speed until blended.

Slowly add remaining flour to make a soft dough, blending thoroughly. Place dough in greased bowl, cover and let rise until double in bulk, about 40 min.

Punch down, fold and turn and place on a lightly floured dish towel. Divide dough into two portions and roll out on floured board and form rolls.

CINNAMON ROLLS

2 pkg yeast — ¼ c barely warm water
2/3 c instant dry milk — 1 3/4 c very hot water
3/4 c melted shortening — ½ c sugar
2 ts salt — 5½ c flour leveled
4 well beaten eggs — ½ c melted butter

Make mixture of 6 Tb sugar, 2 ts cinnamon, set aside. Soften yeast in ¼ c water. Combine milk, hot water & oil. Add sugar, salt and cool to lukewarm. Beat in 2 c flour. Add yeast mixture, flour etc., to make soft dough. Cover and refrigerate overnight. Divide into 2 parts and roll 8 x 12". Spread with butter and cinnamon sugar. Cut into 1" pieces. Cover and let rise 1 3/4 hrs. Bake at 400° for 8-10 min. Frost with icing of 4 c powdered sugar, 1 c butter and vanilla. Makes 2 dozen large rave-getting rolls.

WHOLE WHEAT ROLLS

In large bowl combine:
½ c mashed potatoes
½ c shortening
1/3 c sugar
2 c scalded milk

Cool to lukewarm. Then add 1 pkg yeast dissolved in ½ c warm water.

Add:
2 beaten eggs — ½ ts salt
1 ts baking powder — ½ ts soda
¼ c molasses or honey

Add 2 c white flour and beat well. Then stir in 4 c whole wheat flour. Roll out and shape. Let rise 1 hr or refrigerate 4-5 days. When needed, roll out, shape and let rise 2 hr. Bake at 400° for 15 min.

* * * *

When making whole wheat bread, blend a whole orange and add to dough. It keeps it moist and less crumbly when slicing, as well as creating a delightful aroma when baking.

HOMEMADE PIZZA

Crust: 1 c warm water and 1 pkg dry yeast
1 ts sugar, 1 ts salt, 2 Tb oil or olive oil
Stir until dissolved.

Add 2 c sifted flour and beat until smooth. Then add 1½ c flour or less. Turn out on floured board and knead until smooth and elastic. Place in greased bowl. Let rise 45 min.

Sauce: 6 oz can tomato paste ½ c water
1 ts salt 1 ts crushed oregano

Top with Mozzarella cheese, 2 Tb olive oil, 2 Tb grated Parmesan cheese, mushrooms, pepperoni, Canadian bacon, black olives, sliced, or whatever turns you on!

PEPPY APPLE-CHEESE BREAD

2 9x5x4" or 3 7x3x2" pans
350°

3 eggs
1 c oil
1 c sugar
1/3 c molasses
2 ts vanilla
2 c flour (white) and ½ c whole wheat flour
1 ts salt
1 ts baking soda
½ ts baking powder
2 ts cinnamon
2 c shredded apples
1 c nuts, chopped
1/3 c shredded cheddar cheese

Beat eggs. Add oil, sugar, molasses, and vanilla; beat mixture until thick and foamy. Combine flours, salt, soda, baking powder, and cinnamon, and add to egg mixture. Stir just until blended. Add apples, nuts and cheese. Combine well.

Divide batter between greased and floured loaf pans. Bake for 1 hr or until bread tests done, or use three smaller pans and bake for 45 minutes. Leave bread in the pan for about 10 min. to cool; then turn out on rack and cool thoroughly.

STAR LITE TWISTS

1 yeast cake
3 3/4 c flour
1 c butter
½ c sour cream
2 ts vanilla
¼ c water
1½ ts salt
2 beaten eggs
1 c sugar

Soften yeast cake in ¼ c warm water. Sift together the flour and salt, cut in the butter to particles the size of peas. Blend together the beaten eggs, sour cream and vanilla. Add the softened yeast to this mixture and combine this with the dry ingredients. Chill about 2 hrs. Roll dough into a large rectangle. Use about 1/3 of the sugar. Fold the dough in half and sprinkle with more sugar mix. Use the rolling pin to press sugar into dough. Fold again. Cut into 1" thick strips. Twist each strip and place on ungreased cookie sheet. Bake as directed. Makes 1½ doz. rolls.

MOLASSES WHOLE WHEAT ROLLS

2 pkg dry yeast
½ c lukewarm water
1½ scalded milk
(use ½ c canned milk)
2/3 c molasses
2 t salt
2 eggs, unbeaten
3 3/4 sifted white flour
3 c unsifted wholewheat flour
1/3 c melted butter

Dissolve yeast in water. Cool milk to lukewarm, add to yeast. Stir in molasses, salt and eggs. Combine both flours, add 4 c of this mixture to yeast. Beat in mixmaster or with spoon, <u>well</u>, until smooth. Beat in melted butter. Add remaining flour, working in well. Knead thoroughly on lightly floured board. Place in well-greased bowl, brush dough with soft butter. <u>Cover bowl</u>. Place in frig until ready to use (will keep 4-5 days). When ready to bake, knead dough for a few seconds. Shape into rolls, brush with melted butter, set in a warm place until double in bulk. Bake at 400° for 15 min. Makes 5 doz.

MOM'S REFRIGERATOR ROLLS

2 c milk
10 Tb sugar
2 yeast cakes
4-6 c flour, sifted
1 sq butter or margarine
2 ts salt
3 eggs, beaten

Scald milk, butter, sugar and salt in large pan. Cool to lukewarm. Dissolve or sprinkle 2 yeast cakes over scalded ingredients. Add the beaten eggs, then add the flour gradually. Don't add too much so mixture becomes stiff. They should be quite sticky. Refrigerate. Shape and let rise 2 hrs. Bake 15-20 min. at 375°. Makes about 50 med. rolls. Can be made into 3 Swedish Tea Rings.

SUPFE SWISS SALT BREAD

½ lb butter
¼ c Crisco
2 yeast cakes
3 Tb sugar
1 sq margarine
8 eggs
4 level Tb salt
12 c liquid (half dry milk and half water)

Have eggs & crisco room temp. Whip eggs. Place yeast, eggs, sugar and flour in bowl. Sift flour in warm liquid. Let start to bubble and add more flour. Grease dough, punch down and let rise 1 hr. Braid with 5 ropes or make 6 loaves. Brush with slightly beaten whole eggs. Bake 1 hr at 375°

CORN MEAL BREAD

1 c corn meal
4 Tb sugar
1 ts salt
1 c milk
1 c flour
1 Tb baking powder
1/3 c soft shortening

Blend all ingredients. Pour into square cake pan. Bake at 400° for 25 min. Double recipe for 2 loaves. *For a more fluffy bread, add 1 lg pkg instant vanilla pudding. Incredibly good!

CHEESE PIMIENTO BISCUIT RING

Beautiful, elegant eating--this treat alone will establish your reputation as a top flight cook!

3/4 c corn meal
2 c once-sifted flour
2 ts salt
5 ts baking powder
1/3 c shortening
3 Tb chopped drained pimiento
3/4 c milk
½ c grated sharp cheese
melted butter or margarine

Sift together corn meal, flour, salt and baking powder; cut in shortening until mixture resembles coarse crumbs; mix in pimiento. Add milk all at once, stirring only until ingredients are dampened (add a little more milk, if necessary, to make a soft dough).

Turn out on lightly floured cloth or board; knead gently several times.

Roll out to 3/4" thickness; brush with melted butter or margarine. Cut with floured biscuit cutter (small size).

Dip the greased side of each biscuit in the grated cheese. In a well-greased 8" ring mold stand the biscuits on their cut edges, with flat sides of biscuits together; sprinkle remaining cheese over the top.

Bake in hot oven (400°) 20 to 25 minutes.

Let stand in ring mold 2 or 3 min, then turn out. Turn rightside up and brush with melted butter or margarine. Serve hot.

DATE NUT BREAD

1 c dates
1 scant c shortening
1 ts soda
¼ ts salt
3 c flour
1 c boiling water
1 egg unbeaten
1/3 c sugar
½ c nuts

Cut dates fine and sprinkle soda over them. Add boiling water and let cool. Cream shortening, sugar, salt and eggs. Add nuts, dates and flour. Bake in greased cans (4) for one hr. at 375°.

LEMON NUT BREAD

4 Tb shortening
2 ts grated lemon rind
3¼ c flour
½ ts salt
6 Tb lemon juice
1 c sugar
2 eggs, beaten
3 ts baking powder
½ ts soda
2/3 c milk
3/4 c broken pecan or walnut meats

Cream shortening and sugar; add lemon rind and beaten eggs and blend well. Sift together the flour, baking powder, salt and soda. Add to shortening and sugar mixture alternately with lemon juice and milk. Fold in nuts. Spoon batter into greased 9 x 5 x 2½" loaf pan. Be sure batter is pushed into corners of pan. Bake at 350° for 1 hr, or until a toothpick inserted into center of loaf comes out clean. Remove from pan to cool. Wrap to keep fresh. Loaf mellows for easier slicing after 24 hrs. Delicious toasted or plain, spread with butter.

LEMON LOAF

½ c shortening
rind of 1 lemon grated
½ ts salt
2 eggs beaten
1 c sugar
1½ c flour
1 ts baking powder
½ c milk

Mix dry ingredients & blend with wet ingredients. Bake at 350° for 45 min. Mix juice of 1 lemon & ¼ c sugar. Spoon over hot loaf.

GOOD NEIGHBOR LOAF

½ c boiling water
1/3 c orange juice
1 c sugar
2 ts vanilla
½ c chopped nuts
1 ts baking powder
¼ ts salt
2 Tb grated orange rind
¼ c raisins
2 Tb melted butter
1 egg slightly beaten
2 c flour
1 ts soda

Place boiling water in large bowl, add orange juice and rind, raisins, sugar, melted butter, vanilla, beaten eggs & nuts in order given. Stir to blend. Add sifted dry ingredients and blend. Pour batter into greased loaf pan. Bake 350° for 1 hr. Cool on rack.

CROWN RING BREAD

2 c milk scalded
2 Tb yeast)
½ c warm water) Dissolve
1 ts sugar)
1 c sugar added to lukewarm milk and then add yeast mixture. Then add 3½ c flour. Let rise till bubbly (about ½ hr) Then add:

		(reserve
4 beaten eggs	1 c sugar	(3/4 c sugar)
1 c flour	1½ ts soda	(1 ts cinnamon)

Mix together. Add enough flour till dough loses shine. (about 6 to 7 c in all including what already has been used. Stir and put in greased bowl. Cover and let double in bulk. Grease 2 angel food cake pans, melt butter, pick off pieces of dough about the size of golf ball. Dip in butter and then cinnamon and sugar mixture. Put in pans in honeycomb fashion. Stick cherries and pecans as desired. Let rise until double and bake at 350° for 40 min. Serve upside down.

CRANBERRY BREAD

2 c flour	1 c sugar
1½ ts baking powder	1½ ts soda
½ ts salt	

Combine juice and grated rind of 1 orange with 2 Tb shortening and enough boiling water to make 3/4 c. Add 1 egg well beaten.

Blend the liquid into dry ingredients and stir them only until the flour mixture is damp. Add 1 c chopped nuts and 1 c raw cranberries halved.

Pour the batter into a greased loaf pan 3" deep. Push the batter into the corners of the pan, leaving center slightly hollowed.

Allow batter to stand at least 20 min. before baking. Then bake in a moderate oven at 350° for 60-70 min. Allow to cool thoroughly before slicing. Very festive for the holidays, but good the year around! Can use canned cranberries as well.

SESAME POPPY SEED LOAF

3/4 c flour
3/4 c whole wheat flour
3 ts baking powder
½ ts salt
1/3 c (about 1 3/4 oz) sesame seed
2 ts poppy seed
3/4 c orange juice
¼ c honey
2 eggs
¼ c oil
½ c All Bran

Sift together flour, whole wheat flour, baking powder, salt and seeds; set aside.

In large mixing bowl beat orange juice, honey, eggs, oil and cereal until well combined. Let stand about 2 min, or until cereal is softened.

Add flour mixture, stirring only until combined. Spread batter evenly in greased 8½ x 4½ x 2½" pan. Bake at 375° for 1 hr or until toothpick test comes clean.

ANADAMA BREAD

2/3 c corn meal
2 c boiling water
2 Tb shortening
½ c molasses
1 ts salt
1 cake or pkg yeast
1 c warm water
6 c flour

Stir the cornmeal slowly into the boiling water and mix well. Add shortening, molasses and salt. Set aside to cool. Dissolve the yeast in the warm water about 5 minutes; then add alternately with flour to the lukewarm cornmeal mixture. Knead until smooth and place in large greased bowl, in a warm place. Cover and let rise until double in bulk.

Turn out onto floured board, divide into a loaf. Place in greased bread pan and let rise again until double it's bulk. Bake at 375° for 1 hr.

*This recipe came from the early settlers of Massachusetts.

APPLESAUCE PUMPKIN BREAD

2/3 c shortening
2½ c sugar
4 eggs
1 c applesauce
1 c mashed pumpkin
3 1/3 c flour
2 ts baking soda
½ ts baking powder
1½ ts salt
1 ts cinnamon
½ ts mace
2/3 c apple juice
1 c chopped nuts

Cream shortening and sugar. Add eggs one at a time, beating after each. Stir in applesauce and pumpkin. Sift together dry ingredients and add alternately with applesauce. Stir in nuts. Pour in 2 loaf tins. Bake at 350° for 1 hr.

APRICOT NUT BREAD

3/4 c water
2 c flour
½ ts soda
½ c chopped walnuts
1/3 c shortening
3 Tb orange juice
2 c apricots, dried
1 ts baking powder
½ ts salt
2/3 c sugar
2 eggs
½ c raisins (optional)

In small saucepan, combine water and apricots; simmer, covered, until apricots are tender. Drain, reserving syrup. Puree apricots in blender. Add enough apricot syrup to measure 1 c. (Canned apricots can be used in similar method but must be drained and then measured).

Sift together flour, baking powder, soda, salt; mix with nuts.

Cream together sugar and shortening in bowl; beat in egg. Stir in orange juice and apricot puree. Add flour-nut mixture and mix well.

Pour batter into greased 9x5x3" loaf pan or 3 greased and floured 12 oz. fruit juice cans. Bake at 350° for 40-45 min or till cake tests done. Cool 10 min; remove from pans and cool on rack. Makes 1 lg loaf or 3 small round ones. A real family pleaser!

* * * *

By the time a man realizes that maybe his father was right, he usually has a son who thinks he's wrong.

QUICK STOLLEN BREAD

Combine: 2½ c flour, 2 ts baking powder, ¼ c sugar, ½ ts salt, ¼ ts mace, 1/8 ts cardamon, 3/4 c ground blanched almonds

Cut in with a pastry blender until mixture resembles coarse crumbs ½ c cold butter (1 sq)

Blend together and stir into flour mixture until all ingredients are moistened:

1 c cottage cheese (whirled smooth in a blender or forced through wire strainer)

1 egg	½ ts vanilla
1 ts almond extract	1½ Tb water
1 ts rum flavoring	½ c currants
½ c golden raisins	¼ c chopped candied lemon peel

Mold dough into a ball, place on a floured board and knead 6 to 10 turns or until dough is smooth. Roll dough out to form an oval about 8½ x 10". With knife, lightly crease dough just off center, parallel to the 10" side. Brush dough with 1 Tb melted butter. Fold smaller section over the larger. Place on ungreased baking sheet and bake in 350° oven for approximately 45 min. or until crust is well browned and bread tests done in center. Brush with 2 Tb melted butter. Sprinkle with 2 Tb vanilla sugar. Serve warm, or cool on a wire rack. Wrap airtight to mellow for 2-3 days, or freeze. To reheat, wrap loaf in foil and place in a 350° oven for 30 min.

DRY HOT CAKE OR WAFFLE MIX

Mix and store in covered container:

8 c whole wheat flour	1 c wheat germ
1 c bran	8 ts baking powder
4 ts salt	3 c powdered milk

To serve: Put in blender 1 c dry mix, 1 or more Tb vinegar, yogurt or buttermilk, 2 eggs, 1-1½ c water. Mix in blender. Cook as hotcakes or waffles. Serves 2-3. Batter is thin.

<u>Maple Syrup</u>

4 c sugar — 2½ c water

Boil 3 min, remove from heat and add 1 ts maple extract and 1 ts vanilla. Makes almost one quart. Heat before serving.

QUICK ORANGE LOAF

Put all ingredients in the blender except raisins.
First, blend the following:

1 large orange, quartered
¼ c oil
3/4 c hot water
1 egg

Add: 2 c flour
1 ts soda
1 c brown sugar
2 ts baking powder
1 ts salt

Add: 3/4 c raisins

Bake in 375° oven for 40-45 min.

BANANA NUT BREAD

4 ripe bananas, mashed
1½ c brown sugar
3 Tb milk
1 ts baking powder
½ ts salt
3 Tb butter
1 egg beaten
2 c flour
½ ts soda
1 c nuts

To mashed bananas, add melted butter, egg, sugar and milk. Beat well. Sift together flour, baking powder and soda. Add nuts and mix well. Bake in moderate oven 350° for 1 hr. Makes 2 small loaves.

ZUCCHINI BREAD

1 c white sugar
3 eggs beaten
2 c zucchini grated
3 c flour
1 ts salt
¼ ts baking powder
1 c brown sugar
1 c oil
3 ts vanilla
1 ts soda
3 ts cinnamon
½ c nuts chopped

Bake 1 hr at 325°.

* * * *

A woman is a person who will spend $30 on a beautiful slip and then be annoyed if it shows.

Women can keep a secret just as well as men, but it takes more of them to do it.

The woman's work that's never done is most likely what she asked her husband to do.

GERMAN PANCAKES

1 c milk
6 eggs
1 sq butter

1 c flour
¼ ts salt
2 Tb sugar

Melt butter in pan. Mix flour, sugar, eggs, milk and salt. Pour into melted butter. Bake 20 min. at 450°.

Topping Suggestions:

Powdered sugar: Have a shaker or bowl of powdered sugar and thick wedges of lemon at the table. Sprinkle sugar on hot pancake, then squeeze on lemon juice.

Fruit: Arrange sliced strawberries or peaches, sweetened to taste, in pancake, or serve with any fruits in season, cut and sweetened. Or substitute canned or frozen fruit.

Hot Fruit: Glazed apples or pears make a good topping; offer with sour cream or yogurt. Or heat banana or papaya slices in melted butter or margarine over medium heat, turning until heated through; serve with lime wedges.

Canned Pie Filling: To cherry or apple pie filling, add lemon juice and ground cinnamon to taste. Serve warm or cold, topped with yogurt or sour cream.

Syrups: Pass warm or cold honey, maple syrup, or fruit syrup.

COCONUT-PUMPKIN BREAD

Beat together:	1 1/3 c oil	5 eggs
	2 c pumpkin	
Add:	2 c flour	2 c sugar
	1 ts salt	1 ts cinnamon
	1 ts nutmeg	1 ts soda
	2 3-oz. pkg coconut pie filling mix	
	1 c chopped nuts	

Place batter in two well greased loaf pans. Bake at 350° for 1 hr. or until toothpick inserted in center comes out clean. Slices best when cool. Keeps well.

WHOLE WHEAT HOT CAKES

3/4 c whole grain wheat 1 c water

Bring to a boil and let stand overnight. Drain in the morning and add 3/4 c milk. Blend in blender 3 to 5 min, or until creamy. Add 3 egg yolks, 2 Tb oil, 3/4 ts salt, 1 Tb honey. Beat for 1 min. Beat whites until stiff but not dry. Fold all together and put on hot griddle. A delicious new experience in pancakes!

GERMAN APPLE FRITTERS

1½ lb apples (4 or 5 medium) 2 c flour
3 ts baking powder ¼ c sugar
1 egg 2 Tb oil
Dash salt 1 c milk

Peel apples and carefully remove core from center. Slice apples into ¼" slices.

To make batter, blend together flour, baking powder, sugar, egg, oil, salt and milk. Batter should be smooth and of good dropping consistency. Add more milk if necessary.

Dip apples into batter and put into very hot fat. Fry quickly on both sides in ½" or more hot fat in skillet. When golden brown on both sides, remove from fat, drain and while still hot, sprinkle with a mixture of cinnamon and sugar. Serve either hot or cold, but be prepared, they may not have a chance to get cold!

SCALIDI'S

12 eggs 1 ts sugar
½ c oil 1 ts baking powder
5-6 c flour

Beat with fork until egg yolks are broken up, then add remaining ingredients. Knead until smooth. Let stand ½ hr before rolling into shape. Roll out small portions and twist. Fry in deep fryer of olive oil. Let cool and dip in hot honey.

DANISH DUMPLINGS

These dumplings were a tradition in Connie's family. Whenever anyone was sick, her Grandmother Iverson prepared this recipe, along with chicken broth accented with carrots and parsley, and people got well as if by magic!

1 c milk	scant c flour
¼ c butter	2 eggs
½ ts salt	1 Tb sugar
1 slice white bread	

Place milk, shortening and bread in a heavy skillet on the stove and mix until bread is all mixed with milk. Add salt, sugar, flour, and continuing cooking, stirring constantly until mixture sticks together. Remove from heat and add eggs, one at a time, beating after each addition. Drop from tablespoon into gently boiling soup. Dip spoon into soup between spoonsful so dumplings will slide off spoon easily. Cover kettle and simmer about 7 min. or until dumplings come to top of soup.

DATE & NUT MUFFINS

2 c boiling water	2 c chopped dates
5 ts soda	1 c walnuts
1 c shortening	2 c sugar
4 eggs	1 qt buttermilk
5 c flour	1 ts salt
4 c All Bran	2 c 40% Bran Flakes

Add soda to boiling water and cool. Cream shortening, add sugar and eggs separately. Stir in buttermilk. Add flour and salt. Add water and soda to mix. Mix all bran flakes, dates and nuts. Add buttermilk and mix. Store in well-covered container in frig. Spoon into well greased muffin tins without stirring. (I use the paper liners in muffin tins). Bake at 375° for 20 min.

This recipe keeps well for up to 6 weeks in the frig. A real meal picker-upper when you are in a hurry!

MOCK RYE BREAD

(This makes 12 46-oz cans. Cut down recipe for less, but it freezes wonderfully well--share with friends, family for compliments galore!)

11 c potato water, lukewarm
4½ Tb salt
4½ Tb caraway seeds
15 Tb cooking oil
12 Tb whey or sugar
4½ Tb yeast
4½ Tb anise seeds
16 c whole wheat flour
16-17 c unbleached white flour

Mix all ingredients except flour. Add flour 3 cups at a time, mixing well. Knead dough. Let rise twice. Fill greased cans (or pans) 1/3 full and let rise 2/3 full. Bake at 400° about 45 min. Shake out of cans and let cool on towels or racks.

DILLY BREAD

1 pkg yeast
¼ c warm water
1 c cottage cheese (heat till warm)
2 Tb sugar
½ Tb butter
2 ts dill seed
1 ts salt
¼ ts soda
1 egg, unbeaten
2¼ c flour

Dissolve yeast in water. Combine all other ingredients. Add yeast and flour. Put in 8" round casserole. Let rise until double. Bake at 350° for 40-50 mins. Rub with butter and salt. An unforgettable savory experience!

BREAD STICKS

1 loaf frozen bread or roll dough, thawed
1 stick butter or margarine
garlic salt
Parmesan cheese

Roll thin with hands about the size of finger. Roll in butter or margarine and place in width of loaf pan. Pour remaining butter or margarine over top. Sprinkle with PLENTY of garlic salt and parmesan cheese. Let rise 3 hrs. Bake at 375° 15 or 20 mins.

FRUITY MUFFINS

2 c whole wheat flour
½ c wheat germ
1 ts baking soda
1 c chopped apples
2 ts grated orange rind
Juice of 1 orange
1 egg, beaten
2 Tb oil
1 c wheat bran
¼ ts salt
1 ts nutmeg
½ c raisins
½ c chopped nuts
1 2/3 c yogurt or buttermilk
½ c molasses

Lightly toss together dry ingredients. Stir in apples, raisins, nuts and orange rind. Combine juice, yogurt, egg, molasses and oil.

Stir liquid into dry ingredients, but do not overmix. Pour into greased muffin tins, and bake in a preheated oven at 350° for 25 min.

FUNNEL CAKES

2 eggs
pinch salt
1½ c milk
1 ts baking powder
2 c flour

Mix together well and pour a portion of above mixture into a funnel, keeping finger under opening. Remove finger and let batter drop into hot oil, moving funnel in a circular motion, making a pinwheel-like cake. Turn when brown. Lift out and drain. Using a sieve, sprinkle with powdered sugar. Great when accompanied with a drink of hot, spiced apple juice. A teen-pleaser for any event!

BAKE DAY SURPRISES

The aroma of these bake-day surprises made coming home from school memorable. Equally good hot or cold.

Pinch off dough the size of an egg. Roll in buttered hands and put in deep greased dish, letting them touch as rolls. Let raise until light. Mix 1 c sour cream or canned milk, 1 c brown sugar, 1 ts soda and 1 ts cinnamon. Mix all together and pour over buns just before putting in the oven. Bake in slow 300° oven for 30-40 minutes. Watch closely and do not burn. Turn out on to plate, serve upside-down.

FABULOUS FRENCH LOAVES

1. Dissolve 2 pkg dry yeast in ½ c warm water.
2. Allow to stand 10 min.
3. Combine in large bowl

   2 c hot water — 3 Tb sugar
   1 Tb salt — 5 Tb shortening, melted or oil
   3 c flour
4. Stir in dissolved yeast
5. Stir in mixing well 3 c flour
6. Leaving spoon in batter, allow to rest 10 min.
7. Stir vigorously. Allow to rest 10 min. Repeat step No. 7 three more times.
8. Turn dough onto floured board. Knead until lightly coated with flour. Divide dough in half.
9. Roll each half into a 9 x 12" rectangle. Starting at long edge, roll loosely as for jelly roll. Seal edges.
10. Place both rolls seam side down, on one large baking sheet.
11. Using a sharp knife slash top of each loaf diagonally 3 times.
12. Brush with 1 beaten egg white.
13. Sprinkle with sesame seeds
14. Allow to rise 30 min. Makes 2 loaves.
15. Bake in a 400° oven 35 min. until golden brown.

You'll be the talk of the town with this recipe!

WHOLE WHEAT BUNS

1 c plus 3 Tb warm water — 1/4 c sugar or honey
1/3 c oil — 2 pkg yeast (2 Tb)

Combine the above ingredients. Let rest 15 min. (Mixture will double) Then add:

1 ts salt
1 beaten egg
3½ c whole wheat flour

Mix well. Roll 3/4" thick and cut into 10-12 4" rounds. Place on cookie sheet and let rise 10 minutes. Bake at 425° for 10 minutes or lightly browned.

BACON BISCUIT BALLS

1. Combine in a bowl
   2 c biscuit mix
   2/3 c milk
   1/8 ts pepper
   ½ lb cooked crumbled bacon
   3 Tb minced green pepper
   ½ pkg onion soup mix or
   ½ ts chopped dill weed plus 1 Tb chopped onion
2. Shape into small balls or roll dough out on a floured surface to ½" thickness, cut dough with a 1½" round cookie cutter. Place on ungreased cookie sheet.
3. Brush balls with 1 egg, beaten.
4. Bake in 450° oven for 8-10 min or until golden brown.
5. Serve balls, warm or cold, with dill dip (below). Makes two dozen.

DILL DIP

1. Combine together
   1 c sour cream
   1 pkg onion soup mix
   ½ ts dill weed

Use as dip for bacon biscuit balls.

RABANADAS

Portuguese French Toast

4 Tb honey
4 Tb sugar
2 Tb grated lemon rind
Pinch of salt
3 c milk
½ c light salad oil
10 slices of bread
3 eggs, beaten
4 Tb powdered sugar
4 Tbs cinnamon

Combine honey, sugar, lemon rind, salt and milk in sauce-pan; simmer for 45 minutes. Remove from stove. Heat oil in frying pan. Dip bread slice in cooked mixture, then in beaten egg. Fry in hot oil until light brown on both sides. Place on dish and let cool for 30 min. Sprinkle with powdered sugar and cinnamon. Serve. Makes 10 servings.

* * * *

Ideas are a lot like children. Our own are wonderful!

VEGETABLE BREAD

2 pkg active dry yeast
4 c milk, scalded
4 ts salt
3 eggs, beaten
½ c warm water
4 Tb sugar
4 Tb shortening or butter
11-12¼ c flour

½ c finely chopped red cabbage
½ c finely chopped onions
3/4 c grated carrots
1/3 c finely chopped celery
¼ c finely chopped green pepper
¼ c finely chopped cucumber, peeled
¼ c alfalfa sprouts
1 clove garlic, minced

Soften yeast in warm water. Combine hot milk, sugar, salt and shortening. Cool to lukewarm. Stir in beaten eggs.

Add 6 c flour, softened yeast and beat until well blended. Stir in finely chopped and grated vegetables, mixing until blended.

Add enough of the remaining flour to make a soft dough and mix well.

Place dough in greased bowl, turning once to grease surface. Cover and let rise in warm place until double, about 1¼ hours. Punch down.

Cover and let rise again until double in bulk. Punch down; divide into four portions. Shape each into a smooth ball; cover and let rest 10 min.

Shape into loaves. Place in four greased loaf tins. Cover and let rise until about double. Bake at 375° or until dough leaves the sides of pan.

Brush tops with butter if desired. Makes four delicious loaves. Try toasting the slices for added goodness.

* * * *

Usually parents who are lucky in the kind of children they have, have children who are lucky in the kind of parents they have.

BRAN BREAD STICKS

A quick yeast bread that's really nutty and nutritious--made with breakfast cereal.

1. In large bowl, dissolve 1 pkg dry yeast, 1c warm water
2. Add and mix thoroughly:
   1 13-oz can evaporated milk
   1 c All Bran cereal
   ½ c sugar
   1 ts salt
3. Stir in 3½ c flour.
4. Cover and let rise until double in bulk.
5. Stir dough down and divide into well-greased bread stick pans or muffin tins. Fill only half full.
6. Allow bread sticks to double in size about 1½ hrs.
7. Bake at 350° for 20-25 min.

Makes 3 long bread sticks OR 2 dozen muffins.

CRESCENT LAYER HERB BREAD

1. Combine in a bowl:
   ¼ c grated Parmesan cheese
   1 Tb dill weed
   1 ts poppy seed
   1 Tb sesame seed
   1 ts seasoned salt
   ½ ts garlic powder
2. Separate into 8 rectangles 2 pkg crescent rolls
3. Cut rectangles in half crosswise.
4. Place 3 of these in an ungreased 9 x 5" loaf pan.
5. Sprinkle over dough 1-2 Tb seasoning mixture
6. Repeat, forming 3 more layers.
7. Place remaining rectangles on top and sprinkle with:
   1 Tb sesame seeds and 1 Tb grated Parmesan cheese
8. Bake in 375° oven for 35-40 min.
9. Remove from pan immediately. Makes one loaf.

* * * *

There are four things a woman should know. She should know how to look like a girl, act like a lady, think like a man and work like a dog.

It's true that women like the simple things in life--such as men.

There is no cure for laziness, but a large family helps.

SWEET POTATO FRUIT LOAVES

2 ts grated orange rind
2 3/4 c sugar
2 c mashed sweet potatoes
3½ c flour
1 ts salt
2 ts pumpkin pie spice
½ c maraschino cherries, chopped
½ c crushed pineapple, well drained
2/3 c margarine
3 eggs
½ c orange juice
1 ts soda
½ ts baking powder
3/4 c pecans, chopped

In large bowl, combine orange rind, margarine and sugar and cream together until light and fluffy. Add eggs, one at a time, mixing well after each addition. Blend in sweet potatoes and orange juice.

Combine dry ingredients in separate bowl; add to creamed mixture and mix well. Stir in pecans, cherries and pineapple. Pour into greased and floured 9x5" loaf pan. Bake at 350° for about 1 hr or until toothpick inserted comes out clean.

SPUDNUTS

2 c milk
½ c white sugar
½ c shortening
1 c mashed potato
(instant works fine)
3 eggs
1 pkg yeast
1 Tb salt
2 ts cinnamon
7 c white flour

Scald milk, dissolve yeast in ½ c warm water. Add 1 Tb white sugar to water and yeast and let stand for 15 min. When milk has cooled to lukewarm, add 2 c of the flour. Beat to a smooth batter and add the yeast. Let this rise for 20 min. Add the eggs to the mashed potato, add the melted shortening and whip until very smooth. Potato mixture must be warm. Add to the batter and mix well. Add the rest of the flour to which the salt and cinnamon has been added. Mix and knead to a smooth dough. Let rise once and knead down. The second time it rises roll out to ½" thickness and cut as for doughnuts. Let rise and drop into hot grease (350°) and cook for 3-4 minutes or until light and golden brown. Drain on paper towel. Coat with sugar or when cool dip in a thin icing on one side.

ONE-RISE WHOLE WHEAT BREAD

About 4½ c whole wheat flour
2 pkg active dry yeast
2 Tb molasses or honey
1 3/4 c warm water (about 110°)
¼ c salad oil
1½ ts salt
1/3 c wheat germ

Measure 4½ c flour into a bowl; place in warm oven (about 150°) until warmed through (about 10 min.)

Meanwhile, in large bowl of a heavy-duty electric mixer or another large bowl, dissolve yeast and molasses in 3/4 c of the water; let stand until bubbly (about 15 minutes). Stir in remaining 1 c water, oil, salt and wheat germ. Add flour about 1 c at a time, beating well with a heavy-duty mixer or vigorously by hand after each addition.

When dough begins to clean sides of bowl, turn out onto a board sprinkled with about 1 Tb flour. Knead just enough to shape into a smooth loaf. Place in a greased 9x5" loaf pan and cover lightly with plastic wrap. Let rise in a warm place until dough is about 1" above rim of pan (30-40 min.).

Bake in preheated 400° oven (375° for a glass pan) for 35 min. or until loaf is well browned and sounds hollow when tapped. Turn out onto a rack to cool. Makes one loaf.

EASY WHITE BREAD

6 Tb shortening
1½ c dried milk
9 Tb sugar
3 Tb salt
6 c hot water
3 Tb yeast
12 c flour (approx.)

Dissolve shortening, dried milk, sugar and salt in hot water. Cool and add yeast. Wait 5 min., then add flour. Keep dough soft. Knead 10 minutes. Cover, let rise until double.

Punch down. Shape as desired or make 6 loaves. Place in greased pans. Let rise until double. Bake in preheated 400° oven for 15 min. Turn oven down to 325° and continue baking for 20 min. Remove immediately from pans and cool on wire rack. Makes 6 loaves.

Notes

Notes

Notes

Notes

salad & dressing

Notes

POTATO SALAD

Dressing

2 ts salt — 2 ts dry mustard
¼ c sugar — ¼ c flour

Mix the above ingredients well. Add:

2 eggs — 3/4 c vinegar
3/4 c water

Bring to a boil, stirring constantly until thickened. Remove and stir in 1 Tb butter. Let cool.

Salad

11 med. potatoes (cook & dice)
1½ ts salt
3/4 ts Beaumonte
6 green onions, sliced w/tops

To 1 c dressing add 1 c sour cream. Fold into potatoes while still warm using rubber spatula. Chill for 6 hrs. Can moisten with a little milk before serving. Makes 10 cups. A favorite with every family!

LENTIL SALAD

1 c dried lentils
1 ts salt
¼ c vinegar
½ ts dry mustard
¼ ts pepper
½ c green onion, sliced
1 qt water
½ c salad oil
1 ts salt
½ ts paprika
¼ c sweet pickle relish
¼ c shallots, finely chopped (optional)

Pick over lentils and rinse in cold water. In large saucepan cover lentils with 1 qt water and 1 ts salt. Bring to boil; simmer 20-30 min, uncovered, or until tender. Drain. Combine remaining ingredients in large bowl. Add hot, drained lentils to dressing mixture; toss until lentils are well coated. Refrigerate for at least 2 hrs.

Note: For lentil and tomato salad, wash and trim six medium tomatoes and section partly through. Open up as for petaled flowers and serve lentil salad inside. Very colorful, but tasty too!

TABBOULAH (LEBANESE SALAD)

1 head romaine lettuce
½ c bulgur wheat (available at Mideastern stores)
1 lg tomato, finely diced
1 med onion, chopped fine
¼ c salad oil
salt and pepper
1 sm bunch parsley
1 lg cucumber, peeled & diced
½ c lemon juice

Wash lettuce, drain thoroughly and dry, cover and chill. Wash, stem and shake parsley dry; cover and chill. Thirty minutes before assembling salad, set bulgur wheat to soak in water that measures a little more than measurement of wheat. Set aside. Wrap parsley in leaves of lettuce, shred as finely as possible. (The secret of Tabboulah is in the finely chopped vegetables.) Combine greens with bulgur, which should have absorbed all water. At this point salad may be covered tightly and refrigerated. When time to serve, add finely diced vegetables, salad oil and lemon juice. Toss until well mixed. Season generously with salt and pepper. Be sure to add enough lemon juice and salt to get characteristic flavor. It's nutty and chewey and so good for you!

CAULIFLOWER WITH BLACK OLIVES

1 med-size head cauliflower
6 Tb olive oil or salad oil
1 Tb each chopped capers, minced parsley, choppedpimento
1 green onion, chopped
1/8 ts each dry mustard and pepper
½ c sliced pitted black olives
boiling, salted water
3 Tb white wine vinegar
½ ts salt

Cut apart cauliflower carefully, keeping the flowerets fairly large. Drop into boiling salted water, boil 4-5 min, until just slightly tender. Pour into a colander and cool in running cold water.

Drain well and reassemble by arranging top-side down in a bowl (one about the same shape on the bottom as the cauliflower). Combine the oil, vinegar, capers, parsley, pimento, onion, salt, mustard, and pepper; spoon over the cauliflower. Cover bowl and refrigerate for at least 2 hrs or overnight.

To serve, hold cauliflower in bowl with one hand and drain off the marinade into another bowl. Flip cauliflower over onto serving plate. Add olives to the marinade and spoon over cauliflower. Makes 6 servings.

SUPERB SALAD

1 head romaine
1 small head lettuce
2 oz bleu cheese, crumbled
1 cucumber, pared and sliced
6 slices bacon, crisp-cooked & drained
1 head Bibb lettuce
½ c shredded Parmesan
3 medium avocados
18 cherry tomatoes, halved
Red & green pepper slices
½ c sliced pitted ripe olives
Italian dressing. Toss it altogether and you'll call it SUPERB!

SEVEN LAYER SALAD

½ head crisp lettuce
3/4 c green pepper
½ pkg frozen peas
3/4 c celery
½ c green onions
3/4 c mayonnaise
1 c coarsely grated sharp cheese
4-6 slices bacon (crisp & crumbled)
Chop vegetables. Put in layers according to list. Spread mayonnaise on top and sprinkle cheese then bacon over ingredients. Refrigerate several hrs or overnight. Toss just before serving.

SPECIAL GREEN SALAD

½ jicama, sliced or cut into chunks
½ to 1 c bean sprouts
1 pkg (1½ lb) mixed salad greens
1 c sliced carrots
1 avocado, sliced
½ to 3/4 c sliced fresh mushrooms
2 tomatoes, coarsely chopped
½ to 1 c small raw broccoli flowerets
½ c thinly sliced raw zucchini
½ c alfalfa sprouts
Ranch-style dressing
Cut jicama (pronounced HIC-amuh, available in produce section) in half and cut skin off. Slice or cut into chunks and combine with remaining ingredients in large salad bowl. Sprinkle alfalfa sprouts over top and serve with Ranch-style dressing. Serves 18-20.
(When you're in the mood for a new adventure in salad!)

CUCUMBER SALAD WITH SOUR CREAM (GERMAN)

1 egg, hard-cooked
½ c dairy sour cream
1 Tb chopped chives
1/8 ts white pepper
1 lg cucumber, rinsed & pared
1½ Tb vinegar
3/4 ts salt

Hard cook egg; peel and set aside. Rinse and pare cucumber. Score cucumber 1/8" deep by pulling tines of fork lengthwise. When entire cucumber is scored, cut into thin slices. Place in bowl.

Combine sour cream, vinegar, chopped chives, salt and pepper. Pour mixture over sliced cucumbers. Chill and refrigerate.

When ready to serve, cut peeled egg into halves. Remove egg yolk and chop finely. Garnish salad with chopped yolk. Use white of egg for other dishes. Serves 4-6.

COMBINATION SALAD

1 lg cucumber or 2 small
1 can cut green beans
¼ green pepper, diced
3 lg sliced tomatoes
2 chopped green onions

Dressing

½ t black pepper
1/8 t paprika
1 Tb Maggi's seasoning
4 Tb salad oil
½ ts salt
2 Tb sugar
½ Tb dill weed
4 Tb vinegar

Pour dressing over salad. Mix well and refrigerate 1-4 hrs. Mix again before serving.

ITALIAN MARINATED CAULIFLOWER

1 lg head cauliflower cut into flowerets
½ c wine vinegar
2 ts sugar
1½ ts basil, crushed
¼ ts pepper
1 bunch radishes, sliced
2 med. carrots, sliced
1/3 c olive oil
4½ ts oregano, crushed
1 ts tarragon, crushed
2 green peppers, thinly sliced
1 small purple onion, thinly sliced

In large saucepan of boiling water, blanch cauliflower 5 to 7 min. Plunge into cold water, then drain. Place in large bowl. In small bowl, mix vinegar, oil, sugar, herbs and pepper. Pour over cauliflower. Add remaining ingredients. Toss lightly, cover and chill 6 hrs or overnight.

FIVE MINUTE OSTERIZER SALAD

Put in blender 2 envelopes gelatin and 2/3 c boiling water. Blend for 40 seconds. Add ½ c sugar and blend again. Add small can frozen juice, either orange, pink lemonade or grape and 2 c cracked ice. Blend well and pour in mould. Salad is ready immediately.

ORANGE JELLO

Dissolve in 2 c boiling water: 1 pkg each orange and lemon jello

Grate one orange. Section orange and mix in blender. Add 1 can crushed pineapple, 1 apple in small pieces, 1 banana cut up. Let partially set. Fold in 1 c cream whipped. Let set in refrigerator.

JELLO SALAD

1 lg pkg lemon jello)
2 c hot water) Dissolve together
8 large marshmallows)

Add 2 cubed bananas to boiling water and they won't go brown. Add 1 can crushed drained pineapple.

Topping:

1 c pineapple juice and water together
½ c sugar
2 Tb cornstarch

Cook until thickened. Cool and add 1 c dream whip or whipped cream. Spread over set jello and sprinkle with grated cheese. An old family favorite!

PINEAPPLE MINT FREEZE

1 15½-oz crushed pineapple
1 10-oz jar mint jelly
1 ts powdered sugar
1 Tb Knox gelatin
1 c whipped cream

Drain pineapple. Put syrup in saucepan and soften gelatin. Add jelly and heat until dissolved. Add dash of salt. Stir in pineapple. Chill till mixture is thickened & syrupy. Whip cream and add sugar. Fold into thickened mixture. Tint with green coloring. Freeze until firm. Unmold, cut into squares and put on lettuce leaf. Very good with ham loaf, baked potato & vegetables.

CRANBERRY SALAD

1 pkg cranberries, ground
1 whole orange, ground
1 c nuts
1 c sugar
Let stand and prepare:
2 pkg raspberry jello
3 c hot water
1 small can crushed pineapple, drained
Mix altogether and let stand overnight until chilled and set.

BLUEBERRY SALAD

1 (6 oz) pkg blackberry jello
1 (8¼ oz) can crushed pineapple
1 (8 oz) pkg cream cheese
1 c sour cream
½ c chopped pecans
2 c boiling water
1 (15 oz) can blueberries
½ c sugar
½ ts vanilla
Dissolve jello in boiling water. Drain blueberries and pineapple and save pineapple juice. Add enough water to this to make 1 c. Then add to jello mixture. Stir in fruit. Pour into a 2 qt container with a flat bottom and put into frig. When set, prepare topping using the cream cheese, sugar, sour cream and vanilla. Blend. Spread over entire set jello mixture and sprinkle with chopped pecans. A sure winner!

LEMONADE SALAD

1 sm pkg lemon jello
1 c boiling water
½ c sugar
1/8 ts salt
1 sm can pink lemonade
1 c whip cream
Mix all but whip cream and let thicken. Then fold in whipped cream. Can add any fruit such as grapes, melon balls, etc. Place in jello mould and garnish with summer fruits and berries.

* * * *

Most non-negotiable demand you'll ever hear: the baby calling for his 3 a.m. feeding.

Years ago the perfect gift for a girl graduate was a compact. It still is--provided it has four wheels and bucket seats.

CHRISTMAS RIBBON SALAD

2 3-oz pkg lime jello
1 3-oz pkg lemon jello
2 3-oz pkg cherry or strawberry jello
1 c hot pineapple juice and water
½ lb small marshmallows
1 #2 can crushed pineapple
1 8-oz pkg cream cheese
½ c mayonnaise (or less)
1 pt whipping cream whipped

Prepare lime jello according to pkg instructions. Pour into a 15 x 10 x 2 pan or 2 qt pyrex pans and chill till almost set, then drain juice from pineapple and add water to make one cup. Bring to boil in top of double boiler or heavy pan and dissolve lemon jello in it. Add cut up marshmallows and melt. Remove from heat and cool and add whipped cream, mayonnaise, and cream cheese. Beat with beater till blended and stir in drained pineapple. Cool till slightly thick and pour over lime jello. Chill till almost set. Then prepare cherry jello according to pkg. Chill to slightly thick and pour over pineapple layer and chill till firm. Makes 24-36 servings, and it's so very pretty!

WALDORF SALAD DELUXE

4 apples, cut small (leave skins on, dip in pineapple juice)
6 bananas cubed
½ c chopped dates
½ c nuts

Mix these together and whip ½ c cream, add ½ c salad dressing, 3/4 ts vanilla, and 4 ts sugar. Add ½ c drained pineapple. Serve over fruit or very gently mix together.

OVERNIGHT FRUIT SALAD

5 c fruit (blueberries, frozen, bananas, apples, grapes, pears or orange segments)
1 c drained chunk pineapple
2 c miniature marshmallows
2 Tb lemon juice
1 egg, beaten
2 Tb sugar
½ c fruit syrup from pineapple
½ c whipped cream, whipped

Fold together and refrigerate over night.

SPINACH AND MUSHROOM SALAD

1/3 c vegetable oil
2 Tb lemon juice
1 egg yolk
1 clove garlic, mashed
3/4 ts salt
¼ ts sugar
1/8 ts dry mustard
1/8 ts ground pepper
1 lb fresh mushrooms, sliced
6 strips bacon
1 pkg (10 oz) fresh spinach
6 green onions, sliced

Combine vegetable oil, lemon juice, egg yolk, garlic, salt, sugar, mustard and pepper. Pour over mushrooms. Refrigerate several hours. Fry bacon until crisp. Crumble. Set aside. Just before serving toss mushrooms with liquid, bacon, spinach and onions.
Serves 6.

CANDIED APPLE SET SALAD

1 pkg cherry jello
½ c nuts
½ c cinnamon candies (red)
1 c apples cut fine
½ c celery cut fine

Set jello as directed; add candy with hot water. Mix in celery, apples and nuts. Top with whipping cream.

LEMON SALAD

Dissolve 2 pkg lemon jello in 1 c boiling water
Add: 2 Tb lemon juice
Mix in blender: 1 c cottage cheese, 1 can (13 oz) pineapple tidbits
Add to jello mixture. Chill until partially set.
Fold in: 1 c heavy cream-whipped and ½ c slivered almonds. Chill until firm. Garnish with slivered almonds.

* * * *

It now costs more to amuse a child than it once did to educate his father.

For adult education nothing beats children.

The frightening thing about heredity and environment is that we parents provide both.

CINNAMON APPLE SALAD

4 apples, peeled, cored and sliced
1 c water ½ c red cinnamon candies
1 pkg (3 oz) cream cheese, softened
1 Tb lemon juice
2 Tb chopped walnuts

In saucepan combine apples, water and cinnamon candies. Bring to boil and cook uncovered, about 10 min or until tender, carefully stirring occasionally.

Cool and chill. To serve, drain apples and arrange on lettuce. Combine cream cheese and lemon juice, beating until creamy. Spoon over apples; garnish with walnuts or pecans. Makes 4-5 servings.

ORANGE SOUR CREAM SALAD

1 c diced oranges 1 c pineapple tidbits
1 c marshmallows diced 1 c coconut
1 c sour cream

Mix altogether and let stand overnight. A diet-buster, for sure!

FROZEN FRUIT SALAD

1 lg can fruit cocktail (drained)
3 cans pineapple tidbits (drained)
1 lg bottle maraschino cherries (drained)
2 c quartered marshmallows
1 pkg Philadelphia cream cheese (8 oz)
1 c whipping cream whipped
2 Tb salad dressing

Whip cream; add to cream cheese and salad dressing. Add to fruit and marshmallows. Set in pan and freeze overnight. Serves 20-30.

* * * *

The two most difficult careers are entrusted to amateurs--citizenship and parenthood.

Between marbles, courtships and crab grass, a man can wind up spending half his life on his knees.

PATIO SALAD

1 12-oz pkg frozen green peas
½ ts salt and 1½ c tomato juice
½ c chopped dill pickle
1 ts grated onion
1/8 ts pepper
2 c cooked shrimp, cut in half
3/4 c mayonnaise 1½ c minute rice

Cook frozen peas as directed and drain. Meanwhile, combine salt and tomato juice in saucepan. Bring to boil. Stir in 1½ c minute rice. Cover, remove from heat, and let stand 5 min. Then add peas, pickles, onion and pepper , mixing lightly with fork. Chill. Just before serving add shrimp and mayonnaise. Toss lightly and serve on crisp salad greens. Serves 6.

SHRIMP SALAD

1 can tomato soup
3 pkg cream cheese
1 envelope gelatin
1 c salad dressing
1½ c celery, green onions, red and green peppers, sliced stuffed olives (combined to make 1½ c, not each)
1 can shrimp (5 oz)

Heat soup, add gelatin softened in a little water. Add cheese and beat. Add rest of ingredients. Set. Serves 9.

SHRIMP SALAD SUPREME

1 pkg (3 oz) lemon jello 1 c boiling water

Chill until partially set. Fold in ½ c whipping cream whipped to soft peaks. Add ½ c salad dressing.

Add: 3 hard cooked eggs, chopped
2 c finely chopped celery
4 oz pimento cheese, diced
1 can (4 oz) deveined cocktail shrimp, drained and rinsed
2 Tb minced onion, 2 Tb diced green pepper
1 Tb lemon juice ½ ts salt

Spoon into greased 2 qt ring or mold. Chill until firm. Serve on lettuce. Serves 12.

WALKING SALADS

¼ c honey
1 c sliced bananas
1 c heavy cream, whipped
2 c miniature marshmallows
1 8-oz pkg cream cheese
1 10-oz pkg frozen raspberries (partly thawed)

Gradually add honey to softened cream cheese. Stir in fruit, fold in cream and marshmallows. Pour in 8 6-oz paper cups. Insert wooden stick or plastic popsickle stick in center of each. Freeze until firm.

APPLE STRAWBERRY SALAD

1 3-oz strawberry jello dissolved in 1 1/8 c boiling water
½ c orange juice) add to the jello
1 T sugar)

When jello starts to jell, add 3 big or 6 small red, unpeeled apples, grated, 1 c crushed pineapple drained, and rind of 1 orange grated fine. Tastes delightfully like cranberry salad!

FLUFFY FRUIT SALAD

1 sm pkg lemon pudding (instant)
2 c whipping cream
1 can fruit cocktail (drained)
1 can mandarin oranges (drained)
1 sm pkg miniature marshmallows
½ c pecans or almonds

Make pudding as directed. Whip cream, adding sugar and vanilla to taste. Mix cream with pudding, then add fruit, nuts and marshmallows. Cover and let sit overnight. Scrumptuous!

* * * *

Honeymoons are short periods of adjustment; marriages are long ones.

A perfect wife is one who doesn't expect a perfect husband.

CRANBERRY RICE SALAD

3 c fresh cranberries, rinsed and drained
1 c sugar
½ c water
Combine in a saucepan and simmer for 10 minutes or until cranberries are tender. Chill.
3 c cold cooked rice
1 c heavy cream, whipped
1/3 c confectioner's sugar
1 c or 1 11-oz can mandarin oranges, drained
½ c pecan halves
Combine 2/3 of the cranberry mixture with above. Place alternate layers of cranberries and rice mixtures in large serving dish, and garnish. For individual salads use an icecream scoop to place a generous portion of the rice mixture onto a lettuce leaf. From remaining cranberry mixture spoon about 1 Tb on top of each salad. Garnish with pecan halves. Serves 6-8.

FROZEN CRANBERRY SALAD

1 pkg cranberries (frozen)
Grind cranberries and 2 c apples
Add 1 lb tiny marshmallows and 1 c sugar
Refrigerate over night. Fold in 1 pt cream (whipped) and ½ c chopped nuts. Freeze and serve.

ORANGE FRUIT SALAD

1 lg can peaches, 1 lg can pears, 1 lg can pineapple
Drain the juice off and dice fruit. Sprinkle with one 3-oz package of orange jello (do not dissolve in water). Let set 3 hrs or overnight. Add one 8 oz carton cool whip and 1 8 oz carton of sour cream.

* * * *

Give a woman an inch--and right away the whole family is on a diet.

Mother Nature is providential. She gives us twelve years to develop love for our children before turning them into teenagers.

PASTA SALAD

4 tomatoes, chopped
2 green peppers, chopped
1 sm onion or 6 green onions cut up
½ bottle salad supreme (Schilling)
1 16 oz bottle Kraft Italian dressing
Let marinate over night. Add 6 oz cooked spaghetti. Don't over-cook. Will keep for several days under refrigeration. Can add cucumber or fresh mushrooms if desired.

MACARONI SHRIMP SALAD

3 c cooked and drained salad macaroni
½ c finely diced green pepper
¼ c finely diced green onion
2 Tb chopped pimento
3 hard-cooked eggs, chopped
½ c chopped celery
1 can (4½ oz) broken shrimp
¼ c mayonnaise
2 Tb chili sauce
1 ts prepared horseradish
Cook and drain macaroni according to package directions. In a large bowl toss cooked macaroni with green pepper, onion, celery, pimento, chopped egg and shrimp. Combine mayonnaise with chili sauce and horseradish. Fold into macaroni-vegetable mixture. Chill. Serves 6-8.

FRUIT PASTA SALAD

1 pkg Acine DePeppi (macaroni) Bring to boil, cook 10 min. and cool.
1 c sugar)
2 eggs) Mix together in saucepan
1½ c pineapple juice)
Bring to a boil over med heat, stirring constantly until thick. Cool and mix with macaroni. Refrigerate overnight. Remove from frig and add:
1 can chunk pineapple, 2 cans mandarin oranges, 10 oz. pkg marshmallows, 1 17-oz container of Cool Whip.
Mix gently and serve. They'll think you hired a new cook!

TUNA-CHICKEN SALAD

1 3 oz pkg lemon jello
1 can tuna
1 can chicken soup w/rice
1 c whipping cream, whipped ½ c salad dressing
1 c celery chopped fine
1 c peas
½ c walnuts
Strain chicken soup and add enough water to make 2 c of hot liquid for jello. Set and add whip cream and salad dressing. Then add other ingredients. Makes 9-10 servings. Very flavorful!

FRUITY HAM & CHICKEN SALAD

3 c diced cooked chicken
3 c diced cooked ham
1 c toasted slivered almonds
2 lg red-skinned apples
2½ Tb lemon juice
1½ c halved seeded grapes or mandarin oranges
1-1½ c salad dressing (as desired)
Optional:
1½ ts curry powder, added to salad with salad dressing
2 ts soy sauce
Combine the chicken, ham and almonds. Thinly slice the unpeeled apples and coat with lemon juice. Add apples to salad with the grapes or mandarin oranges. Pour salad dressing over salad, mix, chill and serve. Serves 6-8.

PEACHY CHICKEN SALAD

3/4 c mayonnaise
1 Tb Dijon mustard
1/8 ts pepper
3 c diced cooked chicken
6 fresh peaches, peeled and sliced
½ c chopped walnuts
½ c chopped celery
¼ c sliced green onions
In small bowl, combine mayonnaise, mustard and pepper, mixing well. In large bowl, combine remaining ingredients. Spoon dressing over salad and toss to coat evenly.

HERBED MACARONI SALAD

2 c shell macaroni, cooked and drained (abt 4 c)
½ c chopped celery
¼ c chopped green onion
¼ c chopped pimento or red pepper
1 envelope herb dressing mix with buttermilk
1 c mayonnaise or mayonnaise-style salad dressing
½ c milk
1 c (4 oz) process cheese with onion, cubed
3 hard boiled eggs, sliced
1 c cheese croutons
Paprika

In large bowl mix macaroni, celery, green onion and pimento; set aside. In small bowl, mix dressing mix, mayonnaise or salad dressing and milk. Beat with whisk until smooth. Fold 3/4 c dressing into macaroni mixture. Cover and refrigerate salad and remaining dressing 3 hrs or overnight. Just before serving, fold in cheese, eggs and croutons. Add enough remaining dressing to moisten. Sprinkle with paprika. Serves 8-10.

HOT CHICKEN SALAD

4 c cooked diced chicken
2 Tb lemon juice
3/4 c mayonnaise
1 ts salt
½ ts accent
2 c chopped celery
4 sliced hard boiled eggs
3/4 c cream of chicken soup
1 Tb chopped onion
2 pimentoes chopped fine
1 c grated cheddar cheese
1½ c crushed potato chips
2/3 c finely chopped toasted almonds

Combine all except cheese, chips and almonds. Let stand overnight in refrigerator in long rectangular pan. Top with cheese, chips and almonds. Bake 20 to 25 minutes at 400°. Serves 10.

* * * *

There's nothing that so often seems to go with a narrow mind as a wide mouth.

Before giving someone a piece of your mind, be sure that you have enough to spare.

HAM AVOCADO SALAD

3 c cubed cooked ham
2 sweet pickles, chopped
1½ c celery, chopped
2 Tb sweet pickle juice
4 hard cooked eggs, chopped
2 green onions, chopped
½ c mayonnaise
2 sliced avocados

Combine above, mixing well. Place salad on lettuce bed and garnish with ½ c cashew nuts. Serves 4-6.

CHICKEN VEGETABLE SALAD

1 c mayonnaise
¼ c chopped parsley
½ ts salt
¼ c thinly sliced green onion
½ ts dried basil
1/8 ts pepper
3 c cooked chicken cut into strips
1 c broccoli flowerets, cooked and well-drained
1 c frozen peas, thawed and well-drained
1 c matchstick-sliced carrots
1 small zucchini, cut in half and thinly sliced
¼ c chopped red pepper

In large bowl, stir together mayonnaise, onion, parsley, basil, salt and pepper. Add remaining ingredients. Toss to coat well. Chill at least 2 hrs to blend flavors.

CHICKEN ICEBERG MEXICALI

1 head lettuce
3/4 c orange juice
2 Tb red wine vinegar
1 ts salt
1/8 ts cinnamon
2 oranges
3 Tb corn oil
1 ts sugar
¼ ts powdered cumin seed
1/16 ts white pepper
3 drops tabasco pepper sauce
2 c cooked chicken strips or cubes

Core, rinse and thoroughly drain lettuce. Chill in disposable plastic bag or lettuce "crisp-it." Pare and slice oranges; cut slices in half, then chill. Combine all remaining ingredients except chicken and blend well.

When ready to serve, cut lettuce into chunks to measure 1½ qts. Combine with oranges and chicken. Serve with dressing. Makes 4 or 5 servings.

OVERNIGHT LAYERED CHICKEN SALAD

6 c shredded iceberg lettuce
¼ lb bean sprouts
1 can (8 oz) water chestnuts, drained and sliced
½ c thinly chopped green onions, including tops
1 med size cucumber, thinly sliced
4 c cooked chicken, cut in 2-3" strips
2 pkg (6 oz) each frozen pea pods, thawed
2 c mayonnaise
1 Tb sugar
½ c Spanish peanuts
2 ts curry powder
½ ts ground ginger
12-18 cherry tomatoes, halved

Spread lettuce evenly in a wide 4 qt glass serving bowl. Top with a layer each of bean sprouts, water chestnuts, onions, cucumber and chicken. Pat pea pods dry and arrange on top.

In a small bowl, stir together mayonnaise, curry powder, sugar and ginger. Spread mayonnaise mixture evenly over pea pods. Cover and refrigerate for several hrs or until next day.

Just before serving, garnish with nuts and tomato halves. To serve, use a spoon and fork to lift out servings, scooping down to bottom of dish to include all layers. Makes 10-12 servings. An absolute knockout!

MEXICAN CHEFS SALAD

1 lb ground chuck
1 can kidney beans
4 tomatoes
1 onion, chopped
1 head lettuce
1 green onion
1000 Island Chart House Dressing (see p. 66)
avocado
4 oz cheddar cheese, grated
ripe olives (optional)
1 small bag corn chips

Brown ground chuck and onion, add kidney beans, salt and pepper to taste. Simmer 10 min. Make salad with lettuce tomato, green onion. When ready to serve, place salad on invividual plates, and then add dressing. Add crushed corn chips. Add the hot meat mixture to salad. Top with grated cheese. Ripe olive (optional). Garnish with slices of avocado. A zesty, hearty salad!

FRENCH SALAD DRESSING

1 can Campbell's tomato soup
½ c Wesson oil
½ c sugar
½ c vinegar
1 ts salt, pepper to taste

Combine and beat well with beater.

SAVORY DRESSING

1 c sugar
1 ts paprika
1 ts onion juice
½ ts salt
1 ts celery salt
4 Tb lemon juice
½ t dry mustard or 1 Tb prepared mustard
1 c salad oil
1 ts celery seed

Mix in bowl everything but oil and celery seed. Add oil, a little at a time, beating well between each addition. Beat about ½ hr after all the oil is in. Add celery seed.

ROQUEFORT DRESSING

1½ c commercial salad dressing
1 triangle pkg bleu or roquefort cheese
1 sm pkg cream cheese, thinned
¼ ts celery salt
¼ ts garlic salt
¼ ts onion salt
2 Tb chopped green pepper

Add everything but green pepper and beat until creamy. Add green pepper and beat again.

APRICOT FRUIT DRESSING

1 c mashed ripe apricots (6-8)
1 fresh lime, juiced
3 Tb sugar
2 Tb mayonnaise
1 c heavy cream, whipped
Few drops of yellow food coloring

Halve apricots and remove pits. Whirl in blender for 3 seconds or force through a sieve to make a puree. Add lime juice and sugar, stir until well blended. Add mayonnaise and fold mixture into whipped cream. Add food coloring if/as desired. Pile on fruit salad. For sophisticated garnish, top with a few pistachios. Makes 2½ c.

CHICKEN-MUSHROOM MOLD

1 can cream of mushroom soup
1 envelope unflavored gelatin
¼ c cold water
2 pimentos cut fine
½ c salad dressing
1 ts lemon juice
1 c celery chopped fine
1½ c diced chicken or tuna (chunk)

Add salad dressing and lemon juice to soup. Soften gelatin in cold water and dissolve over hot water. Add gelatin and soup mixture with celery, pimento and chicken. Turn into oiled mold and chill.

AVOCADO SALAD

1 pkg lime jello
½ ts salt
1 Tb green pepper
1 Tb lemon juice
½ Tb onion juice
1 c avocado, diced
½ c mayonnaise
½ c whipped cream
1 1/3 c boiling water
1/3 c celery diced

Prepare jello, cool and partially set. Add other ingredients, chill, set and enjoy!

BEET SALAD

1 pkg strawberry jello, 1 raspberry and 1 cherry (3 oz)
Dissolve in 4 c boiling water and add:
1 #303 can julienne beets and juice
1 #303 can crushed pineapple and juice
½ c sweet pickle juice

Dressing

1 c sour cream
2 Tb chopped green onion
2 Tb chopped green pepper
½ c miracle whip
dash of salt

Spread over top of set jello mixture.

COLE SLAW

1 head cabbage
3/4 c vinegar
2 carrots
3/4 c oil
1 med. onion
1 Tb salt
1½ c sugar
1 Tb celery seed

Shred vegetables. Bring to a boil sugar, vinegar, oil, salt and celery seed. Pour over vegetables and mix well. For best results, make this 3-4 days before serving.

VEGETABLE SET SALAD

2 pkg lemon jello 2 c boiling water
1 sm can crushed pineapple)
1 c grated cheddar cheese) Set in frig and top with:
1 c chopped nuts)
1 c salad dressing miracle whip
½ c cream, whipped
1 c finely chopped celery
3 sm green onions chopped (with tops)
½ green pepper, chopped

TOMATO ASPIC SALAD

2 c tomato juice
2 Tb sugar
2 c hot water
dash of cinnamon
Pour over 2 pkg lemon jello. Add 2 Tb vinegar and 1 c diced celery, 1 bottle of green olives stuffed with pimento. Set and serve. May set with shrimp, crab, tuna or chicken.

BIRTHDAY LUNCHEON SALAD

1½ c chopped celery
2 Tb lemon juice
½ ts salt
1 sm bottle stuffed olives (sliced)
½ c chopped green pepper
8 hard cooked eggs, chopped
1/4 c minced onion
1 c mayonnaise
1 c cream, whipped
2 envelopes Knox gelatin dissolved in ½ c cold water (Put over hot water until completely dissolved)
1 sm bottle sweet pickles, chopped
Chop all ingredients, mix together with mayonnaise and cream. Add dissolved gelatin. Put into molds. Set.

Sauce

1 c whipped cream
1 bottle cocktail sauce
1 can crab
1 c mayonnaise
1 can shrimp

Whip cream and add all ingredients and chill. Garnish molds with fruit & top with sauce. (Mandarine oranges and fresh sectioned grapefruit were used as fruit.) Serves 10-12.

HOMESPUN THOUSAND ISLAND

1½ c mayonnaise
1½ c chili sauce
1 hard cooked egg, finely chopped
3 Tb minced pimento
2 Tb minced green pepper
1½ ts minced onion
3/4 ts worcestershire sauce
3/4 ts salt
½ ts paprika

Combine and mix well.

MIDNIGHT SUN DRESSING

1. Combine in medium bowl
   1 ts salt
   1 clove crushed garlic
   1 Tb hot pepper sauce
   1 ts Dijon style mustard
   1 egg yolk
   juice of ½ lemon
   1 Tb red wine vinegar
2. Using a wire whisk, beat in a small amount at a time 1 c olive oil
3. Stir in 2½ Tbs sour cream
   2 ts tomato sauce
4. Serve dressing over tossed salad greens.

EASY FRENCH DRESSING

½ c salad oil
¼ c white vinegar
½ c chili sauce or catsup
1 clove garlic
1/3 c sugar
1 ts salt
1 ts paprika
2 green onions, chopped fine

Put all ingredients in quart jar and shake well. Remove garlic clove in a couple of days. Sweet, rich and tangy!

CATALINA DRESSING

¼ c vinegar
½ c ketchup
½ c sugar
1 Tb grated or minced onion
½ ts salt
¼ ts pepper
1 c salad oil

Using egg beater or electric mixer, combine all ingredients except oil. Gradually add salad oil while beating. Chill and pour over favorite salad greens. Makes 2 c.

1000 ISLAND CHART HOUSE DRESSING

2 c mayonnaise
½ c ketchup

Add the following ingredients, chopped fine:
¼ medium onion
2 celery stalks
2 sweet pickles
¼ bell pepper
1 sprig parsley
1 Tb pimento
1 hard boiled egg.
Mix and store in refrigerator.

This recipe is given to guests who dine at any of the many Chart House restaurants throughout the State of California.

PINEAPPLE DRESSING

1/3 c sugar
4 ts cornstarch
¼ ts salt
1 c pineapple juice
¼ c orange juice
3 Tb lemon juice
2 beaten eggs
2 3-oz pkg cream cheese, softened

Blend in dry ingredients; add juices. Cook and stir till thickened and bubbly. Cook 2 min. Add small amount of eggs. Return to hot mixture. Cook and stir over low heat till slightly thickened, 3-5 min. Cool 5 min. Beat into cream cheese. Chill. Makes 2 1/3 c dressing.

HONEY-LIME DRESSING

1 beaten egg
¼ c lime juice
½ c honey
dash salt
dash ground mace
1 c sour cream

In saucepan, combine egg, juice, and honey. Cook and stir over low heat till mixture thickens. Blend in salt and mace; cool. Fold in sour cream. Chill. Makes 1½ c dressing.

* * * *

Love is an ocean of emotion surrounded by expanses of expenses.

EASY ROQUEFORT DRESSING

1 c dairy sour cream
½ ts worcestershire sauce
2 oz Roquefort cheese, crumbled
1 c mayonnaise
½ ts garlic salt

Combine all ingredients. Cover and refrigerate for 24 hrs before serving. Makes approximately 2 c.

GREEN GODDESS DRESSING

¼ c tarragon wine vinegar
1 Tb anchovy paste
1 Tb minced green onion
1½ c dairy sour cream
¼ c chopped parsley
1 Tb lemon juice
1/8 ts garlic powder

Combine vinegar, parsley, anchovy paste, lemon juice, onion and garlic powder in small mixing bowl. Fold in sour cream. Cover and refrigerate one to two hours to allow flavors to blend. Makes approximately 2 c.

DILLED COTTAGE CHEESE DRESSING

1½ c creamed cottage cheese
1 c peeled seeded shredded and well drained cucumber
3 Tb white wine vinegar
1½ ts sugar
½ ts salt
2 ts instant minced onion
1/2 ts dill weed

Beat cottage cheese in small mixing bowl on high speed of mixer until almost smooth, about 5 min. Fold in remaining ingredients. Cover and refrigerate one to two hrs to allow flavors to blend. Makes approximately 2¼ c dressing.

GERMAN SALAD DRESSING

1 c cider vinegar
1½ Tb onion salt
½ Tb whole thyme
¼ Tb sweet basil
¼ ts dill, whole
½ c orange juice
1 c sugar
1 Tb garlic salt
¼ Tb rosemary
¼ Tb capers, with juice
¼ c lemon juice

Shake well in a quart jar until salt and sugar are dissolved, then fill the bottle with Wesson oil. Makes 1 qt.

MARINATED VEGETABLES

1-2 heads cauliflower
1-2 boxes cherry tomatoes
1 bunch broccoli with stems
3-4 carrots cut in small strips
1 bunch chopped green onions
2-3 stalks celery cut in 1" pieces
1 8 oz bottle Italian dressing
pitted black olives

Prepare vegetables, cutting into bite-size pieces. Cherry tomatoes either left whole or halved. Put all vegetables in a sealed plastic bowl. Pour dressing over all to cover. Marinate and refrigerate 24 hrs, turning often. Drain before serving and arrange attractively on platter.

CHRISTMAS APPLE-CRANBERRY SALAD

2 c cranberries, chopped
1 lg orange, ground
1 c sugar
2 sm. pkg strawberry jello
3 c hot water
2 c apple, ground
1 c pecans, chopped
1 c crushed pineapple
1 c min iature marshmallows

Combine cranberries, orange and sugar; let stand till it draws juice (3-4 hrs). Make gelatin; cool. Add remaining ingredients to gelatin. Serves 8-10.

AMBROSIA

1 lg can pineapple bits
1 can mandarin oranges
2 c marshmallows
1 c cocoanut
1 c sour cream

Drain fruit and add marshmallows and cocoanut. Fold in sour cream. Set overnight.

Notes

Notes

soups

Notes

HINTS ON MAKING SOUP STOCK

1. Brown soup meat before adding water and vegetables to make stock. It will improve flavor and color. Saw or crack the bone in several places. The more surface exposed, the better the flavor.
2. Heat slowly to simmering point. Skim at this point. Simmer 3 to 4 hrs. Simmering in contrast to boiling produces finer flavored soup.
3. Save drippings from broiler pan, frying pan, roaster pan, and add to stock for richer flavor and color. Keep container in freezer and add drippings until ready to make stock.
4. Store stock covered in the refrigerator. Remove fat later, when stock is used, as it improves the keeping quality.
5. Use turkey or chicken carcass for delicious broth. Cook in water to barely cover and add several peppercorns and pieces of onion, carrot and celery. Also use chicken necks, backs, wings, that do not yield much meat when fried.
6. For easy removal of fat, refrigerate soups for a few hours.

TO CLARIFY STOCK: Crush 1 egg shell and ¼ c water. Stir into hot stock. Bring to boiling. Let stand 5 min and strain.

GARNISHES TO MAKE YOUR SOUP DELICIOUS & ATTRACTIVE:

Shredded carrots, sliced green onions, crisp bacon bits, chopped parsley, toasted croutons, parmesan or grated swiss cheese, chives, pimento, dash of paprika.

<u>Bouquet Garni</u>: Wrap several sprigs parsley, garlic cloves, fresh or dried thyme, and a whole bay leaf in cheesecloth. Drop 1-3 in a simmering soup, stew or sauce

COLD TOMATO SOUP

1 10 oz can tomato soup
½ c cold water
salt and pepper
1 c orange juice
¼ ts basil

Blend and chill. Season with salt and pepper. Serve with a dallop of sour cream or yogurt and minced parsley.

ORANGE CANTALOUPE SOUP

1 lg cantaloupe, halved, seeded
2 c water, divided
1 can (6 oz) frozen concentrated orange juice, thawed and undiluted
½ ts salt
dash of mace
1/8 ts cinnamon
2 Tb corn starch

Using a lemon ball scoop, scoop balls from one half cantaloupe; set aside. Scrape out pulp, reserve. Peel remaining half and cut into chunks. In blender container, place chunks and pulp. Cover and blend until pureed (there should be 1 cup). Add 1 c water, orange juice, salt cinnamon and mace. Cover and blend 5 seconds. Pour into large bowl. In small saucepan, combine corn starch and remaining 1 c water. Stir to dissolve corn starch. Cook over medium heat, stirring constantly, until mixture boils and thickens, about 3-5 min. Gently stir into cantaloupe mixture. Add melon balls. Cover and chill 2-3 hours before serving.

SUMMER PEACH SOUP

1 Tb butter or margarine
2 Tb chopped onion
1 can (11 oz) cheddar cheese soup
1 c drained canned sliced peaches
1 c vanilla yogurt
½ c milk plus additional milk, if necessary
Peach slices, optional

In med. sized saucepan over med. heat, melt butter. Add onion and cook about 5 min, or until tender. Add soup, peaches and yogurt. Pour into blender container or food processor. Cover securely and blend at med. speed until smooth. Return mixture to saucepan. Gradually stir in ½ c milk. Cook over med. heat, stirring occasionally, until hot, but do not boil. Pour into med. sized bowl. Cover and chill 4 hrs or overnight.

BASIC RAW MEAT STOCK

2 lbs veal or beef (brisket, shinbone, ribs or other meat and bone which have been cracked)
2 lg carrots
2 celery stalks
1 onion cut in half and stuck with 2-3 cloves
2 bay leaves
3/4 c tomatoes or 3 T tomato puree
Pinch of thyme, crushed

Rub meat bones with oil. Place in a shallow pan. Bake at 400° for 20 min. Rub carrots, onion, celery, and green pepper with oil. Add to bones and cook another 20 minutes until all are a rich dark brown. Remove from oven. Place in large pot with other ingredients. Bring to boil and simmer 4 to 5 hrs to reduce by 1/3. Strain and refrigerate, remove fat and reheat or freeze.

BASIC CHICKEN STOCK

2 qt water
Bones, gizzard and neck and back of one chicken
1 onion, cut in half stuck with 2 cloves
2 carrots sectioned or coarsely chopped
2 stalks celery, sectioned or coursely chopped
6 parsley stems 2 bay leaves
salt and 4-5 pepper corns
pinch of thyme

Place cold water in large saucepan. Add remaining ingredients. Bring to boil. Simmer slowly for 4 hrs to reduce by 1/3. Strain, refrigerate, remove fat, reheat or freeze.

SCRAP STOCK

2½ c water 1 c scraps (basic proportion)

Place every bit of food suitable for soup (also a Tb or two of raw or left-over cereal) in saucepan. Simmer for 1-2 hrs (the longer period when cooked meat or bone used). Can be pressure cooked with only 1½ c water for 12 min. Serve it or cool and store.

SOUP STOCK MADE WITH COOKED MEAT

2 c meat and fat, cut meat from bone
4-5 c water ¼ ts salt

Soak meat and bone, bring it to the boiling point, simmer covered for 1½ hrs. Add and simmer covered for ½ hour longer. Add:

1 c chopped vegetables, carrots, turnips, celery, parsley, etc.
1 small onion
1 c tomatoes or 4 Tb tomato puree
½ ts sugar ¼ ts salt
¼ ts paprika ¼ ts celery salt

Strain or blend soup. Chill, remove fat and reheat soup.

VICHYSSOISE

1 can (10 3/4 oz) condensed chicken broth
1 can " " cream of potato soup
1 soup can of milk
1 pkg (8 oz) cream cheese, softened
2 Tb sliced green onions
chopped chives, optional

In blender container, combine all ingredients except chives. Blend until smooth. Pour into medium saucepan and cook over medium heat, stirring occasionally until hot, but do not boil. Pour into bowl and chill 4 hrs or overnight. Garnish with chopped chives. Serves 4-5. Absolutely wonderful!

ICED CARROT SOUP

1 10½ oz. can condensed cream of celery soup, undiluted
1 soup can of milk 1 c shredded, peeled carrot
2 Tb creamy peanut butter 3/4 ts onion salt
few grains pepper water cress sprigs

Place celery soup, milk, carrot, peanut butter, onion, salt and pepper in the container of a blender or food processor. Cover and blend 30 seconds at high speed. Chill soup several hours. Garnish with water cress or parsley. Serves 3.

FRUIT SOUP

3 c dried prunes
1 c dried apple slices
½ ts salt
2 ts vanilla
3 c raisins
1 c honey
½ c quick cooking tapioca
¼ c butter
2 sticks cinnamon or 1 ts ground cinnamon

Cover prunes with water and soak over night. Cover fruit with water, using prune water as part of it; cook until fruit is soft. Drain liquid from fruit into measuring cup and add enough more water to make 1½ qts liquid. Return liquid to fruit; add honey, tapioca, vanilla and cinnamon. Cook until tapioca thickens and becomes clear.

Serve hot or cold with whipped cream. Note: other dried fruits may be used in any desired combinations. A refreshing change!

SWEET SOUP (SWEDISH DESSERT)

1. Soak overnight ½ lb pkg of pearl tapioca.
2. Next morning discard water and rinse well.
3. Cook tapioca with 2 c sugar and 3 c water until thick.
4. Add 1 can undiluted concentrated orange juice to hot tapioca mixture and mix.
5. Add dash of salt and 1 Tb lemon juice.
6. Add choice of fruits such as cherries, oranges, peaches, mandarin oranges, watermelon, grapes, bananas, strawberries, pineapple chunts, boysenberries, etc.
7. Serve cold.

CHICKEN AVOCADO SOUP

4 c cold chicken bouillon
¼ c lime juice
2 c diced avocado (2 med)
1 ts salt
freshly ground pepper (black)

Combine ingredients. Blend in electric blender. Chill at least 1 hr. Serves 6.

ROUND-UP STEW

2 lb stew meat
3 potatoes
3 carrots
2 onions
1 can consomme
¼ lb mushrooms, sliced
1 ts salt
½ c bread crumbs
1 Tb brown sugar
1 can stewed tomatoes

Dice vegetables as desired. Mix all ingredients in large oven-proof container. Bake at 300° 5-6 hrs.

OXTAIL STEW

2 oxtails, disjointed
2½ c water
8 small boiling onions
1 c thickly sliced celery
1 Tb cold water
1 Tb oil
1½ ts salt
4 lg carrots
1 Tb flour

Parsley dumplings:
2 c biscuit mix
3 Tb chopped parsley
2/3 c milk

Brown oxtails slowly in heated oil. Add water and salt, cover and cook slowly until meat is tender (about 1½ hrs). Meanwhile, peel onions and carrots, and cut carrots into large chunks. Add onions and carrots to oxtails, and cook 20 min. Add celery and Parsley dumplings. Cover closely, and cook 15 min longer without removing lid. Stir flour into cold water to make a smooth paste, and stir into liquid on stew. Cook, stirring gently until gravy clears and thickens slightly. Serve at once.

Parsley Dumplings: Combine mix and parsley. Stir in milk to make a soft dough. Drop by tablespoonsful onto top of simmering stew. Makes 4-5 servings.

* * * *

He that falls in love with himself will have no rivals.

Children are a great comfort in our old age. They can help you reach it sooner too.

A wise man never plants more garden than his wife can hoe.

COLD STRAWBERRY SOUP

3 10-oz pkg frozen sliced strawberries in syrup, defrost
(if using fresh use no water)
2 c sour cream
1 c water
1/3 c claret wine or water

2 ts lemon juice
A few grains of salt
whipped cream

Put strawberries, one pkg at a time, into the container of an electric blender. Blend at high speed for a few seconds until pureed. Put the pureed strawberries in large bowl. Add the sour cream, water, claret wine, lemon juice, and salt. Beat with an electric or rotary beater until smooth and well blended. Chill. To serve, top each bowl with a tablespoon of whipped cream. Makes 2 qts. Serves 6-8.

OLD FASHIONED BEEF STEW

½ c flour
½ ts paprika
¼ ts pepper
2 lb stew meat
1 Tb shortening
1 qt hot water
3 pared potatoes, cubed
4 carrots, quartered
1 c diced celery
1 green pepper, diced
½ c diced onion
2 ts salt
2 beef bouillon cubes

Mix flour, paprika and pepper; roll meat in flour mixture. Brown thoroughly in hot shortening. Add water, simmer covered for 2 hrs. (Add more water if needed). Add remaining ingredients. Cook until vegetables are tender, about 30 min. Serves 8.

* * * *

It is absurd to pretend that one cannot love the same companion always, as to pretend that a good artist needs several violins to play a piece of music.

A bride should make sacrifices for her husband, but not in the form of burnt offerings.

DELICIOUS STEW

1½ lb stew meat — 2 cans tomato soup
1 can water — 2 onions
4 carrots (diced) — 4 potatoes (diced)
1 pkg frozen green beans or a can of same
4 stalks of celery (diced)
salt and pepper to taste
worcestershire (1-2 Tb as desired)

Flour meat and put everything in pan and bake at 250° for 6-7 hrs. Serves 4 or 5.

PARK CITY OVEN STEW

2½ lb beef cubes — 1 pkg dried onion soup
8 med potatoes, qt'd. — 1 can cream mushroom soup
8 lg carrots, cut in lg chunks
2 bay leaves — 1 can cream of celery soup
1 8-oz can tomato sauce — 1 or 2 soup cans of water

In large casserole or pan with a tight lid, make a layer of half the beef, then half the vegetables, then remaining beef and vegetables. Sprinkle dried soup over top, add bay leaves, then soups and sauce mixed together. Cover tightly and bake at 250° for 6-8 hrs. Serves 8-10.

WARM-UP STEW

4 slices bacon, chopped — 1/8 ts pepper
1 c diced onion — ½ c chopped red pepper
1 c diagonally sliced celery — 1 c cooked sliced carrots
1 pkg (9 oz) frozen cut green beans, thawed or 2 c fresh cut green beans, cooked crisp tender
1 can (40 oz) beef ravioli in sauce
½ c red wine or chicken broth
1 ts grated Parmesan or Romano cheese

In large heavy saucepan, cook bacon, onion and celery until onion is tender. Stir in carrots and green beans; heat through. Stir in beef ravioli, wine or broth, cheese, pepper and red pepper. Bring to a boil; cover and simmer 10 min or until heated through, stirring frequently. Makes 6-8 servings (about 7 cups).

PIONEER STEW

1¼ c dried pinto or kidney beans
3 c cold water
1 ts salt
½ to lb ground beef
½ c chopped onion
½ c finely diced green pepper
½ c sharp process American cheese, shredded
1 lg can whole kernel corn
1 lg can tomatoes, undrained
3/4 ts salt
1 ts chili powder

In large saucepan, place washed and drained beans, cold water and 1 ts salt. Bring to boil, cover and simmer 2 mins. Remove from heat and let stand 1 hr. Return to heat and simmer 1¼ hrs. In skillet, cook ground beef, chopped onion and green pepper till meat is browned and vegetables are tender; drain off fat. Add meat mixture, corn and tomatoes, chili powder and salt to beans; simmer 20 min. Combine 1 Tb flour with 2 Tbs water. Stir into stew. Cook and stir till thickened and bubbly. Stir in cheese till melted. Makes 6 servings.

CORN CHOWDER

8 slices bacon
4 Tb chopped onion
4 med. large potatoes, cubed
1-2 small carrots, cubed

Fry bacon light brown. Remove from pan and take out 2 Tb fat. Add vegetables and almost cover with water. Let simmer until vegetables are tender. Add 2 cans of corn (either whole kernel or creamed) with liquid. Add 1 can evaporated milk and crushed bits. Heat thoroughly, but do not boil. Inexpensive, but impressive with one and all!

SEAFOOD SOUP

2 Tb salad oil — 2 med onions chopped
2 cloves garlic or ¼ ts garlic powder
1 green pepper chopped or ¼ c dried bellpepper
1 ts basil leaves — ½ ts rosemary leaves
½ ts thyme leaves — 1 lg (26 oz) can tomato soup
2/3 c clam juice — 1 14-oz can chicken broth
1 lb fresh or frozen clams or 2 cans 8-oz minced clams
8 oz shrimp (fresh or frozen or canned)
1 lb white fish, cut into 1" chunks
1 can crab (optional)
2 oz spaghetti

Heat oil in Dutch Oven. Add onion, garlic and green pepper. Cool, stirring until onion is limp. Stir in basil, rosemary, thyme, tomato soup, clam juice and broth. Bring to boil. Add clams, shrimp, fish. Cover. Reduce heat and simmer until clams pop or white fish flakes with fork. Makes 5 servings. (Serve with raw vegetables and French bread)

CLASSIC OYSTER SOUP

¼ c flour — 4 ts salt
4 ts Worcestershire sauce — 2 containers (8 oz) shucked oysters
1 qt milk — 3 Tb butter or margarine
4 c heavy cream

In med. saucepan, blend flour, salt, Worcesterhire and ¼ c water; add oysters and their liquid. Simmer over low heat, stirring for 10 min or until oyster edges curl. Add remaining ingredients. Heat almost to boiling. Remove from heat. Cover and let stand 10 min to mellow flavors. Makes 10 c or six servings.

* * * *

The human brain is a wonderful thing. It starts working the moment you are born, and never stops until you stand up to speak in public.

CORN CHEESE CHOWDER

6 bacon slices, cut into ½" pieces
1 sm onion, cut in half and sliced
2 cans (16 oz each) cream-style corn
2 c cubed, cooked potatoes
2 1/3 c hot water
2/3 c evaporated milk
1 ts salt
¼ ts garlic salt
1½ c Cheddar cheese, cut into small cubes

Cook bacon until almost crisp; remove from fat with slotted spoon. Saute onions in hot fat. Remove from fat before they begin to brown.

Cube raw potatoes and cook in 2 c water just until tender. Drain water and reserve.

Use the potato water to make up the 2 1/3 c hot water adding water as needed. Put all ingredients, except cheese, in heavy kettle and heat to simmering point. Remove from heat; stir in cheese and serve immediately.

CREAM OF CORN SOUP

½ c (2 slices) bacon, diced
1/3 c flour
1 ts salt
¼ ts celery salt
¼ c onion, minced
4 c milk
¼ ts pepper
1 can (17 oz) cream style corn

Cook bacon in heavy saucepan over med. heat until almost crisp. Add onion; cook until soft but not brown. Blend in flour and milk; cook and stir until thick and smooth. Season. Add corn; bring to boiling point. Season to taste and serve. Note: If desired, top with spiced whipped cream made by combining ½ c heavy cream, whipped, and ½ ts cinnamon.

BRATTEN'S BOSTON CLAM CHOWDER

3/4 lb minced clams, or two 6½ oz cans minced clams
1 c onions chopped fine
1 c celery, diced fine
2 c potatoes diced fine
3/4 c butter (1½ sticks)
3/4 c flour
1 qt half n'half cream
1½ ts salt
few grains of pepper
½ ts sugar

Drain juice from clams and pour over vegetables in med. saucepan, add enough water to barely cover and simmer, covered, over med. heat until potatoes are tender, abt 20 min. In meantime, melt butter, add flour and blend and cook a minute or two. Add cream, cook and stir until smooth and thick, using wire whisk to blend. Add undrained vegetables and clams and heat through. Season with salt, pepper and sugar to taste. Serves 8.

CLAM AND AVOCADO SOUP

1 can (10 3/4 oz) cream of chicken soup
1 soup can half and half
1 can (7 oz) minced clams, drained
1 small onion, minced and sauteed in butter
Juice from ¼ lemon   Dash of Tabasco sauce
Salt & pepper   1 avocado, chopped
Dairy sour cream for garnish if desired

In a saucepan, combine cream of chicken soup, half and half, clams and onion. Heat to boiling and add lemon juice, dash of Tabasco and salt and pepper. Remove from heat and stir in avocado. Serve with dairy sour cream, if desired. (Ingredients lose their identity, and invariably your diners will end up guessing what magic went into this tasty treat!)

CIOPPINO (Originated with a good Italian cook in San Francisco)

3/4 c (1/8 lb) butter or margarine
med size onions, chopped
2-3 whole garlic cloves 1 c packed chopped parsley
2 lg cans whole tomatoes
2 cans (about 14 oz each) regular strength chicken broth
1 bay leaf 1 Tb basil leaves
½ ts each thyme and oregano leaves
1 c water 1½ c dry white wine
1½ lbs large shrimp (or boneless, skinless, chunks of rock fish or ling cod)
2 lg Dungeness crab, live, cleaned, and cracked (have your fisherman do this for you)
1½ lbs scallops

Melt butter in a large kettle and add onions, garlic, and parsley; cook, stirring, until onion is soft. Add the tomatoes (breaking into chunks) and liquid, broth, bay, basic, thyme, oregano, water, and wine. Cover and simmer for about 30 min.

Devein the shrimp in this manner: insert a small metal or wooden skewer along the back of each shrimp (in shell) beneath the vein. Gently pull the skewer to surface, drawing out vein as you do so; repeat as often as necessary to remove the entire vein. Set shrimp aside.

Add crab to the simmering sauce and cook, covered, for 10 min. Then add shrimp and scallops and return stew to boiling, then cover and simmer 5-7 min. more or until scallops are opaque throughout.

Serve stew from the kettle or a tureen into large soup bowls; have a large bowl availabcle to hold shells as they are emptied. Makes 8-10 servings. Note: if you cannot get live Dungeness crab, use cooked, cleaned, cracked crab and add it to the sauce when you add the shrimp.

U.S. SENATE BEAN SOUP

1 lb white beans
1 ham hock or ham bone w/meat
3 qts water
1 c mashed potatoes
3 onions
1 small bunch celery, incl. tops
2 garlic cloves, finely chopped
¼ c chopped parsley

Soak beans overnight, drain and put in soup pan with ham bone. Bring to boil and simmer for 2 hrs. Stir in potatoes and add onions, celery, garlic cloves and parsley. Simmer soup for 1 hr longer until beans are thoroughly cooked. Remove ham bone, dice meat and return meat.

ROCKY MOUNTAIN SOUP

6 slices bacon, diced
2 cloves garlic crushed
3 c pinto beans, parboiled 15 min
½ c minute rice, cooked as directed on pkg
1 8-oz can stewed tomatoes
pepper and paprika
½ c chopped onion
2 ts salt
4 c water

Fry diced bacon, cook the onions and garlic in bacon fat until onions are golden. Add to all remaining ingredients in soup kettle, cover and simmer 1½ hrs or until beans are tender, stirring occasionally.
Makes 6 cups.

SPLIT PEA SOUP WITH SAUSAGE BALLS

1 lb (2¼ c green split peas)
3 qts water
2 ts salt
½ ts pepper
¼ ts marjoram
1 c diced celery
1 c diced potatoes
1 c chopped onion
1 lb pork sausage

Wash and sort split peas. In a large saucepan combine water and seasonings and bring to boil. Add peas gradually to hot water. Shape sausage into 1" balls and roll in flour. Drop into soup, cover and simmer for 2-3 hrs. Add vegetables about 30 min. before serving time and cook until tender.

PRINT SHOP CHEESE SOUP

2 carrots, peeled and sliced
3 celery sticks, cleaned and sliced
½ med onion, finely diced
½ 10 oz pkg frozen peas
1 jar (8 oz) Kraft's Cheez Whiz
3 sticks (3/4 lb) butter (no substitute)
1½ c flour
2 chicken bouillon cubes
3 qts boiling water
salt and pepper to taste

Cook vegetables in small amount boiling salted water until tender; set aside. Set jar of Cheez Whiz in pan of boiling water to melt. Heat butter in large saucepan; stir in flour; cook and stir until bubbly, then remove from heat.

Add half of water to roux and stir until well blended. Stir in remaining water in which bouillon cubes have been dissolved. Return soup to heat and cook on med. heat, stirring until thick and smooth.

Stir in melted cheese and undrained vegetables. Season to taste, heat and serve. Makes 10 servings. (if little more color desired, add a few drops of egg-shell coloring or yellow food coloring to bring up soup color.) An epicurian experience that is out of this world!

MONTEREY JACK CHEESE SOUP

1 c finely chopped onion
1 lg tomato, peeled, seeded and chopped
1 can (4 oz) diced green chilies, drained
1 clove garlic, minced
1½ c Med. White Sauce
1½ c milk
1½ c grated Monterey Jack cheese
1 c chicken stock or bouillon
salt & pepper to taste

Put the onion, tomato, garlic and green chilies in a sauce pan with the chicken stock and simmer until vegetables are tender. Remove from heat; slowly stir in white sauce, stirring constantly. Add milk slowly. Add salt, pepper and grated cheese. Simmer over low heat, stirring until cheese melts. Serve immediately. Serves 6. (White sauce follows.)

White Sauce accompaniment for Monterey Jack Cheese Soup

1½ Tb butter ½ ts salt
1½ Tb flour 1½ c milk

Melt butter in saucepan; stir in flour. Stir and cook for 1 min. Add salt and milk and cook, stirring constantly, until mixture thickens and is smooth.

NAVY BEAN OR LIMA BEAN SOUP

Wash 2 c beans and let stand in 4 qts water overnight or for 6-7 hrs. Then add:

4 finely chopped onions
3-4 carrots, cut fine
4 bay leaves
2 Tb salt
1 stalk celery
few sprigs of parsley
¼ ts pepper
2 Tb cider vinegar

It is a good idea to cook a ham bone, beef bones, or soup meat, then cook altogether 2½ to 3 hrs. Taste for salt before serving. Great on a cold day!

THRIFTY LIMA POT

1½ c large dry lima beans (12 oz)
3 c cold water
1 can tomatoes (1 lb) cut up
¼ c chopped onion
½ ts salt
1 can (12 oz) luncheon meat, cubed
1 beef bouillon cube
1/8 ts pepper
1 c milk, regular or skim
3 Tb flour
1 ts Kitchen Bouquet, if desired.

Rinse beans; place in lg saucepan and add water. Bring to boiling; cover and simmer 2 min. Remove from heat and let stand 1 hr. Do not drain. Add tomatoes, onion and salt. Cover and simmer for 1¼ hr. Add luncheon meat, bouillon cube and pepper. Bring to boiling; reduce heat and simmer 15 min, stirring occasionally. Combine milk and flour; add to stew mixture. Cook, stirring constantly, till thickened; stir in Kitchen Bouquet. Makes 8 servings.

GERMAN BEAN SOUP

1 c beans (black or pinto) 1 c diced salt pork or ham
1 c finely diced potatoes 1 c finely diced celery
½ c finely sliced or chopped onion
2 qts water 2 c cream or evap. milk
1 slice well buttered toast

Cook beans in plenty of water. Run through sieve when tender, discard hulls. Add all other ingredients except cream and toast. Cook 4-5 hrs. Just before serving add cream and garnish with toast triangles or croutons.

CALORIE WATCHERS MINESTRONE SOUP

1-46 oz. can tomato juice 4 c water
6 cubes or tsp instant beef bouillon
Garlic powder to taste (about 1 ts)
salt and pepper to taste
½ head of shredded cabbage
3 zucchini, sliced
1 Tb dry minced onion

Add mushrooms, celery, cauliflower as desired. Simmer for 1 hr. Aroma alone is delicious!

TORTILLA CHEESE SOUP

4 c chicken broth 2 c vegetable broth
1 7-oz can Mexican green chili sauce
2 cloves garlic minced
2 c shredded Monterey Jack cheese
1 bunch green onion, thinly sliced (green tops only)
2 c tortilla chips slightly crushed

Place broths, chili sauce and garlic in saucepan. Bring to boil, lower heat, simmer, covered for 1 hr. When ready to serve, sprinkle each soup dish with ½ c of cheese. Pour hot soup over cheese and sprinkle with sliced green onions and tortilla chips.

HAMBURGER SOUP

Saute in large pot, 1 onion chopped, 1 Tb salad oil
Add and brown lightly: 1½ lb ground beef
Add together and simmer covered 45 minutes. Then add:
1 2½ can tomatoes, cut up
3 cans consomme and 2 cans water <u>or</u>
6 c water and 1½ ts stock base
1½ ts thyme 1 bay leaf
1 Tb salt 10 pepper corns
4-5 sliced celery stalks) Simmer at least 2 hrs
6-8 sliced carrots)
4 sliced potatoes or 8 Tb pearl barley)
Makes 5 qts. Freezes well.

POTATO HAM CHOWDER

4 lg potatoes
2 Tb butter
¼ c sliced green onions
½ c chopped green pepper
2 c diced ham
chopped parsley
1 ts salt
1/8 ts pepper
3 Tb flour
2 c milk
2 c water
¼ ts paprika, 1 lg can corn

Peel and dice potatoes. In large saucepan melt butter. Add onion and green pepper and cook until tender. Add potatoes, water and seasonings. Cover and simmer until potatoes are tender. Make paste of flour and 1/3 c water. Add to potato mixture. Add milk and cook until slightly thickened, stirring constantly. Stir in undrained corn and diced ham. Heat thoroughly. Before serving sprinkle with chopped parsley.

* * * *

Some people will believe anything if it is whispered.

Nothing happens in a small town; but what you hear makes up for it.

A rumor is about as hard to unspread as butter.

MEXICAN SOUP

1 can tomato sauce
1 can chicken broth
1 onion chopped
Tortilla, cut in thin strips
2 cans beef broth
3 cans water
2 c Monterey Jack cheese (shredded)

Simmer onion in broth, water, and sauce until onion is tender, about 20 min. Saute tortilla strips in a little oil until crisp, just a min or two. When ready to serve sprinkle tortilla strips and ½ c cheese over each bowl.

BROCCOLI BISQUE SOUP

2 10-oz pkg frozen chopped broccoli
2 13 3/4-oz cans chicken broth
1 med. onion, quartered
2 T butter or margarine
dash of pepper
8 lemon slices
1 ts salt
1-2 ts curry
2 Tb lime juice
1 Tb snipped chives

Place broccoli in large saucepan. Add broth, onion, butter, salt, curry & pepper. Bring to boil. Reduce heat & simmer, covered for 8-12 min. or until tender. Place half of broccoli & broth mixture in blender. Cover and blend until smooth. Repeat with remaining mixture. Stir in lime juice. Cover & refrigerate for at least 4 hrs. Ladle into small bowls. Top with lemon slice and spoon on sour cream & chives. Serves 8.

* * * *

God gave man a mouth that closes and ears that don't-- which should tell us something.

When all is said and done, it is best to leave it that way.

A busybody is a person who burns the scandal at both ends.

MONGOLIAN HOT POT

1. Combine and simmer 8 med tomatoes peeled and quartered
   or 1 lb canned tomatoes
   3 c celery, slant cut
   1 onion, shredded
   1 green pepper, diced
   2 med zucchini
   1½ qts water
   salt and pepper to taste
   1 (10 oz) pkg frozen mixed vegetables or assorted fresh vegetables, not more than 1 sm carrot
2. Combine into balls and brown:
   1 lb lean hamburger
   1 Tb soy sauce
   1/8 ts pepper
3. Add meat to vegetables and simmer for 1 hr.
4. Serve over buckwheat, wheat noodles, or just as soup.

MASTER BEEF VEGETABLE SOUP

2 lb beef shank, short ribs or beef plate
2½ qt cold water. Cover, bring to boil. Reduce heat and simmer 4 hrs. Remove bone, return meat to soup. Add

½ c minced onion	1 clove garlic
½ ts pepper	½ ts Tabasco sauce
1 c green cut beans	3/4 c celery & tops
1 c diced raw potato	1/3 c rice
1 c diced carrots	2⅓ c tomatoes

Cover and simmer 30-40 minutes. When ready to serve add 4 Tb minced parsley.

* * * *

When you throw a little mud, you lose a little ground.

No man ever told a woman she talked too much when she was telling how wonderful he is.

A man shouldn't drop his mind into neutral and let his tongue idle on.

MANHATTAN CLAM CHOWDER

2 7½ oz cans minced clams
1 lg onion diced
1 c diced celery
¼ c diced green pepper
¼ ts white pepper
1½ ts leaf thyme, crumbled
¼ c sweet butter
1½ c diced potatoes
3/4 c diced carrots
1 35 oz can Italian-style plum tomatoes, drained
1/8 ts curry powder

Drain clams, reserve broth. Broth should measure 2 c; if not, add water or bottled clam broth. Melt butter in a large saucepan and saute onions until lightly browned. Chop tomatoes and add with remaining ingredients. Add extra water if needed to cover vegetables. Bring to boil; lower heat; cover and simmer 30 min. or just until vegetables are tender. Add clams; turn off heat. Cover and let stand 2 min. or just until clams are thoroughly hot. Serve with warm buttered pilot crackers.
Serves 6.

* * * *

Always tell the truth and you won't have to remember anything.

Forbidden fruit is responsible for many a bad jam.

It would be a lot easier if sin didn't always seem to be in such jolly company.

The way some folks go out of their way to look for trouble, you'd think trading stamps came with it.

PUMPKIN SOUP

4 green onions & tops thinly sliced
1 onion thinly sliced
2 carrots sliced
4 Tb butter, melted
1 29-oz can pumpkin
5 c chicken stock
salt to taste
½ ts garlic powder
2 Tb flour
1 c whipping cream
½ c tiny homemade croutons
½ c heavy cream, whipped

Saute all the onions and carrots in 3 Tb butter until soft. Add the pumpkin and stock; blend well. Add salt to taste and garlic powder. Simmer about 25 min. Mix the flour and 1 Tb softened butter. Stir into soup. Bring to boil. Remove from heat and puree in blender or food processor. Add the cream. Return to heat and bring to boil. If served cold, chill thoroughly. Garnish with whipped cream and croutons.

MINESTRONE SOUP

Saute 1 c celery and tops and 1 c chopped onion
1 can carrots
2 c beef broth
1 can water
1 lg can tomatoes
1 can kidney beans, drained
1 can pork and beans (lg size)
½ ts salt
½ ts pepper
1 c cooked macaroni
1 can SPAM cut in strips

Simmer 10 min before adding the spam. Simmer another 10.

* * * *

Sign in a California residential area: "Free kittens! Last Chance! Mother going out of business!"

My daughter, a college student, wrote to her grandmother in the hospital. "Dear Grandmother," she began, "Mother told me you were in the hospital for tests. I hope you get an A."

What is more mortifying than to feel that you have missed the plum for want of courage to shake the tree?

SPICY LAMB MEATBALL SOUP

2 lb ground lamb
1 c bread crumbs
1 4-oz can green chilies, chopped
1 clove garlic, minced
½ ts ground cumin
4 c beef or chicken broth
3 c water
1½ ts chili powder
¼ ts ground cumin
1 16-oz can corn
2 eggs
1/3 c chopped onion
2 ts chili powder
2 Tb cooking oil
2 cans (16 oz each) tomatoes
1 green pepper, chopped
1¼ ts salt
1/8 ts cayenne pepper

Combine ground lamb with eggs, bread crumbs, onion, chopped green chilies, garlic, 2 ts chili powder and ½ ts ground cumin. Blend well and shape into 1" meatballs. Brown lightly. Remove from heat; drain and set aside.

In large kettle combine all the remaining ingredients, except corn and bring to boil. Drop in meatballs, a few at a time. Cover and cook about 1 hr or until meatballs are thoroughly cooked. Skim grease from top of soup. Stir in corn and heat to serving temperature. Serves 8-10.

GYPSY CHOWDER

1 c dried lentils
1 15-oz can tomato sauce
½ c onion chopped
½ lb ham scraps or seasoning ham or can of SPAM cubed
½ ts marjoram
5 c water
1 c carrots, finely cut
1½ ts salt
optional (dairy sour cream
(ground nutmeg

Combine all ingredients except sour cream and nutmeg in 3 qt kettle. Bring to boil, reduce heat and simmer, covered, about 2 hrs or until lentils are very tender. Top each serving with a dollop of sour cream and sprinkle of nutmeg, if desired.

* * * *

Criticism is the one thing that most of us think is more blessed to give than to receive.

If no one knows the trouble you have seen, you're not living in a small town.

LENTIL SOUP

4 c dried lentils — 2 cloves garlic, minced
16 c water — 5 ts salt
6 slices bacon, diced (raw) — ½ ts pepper
2 onions, chopped — 1 ts dried oregano, crushed
3 stalks celery, chopped
1 qt canned tomatoes — 4 carrots, chopped
2 Tb dried parsley or — 6 Tbs fresh, chopped parsley
4 Tbs wine vinegar

Rinse lentils, drain. Place in large kettle. Add remaining ingredients except tomatoes and vinegar. Cover and simmer 1½ hrs. Add undrained tomatoes, breaking up any large pieces. Add vinegar, simmer, covered, 30 min more. Season to taste. A dash of Tabasco sauce adds character. Serves 16 to 20.

HEARTY SOUP

Saute 1 c chopped onion and ½ c chopped celery
Add: ¼ ts garlic powder — 1 ts basil leaves
1 can beef broth — 1 can bean & bacon soup
1½ c water — 1 can tomatoes
½ c macaroni — ½ ts salt
1 c cabbage — 1 c cubed zucchini

Mix all ingredients and simmer for 2 hrs or until macaroni is tender.

CREAM OF MUSHROOM SOUP

1 c (¼ lb) mushrooms — 2 Tb chopped onion
2 Tb butter — 2 Tb flour
2 c chicken broth or beef broth
½ c light cream — ¼ ts salt
¼ ts ground nutmeg — 1/8 ts white pepper

Slice mushrooms through cap and stem; cook with onion in butter 5 min. Blend in flour; add broth. Cook and stir until slightly thickened. Cool slightly; add cream and seasonings. Heat through. Serve at once. Makes 4-6 servings.

DIVINE MINESTRONE SOUP

1 lb mild bulk pork sausage
1 qt water — 2 onions, chopped
2 lg carrots, sliced — 2 lg celery sticks, diced
1 28-oz can tomatoes, pureed — 2 cans (8 oz ea) tomato sauce
2 c beef bouillon — 1 Tb parsley flakes
½ ts leaf basil — 1 ts leaf oregano
salt & pepper to taste — Garlic salt to taste
1 can (1 lb) garbanzo beans (drained)
1 can (1 lb) green beans (drained)
1 c egg dumpling macaroni, uncooked

Brown pork sausage in heavy kettle, drain. Add water and simmer for 5 min. Add onions, carrots, celery, tomatoes, tomato sauce, parsley, bouillon and seasonings, and simmer, covered, for 6 hrs.

Thirty minutes before serving time, add drained garbanzo and green beans and noodles and simmer until noodles are tender. Serve hot with Parmesan cheese, if desired. Makes 10-12 servings.

YORKSHIRE-STYLE FRENCH ONION SOUP

2½ Tb butter — 1 Tb olive oil
1 lb red onions, thinly sliced
2 ts sugar — salt & pepper to taste
5 c boiling beef stock (instant may be used, reconstituted)
2 Tb cherry, optional
Bread croutes (toast 2 slices French bread and cut 2 triangle pieces from each slice)
Parmesan cheese — Grated Swiss cheese

Heat butter and oil in heavy pan; add onions and stir over moderate heat for 2 min. Cover and cook over low heat until soft, 15 to 20 min.

Sprinkle with sugar and stir over moderate heat about 5 min longer. Add stock. Season to taste. Cover and simmer gently for 30 min.

Place bread croutes into individual flame-proof bowls. Sprinkle with olive oil, then sprinkle liberally with Parmesan cheese. Pour boiling soup over croutes, sprinkle liberally with grated Swiss cheese and slip under broiler grill under bubbling and golden. Serve with loaf of crusty French bread. Eat and enjoy!

RUSSIAN BORSCHT

2 16-oz cans sliced beets blended
1 can (13 3/4 oz) chicken broth
1 ts accent
2 Tb cornstarch
1 pt sour cream
1 ts salt
2 ts fresh lemon juice
4 egg yolks

Bring blended beets and chicken broth to boil; dissolve cornstarch in cold water and add to hot liquid. Boil slowly for 5 min. Mix egg yolks and sour cream thoroughly. Add to this some of the hot beet mixture and then slowly combine with the hot soup. Heat well but do not boil. Serve cold and garnish with parsley chopped or finely chopped hard cooked egg.

CREAM OF CAULIFLOWER SOUP

3 pkg Knorr Swiss Leek soup mix
2 heads cauliflower

Pour contents of Leek soup into saucepan with 6 c cold water. Bring to boil (stirring constantly). Reduce heat and simmer for 10 min. Set aside.

Boil rosettes of cauliflower in 6 c boiling water until done, not mushy but rather a little on the crisp side.

Strain (optional) leek soup and the cauliflower water into a saucepan and bring to a boil.

In the soup turine, mix 3 Tb butter, 3 egg yolks, ½ c heavy cream.

Pour boiling soup slowly into turine. Add the cauliflower rosettes. Sprinkle with nutmeg.

* * * *

The cemetery just raised the price of its burial plots--and blamed it on the cost of living!

You know it's time to diet when you nod one chin and two others second the motion.

Every man needs a wife, because sooner or later something goes wrong that you just can't blame on the government.

POTATO SOUP

3/4 c butter, melted)
3/4 c flour)
1 pt half and half) white sauce
1 pt milk)

3/4 c celery, sauted with ½ c onion
Boil 4 potatoes, dice and add to white sauce with onions. Simply delicious!

CREAMY FRESH CARROT SOUP

4 c beef broth
1 c sliced onion
½ c instant mashed potatoes
1 Tb lemon juice
2 Tb chopped parsley
3 c sliced carrots
1 bay leaf
2 c milk

In large stockpot, combine broth, carrots, onion and bay leaf. Cover and bring to boil. Reduce heat; simmer 10 min or until vegetables are tender. Do not drain. Remove bay leaf. In container of food processor or blender, puree vegetables with cooking liquid in several batches. Return to pot. Stir in potato granules and lemon juice. Add milk, mix well. Cover; place over medium heat, stirring occasionally until heated through, about 5 min. Sprinkle with parsley just before serving.

FRESH PEA SOUP

1 lg onion minced
2 lg potatoes, peeled & cubed
3 pkg frozen peas (10 oz)
¼ ts pepper
½ c fried crisp bacon or
½ c diced ham
2 ts salt
2 c water
2 c milk
2 Tb bacon drippings or butter

Combine onion, potatoes, salt and 1 c water in saucepan with 2 Tb bacon drippings. Bring to boil, reduce heat and simmer until tender. In another saucepan boil 1 c water, add frozen peas and simmer until tender. Combine peas and potatoe mixtures. Place in blender or food processor. Return to saucepan, add milk, pepper and season to taste. Heat slowly until hot but not boiling. If thinner soup is desired, add more milk. Serves 12.

ZUCCHINI SOUP

2 c onion chopped
¼ c butter
4 c chicken stock or bouillon
8 c chopped zucchini
¼ c chopped parsley
¼ ts garlic salt
¼ ts celery salt
¼ ts seasoned salt

Saute onions. Add broth and zucchini until barely soft. Put through blender and add 2 tomatoes if desired. Heat through before serving. Freezes very well!

CREAM OF ZUCCHINI SOUP
(from the Gable House in St. George)

½ lb (2 med.) onions
2 Tb butter
1½ lb zucchini
3 c chicken broth
½ c half & half
1/8 ts pepper
1/8 ts nutmeg
1/8 ts salt
pinch cayenne pepper
grated cheddar cheese

Chop and cook onion in butter until clear & soft but not browned. Wash and slice zucchini. Combine onion, zucchini and broth in heavy saucepan and bring to boil. Simmer for 15 min or until squash is tender. Add seasonings and put mixture into blender until smooth. Add half and half, adjust seasonings to taste and reheat, but do not boil. Serve immediately garnished with grated cheddar cheese. Serves 6-8.

HOTEL UTAH BORSCHT

4 c beet juice
¼ c cornstarch
3½ c chicken or beef stock
juice of 1 lemon
1 c sour cream
sugar to taste
1 or 2 egg yolks
salt to taste
chopped parsley
½ c chicken or beef stock
hard-cooked eggs, diced

Bring beet juice and 3½ c stock to boil, stir in lemon juice, sugar and salt . Combine ½ c stock and cornstarch until smooth. Stir into soup. Cook and stir until thickened. Combine sour cream and egg yolks. Gradually stir 1 c of hot liquid into egg mixture. Then, stirring constantly, slowly add warmed eggs to hot liquid. Heat without boiling. Strain. Serve hot or cold garnished w/sour cream, parsley and eggs. Serves 8.

BAVARIAN CABBAGE SOUP

1 med. onion, sliced
½ shredded cabbage (abt 1½ lbs)
1 Tb butter
¼ c sugar
6 c consomme or vegetable juices
¼ lb wide egg noodles
1 ts salt
½ ts white pepper
Poppy seed

½ ts celery seed
Pinch dill weed
Pinch rosemary
3-4 dashes Tabasco sauce

¼ c lemon juice
¼ to ½ c dry sherry
(to suit taste)

In saucepan saute over low heat the onion and cabbage in melted butter. Cook until bulk is reduced by half, about 30 min, stir occasionally.

Uncover and cook over high heat until all moisture has evaporated. Stir constantly. Add sugar, stirring constantly, until cabbage is glazed and looks slightly caramelized.

Add consomme or vegetable juices. Lower heat, cover and simmer for 30 to 45 min, or until cabbage is tender.

Meanwhile, cook egg noodles; drain and set aside.

To the soup add the 1 ts salt, pepper, celery seed, dill weed and rosemary. Stir in lemon juice, Tabasco and simmer, uncovered, for 15 min.

Add the cooked noodles, dry sherry and heat. Taste for additional salt. Serve very hot sprinkled with poppy seed. Serves 4-6.

* * * *

Psychiatrist on phone to patient: "That's right, Mr. Hartly. I've sent you two bills. One for each personality."

If at first you don't succeed, you're running about average.

Overheard at luncheonette: "I don't mind going to work. It's that long wait to go home that bothers me."

CHICKEN-CABBAGE SOUP

2 Tb butter
¼ c chopped onions
4 chicken bouillon cubes
2½ c shredded cabbage
¼ c grated sharp cheese
¼ c raw rice
1 qt water
½ ts salt
dash paprika

Melt butter, add onions. Cook 5 min. Add rest of ingredients except cabbage and cheese. Cover and simmer 15 min. Add cabbage and cook uncovered for 5 min. Sprinkle cheese on each serving. Makes 4 servings.

CHICKEN VELVET SOUP

Make sauce of 1/3 c butter, 3/4 c flour and 2 c warm chicken stock. Add 1 c warm milk and 1 c warm cream (can use all milk if desired). Cook slowly, stirring until thick. Add 4 more cups chicken stock and 1½ c diced chicken. Season with salt and pepper.

CREAM OF PUMPKIN SOUP

2 Tb butter
¼ c chopped onion
1 ts curry powder
1 Tb flour
2 cans (14 oz) chicken broth
1 lb pumpkin
1 ts brown sugar
1/8 ts nutmeg
1/8 ts pepper
¼ ts salt
1 c milk or half n'half
chopped chives or parsley

Heat butter in 2 qt saucepan and saute onions until limp. Stir in curry and flour. Cook until bubbly. Remove from heat and gradually stir in chicken broth. Add pumpkin, sugar nutmeg, salt and pepper. Cook until it begins to simmer. Stir in milk and continue heating but do not boil. Sprinkle a few minced chives or parsley into each bowl before serving. Serves 6.

GASPACHO (SPANISH)

1 clove garlic
1/3 c green pepper, minced
1/3 c onion, minced
1 lg cucumber, peeled and diced
2 c tomato juice
Dash of cayenne pepper
1 lb can tomatoes or 3 lb fresh tomatoes peeled
¼ c olive oil
salt & pepper to taste

Combine all ingredients. Press garlic through a garlic press or grate. Combine with the rest of the ingredients and blend in blender. Chill for several hours and serve cold. Serves 8.

AUSTRIAN CREAM SOUP

1. Melt in Dutch oven over med. heat, 3 Tb butter or margarine
2. Saute until tender and transparent, 2¼ c chopped leeks, white portion only, and 1 c chopped celery
3. Stir in and cook 3 additional min, ¼ c flour
4. Add and bring to boil stirring occasionally, 2½ c chicken broth, 1½ c water, ½ ts salt
5. Reduce flame, cover and simmer 15 min.
6. Blend together in medium bowl, 1 pkg (8 oz) cream cheese, 3/4 c plain yogurt, 2 eggs well beaten
7. Gradually add 1 c of hot broth to cream cheese mix.
8. Add 3 c cooked cubed potatoes.
9. Stir over low heat until heated through. DO NOT BOIL.
10. Sprinkle with white pepper, chives and parsley.

Serves 6-8 and so tasty!

* * * *

Here, in its entirety, is the text of a post card received by the parents of an eight-year-old camper:

Dear Folks. I knew all along that something awful was going to happen. Well, last night it did. Love Jimmy.

FRESH TOMATO SOUP

2 c water	3 lg onions
5 lbs fresh tomatoes	bunch of parsley
½ c sugar	1 stalk of celery
2 Tb salt	5 strips of bacon
1 Tb mixed spices	2 Tb flour

Cut tomatoes in quarters; add the sugar, water, salt spices, onion, celery, parsley and bring to boil. Simmer 1½ to 2 hrs.

Cut bacon fine and brown; add flour and brown lightly. Put the tomatoes and vegetables and spices through a foodmill. Then add bacon with the flour and bring to a boil.

Make only from fresh tomatoes when in season. Keeps good frozen. Makes 10-12 servings. When serving, add 1 ts of cream to each serving.

FRESH ASPARAGUS BISQUE

2 lb fresh or frozen asparagus (if fresh, snap off tough ends, cut in 1" pieces and set aside)
2 Tb butter
4 green onions (sliced, including part of tops)
1 small potato peeled and diced
1 lg 47 oz regular strength chicken broth
½ ts salt 1/8 ts pepper
½ ts worcestershire sauce
½ ts dill weed

In large dutch oven melt butter over med heat. Add onions and saute until limp (3-4 min). Add potato, broth, salt & pepper, worcestershire sauce, and dill weed. Add asparagus, cover and simmer until vegetables are tender (about 30 min). Remove from heat, pour into food mill or blender a small amount at a time. Return to pan, blend in the following: 2 egg yolks beaten and added to ½ c whipping cream or half and half. Heat through but do not boil. Serves 8-10.

Notes

Notes

vegetables

Notes

POTATO PUFF

Has to be the best camouflage job of instant mashed potatoes ever!

1. Prepare potatoes according to package directions, adding onions to boiling water:
   4 servings instant mashed potatoes
   1 Tb instant minced onions
2. Fold in: 1 c cottage cheese, whirled smooth in blender
3. Place into 1 qt casserole.
4. Dot with: 1 Tb butter
5. Sprinkle with paprika.
6. Bake, uncovered in 350° oven for 30 min or until top is lightly browned.

Makes 4-6 servings.

BEST AU GRATIN POTATOES

6 c finely diced cooked potatoes
1½ c grated sharp cheddar cheese
3 Tb finely chopped onion
3 Tb butter or margarine
3 ts salt
3 eggs
½ c milk
¼ ts white pepper
Additional grated cheese (about 1½ c)

In buttered 3-qt baking dish, arrange alternate layers of potatoes and cheese, sprinkling each layer with onion and dotting with butter. Mix eggs, milk and seasonings and pour over potato mixture. Sprinkle with additional grated cheese. Bake at 325° for 45 min or until set. Makes 12 servings.
Could use green peppers and pimento as well, adding 2 potatoes for larger serving.

INDIAN SPICED LENTILS

1 c minced onion — ¼ c butter or margarine
2 cloves garlic, minced — 2 ts crushed coriander seed
1 ts minced peeled fresh ginger root
½ ts crushed red pepper — ¼ ts turmeric
1 c dried lentils — 2½ c water
salt

In large saucepan saute onion in butter until it is golden. Stir in garlic, seasonings and lentils that have been picked over and rinsed. Saute over moderate heat for 5 min. Add water and bring to a boil over mod. heat. Reduce heat and simmer, covered, for 45 min. or until lentils are soft. Continue cooking, uncovered, over low heat until most of the moisture has evaporated. Season to taste with salt. Makes 4-6 servings.

POSH SQUASH

2 lb crookneck or patty pan squash cooked
2 eggs — 1 c mayonnaise
1 sm onion finely chopped
¼ c green pepper, chopped — ¼ ts thyme
salt & pepper — 3/4 c grated parmesan cheese
1 lb butter

Cut squash into ½" thick slices. Cook in small amount boiling water 4 or 5 min. Drain well. Beat eggs, then blend in mayonnaise, green pepper, onion and thyme. Stir in squash and season to taste with salt and pepper. Spoon into greased 2½ qt casserole. Sprinkle evenly with cheese and dot with butter. Cover and chill if made ahead. Bake uncovered in 375° oven for 25 min. or 30 if refrigerated or until puffy and brown. Serves 6-8.

* * * *

When trouble strikes, take it like a man. Blame it on your wife.

It's an odd thing, but internationally speaking, oil seems to cause a lot of friction.

The best eraser in the world is a good night's sleep.

OVEN FRENCH FRIES

3 lg potatoes
¼ c butter
¼ c Parmesan cheese (grated)
ice water
onion salt or garlic salt and paprika

Scrub potatoes, do not peel. Cut into sticks as for French fries. Cover with ice water; allow to stand 30 min. Drain and dry. Melt butter in 2 baking pans (about 10 x 15" each) Add potatoes and toss until all sides are butter-coated. Spread out in a single layer. Sprinkle to taste with onion salt or garlic salt and paprika. Bake at 450° for 25 min. or until tender and brown. Turn occasionally. Remove from oven, sprinkle with cheese, shaking pan so potatoes are evenly coated. Makes 4 generous servings.

BEST SCALLOPED POTATOES

Slice or cube 6-8 boiled potatoes in baking dish.
Mix together and pour over potatoes:
1 can cream of chicken soup
¼ c butter or margarine
1 pt sour cream
1/3 c green onion, chopped
½ c shredded cheddar cheese
Top with:
2 Tb butter
½ c corn flakes, crushed
Bake at 350° for 45 min. Serves 12.

COMPANY POTATO CASSEROLE

2 c mashed potatoes
1 sm onion chopped
2 Tb flour
1 can French onions
1 8 oz pkg cream cheese
2 eggs
Salt & pepper to taste

Mash potatoes as you would normally. Add cream cheese. chopped onion, egg, flour, salt and pepper. Put in 1 qt baking dish and top with French onions. Bake 35 min. at 300°. Serves 8.

CREAMED POTATOES

10 med. sized potatoes, cooked with skins on, peeled and diced
2 10½ oz cans cream of celery soup
1 soup can fresh milk
½ ts salt

Cook potatoes with skins on, peel and dice. Mix the milk and salt with celery soup and pour over the hot diced potatoes. Heat through (350°for 30 min.) Sprinkle parsley over potatoes just before serving.

ZUCCHINI CASSEROLE SUPREME

6 c grated zucchini
½ c grated onion
1 c grated carrots
2 c diced chicken
1 pt. sour cream
1 can cream of chicken soup
1 pkg herb dressing
2 c grated cheese

Cook vegetables in ½ c water until soft. Drain. Mix sour cream and soup together. Prepare dressing as per instructions on pkg. Grease a 9x13" pan and line with dressing. Layer chicken and vegetables and ending with 2 c cheese sprinkled on top. Cover and bake at 350° for 35 min. Remove cover and cook additional 15 min. Let set 15-20 min. before serving. Serves 10-14.

SAVORY GREEN BEANS

1 lb green beans
1 clove garlic
1½ ts salt
½ ts sugar
½ c boiling water
2 Tb oil
1 Tb chopped onion
1 ts basil
1/8 ts pepper

Heat oil and add onion and halved garlic clove. (Remove garlic when soft.) Add beans and remaining ingredients. Cook 25 min. adding more water if needed.

BRUSSEL SPROUT CASSEROLE

1. Cook according to directions, 2 pkg (10 oz) each, frozen brussel sprouts.
2. Remove from stove, drain and turn into 1½ qt casserole.
3. Arrange over brussel sprouts, 1 can water chestnuts, sliced and drained.
4. Combine: 1 can (10¼ oz) condensed cream mushroom soup
   1 c grated mild cheddar cheese
   ½ c sour cream
   ½ ts salt
   ¼ ts pepper
5. Pour mixture over brussel sprouts.
6. Top with ½ c slivered almonds, toasted.
7. Bake at 350° for 20-25 min.

FRENCH PEAS

1. Cut into ½" pieces and cook until crisp
   4 slices bacon
2. Add and cook 1 min. 2 c finely shredded lettuce
   4 green onions, sliced
3. Stir in: 2 Tb flour
4. Add and cook until thick, stirring constantly,
   1 c chicken broth
5. Add and simmer 10 min. 2 pkg (10 oz) each
   frozen peas
   1 5-oz can water chestnuts,
   drained and sliced
   ½ ts salt

* * * *

One of life's briefest moments is the time between reading the sign on the expressway and realizing you have just missed the exit ramp.

Saying <u>Gusundheit</u>! doesn't really help the common cold--but it about as good as anything the doctors have come up with.

BAKED SAURKRAUT

Combine: One 1 lb can saurkraut, drained, with
1 apple, peeled and chopped
3 Tb tomato paste
1 Tb chopped onion
1 c sour cream
½ ts caraway seeds
2 Tb brown sugar
3/4 ts salt

Place the mixed ingredients in a buttered casserole. Bake in a 350° oven for 20 mins.

STUFFED CABBAGE LEAVES

1 can (12 oz) luncheon meat
½ c cooked rice (or mashed potatoes)
1 egg, slightly beaten
2 Tb chopped onion
1/8 ts black pepper
8 lg cabbage leaves
½ ts poultry seasoning
¼ ts salt
3/4 c beef broth or water

Put luncheon meat through food chopper using medium blade. Thoroughly mix with potatoes, egg, onion, poultry seasoning, salt and pepper. Cook cabbage leaves in boiling water about 3-5 min. Place ¼ cup of meat mixture on each leaf. Roll or fold over. Fasten ends with toothpicks. Place in 10" skillet. Add beef broth or water. Cook 10 min. or until done.

SOUTHERN HOMINY CASSEROLE

3 lg cans hominy, drained
1 16-oz ctn. sour cream
1 7-oz can Ortega diced green chiles
1 ts onion flakes
1 lb grated jack cheese

Season with salt, pepper and Accent. Mix well and put in greased 9 x 13 baking dish. Bake at 325° until bubbling. Serves 12. This is delicious with baked ham!!

BROCCOLI BENEDICT

1 pkg (10 oz) frozen cut broccoli with cheese sauce in a pouch
¼ ts dry mustard
2 slices bread, toasted or 1 English muffin, split & toasted
2 slices cooked ham
1 egg, hard-cooked and chopped

Place unopened broccoli pouch in vigorously boiling water in saucepan. Do not cover. Bring water to a second vigorous boil; heat for 18 min.

In small bowl combine broccoli and mustard. Place toast on serving plate. Top each with ham slice and broccoli mixture. Garnish with egg to serve. Makes 2 servings.

STEAMED CAULIFLOWER

1 lg cauliflower
3 Tb browned butter
1 or 2 chopped hard cooked eggs
2 Tb chopped parsley
2½-3 Tbs. bread crumbs

Clean cauliflower; soak 1 hr in salt water. Cook whole head in small amount boiling salted water in covered container for 20 min. Brown butter in frying pan, then add chopped cooked eggs, bread crumbs and parsley. Cook until thick. Pour over hot cauliflower. Makes 4-6 servings.

NORWEGIAN RED CABBAGE

1 med head red cabbage
4 Tb (½ stick) butter
1 Tb sugar
1 ts salt
1/3 c water
1/3 c vinegar
¼ c currant jelly (or any red jelly)
2 Tb or more grated apples

Wash cabbage, core and cut finely. Preheat oven to 325°. Combine butter, sugar, salt, water and vinegar in lg. casserole with lid. Let come to boil, add cabbage and toss with spoon. Bring to boil again, cover and place in center of oven for 2 hrs. If more liquid required, add a little water. About 15-20 min. before serving, add jelly and apples. Flavor improves if served second day. Delicious!

RED CABBAGE

3 Tb shortening
6 Tb sugar
½ c vinegar
1 Tb salt
½ ts pepper
1 red cabbage
1 green cooking apple

Melt pork fat in cooking pot. Add salt, sugar, pepper and vinegar. Let come to boil to melt all ingredients; then turn low and simmer. Cut cabbage fine, wash in cold water, then drain in colander and add to melted ingredients in pot. Keep stirring until all melted. Add apple cut in quarters and let simmer for 1½ hours. Don't add water.

NOODLES ROMANOFF

2 pkg (8 oz. each) noodles
3 c lg curd cottage cheese
2 ts worcestershire sauce
1 bunch green onions, chopped
½ ts Tabasco sauce
2 garlic cloves, mashed
2 c sour cream
1 c Parmesan cheese

Cook noodles as package directs. Drain. Combine with all other ingredients. Pour into a buttered 2-3 qt casserole. Bake at 350° for 25 min. Makes about 16 servings.

CALICO BEANS

½ lb bacon, chopped
½ lb ground beef
½ c catsup
2 ts salt
1 c onion, chopped
3/4 c brown sugar
2 Tb vinegar
2 ts mustard
1 can (1 lb 12 oz) pork and beans
1 can (15 oz) kidney beans, drained
1 can (15 oz) lima beans, drained
1 can (15 oz) garbanzo beans, drained

Fry bacon until crisp. Remove from pan. Saute onion and ground beef until meat browns. Combine bacon, onions and ground beef with remaining ingredients in 3 qt casserole. Bake at 350° for 40 min.

CAULIFLOWER IN CHEESE PUFF

1. Cook until tender crisp in boiling, salted water:
   1 head cauliflower, washed and broken into flowerets
2. Place cauliflower in lightly greased shallow baking-dish, reserving 2-3 flowerets for garnish.
3. Combine in saucepan:
   3 Tb butter or margarine   3 Tb flour
   3/4 ts salt   ¼ ts pepper
4. Add, stirring constantly over low heat until thickened: 1½ c milk
5. Add to sauce: 3/4 c grated Cheddar cheese
6. Beat and add to sauce: 4 eggs and 1 ts sugar
7. Beat until stiff and fold into cooked sauce:
   4 egg whites
8. Pour over cauliflowerets and bake at 350° for 20 min. or until sauce is firm.
9. Garnish with reserved flowerets.

EGGPLANT PARMESAN FRITTATA

1 egg   1 ts water
½ ts salt   2 c diced pared eggplant
½ c fine dry bread crumbs   ¼ c butter or oil
8 eggs   ½ c milk or tomato juice
½ c shredded Mozzarella cheese
¼ c grated Parmesan cheese
½ ts oregano leaves, crushed
Parsley sprigs, optional

In med. bowl beat together the 1 egg, water and salt. Add eggplant and toss gently until eggplant is completely coated with egg mixture. Let stand 10 min and drain. Return eggplant to bowl; sprinkle with crumbs and toss until completely coated with crumbs.

In 10" omelet pan or skillet with ovenproof handle over med. heat, cook eggplant in butter, stirring frequently, until lightly browned on all sides, about 5 min.

Beat together remaining ingredients except parsley. Pour over eggplant. Cook over low to med. heat until eggs are almost set, 12 to 15 min. Cover pan, remove from heat and let stand 8-10 min. Or broil about 6" from heat until eggs are completely set, 4 or 5 min. longer. Cut into wedges and serve from pan. Garnish with parsley.

YANKEE ROLL-UPS WITH CHEESE SAUCE

1. Roll four to 5 spears of asparagus diagonally on one slice of baked ham.
2. Place in drip pan, seam down.
3. Add enough asparagus juice to the bottom of the pan to cover slightly.
4. Cover pan with foil and place in 350° oven for 15-20 minutes.
5. To serve, remove from pan and cover with one tablespoon cheese sauce. (Easy sauce is undiluted cream of cheese soup.)
6. For 50 servings of two rolls apiece, use 100 slices of ham and 18 cans of 16 oz. asparagus spears.

CHICK-PEA CHILI

1 sm onion, minced
2 cloves garlic, minced
1 Tb oil
2 8-oz cans tomato sauce
1 15-oz can chick-peas, drained
1 Tb ground cumin
½ ts oregano
1/8 ts cayenne pepper
1/3 c low-fat yogurt
1/3 c sour cream
2 c hot cooked rice (optional)
chopped green peppers (garnish)
chopped tomatoes (garnish)
shredded lettuce (garnish)

In large saucepan, cook the onion and garlic in oil over med. heat until the onion is limp and translucent. Stir in the chick-peas, tomato sauce, chili powder, cumin, oregano and cayenne. Simmer, uncovered, about 30 min.

In small bowl, stir together the yogurt and sour cream. Serve with rice and topped with yogurt mixture, peppers, tomatoes and lettuce.

TOMATOES OREGANO

Cut 6 lg ripe tomatoes in half. Place each half cut side up in a baking dish. Sprinkle liberally with oregano, garlic salt and pepper. In a small bowl moisten 1 c soft bread crumbs with 1 Tb salad oil. Top each tomato with some crumbs and 1 ts grated Parmesan cheese. Bake 25 to 30 min. in a moderate 350° oven. Serves 12.

EXTRA FANCY STRING BEANS

1 8 oz. can mushrooms) saute
1 med. onion sliced)

Make white sauce in double boiler:

½ c butter	¼ c flour
2 c milk	1 c light cream

Add the following ingredients:
3/4 lb sharp cheddar cheese

1/8 ts tobasco sauce	1 ts salt
2 ts soy sauce	½ ts pepper

3 pkg French frozen beans (no salt)
Cook and pour above sauce over beans. Garnish with 15 oz. can of water chestnuts and ½ c toasted sliced almonds. Bake 375° for 20 min. Serves 12-18.

SCRUMPTIOUS BEANS

1 lg can pork and beans	4 Tb catsup
2 Tb molasses	2 Tb brown sugar
3 drops tobasco	1 lb bacon, browned & crushed

In 2 Tb of bacon fat saute 2 green peppers and 1 med. onion
Mix together and bake 2 hrs. at 275° or 30 min. at 350°.

STIR FRIED BEANSPROUTS

1. Heat in heavy skillet 2 Tb salad oil
2. Add and stir fry until limp on high heat (3 min) 1 lb washed beansprouts
   2 stalks green onions and tops, finely sliced diagonally
   salt & pepper to taste
   sprinkle lightly with Accent
3. Serve immediately

Makes 4-6 servings.

SESAME BROCCOLI

1. Prepare according to package directions:
   2 pkg (10 oz) frozen broccoli spears
2. Combine in small sauscepan and heat to boiling:
   1 Tb salad oil 1 Tb vinegar
   1 Tb soy sauce 2 ts sugar
   1 Tb sesame seed, toasted
3. Pour sauce over hot broccoli, turning spears to coat. Serve immediately.

Makes 4-5 servings

PUMPKIN SUCCOTASH

4 slices bacon, chopped
½ c chopped onion
1 clove garlic, chopped fine
1 green pepper, seeded and chopped fine
3 c peeled, seeded pumpkin cut in 3/4" cubes
1 pkg (10 oz) frozen whole kernel corn, thawed
2 ts salt
1 can (1 lb) tomatoes
1 c uncooked sliced green beans
dash of pepper

Fry the bacon until it is crisp. Drain and reserve. Measure the drippings and return ¼ c to a frying pan. Add the onion, garlic, green pepper and pumpkin. Cook, stirring constantly for 5 min. Stir in tomatoes, beans. corn, salt and pepper. Cover and simmer until pumpkin is tender (about 25 min.) Serve topped with bacon. Makes 6-8 servings.

STUFFED TOMATOES

6 lg tomatoes (cut center out & cut in small pcs.)
Add 1 good sized onion, chopped
1 green pepper, chopped
2 c bread crumbs
2 sm cans deviled ham

Mix well and put in buttered casserole. Dot with dried bread crumbs. Bake 1 hr at 375°. Salt & pepper to taste.

ITALIAN ZUCCHINI CRESCENT PIE

4 c thinly sliced unpeeled zucchini
1 c coarsley chopped onion
½ c butter or margarine
½ c chopped parsley or 2 Tb parsley flakes
½ ts salt ½ ts pepper
¼ ts garlic powder ¼ ts basil leaves
¼ ts oregano leaves 2 eggs, well beaten
8 oz (2 c) shredded muenster or mozzarella cheese
8 oz can refrigerated crescent dinner rolls
2 ts dijon or prepared mustard
Heat oven to 375°. In 10" skillet, cook zucchini and onion in margarine until tender, about 10 min. Stir in parsley and seasonings. In large bowl, blend eggs and cheese. Stir in vegetable mixture.

Separate dough into 8 triangles. Place in ungreased 11¼ quiche pan, 10" pie pan or 12 x 8" baking dish; press over bottom and up sides to form crust. Spread vegetable mixture evenly into crust.

Bake at 375° for 18-20 minutes or until knife inserted near center comes out clean. (If crust becomes too brown, cover with foil during last 10 min.) Let stand 10 min. before serving. Cut into wedges to serve; serve hot. 8 servings.

Tips: If using 12 x 8" baking dish, separate dough into 2 long rectangles; press over bottom and 1" up sides to form crust.

To reheat, cover loosely with foil; heat at 375° for 12-15 minutes.

ZUCCHINI FLATS

Use large zucchini for this dish--that way, you'll come out with wide, flat, succulent strips.

About 3/4 c grated Parmesan cheese
2 eggs 2 Tb each flour and parsley
3/4 ts salt ¼ ts pepper
2 cloves garlic, minced or pressed
¼ c milk 2 lg zucchini (about 7" long)
All purpose flour ¼ c salad oil
Directions on following page.

ZUCCHINI FLATS (continued)

Directions:

In a shallow bowl, combine 3/4 c of cheese, eggs, the 2 Tbs flour, parsley, salt, pepper, garlic and milk. With a wire whisk or rotary beater, beat until smooth. Cover and refrigerate for at least 15 min.

Cut zucchini in half cross-wise, then into length-wise slices about ¼" thick. Lightly dust each piece with flour.

Heat oil in a wide frying pan over medium heat. Using a fork, dip each zucchini slice into cheese mixture, thickly coating both sides. Place in pan, a few pieces at a time, and cook, turning once, until golden brown on both sides.

Drain briefly on paper towels, then transfer to a serving plate and keep warm until all are cooked. Sprinkle to taste with additional cheese. Makes 4 to 6 servings.

ZUCCHINI PIZZA PIE

Zucchini forms the foundation for this no-bread pizza

About 1½ lb zucchini　　2 eggs
1 c (4 oz) each shredded mozzarella cheese and sharp cheddar cheese
1 lb lean ground beef　　¼ ts each salt and garlic salt
1 medium size onion, chopped
1 can (8 oz) tomato sauce
2 ts oregano leaves
1 green pepper, seeded and cut into thin strips
¼ lb mushrooms, sliced
1/3 c grated Parmesan cheese

Shred zucchini (4 c, lightly packed) squeeze out any moisture.

In large bowl, beat eggs lightly; stir in zucchini and ½ c each of cheeses. Press zucchini mixture in a greased 10 x 15" pan. Bake in a 400° oven for about 10 min. Meanwhile, crumble beef into a frying pan over med. heat and cook, stirring to break up meat, until browned. Sprinkle with salt and garlic salt. Add onion and cook until soft. Drain off and discard drippings, then stir in tomato sauce and oregano.

Spoon meat mixture over zucchini crust. Arrange pepper strips and mushrooms on top; sprinkle w/Parmesan and other cheeses. Bake on lowest rack at 400° for 30 min.

SUNSHINE CARROTS

5 med. carrots
1 ts cornstarch
¼ ts ginger
2 Tb butter or margarine
1 Tb sugar
¼ ts salt
¼ c orange juice

Peel carrots and slice crosswise on the bias, about 1" thick. Cook, covered, in small amount of boiling water until just tender, about 20 min. Drain.

Meanwhile, combine sugar, cornstarch, salt and ginger in saucepan. Add orange juice and cook, stirring constantly until mixture thickens and bubbles. Boil one minute. Stir in butter.

Pour sauce over hot, cooked carrots, tossing to coat evenly. Makes 4 servings.

COPPER PENNIES

5 c cooked, pared and thinly sliced carrots (12-16)
1 green pepper diced
1 8-oz can tomato sauce
½ c salad oil
3/4 c vinegar
1 ts worcestershire sauce
3 bunches green onion, thin slice
1 c sugar
1 ts dry mustard

Peel, thinly slice, and cook carrots just until tender. Dice green pepper, sliced onion and blend with sliced cooked carrots.

Blend tomato sauce, salad oil, sugar, vinegar, dry mustard and worcestershire sauce. Pour over vegetables in a shallow dish. Refrigerate, covered for at least 24 hrs before serving. Marinade keeps indefinitely.

* * * *

Too many people who try to use the weekend to unwind simply unravel.

We're not primarily put on this earth to see through one another, but to see one another through.

Those who complain about the way the ball bounces are usually the ones who dropped it.

FLEMISH CARROTS

1. Cut into julienne strips, 8 med. carrots
2. Plunge carrots into a saucepan full of boiling water. Cook 2-3 min. Drain, reserving ½ c water.
3. Add to carrots:

   ½ c reserved water — ¼ c butter
   ¼ ts salt — 1/8 ts freshly ground pepper
   1 ts sugar

4. Bring to boiling point and reduce to simmer. Cook covered for 5-10 min or until just tender and dry. Stir or shake to prevent sticking. If carrots are soupy, cook without a cover to reduce cooking liquid. Remove from heat.
5. Beat together 2 egg yolks ½ c heavy cream
6. Return to low heat and cook only long enough to heat through.
7. Remove from heat and stir in

   2 Tb fresh lemon huice
   2 Tb minched parsley

Serves 4-6.

SAUCY POTATOES AND CARROTS

1. Combine in heavy saucepan

   2 Tbs butter — ½ c water
   7 green onions, minced
   7 carrots, peeled and sliced 1/8 inch thick
   1/8 ts salt

2. Bring to boiling, reduce heat, simmer 20-30 min. until carrots are tender and liquid has evaporated.
3. Butter bottom and sides of a 2 qt casserole.
4. Peel and slice 1/8" thick 5 white potatoes
5. Starting with potatoes, form layers of potatoes and carrots, finishing with potatoes.
6. Sprinkle each layer with salt and white pepper.
7. Pour over potatoes and carrots, 2 c heavy cream.
8. Bake at 350° for 1 hr, until potatoes are tender.

Makes 8 servings.

FRENCH PANCAKES (CREPES)

3 eggs
3/4 c flour
¼ ts salt
1 c milk
1 Tb sugar

In a blender, combine milk and eggs, then add flour, sugar and salt. Cover and whirl smooth. Set aside in a cool place for at least one hr.

Pour about 2 Tb batter for each crepe onto a lightly buttered, heated 6-8" pan over medium heat. Turn once, baking until golden brown on both sides. Makes 16 or more crepes.

To freeze: Make stacks of from 6 to 12 crepes, wrap together tightly in foil or in plastic bags and freeze. To thaw, set in a warm place over a wire rack for 2-3 hrs or place the foil wrapped crepes in a 175° oven for 15 to 20 min.

GATEAU DE CREPES A LA FLORENTINE

(Mound of French Pancakes filled with cream cheese, spinach and mushrooms)

Sauce Mornay

5 Tb flour
2 3/4 c milk
1/8 ts pepper
4 Tb butter
½ ts salt
Big pinch nutmeg

¼ c whipping cream
1 g grated Swiss cheese
Add the cream slowly to the white sauce, stirring constantly. Stir in all but 2 Tb of cheese. Cover and set aside.

Spinach filling

1 Tb minced green onions
2 Tb butter
1 pkg cooked chopped spinach (drained)
¼ ts salt
Cook onions in butter for a moment. Add spinach and salt and stir over moderately high heat to evaporate moisture. Stir in ½ to 1/3 c of the above cheese sauce. Cover and simmer slowly for 8-10 minutes. Stir occasionally.

CHEESE & MUSHROOM FILLING FOR CREPES

1 c cottage cheese or 8 oz cream cheese
salt and pepper — 1 egg
¼ lb (1 c) minced mushrooms
1 Tb minced green onion — 1 Tb butter
½ Tb oil
Forming the mound:
3 Tb grated cheese — ½ Tb butter
9" baking dish

Mash cheese in a bowl with seasonings. Beat in raw egg. Saute mushrooms and green onions in butter and oil for 5-6 min. Stir them into the cheese mixture.

Butter cooking dish and center crepe in bottom. Spread it with a layer of cheese and mushroom filling. Press a crepe on top and spread with spinach filling. Continue with alternating layers of crepes and fillings ending with a crepe. Pour over remaining cheese sauce. Sprinkle with 3 Tb cheese and dot with butter.

Bake 25-30 min in preheated oven at 350°. Heat through thoroughly and brown the top lightly. To serve, cut in pie-shaped wedges.

BROCCOLI LORRAINE

1½ lb broccoli — 3 slices bacon, cooked crisp
3/4 ts salt — 1/8 ts of pepper & nutmeg
½ ts dry mustard — 4 eggs
1½ c half and half cream
3 Tb freshly shredded Parmesan cheese

Trim and cut broccoli & drain well. Turn into a 2 qt shallow baking dish; sprinke with crushed bacon.

In a bowl, combine the salt, pepper, nutmeg, and mustard. Add eggs and beat lightly with a fork, then stir in half and half and Parmesan and pour over the broccoli.

Set baking dish inside a pan of hot tap water so that water comes to within ½ inch of dish rim. Bake in a 350° oven for 25-30 mins or until you can shake the pan back and forth and only a 3" circle in the center moves. Serve at once. Makes 8 servings.

REFRIED BEANS

1 lb. dried pinto or pink beans, cleaned
5 c water
1 or 2 med. size onions, diced (optional)
½ to 1 c hot bacon drippings, butter, or lard
salt to taste

Combine beans in a pan with water and onions. Bring to a boil, cover, and remove from heat for 2 hrs (or soak beans in cold water overnight). Return to heat, bring to a boil and simmer slowly until beans are very tender (about 3 hrs). Mash beans with a potato masher and add bacon drippings, butter, or lard. Mix well; continue cooking, stirring frequently, until beans are thickened and fat is absorbed. Salt to taste. Serve or reheat. Makes 6-8 servings or 5 to 6 cups. If frozen, can be used again and again with tasty Mexican recipes.

BAKED BEANS SUPREME

2 cans pork and beans
1 lb bacon, cut in pieces
1 #2½ can crushed or chunk pineapple, drained
1 green pepper, diced
1 onion, diced
1 c brown sugar
1 med. sized bottle catsup
6 Tb. Worcestershire sauce (or less to taste)

Fry bacon, onion and green pepper until bacon is crisp. Drain off fat and discard. Mix remaining ingredients and bake 3 hrs. at 250°. Serves 18-20.

* * * *

Praise does wonders for the sense of hearing.

At a Health Spa: "She's a decided blonde--she decided last night."

CAULIFLOWER & CARROT MEDLEY

About 8 lg carrots, peeled
1 lg head cauliflower
Boiling salted water
2 Tb each butter or margarine and flour
½ ts prepared Dijon style mustard
1 c regular strength chicken broth
½ c whipping cream
1¼ c shredded Swiss cheese
2 green onions, including part of tops, sliced

Cut carrots into ¼" slanting slices (should have 4 c). Break cauliflower into flowerets. Cook vegetables in boiling salted water until just tender (about 5 min.) Plunge in cold water, drain.

In another pan, melt butter over med. heat; stir in flour and mustard and cook until bubbly. Remove from heat; gradually stir in chicken broth and cream. Cook, stirring, until melted.

Combine vegetables and sauce in a 2 qt casserole. Sprinkle with remaining cheese. If done ahead, cover and refrigerate.

Before serving, bake, uncovered in a 350° oven until heated through (15 min if warm or 35 minutes if chilled.) Garnish with onions. Makes 8 delectable servings!

SWEET AND SOUR CARROTS

¼ c plus 3 Tb chicken broth, divided
3 Tb white vinegar
2 Tb packed brown sugar
1 Tb corn starch
1 ts salt
1 Tb vegetable oil
½ ts ground ginger
2 c carrots, cut diagonally
2 c red cabbage, cut into 3/4" chunks
1 c green onions, cut into 1" pieces

In small bowl, mix together ¼ c of broth, vinegar, brown sugar, corn starch and salt; set aside. In large wok or skillet, heat oil over high heat. Add carrots, cabbage. and green onions; stir-fry 2 min. Stir in remaining 3 Tb chicken broth and ginger. Cover, reduce heat to medium. Cook until carrots are crisp-tender (about 4 min). Stir cornstarch mixture, then stir into wok. Cook, stirring constantly, until sauce bubbles and thickens. Serve at once; or chill and serve cold.
They'll think you studied cooking in the Orient!

LIMA-CURRIED BEANS

5 lb fresh lima beans in the pod, shelled or 2 pkg (10 oz each) frozen large lima beans
Boiling salted water
¼ c (1/8 lb) butter or margarine
3 Tb each finely chopped onion and all purpose flour
2 ts curry powder
1½ c milk
½ c salted round butter cracker crumbs
4 Tb melted butter or margarine

Cook beans in boiling salted water until tender; drain thoroughly and turn into greased casserole (about 1½ qts). In a saucepan, melt the ¼ c butter; add onions and saute just until soft. Add flour and curry powder, stirring until smooth. Gradually add milk; stir until thickened. Pour sauce over beans; mix gently to coat beans. Toss cracker crumbs with the 4 Tb melted butter. Sprinkle over top of beans. Bake in a 400° oven for 15 minutes. Makes 6 servings.

LEMON GREEN BEANS BECHAMEL

3 pkg (9 oz) frozen French style green beans, thawed
½ c water 3/4 ts salt
½ c regular strength chicken broth
1 Tb cornstarch 2 c sour cream
2 ts sugar 1/8 ts ground nutmeg
2/3 c slivered almonds 1 Tb butter or margarine
2 Tb shredded Parmesan cheese

Cook beans in the water over highest heat, uncovered, until liquid is boiling, then cook 5 min more, stirring frequently. Drain well. Mix beans with salt and spread in a shallow 2 qt casserole.

Gradually blend broth with cornstarch, then cook, stirring until very thick and clear. Blend in sour cream, sugar, and nutmeg, and cook, stirring, just until simmering. Pour hot sauce over beans. Saute almonds in butter until lightly browned, then spoon decoratively around the side of casserole. Sprinkle with cheese. Cover and refrigerate up to 24 hrs. Bake in a 375° oven for 40 minutes or until well heated and top is lightly browned. Makes 10-12 servings.

CARAMEL SWEET POTATOES

8 med. sweet potatoes, cooked and peeled
1 c butter — 2 c brown sugar
½ c water — ½ c shredded coconut

Cut sweet potatoes into 1" slices. Combine butter, brown sugar and water in a saucepan; cook on med. heat until mixture thickens, about 20 min. Add sweet potatoes, lower heat and simmer 10 min. Sprinkle with shredded coconut before serving. Makes 12 servings.

YAM CASSEROLE

6 med. yams cooked — 7-8 apples
2 c water — 1 sq butter
½ c brown sugar — ½ c white sugar
salt — 3 Tb cornstarch

Mix sugar and cornstarch together. Add to water and butter. In a buttered casserole put a layer of yams and a layer of sliced apples. Repeat until all are used. Pour syrup over yams and apples. Bake in 375° oven for 45 min.

CRANBERRY SWEET POTATOES

1. Slice two 1 lb 12 oz cans sweet potatoes
2. Layer one-half of sliced potatoes in a 2 qt casserole
3. Combine together and heat for 5 min:
   1½ c whole cranberry sauce, canned
   2 Tb water — 2 Tb brown sugar
   ¼ c melted butter — ¼ ts salt
4. Pour half of mixture over layered sweet potatoes.
5. Arrange remaining potatoes over casserole. Top with rest of cranberry mixture.
6. Bake in 350° oven for 45 min or until potatoes are hot and bubbly. Makes 8 servings. A lovely change from the conventional.

* * * *

The trouble with sleeping is the going to and the coming from.

ARTICHOKES WITH MUSHROOMS

¼ lb mushrooms, halved
4 Tb (1/8 lb) butter or margarine
2 pkg (8 or 9 oz each) frozen artichoke hearts
1/3 c whipping cream ½ ts tarragon leaves
salt and pepper to taste

In a saucepan, saute mushrooms in the butter for 5 min over medium heat. Add the frozen artichoke hearts. Cover and simmer 7 or 8 minutes longer. Stir in the cream, tarragon, salt and pepper. Makes 4 to 6 servings.

STUFFED ARTICHOKES

1 c ground cooked meat or chicken
½ c finely minced onion
2 Tb each finely chopped almonds and parsley
1 egg, beaten 1/8 ts nutmeg
salt and pepper to taste
6 large artichokes 1 Tb lemon juice
16 slices tomato 1½ c boiling water

Combine meat, onion, almonds, parsley, egg, nutmeg, salt and papper. Mix well. Wash artichokes well and remove stems; cut off about 1" of the tops. Using a spoon, scoop out all the fuzzy choke and tiny leaves. Stuff meat mixture into center of the artichokes.

Place in a deep casserole or baking pan; sprinkle lemon juice over the artichoke leaves and top each with a tomato slice. Pour boiling water in pan. Cover and bake in a 375° oven for 1 to 1½ hrs, or until artichoke leaves pull away easily and are soft at the ends. Serves 6.

* * * *

A day would be improved a lot if it started at some other time than in the morning.

Endeavor to so live that when you die even the undertaker will be sorry.

RATATOUILLE

Even beyond its rich flavor, Ratatouille has other qualities which account for its popularity: It tastes better made ahead (even a day or more old) and is just as good cold as hot.

About ½ c olive oil — 2 lg onions, sliced
2 lg cloves garlic, minced or mashed
1 med-sized eggplant, cut in ½" cubes
6 med-sized zucchini, thickly sliced
2 green or red bell peppers, seeded and cut in chunks
About 2 ts salt — 1 ts basil
½ c minced parsley — 4 lg tomatoes, cut in chunks
Parsley — sliced tomato (optional)

Heat ¼ c of oil in large frying pan over high heat. Add onions and garlic and cook, stirring until onions are soft but not browned. Stir in the eggplant, zucchini, peppers, 2 ts salt, basil, and minced parsley. Add a little of the oil as needed to keep the vegetables from sticking.

Cover pan and cook over moderate heat for about 30 min; stir occasionally, using a large spatula and turning the vegetables to help preserve their shape. If mixture becomes quite soupy, remove cover.

Add the tomatoes to the vegetables and stir to blend. Also add more oil if vegetables are sticking. Cover and cook over moderate heat for 15 min; stir occasionally. Again, if mixture becomes soupy, remove cover. Ratatouille should have a little free liquid, but still be of a good spoon-and-serve consistency. Add more salt if required. Serve hot, chilled, at room temperature, or reheated. Garnish with parsley and tomato. Serves 8-10.

Ratatouille in the Oven: Using the vegetables and seasonings in the above recipe, layer all ingredients into a 6 qt casserole, pressing down to make fit if necessary. Drizzle only 4 Tb of the olive oil over top layer. Cover casserole and bake in a 350° oven for 3 hrs. Baste top occasionally with some of the liquid. Uncover during last hour if quite soupy. Mix gently and salt to taste. Garnish with parsley and tomato.

YAM SOUFFLE

3 c mashed yams or sweet potatoes (unseasoned)
1/3 c Sherry or orange juice
1¼ c half and half (cream)
6 Tb melted butter or margarine
1½ ts grated orange peel
1/8 ts each pepper and ground nutmeg
1 ts salt
2 Tb firmly packed brown sugar
6 eggs, separated

Combine in the mixer bowl the mashed yams, Sherry, cream, butter, orange peel, pepper, nutmeg, salt and sugar; beat until blended and smooth. Add the egg yolks and beat until fluffy. This much can be done ahead and the mixture held at room temperature for several hours. Just before baking whip egg whites until they hold short, distinct, moist peaks; carefully fold into potato mixture.

Spoon into about 12 well buttered, individual souffle dishes (about 5 oz size) and bake in a 375° oven for about 20 min. (Or bake in a 2½ qt souffle dish about 45 min.) Serve immediately. Serves 12.

YAM CASHEW CASSEROLE

About 2½ lbs yams or sweet potatoes, whole or halved
Boiling salted water
1 ts ground cinnamon
¼ ts salt
1 egg
about ¼ c pineapple or orange juice
about ¼ c sugar
3 Tb melted butter or margarine
½ c salted cashews, coarsely chopped

In a saucepan, cook the potatoes in boiling water until tender (about 30 min); drain. When cool enough to handle, peel potatoes. Using an electric mixer or potato masher, beat until mashed, then measure 3 c. Add cinnamon, salt, egg, juice and sugar. Beat until fluffy, adding more fruit juice if mixture seems dry. Taste and add more sugar or salt, if needed. Mix in 2 Tb of the butter.

Spoon into a qt casserole or souffle dish. (Cover and refrigerate at this point, if desired.) Add the cashews to remaining 1 Tb butter in a small frying pan; heat, stirring until lightly toasted. Sprinkle on top of casserole. Bake, uncovered in 375° oven for 15 min. until heated through (about 35 min if chilled.)

ZUCCHINI TOMATO QUICHE

Pretty as a picture and as tasty as it looks, this impressive entree is perfect for a family breakfast, lunch, dinner or a stylish brunch for guests. Be sure to drain the tomato well as summer tomatoes are often very juicy.

1 baked 9" pastry shell 2 c sliced zucchini
½ c chopped onion 1 Tb butter
½ c shredded Swiss cheese 1 Tb flour
1 med tomato, seeded, chopped and drained
6 eggs 1 c half and half or milk
½ ts oregano or basil leaves, crushed
½ ts salt 1/8 ts pepper

Bake pastry shell; set aside. In large skillet over medium heat, cook zucchini and onion in butter until lightly browned, about 5 min. Place mixture in baked pie shell; top with cheese.

Sprinkle zucchini mixture with flour and top with chopped tomato. Beat together eggs, half and half, oregano or basil, salt and pepper. Pour over vegetables and cheese.

Bake at 375 degrees about 30-35 minutes, or until knife inserted near center comes out clean. Let stand five minutes before serving.

LIMA BEAN CASSEROLE

8 med. onions, sliced
4 Tb or 1/4 c butter or margarine
3 cans (4 oz) sliced mushrooms
2 cans cream of mushroom soup
6 pkg frozen lima beans
1 ts salt 1/4 ts pepper
2 ts dill seed ½ pt whipping cream
2 c shredded cheese

Mix all together and bake at 300° for 30 min.
Top with cheese and return to 350° oven for 20 min.
DO NOT OVERHEAT! Serves 8.

MUSHROOMS STUFFED WITH BRAZIL NUTS

1½ lb large mushrooms
1 onion chopped
1 c chopped or ground Brazil nuts
1 ts salt & dash of pepper
1 Tb lemon juice
¼ c butter
1 c soft bread crumbs
1 Tb catsup
½ c cream

Wash mushrooms and remove stems. Chop stems fine. Melt butter and saute onion and stems about 5 min. Stir in bread crumbs and nuts and cook 2 min. Add seasonings. Stuff mushroom caps with mixture. Arrange in dish, garnish with strips of bacon and pour cream around them. Bake 400° for 25 min. Serves 6. Absolutely wonderful!

STUFFED MUSHROONS

18 med. mushrooms, wipe and remove stems
1 pkg cream cheese (8 oz)
1 Tb milk
1 ts worcestershire sauce
¼ c chopped water chestnuts
1 Tbs minced onion
1 Tb green pepper chopped fine
1 Tb crisp crumbled bacon

Combine above ingredients and fill mushroom caps. Place on cookie sheet and bake at 350° for 15 minutes or until light brown.

MARINATED MUSHROOMS

1½ lb mushrooms (smaller the better)
1 c oil
½ c wine vinegar
2 ts salt
1 ts leaf oregano
2 cloves garlic, crushed
1 ts paprika

Wash mushrooms. Combine ingredients and marinate at least 2 hrs. Serve on toothpicks. Also see marinated mushrooms under Appetizers.

ZUCCHINI CASSEROLE

6 c zucchini sliced
1 c shredded carrot
1 pkg stuffing mix
1 c sour cream
½ c chopped onion
1 can cream chicken soup

Boil onion and squash 5 min and drain. Mix soup, sour cream and carrots together. Fold into zucchini. Make stuffing as directed. Put some in bottom and save rest for top. Bake 25 min and then put grated cheese on top and bake 10 min more at 350°. Serve 6 to 8 depending on quantity of zucchini used. Especially good served with chicken or pork.

SIMPLE ZUCCHINI

3 medium zucchini, sliced
2 Tbs salad oil
1 8-oz can tomato sauce
salt and pepper to taste
1 medium onion, sliced
½ to 1 ts crushed oregano
1 small pkg mozzarella cheese

Simmer onion in oil until tender. Add zucchini and all but cheese. Cook 10 min. Add cheese and return to oven until it is melted. Can cook in oven or in frypan after cheese has been added.

SOUR CREAM ZUCCHINI

½ medium zucchini per serving
1-2 ts dry onion soup per 1 c sour cream

Cook squash in salted boiling water until almost done. Drain. Mix dry soup and sour cream and gently fold in almost cooked squash. Place in greased baking dish. Cover with thick buttered crumbs. Bake until brown and heated through at 350°.

* * * *

A generation ago most men who finished a day's work needed rest; now they need exercise.

THREE KING VEGETABLES

1. Remove outer leaves and stalk from 1 medium head fresh cauliflower
2. Wash thoroughly.
3. Wash, trim off root end, leaving several sections together, 1 bunch celery
4. Tie sections together with string then cut into pieces 1¼" long.
5. Wash, pare, and cut into 2" pieces, 1 lb thin carrots.
6. Bring to boiling in 3 qt pan, 2 c chicken bouillon.
7. Add prepared cauliflower, carrots and celery.
8. Simmer 15-20 min.
9. Remove vegetables from broth.
10. Add to broth: 2 Tb butter
    ½ ts salt dash of pepper
    2 Tb cornstarch
11. Heat, stirring until mixture thickens.
12. Serve vegetables on decorative platter with broth spooned over top.
13. Garnish with dill weed.

Makes 8 servings.

* * * *

The only exercise some people get is jumping at conclusions, running down their friends, sidestepping responsibility, and pushing their luck.

Did you ever know anyone who remarked that ugliness, like beauty, is only skin deep.

A man's character and his garden both reflect the amount of weeding that was done during the growing season.

CHINESE VEGETABLES

1 lb bacon, cooked crisp and crumbled
½ head of good sized cabbage
2 med onions, cut in quarters
1 c bean sprouts
1 c mushrooms (smaller the better)
4 stalks celery cut 1" diagonal pieces
(Can also use broccoli, brussel sprouts, green beans, zucchini, whatever you have fresh)

Cook bacon, remove from fat and crumble. Set aside. Layer vegetables in large saucepan, beginning with large chunks of cabbage, and ending with bean sprouts and mushrooms on top. Steam with minimum amount of water until celery is transparent, but not well done. Drippings from bacon should be added to steaming vegetables at onset of cooking. In another saucepan, cook 2 c rice as per directions, or 2 c rice to 4 c water. Cook for 20 min without removing lid. Add soy sauce to make rice brown. Garnish with bacon bits. Serve in separate bowl from vegetables.

<u>Sauce</u>: 2 c brown sugar 1 c catsup
2-3 Tb white vinegar (may be thicked with cornstarch if desired)
2½ c water

Heat and stir until sugar is dissolved. Just bring to boil. We love to make a bed on plate of rice; add vegetables; pour sauce over all. Delicious flavor and always calls for repeat performance! A generous, filling, nutritious meal.

WHIPPED TURNIPS

3 lbs turnips, peeled
¼ c butter
1½ Tb sugar
1½ ts salt
dash pepper
3 eggs
1 c soft bread crumbs
1½ ts lemon juice

Cook turnips in salted water for at least 2 hrs. Drain and mash. Add sugar, butter, salt & pepper. Beat. Add eggs and continue beating until fluffy. Add crumbs & juice. Pour into casserole. Chill until ready to use. Bake uncovered at 385° for 50 min. You'll be pleased with the enthusiastic response to this new twist to a pioneer staple!

ZESTY WINTER VEGETABLES

1. Cook in medium saucepan containing boiling salted water for 10 min — 5 med carrots, peeled and sliced ¼" thick
2. Add and cook 10 additional minutes until tender crisp — ½ lb fresh brussel sprouts
3. Drain, reserving ¼ c cooking liquid.
4. Place vegetables and reserved liquid in 2 qt dish.
5. Combine in small bowl and spoon over vegetables
   - ½ c mayonnaise
   - 2 Tbs finely chopped onion
   - 1 Tb prepared horseradish
   - ¼ ts salt
   - dash pepper
6. Combine and sprinkle over vegetables
   - ½ c dry bread crumbs
   - 1 Tb butter or margarine melted
7. Bake uncovered in a 350° oven for 20 min or until heated through.
8. Garnish with — 2 Tb chopped parsley.

Makes 10 servings.

SIMPLE SQUASH DELIGHT

1. Peel and cut into ½" cubes and simmer in Dutch oven containing boiling salted water for 15-20 min. — 3 lbs winter squash
2. Melt in large saucepan 3 Tb butter or margarine
3. Remove 1 Tb butter and toss with ½ c soft bread crumbs
4. Add to melted butter in saucepan and saute until tender 1 med onion, chopped and 1 clove garlic, minced
5. Stir in drained, cooked squash and 1 c cooked rice
   - 1 c cubed process American cheese
   - 1 egg, beaten
   - 1 ts salt
   - 1 ts thyme leaves, crumbled
   - ¼ ts pepper
6. Place in 2 qt casserole; sprinkle with buttered crumbs, and bake in a 350° oven for 30 min. Makes 6-8 servings.

CHEEZY VEGETABLE PLATTER

1. Scrub, pat dry and pierce with a fork, 3 lg potatoes
2. Bake in oven at 425° until tender, about 45 minutes.
3. Steam on rack in covered saucepan until tender crisp
   3 med carrots, pared, cut diagonally into 1" lengths
   3 c broccoli flowerets
   3 c cauliflower flowerets
4. Cut potatoes lengthwise in half; arrange on oven proof serving platter.
5. Spoon cooked broccoli, cauliflower and carrots over potatoes.
6. Drizzle with 1 Tb melted butter or margarine
7. Season to taste with salt and pepper.
8. Sprinkle with 3 c shredded Monterey Jack cheese
   1/3 c chopped green onions
9. Bake at 350° F until cheese melts, about 5 min.

Sprinkle with 3 Tb toasted shelled sunflower seeds (optional)

Makes 4-6 servings. NOTE: Potatoes may be steamed along with the other vegetables if desired. Your family will ask for this again and again!

* * * *

There are plenty of rules for attaining success, but none of them work unless you do.

A person who has everything should be quarantined.

The dictionary is the only place where success comes before work.

Great men are those who find that what they ought to do and what they want to do are the same thing.

BAKED LENTIL CASSEROLE

2 c dried lentils 2½ c water
2 ts salt ¼ ts pepper
1/8 ts marjoram leaves, crushed
1/8 ts thyme leaves, crushed
1 bay leaf 1½ c chopped onions
2 cloves garlic, minced 1 can (lb) tomatoes, cut up
2 c thinly peeled carrots 1 c thinly sliced celery
½ c chopped green pepper 2½ c shredded cheddar cheese

Combine lentils, water, salt, pepper, marjoram, thyme, bay leaf, onions, garlic and tomatoes in 9x13" baking dish. Cover tightly with foil and bake at 375° for 30 min. Stir in carrots, celery and green pepper, cover and continue baking about 40 min longer, or until vegetables are tender. Sprinkle cheese over top and return to oven, uncovered, just until cheese is melted. Makes 8 servings.

GREEN BEANS WITH WATER CHESTNUTS

2 Tb vegetable oil 1 lb green beans, trimmed
½ ts minced fresh ginger root 1 Tb sherry
¼ c cold water 1 ts corn starch
1 ts salt-free 14 herb and spice blend
12 water chestnuts, quartered

In medium skillet or wok, heat oil until hot. Stir-fry beans and ginger for 3 min. Add sherry, cover and cook 1 min. Meanwhile, in a small bowl, combine water, corn starch and herb and spice blend, mixing well. Pour half of the corn starch mixture over beans. Stir until thickened about 3 min. Remove to serving dish. Add water chestnuts and remaining corn starch mixture to skillet. Stir until thickened, about 3 min. Arrange decoratively around beans.

FRESH SPINACH CASSEROLE

2½ lb spinach
1½ ts salt
2 Tb melted butter or margarine
2 eggs, slightly beaten
1 c milk
1/8 ts pepper
1 ts finely grated onion
½ c shredded Swiss cheese

Trim stems from spinach and wash leaves well. Put into a large pan or Dutch oven. Add 1 ts salt, cover, and cook quickly in the water that clings to the leaves until tender and bright green (about 3 min). Drain well in a colander, pressing out water lightly with the back of a spoon; chop finely.

In a bowl, gently mix the spinach, remaining ½ ts salt, butter, eggs, milk, pepper, onion, and cheese. Pour into a shallow, 1 qt baking dish (cover and refrigerate if done ahead). Uncover and bake in a 325° oven until set (about 30 minutes; 45 minutes if refrigerated). Serve immediately. Serves 6.

CARROT SOUFFLE

2 c packed shredded carrots
3 Tb water
1 Tb minced chives
1 c skim milk
1 Tb melted butter or marg.
1 ts salt
4 Tb flour
4 eggs, separated

Combine carrots, butter, water, salt and chives. Cover and cook over med. heat, stirring occasionally, until carrots are tender. Sprinkle with flour and stir until mixed. Slowly add the milk, stirring, and cook until thickened. Remove from heat. Beat in 4 egg yolks. Whip the 4 egg whites until they hold soft peaks; fold into carrot mixture. Pour into a deep buttered casserole and bake at 375° for 35 min. Serve immediately.

STIR FRIED GREENS

1. Separate greens Wash and drain well. Cut into 2½" strips.	1½ lbs spinach, Swiss chard, Nappa (celery cabbage), bok choy (chard cabbage), head cabbage, mustard cabbage and/or zucchini, broccoli, green beans
2. Heat oil over high heat Add greens and stir fry about 3 min or until greens are tender-crisp.	2 Tb salad oil
3. Season with	¼ ts salt, 1 Tb soy sauce
4. Combine and stir in Cook until thick	1 c chicken broth 1 Tb cornstarch
5. Serve immediately.	

Makes 6 servings.

VEGETABLE CASSEROLE

2 pkg frozen mixed peas and carrots
2 pkg frozen sliced green beans
1 can mushroom soup
1 can french fried onions
2 c shredded Monterey Jack cheese

Cook vegetables separately until just tender. Drain, saving ½ c vegetable liquid to blend with soup. Toss vegetables with soup mixture; put in buttered casserole or baking dish and sprinkle with cheese. Top with crushed french fried onions. Bake at 350° until bubbly, about 15 min.

LAYERED BAKED VEGETABLES

1 pkg frozen lima beans, cooked
1 pkg frozen peas, cooked
1 pkg frozen French cut green beans, cooked
1 thinly sliced onion 1 c freshly sliced mushrooms

Mix together and pour over vegetables:
1 c cream, whipped 1 c mayonnaise

Top with 1 c grated cheddar cheese. Put under broiler or in microwave until cheese is melted.

HOLIDAY SPINACH

4 pkg (10-oz each) frozen chopped spinach
1 pt dairy sour cream
1 envelope dry onion soup mix
2 c fine bread crumbs (I use stuffing mix, crushed)
Cook spinach 20 min; drain very well. Add dairy sour cream and onion soup mix. Pour into greased casserole dish or use to stuff large tomatoes (8).

Combine bread crumbs with melted butter. Sprinkle over spinach mixture. Bake 20 min. in 350° oven. Serves 8.

WILD RICE

1 c wild rice
6 c water
¼ c butter
1 c diced celery
½ c chopped onion
1 can mushroom soup

Wash rice. Boil rice in 6 c water for 45 min. Do not stir while boiling. Do not cover rice while boiling. Rinse rice with cold water after it is cooked. Saute celery and onion in butter until celery is soft. Add cream of mushroom soup (undiluted) to rice mixture. Mix well. Put rice in casserole and bake for ½ hr in 360° oven. Serves 6.

Wild rice is especially delectable served with Cornish Hens.

STUFFED BAKED SWEET POTATOES

6 med. sweet potatoes
½ c orange juice
1 can (8 oz) crushed pineapple
3 Tb butter
1 ts salt
½ c chopped pecans

Bake scrubbed potatoes in moderate oven (375°) until tender, about 45 min to an hr. Cut strip off top of each potato. Spoon potato out of shell. Combine with butter, orange juice and salt, and whip.

Stir in pineapple. Spoon back into sweet potato shells. Sprinkle with nuts. Bake until thoroughly hot, about 12 min. more.

Variation: Stir in a little whipped cream and season with salt and a touch of nutmeg or cinnamon.

Notes

Notes

pasta & grains

PASTA is made chiefly from flour and water. It is the basic food throughout Italy. Pasta includes spaghetti, macaroni, ravioli, lasagne, and vermicelli. Italy has a Spaghetti Historical Museum in Pontedassio, near Imperia, with exhibits that show the history of the food.

It is becoming more and more into popular use in the Americas, as athletes and nutritionists alike recognize it as a quick and easy source of carbohydrates, and with its usual accompaniment of cheeses it has added protein value. It is very versatile and can be used with vegetables or fruits equally well. Once you use it, you'll find numerous ways to express yourself in pasta!

JAPANESE FRIED RICE

6 c cold cooked long grain rice
2 c onions, diced
1½ c celery diced
12 Tb soy sauce
6 Tb oil or bacon drippings
1 c carrots, diced
1 lg green pepper, diced
4 c cold meat cut bite size, ham, spam, pork, chicken

Use left over rice or cook 3 c of long grain rice & cool. Dice onions, celery, carrots, gr. pepper & cooked meat. Heat frying pan, add oil, then carrots and stir-fry 1 min. Add onion, stir-fry 1 min; add celery and green pepper. Stir-fry one min. Add meat and soy sauce and heat through. Break up cold rice which has been cooked. Stir in rice gently into meat and vegetables, taking care that each grain of rice is coated with oil and liquid in pan. Heat through. Serve immediately.

CHINESE FRIED RICE

2 Tb cooking oil
1 1/3 c water
1 Tb cooking oil
2 slighty beaten eggs
1 Tb chopped green onion
½ c cooked green peas
1½ c Minute Rice
½ ts salt
dash of salt
1 Tb cooking oil
½ c cooked ham in strips
1 ts soy sauce

In first oil, saute rice until golden brown. Gradually add water and salt. Bring to a boil and cover, removing from heat and let set for 5-10 min or until water is absorbed.

Heat 1 Tb cooking oil in frying pan. Add dash of salt to slightly beaten eggs. Scramble in oil breaking eggs into small pieces with fork. Remove and set aside. In last Tb of oil, add onions and ham strips to fry pan until golden brown. Add ½ c peas, rice and eggs. Heat thoroughly, stirring occasionally. Season with 1 ts soy sauce. Serves 3 or 4.

* * * *

Headline from the New York Daily News travel section: "Hawaii invites you to dance in the isles."

From an ad for ski vacations in Utah: "You've got to ski it to believe it."

SAVORY RICE

6 Tb margarine
1 med onion, chopped
1 med gr. pepper, chopped
1 c long grain rice
2 beef bouillon cubes
1 4-oz can mushroom pcs.
1 Tb soy sauce
1 ts oregano
2½ c hot water

Melt margarine in skillet, add onion and green pepper and cook until tender. Stir in rice. Cook until lightly browned. Add mushrooms, soy sauce and oregano. Put in buttered casserole dish. Dissolve bouillon in hot water and add. Cover. Put in 350° preheated oven and bake 45 minutes to 1 hr depending on how well cooked you like your rice. Serves 4.

MICRO-WAVE RICE

1 pkg (11 oz) frozen long grain white & wild rice
2 c herb seasoned dressing (stuffing)
1 can mushroom soup
1 2½-oz sliced mushrooms
2 Tb slivered almonds
½ c chopped celery
½ c chopped onion
¼ c hot water

Cook rice according to directions. Combine all ingredients in 1½ qt casserole. Cover. Cook in microwave 11-13 min. Stir after 6 min. Or cook 30 min. at 325° in conventional oven or until heated through. Serves 6-8.

WHEAT STUFFING

Saute until golden brown 1¼ c chopped onion
1 c finely chopped tart green apples & ¼ c butter

Add ¼ lb ground veal and cook and stir until light brown. Add 1 c cooked wheat or long grain rice and 1 c chicken broth and mix well. Cover and simmer over low heat until all liquid is absorbed. Then add:

1 ts salt
¼ ts marjoram
¼ ts celery seed
2 ts finely chopped parsley
¼ ts pepper
¼ ts thyme
1/8 ts cardamon

Cool and mix with 1 egg. Makes 4 c.

TOASTED RICE STUFFING

2 c uncooked converted rice
2 c chopped onion — 2 c chopped celery
2 c green pepper — 2 ts salt
10 chicken bouillon cubes dissolved in 5 c water or stock
2 eggs, well beaten — 1 Tb poultry seasoning
½ c minced parsley or celery tops
1 c mushrooms, or toasted slivered almonds, chopped pecans, diced crisp bacon, or chopped hard-cooked eggs (all optional)

Spread uncooked converted rice in shallow pan. Toast in moderate oven, 350° for 15-20 min, or until kernels are golden brown. Stir rice or shake pan occasionally for even browning.

Place onion, celery, green pepper and salt in bouillon or stock. Bring to boil. Stir in toasted converted rice. Turn heat low and cover. Cook approximately 25 min. or until liquid is absorbed and rice is tender. Remove from heat. Fold in eggs, poultry seasoning, and minced parsley or celery tops. Add mushrooms or other special ingredients desired. Taste and add more seasoning if needed. Stuff fowl and bake. Makes about 12 c or enough for a 12-15 lb bird.

WHEAT & CHEESE CASSEROLE

1 can (10 oz) cooked wheat — ½ c milk
1 c cream of chicken soup — ½ ts dry mustard
¼ ts salt — 3 oz sharp cheese, grated

In shallow baking dish combine wheat, soup, milk, mustard and salt. Mix. Stir in cheese, reserving some for a topping. Bake at 375° for 30-40 min or until slightly bubbly. Serves 4-6.

HAWAIIAN RICE

14 oz Instant rice — 1 lb bacon cut up
3-4 stalks celery diced (more or less as desired)
1 lg onion — ½-1 gr. pepper
¼-½ c soy sauce

Fry and drain bacon, saute onion, celery & green pepper. Add soy & crumbled bacon to rice and serve.

BARLEY CASSEROLE

6 Tb butter or margarine
1 lg onion, minced
1 c pearl barley
3 c chicken bouillon
1/8 ts pepper
2 c coarsely chopped raw chicken
1 c sliced mushrooms
½ ts salt
1 c raw carrots, bias cut

Heat margarine in a skillet over medium heat. Saute chicken, onion, barley and mushrooms. Add buillon, salt & pepper and carrots. Cover skillet. Bring to a boil, then reduce heat to simmer and cook till barley and carrots are tender and bouillon has been absorbed. Depending on the type of barley used, this will take from 25-45 minutes. Serves 6.

BASIC GLUTEN RECIPE

9 c finely ground whole wheat flour
4½ c warm water

Mix the whole wheat flour and water in a large mixing bowl and using the dough hook, knead for 10 min. on speed no. 1. Remove dough hook and fill the bowl with water barely covering dough. Knead gently by hand until the water is white and starchy. Pour off the starchy water into another bowl. Remove doughy mixture from bowl a handful at a time. Knead dough in hands while rinsing under a trickle of lukewarm running tap water. As the starchy part washes out, the gluten will remain in your hands. It is a brown rubbery substance. Put the gluten you have washed in a colander or a plate until you have washed all of the dough. You should have about 2 c raw gluten. Gluten may be flavored and used in making steaklets, roasts, sausage, meatballs and sweet toppings. For more information on its use and preparation see The Magic of <u>Wheat Cookery</u> or <u>The Gluten Book</u>.

* * * *

Jane Howard, in her book <u>Families</u>, reports on a comment made during a panel discussion of married life. "Well, I've known a lot of couples," said one panel member, "where the rocks in <u>her</u> head seemed to fit the holes in <u>his</u>."

GEORGE MARDIKIAN'S RICE PILAF

(From his handwriting on a paper doilie comes a fantastic method of cooking rice.)
Braise 3 c rice in ¼ lb butter
Add 6 c hot stock or boiling water and
1 Tb salt. Cook, covered, in oven or on top of stove until done, stirring occasionally. Heat can be varied, low or high, depending on when you wish to eat.

PEARL BARLEY CASSEROLE

½ c butter
3/4 lb mushrooms, sliced
2 c broth
1/8 ts cayenne
2 onions chopped
1½ c pearl barley
1 ts salt
½ c fresh parsley

Saute onions, mushrooms and barley in butter. Put all ingredients in covered greased casserole and bake at 350° for 50 min.

WHEAT-LENTIL PILAF

½ c lentils
1 ts salt
1 small onion, chopped
½ c quick cooking cracked wheat
2 c water
3 Tb olive oil
¼ lb mushrooms, sliced
plain yogurt
sliced green onions, including part of tops

Combine the lentils,water and salt in a saucepan. Bring to a boil, cover and simmer for 20 min; set aside.

Heat the oil in a 10" frying pan over medium heat; saute onion, mushrooms, and wheat until onion is soft (about 5 min). Pour lentils and water over wheat, bring to boil, cover, and simmer for 15 min or until wheat is just tender. Serve with yogurt and green onions to spoon on top. Serves 4.

* * * *

And then there's the book being written for people with inferiority complexes. Its title: Looking Out for No. 2.

For a feeling that makes you very much alive, sensitive to every movement of your being, and aware of the vibrations of your environment, there's nothing like a good sunburn!

MACARONI-BEEF CASSEROLE

2 lb ground beef
1 med. sized onion, chopped
½ c butter or margarine
¼ c catsup
1 8-oz pkg macaroni, cooked and drained
¼ c beef bouillon, white wine, or water
1 c shredded Cheddar cheese
1/3 c chopped parsley
½ ts pepper
½ ts cinnamon
3 ts salt
1/3 c flour
2½ c milk
1 ts dry mustard
3 eggs, slightly beaten

Saute ground beef and onion in 2 Tb of the butter until browned and crumbly. Combine with the cooked macaroni, catsup, bouillon, ½ c of the cheese, parsley, pepper, cinnamon and 2 ts of the salt. Turn into a greased 13 x 9 x 3" baking pan. Heat remaining 6 Tb butter; add flour and cook until bubbly. Gradually stir in milk. Add remaining 1 ts salt and mustard and cook, stirring until thickened. Gradually stir the hot mixture into eggs. Pour into the casserole. Sprinkle with remaining ½ c cheese. Bake, uncovered, in a moderate oven (350°) for about 30 min; let stand for about 15 min before serving. Makes 8 to 10 servings.

GLORIFIED MACARONI & CHEESE

2 cans (15¼-oz each) macaroni and cheese
4 hard-cooked eggs, sliced
2 cans (10½ oz each) green asparagus tips, drained, liquid reserved
1 4 oz can chopped ripe olives, drained
½ c shredded Cheddar cheese
¼ c saltine cracker crumbs

Turn one can of the macaroni and cheese into a buttered 1½ qt casserole. Arrange 2 of the hard-cooked eggs in a layer over the macaroni. Arrange asparagus over the egg slices. Repeat these three layers, using the remaining macaroni, eggs, and asparagus. Add the olives, mixing them lightly into top layer with a fork. Pour asparagus liquid (about 1 c) over the mixture. Combine cheese and crackers and sprinkle over the top. Bake, uncovered in a hot (400° oven) for 25 min. Serves 6-8.

CRACKED WHEAT CEREAL

1 qt boiling water
1 ts salt
¼ c honey
1 c cracked wheat
1½ c regular rolled oats
½ c raisins
½ c coconut

Sprinkle the 1 c cracked wheat into the boiling water, stirring constantly. Slowly add the rolled oats, raisins and coconut to the cooking cereal and continue cooking until the desired thickness.

EASY GRANOLA

3 c uncooked rolled oats
1½ c unsweetened grated coconut
½ c wheat germ
½ c sesame seeds
1 ts vanilla
½ c water
raisins, dates, dried fruit to taste
1 c sunflower seeds
½ c honey
¼ c oil
1 c chopped nuts (preferrably almonds)

Combine oats, coconut, wheat germ and seeds. Combine honey, oil and vanilla until well mixed. Add to dry ingredients and stir thoroughly. Gradually add water. Pour mixture into heavy shallow pan, spread evenly, and place in 250° oven. Bake for 1 hr, stirring every 15 min.

Add nuts and bake a little longer, then add raisins. Turn off oven and allow cereal to cool in oven. (If you prefer, you can cook longer to make the cereal more crisp). When cool, store in tightly covered container.

KOLLIVA

2 c unwashed whole wheat kernels
½ c sesame seeds
½ c anise seed
½ c chopped walnuts
2/3 c golden or dark currants
pomegranate seeds
1/4 ts orange rind
1 c confectioner's sugar
1 ts cinnamon
½ c graham cracker crumbs
1/4 c slivered almonds

Cook wheat until the kernels split. Place on clean sheet and let dry out for a couple of days before adding other ingredients. Put in sealed tupperware or tin and let season.

FRUIT-NUT GRANOLA

Blend in large bowl:
6 c rolled oats
2½ c whole wheat, ground
½ c sesame seeds
1 c sunflower seeds
1 c shopped dates
1 c flaked coconut
1 c chopped nuts
1 c raisins*

In blender liquify:
1 c oil
1 Tb salt
1 c brown sugar
½ c honey
1 c water
1½ ts vanilla
1½ ts mapeline

Add liquid to dry and mix thoroughly. Divide between 2 or 3 cookie sheets. Bake at 250° for 1¼ hr. stirring 2-3 times. Mixture is soft and moist when removed from oven. *Add the raisins after it is baked. Cool and place in plastic containers.

ONE-POT MACARONI SUPPER

2 cans (10½ oz each) tomato soup, undiluted
2¼ c water
2 ts chili powder
2 c elbow macaroni, uncooked (8 oz)
1 lb frankfurters, cut in 1" lengths
1 can (6 oz) sliced broiled mushrooms, undrained

In Dutch oven, combine and heat soup, water and chili powder until boiling.

Stir in macaroni, frankfurters and mushrooms; cook covered over low heat until macaroni is tender, about 12 min. Serves 6.

MACARONI CASSEROLE

1 lb ground meat
1 small onion
1 can tomato sauce
½ bottle chili sauce
½ lb cooking cheese
1½ c macaroni

Fry meat and onion until brown. Add tomato sauce, chili sauce and cheese. Simmer 15 min. Cook macaroni in salted water until tender. In 9x13 pan layer macaroni, meat sauce and top with cheese. Bake in 350° oven for 35-40 min. Serves 8.

HOW TO FIGURE PASTA QUANTITIES

	Weight (Uncooked)	Quantity (cooked)
<u>Packaged dried pasta:</u>		
Egg noodles	8 oz	4 c
Spaghetti	8 oz	4-5 c
Elbow macaroni	8 oz.	4-4½ c
<u>Homemade pasta:</u>		
Med.-wide and thin noodles	12-14 oz.	4 c

GREEN NOODLES WITH ZUCCHINI

1 recipe spinach pasta or 8 oz packaged med-wide green noodles
1 lg onion, coarsely chopped
1 red bell or green pepper, seeded and coarsely chopped
1 clove garlic, minced or pressed
3 Tb olive oil or salad oil
1 can (about 1 lb) Italian-style tomatoes
3 Tb chopped parsley
½ ts each dry basil and marjoram leaves
3/4 ts salt ¼ ts pepper
¼ c dry red wine or bouillon
3 med-size (about 1 lb) zucchini, crookneck or patty pan squash, thinly sliced crosswise
Boiling salted water
Grated Parmesan cheese

Cut fresh pasta into med-wide noodles about 10" long.

In a wide drying pan over medium heat, cook onion, red pepper, and garlic in oil until vegetables are limp. Add tomatoes and their liquid (break up tomatoes with spoon), as well as parsley, basil, marjoram, salt, pepper, and wine. Stirring, bring to a boil; then reduce heat, cover, and simmer for 30 min. Stir in squash and cook, covered, until crisp-tender (5-7 min.)

Cook noodles in a large kettle of boiling salted water until tender (2-3 min for fresh noodles, or follow pkg directions). Drain noodles, then place in a serving bowl. Spoon sauce over noodles, toss gently, then serve. Sprinkle Parmesan cheese over pasta. Serves 4.

HOMEMADE EGG NOODLES

5 eggs, slightly beaten
3/4 ts salt
5½ egg shells milk (about ½ c)
4 fingertips baking powder (1 ts)
3½ c flour (about)

Beat eggs slightly; add salt and milk. Stir in baking powder and enough flour to make a soft, elastic dough. Knead until dough is smooth.

Break off pieces of dough and roll paper-thin on lightly floured board. Roll up jelly-roll style; cut into ¼" strips.

Unroll strips and allow to dry on waxed paper about 2 hrs. Pick up every few minutes and turn.

When strips are dry, cook amount desired in rich chicken broth 10-12 minutes or until tender.

Store unused noodles in covered container.

JEWISH NOODLES

3 c water
1 pkg Lipton Noodle Chicken Soup
½ pkg fine spaghetti
½ pt sour cream
2 Tb chopped chives

Bring water to rolling boil; add soup mix and noodles. Cook until tender. Add sour cream and chives. Put in casserole at 350° and cook until bubbly.

STUFFED MANICOTTI

1½ lb hamburger
2 eggs slightly beaten
1 c chopped spinach
4 Tb parsley
½ ts salt
½ c onion
2 slices French bread soaked in
½ c milk
¼ ts pepper
1 c Mozzerella cheese
1 box large shell or Manicotti shells

Brown onion and hamburger. Parboil shells about 6 min. Mix all ingredients together, except shells. Stuff shells with meat filling. Use any spaghetti sauce (I use 1 can tomato sauce with 1 pkg spaghetti sauce). Pour half sauce in bottom of 9 x 13" pan. Place stuffed shells leaving room for shells to expand, cover with remaining sauce. Place a piece of cheese on each shell. Cover and bake for 30 min. in 350° oven. Uncover & sprinkle with Parmesan cheese. Cook 10 min. more.

NOODLES WITH CABBAGE

8 oz pkg wide noodles	1 ts salt
4 c shredded cabbage	6 Tb butter or margarine
2 ts sugar	½ ts caraway seeds
¼ ts pepper	boiling salted water

If using fresh pasta, cut into wide noodles about 4" long. Sprinkle salt over cabbage, toss lightly, and let stand 30 min. Squeeze cabbage to release liquid; discard liquid.

Melt butter in a wide frying pan over medium heat. Add cabbage, sugar, caraway seeds, and pepper. Cook, stirring occasionally, until cabbage is crisp-tender (about 5 min.) Keep warm.

Cook noodles in a large kettle of boiling salted water until tender (1-2 min for fresh noodles, or follow pkg directions). Drain, then toss with cabbage mixture before serving. Makes 6 servings.

OLD FASHIONED CHICKEN & NOODLES

8 oz all-purpose pasta (2" squares)
1 broiler-fryer chicken (about 3 lbs) cut in serving size pieces)
6 small whole onions, peeled
4 Tb butter or margarine
7 c water
1½ ts salt
1/8 ts white pepper
2 carrots, cut in 1" lengths
2 stalks celery, cut in 1" lengths
chopped parsley

In a 6 qt kettle, over medium heat, melt butter. Brown chicken and onions in butter until golden on all sides. Add water, salt and pepper; reduce heat, cover and simmer 15 min. Add carrots and celery and continue cooking, covered, until chicken and vegetables are tender (about 40 min.) Remove chicken pieces from kettle and keep warm. Spoon off excess fat. Bring liquid to a rapid boil; add noodle squares and cook until tender (4-6 min.)

Serve in shallow soup bowls. Place a piece of chicken and some vegetables, noodles, and broth in each; sprinkle with parsley. Serves 4-6.

PASTA WHEELS WITH SAUSAGE & TOMATOES

1 lb mild Italian sausages
1 med. size onion, coarsely chopped
1 clove garlic, minced or pressed
1 can (about 1 lb) Italian-style tomatoes
1 ts oregano leaves
¼ ts each thyme leaves and pepper
2 Tb each minced parsley and catsup
12 oz wheels or other medium-size fancy-shaped pasta
Boiling salted water
Chopped parsley
Grated Parmesan cheese

Remove and discard sausage casings; slice sausages diagonally into ½" thick pieces. In a wide frying pan over medium heat, cook sausages until browned (about 5 min.) Add onion and garlic and continue to cook, stirring occasionally for about 3 min. or until onion is limp. Add tomatoes with liquid (break up tomatoes with a spoon). Stir in oregano, thyme, pepper, parsley, and catsup. Simmer, uncovered, for about 15 min. or until sauce is slightly thickened and reduced to about 3½ c.

Following package directions, cook pasta in a large kettle of boiling water until tender; drain. Stir hot pasta into sauce and turn onto a platter. Garnish with chopped parsley and pass Parmesan cheese at the table. Serves 4-6.

HOMEMADE NOODLES

1 c flour
2 eggs
½ ts salt
¼ ts baking powder
water (½ eggshell full)

Usually don't use any water unless the eggs are very small. Roll out really thin on a pastry cloth, then roll up and cut very thin noodles. Drop in any broth and simmer until tender. Very delicious with stewed chicken.

ONE POT SPAGHETTI SUPPER

1 lb ground beef
1 med. onion, chopped
1 clove garlic, minced
1 c water
1½ ts salt
¼ ts allspice
½ ts dry mustard
¼ ts pepper
6 oz (1½ c) uncooked spaghetti, broken into fourths
2½ c tomato juice
Parmesan cheese

In Dutch oven, brown beef with onion and garlic. Add seasonings; arrange spaghetti on top. Pour water and tomato juice over mixture, moistening all of spaghetti.

Cover and bring to a boil; reduce heat and simmer 15 min. or until spaghetti is tender, stirring occasionally. Serve with Parmesan cheese. Serves 4-6.
If desired, add chopped parsley to mixture just before serving, or add 1/3 c sliced pimiento-stuffed olives, reducing salt to 3/4 ts.

PASTA WITH SAUCE SUPREME

4 Tb butter or margarine
1½ c whipping cream
½ ts nutmeg, freshly grated if possible
4 c hot cooked, drained pasta such as fresh egg noodles, fettucini, tagliarini, or hot or cold tortellini, ravioli, or gnocchi
1 egg yolk
3/4 c freshly grated Parmesan cheese
Grated nutmeg and grated Parmesan cheese

Melt butter with cream and the ½ ts nutmeg in a wide frying pan. Stir in the cooked pasta and bring quickly to boiling, stir gently from time to time. Let boil rapidly for 1 or 2 min, then blend a little of the hot sauce with the egg yolk.

Remove pan from heat and stir in the egg yolk mixture and the 3/4c Parmesan cheese, blending thoroughly. Serve at once, offering additional nutmeg and Parmesan cheese. Makes 4 main dish servings or 6 to 8 first course servings.

VEGETABLE LASAGNE

Your guests may never guess that this vegetable-full lasagne is meatless. Whole wheat noodles and cheese make it a protein-rich entree.

1/3 c olive or salad oil
1 lg onion, chopped
2 cloves garlic, minced or pressed
1 med. size eggplant (about 1 lb) diced, but not peeled
¼ lb mushrooms, sliced
1 can (1 lb) Italian-style tomatoes
1 8-oz can tomato sauce
½ c dry red wine or bouillon
1 med. size carrot, shredded
¼ c parsley
2 ts oregano leaves
1 ts each basil and salt
¼ ts pepper
12-16 packaged lasagne noodles
boiling salted water
2 c (1 lb) ricotta cheese
2 c (8 oz) shredded mozzarella cheese
1½ c (4½ oz) grated Parmesan cheese

In a wide frying pan over medium heat, add oil. When hot add onion, garlic, eggplant, and mushrooms and cook, stirring frequently for 15 min. Add tomatoes and liquid (break up tomatoes with spoon), tomato sauce, wine, carrot, parsley, oregano, basil, salt & pepper. Bring to a boil then reduce heat and simmer 30 min. Uncover and continue cooking until sauce is thick. Should have 5 c sauce; set aside.

Cook 12-16 pieces of noodles in large kettle of boiling water until tender (3-4 min. if using fresh, or follow directions on pkg.) Drain, rinse with cold water, and drain again.

Butter a 9 x 13" baking dish. Spread ¼ of sauce over bottom. Arrange 1/3 of noodles in even layer over sauce. Dot noodles with 1/3 ricotta. Sprinkle over 1/3 mozzarella, then sprinkle with ¼ of Parmesan cheese. Repeat this layering two more times. Spread remaining sauce evenly over top and sprinkle with remaining Parmesan cheese. If made ahead, cover and refrigerate.

Bake, uncovered, in a 350° oven until hot and bubbly 40-50 min. Cut in squares to serve. Serves 8.

FETTUCCINE

6 Tb butter or margarine   1½ c whipping cream
3-4 c hot cooked, drained, tagliarini or egg noodles (dried or freshly made)
1 c shredded Parmesan cheese
salt and pepper
freshly grated nutmeg

In a wide frying pan or chafing dish over high heat, melt butter until it is lightly browned. Add ½ c of the cream and boil rapidly until large shiny bubbles form; stir occasionally. (You can make this part of the sauce earlier in the day then reheat.)

Reduce heat to medium or place chafing dish over direct flame. Add noodles to the sauce. Toss vigorously with 2 forks, and pour in the cheese and remaining cream, a little at a time--about three additions. Noodles should be moist but not too moist. Season with salt and pepper and grate nutmeg generously over the noodles (or use about 1/8 ts of the ground spice). Serve immediately. Makes 4 generous or 6 ample first course servings.

LINGUINE WITH CLAM SAUCE

¼ c each olive oil and butter or margarine
3 Tb finely chopped parsley
3 med-size tomatoes, peeled, seeded & chopped
¼ ts salt   1/8 ts pepper
few drops of liquid hot pepper seasoning
¼ ts oregano leaves, crumbled
3-4 dozen small hard-shell clams, washed well
2 Tb water   6 oz hot, cooked linguine or spaghetti
1 clove garlic, minced

Heat the olive oil and butter in fry pan. Add parsley & garlic and saute on med. heat for 1-2 min. Add tomatoes, salt, pepper hot pepper seasoning & oregano. Simmer gently, stirring occasionally for about 10 min; reduce heat to warm. Meanwhile, put clams and water into heavy pan. Cover & simmer until clams open. When cool enough to handle, pluck clams from shells and put into sauce; save some clams in shells for garnish. Strain the clam juices from bottom of pan through muslin cloth and add juice to sauce. Reheat and serve over the hot linguine. Serves 4.

SHRIMP TETRAZZINI

½ c butter or margarine
1 c thinly sliced green onions, including some tops
5 Tb flour
2½ c chicken broth, canned or freshly made
½ c clam juice ½ c dry white wine or broth
½ c heavy cream ½ ts oregano
½ c shredded Parmesan 2 whole cloves garlic
½ lb mushrooms, sliced salted water
8 oz noodles (spaghetti or vermicelli)
4 c deveined, cooked, shelled shrimp
salt

Melt ¼ c of the butter in a pan, add onions, and cook, stirring until soft. Mix in flour and gradually blend in chicken broth, clam juice, wine, cream, and oregano. Cook, stirring for about 3 min. after sauce begins to simmer. Stir in ¼ c cheese. Set sauce aside.

Melt remaining butter in another pan, add garlic and mushrooms and cook quickly until lightly browned. Discard garlic.

Also bring to a boil a quantity of salted water, add the noodles and cook until they are tender, but not soft; then drain.

Combine sauce, mushrooms, noodles, shrimp (save a few shrimp for garnish if you like), and season with salt to taste. Pour into a large shallow casserole (9 x 13") or individual casseroles. Top with shrimp and sprinkle with remaining cheese. Bake, uncovered, in a moderately hot oven (375°) until bubbling; allow 15 min. for large casserole or 8 min. for small ones. Broil top until lightly browned. Makes 6-8 servings.

* * * *

A pessimist complains about the noise when opportunity knocks.

Opportunity knocks but once, but temptation leans on the doorbell.

CHINESE MEDLEY

1 lb lean pork steak, cut in ½" cubes
Seasoned flour (½ c flour, 1 ts salt, ¼ ts pepper, ½ ts paprika)
1 Tb shortening or salad oil
1 Tb grated fresh ginger or preserved ginger
2 c chopped celery
1 c chopped onion
¼ c chopped green pepper
Boiling salted water
4-5 oz. Oriental noodles or any fine spaghetti
1 10½ oz can mushroom soup
1 3-4-oz can sliced mushrooms
1 ts Accent
½ c soft bread crumbs, mixed with 2 Tb melted butter
¼ c slivered almonds

Toss pork pieces in paper bag with the seasoned flour. Brown on all sides in the fat. Add ginger, celery, onion, and green pepper; cover and cook over low heat about 15 in. Meanwhile, cook the noodles in boiling water (salted) until they are just tender; drain. Arrange half noodles in the bottom of a greased casserole (about 1½ qt size).

To the meat and vegetable mixture, add mushroom soup, mushrooms (including mushroom liquid), Accent; mix well. Spoon half over noodles in casserole. Repeat with second layers of noodles and meat mixture. Top with buttered crumbs and slivered almonds. Bake, uncovered, in moderate oven (350°) for about 45 minutes. Makes about 4 servings.

* * * *

Oblivion is full of men who permitted the opinion of others to overrule their belief in themselves.

The glory of ancestors sheds a light around posterity; it allows neither their good nor bad qualities to remain in obscurity.

GREEK STYLE MANICOTTI

6 manicotti shells
12 oz beef top round steak, cut into ¼" cubes
½ c chopped onion
2 Tb cooking oil
1 c Italian cooking sauce or meatless spaghetti sauce
½ ts ground cinnamon
1/8 ts ground nutmeg
1 Tb butter or margarine
2 Tb flour
1¼ c milk
1 beaten egg
¼ c grated Parmesan cheese

Cook the manicotti in boiling salted water 15-20 min. Drain. In skillet cook meat and onion in hot oil till meat is brown and onion is tender. Drain off fat and juices. Stir in cooking sauce, cinnamon, nutmeg, ¼ ts salt, and 1/8 ts pepper; set aside. In saucepan melt butter or margarine; stir in flour and 1/8 ts salt. Add milk all at once; cook and stir till thickened and bubbly. Cook and stir 1 minute more. Stir half of the hot sauce into beaten egg; return all to saucepan. Stir in 2 Tb of the cheese.

To assemble, use a teaspoon to spoon meat mixture into shells. Place shells in a single layer in greased 10x6x2" baking dish. Pour sauce over manicotti. Sprinkle with remaining cheese. Bake, uncovered in 350° oven for 20 minutes or till heated through. Serves 6.

SAVORY NUT CAKE

½ c raw cashews
½ c raw peanuts
2 eggs ½ small onion
1/4 c wheat germ
½ ts sage
½ ts salt
1/3 c grated cheese
½ c raw almonds
2/3 c sunflower seeds
½ c raw brown rice, cooked
½ c chopped fresh parsley
½ ts thyme
2 Tb brewer's yeast

In blender or food processor grind the nuts to a medium fine consistency. Put onion and eggs in blender for ½ minute. Add to other ingredients and blend well. Bake in loaf pan at 350° for 25 minutes. A nice complement to whole wheat buns, page 39.

CREAMY CLAM SHELLS

2 cans (6½ oz each) chopped clams
¼ c each dry white wine or chicken broth
and whipping cream
6 Tb butter or margarine ½ c chopped green onions
½ lb mushrooms, sliced 1 Tb flour
6 Tb grated Parmesan cheese 3 egg yolks beaten
1 ts lemon juice 18 giant shells
boiling water (salted) 2 Tb butter or margarine
1/3 c fine dry bread crumbs

Drain clams well, reserving clam juice. Combine ½ c of clam juice with wine and cream. Set aside remaining clam juice.

In a wide frying pan over med. heat, melt 4 Tb butter. Add onion and mushrooms and cook until onion is limp & all liquid from mushrooms has evaporated. Stir in flour and cook, stirring until bubbly. Pour in clam juice mixture and cook, stirring until smooth. Add drained clams and 3 Tb of Parmesan. Bring mix to a boil, stirring; then remove from heat. Beat some of hot mix into egg yolks, then stir egg mix into hot mix in pan. Reduce heat to med. and cook, stirring constantly, until thickened. DO NOT BOIL. Stir in lemon juice.

Following package directions, cook giant shells in a large kettle of boiling salted water until tender. Drain, rinse with cold water, and drain again. Brush outside of each shell with melted butter, then fill each shell with about 2 Tb filling. Place filled shells side by side in buttered 8 x 12" baking dish. Melt remaining 2 Tb butter; mix with bread crumbs and remaining 3 Tb Parmesan until well blended. Sprinkle crumb mixture evenly over shells. Pour reserved clam juice into dish around shells. If made ahead, cover and refrigerate until next day.

Bake, covered, in a 350° oven until hot and bubbly (about 30 min.) Makes 4 main-dish servings.

GREENS & PASTA

6 oz udon noodles, somen noodles, or linguine, cooked and drained
1 Tb cooking oil 2 beaten eggs
8 oz fresh spinach or Swiss chard or one 10 oz pkg frozen chopped spinach
½ c thinly sliced green onion
¼ c snipped parsley 4 eggs
1 3 oz pkg cream cheese, softened
1 c buttermilk
½ ts Worcestershire sauce
2 green onions with tops (optional)

Combine noodles, oil and the 2 eggs. Press on the bottom and up sides of a 10" quiche dish or pie plate. Cover edge of pasta with foil; bake in 375° oven 7-10 min. oruntil set. Meanwhile, if using fresh greens, rinse and chop greens, removing stems. In saucepan, cook the greens, covered, with just the water that clings to the leaves till steam forms. Reduce heat and cook 3-5 min. more, stirring often. (Or cook frozen spinach according to package directions.) Drain well. Add sliced onion and parsley.

Beat together the 4 eggs, cream cheese, and buttermilk; stir in vegetables, Worcestershire, ½ ts salt, and 1/8 ts pepper. Spoon into pasta shell. If desired, lay whole green onions atop. Bake in 375° oven for 25-30 minutes or till knife inserted near center comes out clean. Let stand 10 minutes. Serves 6.

* * * *

Many a man grows sage after sewing wild oats.

Some people look at a secret two ways--either it's not worth keeping, or it's too good to keep.

The moon must be made of wonderful stuff. It not only pulls the oceans back and forth to cause tides, but also stops cars along side roads.

They say politics makes strange bed-fellows, but it seems they soon get used to the same bunk.

Notes

Notes

meat

Notes

FILET OF BEEF MADAGASCAR

1 Tb butter
1 3 lb tenderloin of beef
4 shallots, finely chopped
½ c dry red wine or
 ½ c more beef broth
1 Tb vegetable oil
salt & pepper
3/4 c beef broth, double strength
1 ts meat extract (Bovril)
2 Tb green peppercorns (from food specialty shop)
1 ts cornstarch mixed with little water

Heat butter and oil in heavy saucepan. Brown meat well on all sides; transfer to rack in shallow pan. Bake, uncovered, at 375° for 45-60 min or until roast meat thermometer registers 140° (rare).

In the meantime, add shallots to oil and butter in skillet and saute for about 3 min. Add beef broth, wine if used, meat extract and peppercorns that have been rinsed and drained. Simmer over low heat for about 10 min. Just before serving, thicken sauce with cornstarch mixture and serve over slices of tenderloin. Makes 8 servings.

BARBECUED BEEF

1 round-bone beef roast, about 5 lb (rump roast may be used) competely cooked
1 onion, chopped
2 c chili sauce
1 c catsup
1 ts paprika
4 Tb vinegar
½ ts Worcestershire sauce
1 ts paprika
2 c water
2 Tb cornstarch
1 ts chili powder
dash of pepper
½ c brown sugar
½ ts allspice

Cook roast completely. In large skillet, saute onion in 1 Tb oil. Add chili sauce, catsup, Worcestershire, water, cornstarch, chili powder, paprika, pepper, vinegar, brown sugar and allspice. Simmer 5 min.

Slice meat thin and put in roaster pan or large casserole dish, layered with sauce. Cover and bake at 325° for 3 hrs. Serve on buns. Serves 8-10. This is a sure-fire favorite!

LEMON PORK CHOPS

1½-2 lb pork chops (5 chops)
1-2 lemons, sliced
1/3 c brown sugar
dash pepper
½ c chili sauce
5 onion slices
3/4 ts salt (to taste)
1-2 Tb lemon juice

In baking pan arrange chops, cover each with lemon and onion slices. Combine remaining ingredients; pour over chops. Cover closely with lid or foil. Bake in moderate oven (350°) 1½ hrs or until chops are tender.

PORK CHOPS, FILIPINO STYLE

1 3/4 c chicken broth
3 Tb soy sauce
1 bay leaf
¼ ts paprika
1½ Tb cornstarch
½ c distilled vinegar
2 cloves garlic, halved
1¼ ts salt
6 med pork chops
1 Tb salad oil

In a saucepan combine 1½ c of the chicken broth, vinegar, soy sauce, garlic, bay leaf, salt and paprika; add pork chops to mixture. Bring to a boil; lower heat and simmer covered for 45 min. Remove pork chops. Combine remaining ¼ c of the broth with cornstarch; add to liquid in saucepan and heat on low heat until thickened, stirring constantly. Heat oil in pan; fry pork chops 5 min, turning once. Pour gravy over pork chops. Makes 6 servings.

STUFFED PORK CHOPS

6 rib pork chops cut 1" thick-
2 c dry bread cubes
½ c apple, chopped
1/8 ts poultry seasoning
stock to moisten
½ ts salt, 1/8 ts pepper
1½ Tb onion, chopped
½ ts ground sage
2 Tb butter, melted
½ c hot water

Have pocket cut in each pork chop for stuffing. Combine bread cubes, onion, apple and seasonings. Moisten with butter and liquid; toss gently. Stuff dressing loosely into pork chops. Brown chops on both sides in hot fat; season lightly with salt and pepper. Transfer pork chops to casserole. Add ½ c water, cover tightly and bake for 45 minutes or until tender, adding more water, if needed. Or water may be added to pork chops in skillet; cover tightly and simmer over low heat until tender--about 45 min to 1 hr.

SAUERBRATEN

4 lb piece of beef (round, chuck, or rump)
1½ c red wine vinegar
½ c dry red wine
2 onions, sliced
2 carrots, sliced
1 bay leaf
3 allspice berries
3 cloves
1 Tb salt
8 Tb butter
1 Tb oil
5 Tb flour
1 Tb sugar
2/3 c gingersnaps, crumbled optional
1 Tb peppercorns

Ask butcher to tie meat so it will hold its shape. Make a marinade of the mixed vinegar, wine, onions, carrots, bay leaf, allspice, cloves, peppercorns, and salt. Put the beef in a deep bowl and pour the marinade over it. Cover and leave in the frig to soak for 3 days, turning the meat occasionally during this time.

When beef is well soaked, remove from the marinade and wipe dry. Melt 4 Tb of butter with the oil in a heavy dutch oven. Brown the beef on all sides in the hot fat and sprinkle lightly with flour as you turn. Heat the marinade and pour over the browned meat. Cover the kettle, lower the heat and simmer gently until the beef is thoroughly tender, about 3 hrs.

When the meat is done, pour off the sauce and set the kettle on one side to keep the meat warm. Skim fat from sauce and strain it. In a heavy skillet, melt 4 Tb butter and blend in 4 Tb flour and sugar. Cook gently until flour and sugar are slightly browned. Add the strained sauce slowly, stirring it until it is smooth and thickened. Add the gingersnaps to the sauce. Pour over the meat, cover and cook gently for ½ hr. The traditional accompaniment for sauerbraten is dumplings. However, noodles may be served instead. Serves 4-6.

* * * *

Life must be worth living. The cost has more than tripled and folks still hang on!

For some reason, the future seems to get here quicker than it used to.

QUICK ROULADIN

1 Tb dry chopped onion or 3 Tb fresh onion, chopped
1 ts parsley flakes or 1 Tb fresh parsley, chopped
½ ts salt
½ c soft bread crumbs
1 c (¼ lb) mushrooms, cleaned and chopped
5 cubed beef steaks
½ c grapefruit juice
1 can golden mushroom soup
½ c sour dairy cream
5 slices bacon, diced
1 Tb Worcestershire sauce
Flour
1 c beef bouillon
1 c fresh mushroom, sliced

Combine onion, parsley, salt, bacon, crumbs, Worcestershire sauce and 1 c chopped fresh mushrooms. Place equal portions of stuffing on each cube steak. Roll up steaks; fasten securely with wooden toothpicks or tie with string. Dredge rolls in flour. Brown well on all sides in hot oil in skillet. Place rolls into pressure cooker containing grapefruit juice and bouillon. Pour golden mushroom soup over top. Assemble pressure cooker. Cook, according to directions for 20 min. Turn heat indicator off; unplug cord; let pressure drop of its own accord. Add sliced mushrooms; allow to stand, covered, but without heat for 3 min, until mushrooms are heated. Arrange rouladin on serving platter. Top with sour cream.
Note: Rouladin may be baked, covered, at 325° for 1 hr or until tender. Serves 5.

BEEF TENDERLOIN

Take the whole beef tenderloin. Allow 1/3 lb per person. Rub good with onion salt then wrap it in handiwrap and let stand in the frig for 3-4 hrs, or overnight.

Melt ¼ to ½ lb margarine (the amount depends on how much you have) in an electric fry pan at 300°. Brown meat on both sides then turn heat down to 250°-275°. Baste often with the butter you have in pan. Allow about 1½ to 2 hrs to simmer then add some mushrooms and simmer for another 2-3 minutes.

Slice meat ¼" thick and put on a platter. Pour mushrooms and butter over the meat and serve.
*This is a German dish most often requested by the rest of us!!

SWEET & SOUR PORK

2 lb lean pork, about ½" thick
2 Tb cornstarch ¼ c soy sauce
3 Tb oil 2 c carrots, diagonal cut
3 small onions, quartered 1 green pepper, cut in strips
1 can (20 oz) chunk pineapple, drained
3 Tb cornstarch 2 Tb sugar
2 c liquid (drained juice from pineapple, plus water)
2/3 c vinegar ½ c soy sauce
Cooked rice

Cut pork into 2" strips. Mix 2 Tb cornstarch and ¼ c soy sauce, and marinate pork in this mixture for an hour or two, or overnight, in refrigerator. Drain (save marinade). Stir-fry meat in hot oil until evenly browned and tender (about 10 min.) Remove meat from pan. Stir-fry carrots and onions in same pan, using more oil, if necessary. Cover and cook on low heat until tender crisp, about 10 min. Add green pepper and pineapple. Return meat to pan, then stir in marinade.

In the meantime, make the sauce: Mix 3 Tb cornstarch and the sugar in a small saucepan. Add 2 c liquid, vinegar, and ½ c soy sauce. Stir and cook until thickened and clear. Pour over meat and vegetables, and heat until flavors are blended, about 10 min. Taste to correct seasonings. Serve over cooked rice. Makes 8-10 servings.

CHOW MEIN

1 lb sliced pork, ham, beef, shrimp or chicken
2 c shredded onion 3 c celery, slant cut
1 can bamboo shoots 3/4 c mushrooms
1½ lb bean sprouts 1 Tb fresh ginger
3 Tb oil

Make a mixture of 5 Tb soy sauce, 3 Tb cornstarch, 3/4 c soup stock and 1 ts sugar. Set aside.
Heat frying pan, add 3 Tb oil and meat, fry until done. Remove meat from pan. Add onion and saute slightly. Add celery and cook until crunchy. Add bamboo shoots, mushrooms, bean sprouts and ginger. Cook 2 min. Return meat to pan, add mixture of stock, cornstarch, sugar and soy sauce. Heat thoroughly, stirring until cornstarch thickens. Serve hot with fried noodles, boiled noodles or rice.

BARBECUED SPARE RIBS

Cut spare ribs in 2" pieces
2 ts liquid smoke
1/3 c Worcestershire sauce
1 ts salt
2 c water (or pineapple juice from chunks)
½ c brown sugar
1 ts chili powder
¼ ts tabasco sauce
1 12-oz can chunk pineapple
pinch of celery seed (optional)
Place ribs in pan with meat side up and sprinkle with liquid smoke. Bake ½ hr at 450°.

Make sauce and simmer for 30 min. Pour sauce over ribs and bake at 350° for 1 hr. Baste about every 15 min.

QUICK & EASY BARBECUED SPARE RIBS

3 lb button spare ribs
1 Tb salt
1 Tb mixed pickling spice
1 med onion sliced

½ bottle barbecue sauce
1/4 c dark corn syrup

Cut ribs into serving size pieces. In a large kettle, just cover ribs w/water and add first four ingredients. Bring slowly to a boil. Lower heat and cover. Simmer 1 hr. Remove from heat and cool in liquid.

Take out, place on broiler rack. Brush with syrup and barbecue sauce. Broil 4" from heat. Turn and baste and turn again. Watch closely as they burn easily. Serves 6-8.

SUB GUM CHOW MEIN

1 lb lean pork, beef, chicken, shrimp or combination ½" cubes
3 Tb soy sauce
2 Tb sherry
¼ ts Accent
5 c vegetables-choose: carrots, celery, onions, broccoli, bamboo shoots, green string beans, water chestnuts, mushrooms
1/8 to ¼" slice fresh ginger root, mashed
2-4 Tb butter or vegetable oil
1 clove garlic
1 ts salt
½ ts Accent
2 c hot water, soup stock or mushroom liquid
1 c Snow peas, stringed, whole (optional)
½ lb bean sprouts, washed and drained
¼ c cornstarch
3 Tb cold water
1 Tb sugar
1 can (5 oz) chow mein noodles, optional
1 c butter fried almonds, coarsely chopped
1 c slivered cooked ham (optional)
¼ c sliced green onions, including tops

Combine meat, soy sauce, sherry and ¼ ts Accent. Set aside. Cut vegetables into ½" pieces. Set aside. Fry mashed ginger root and garlic in butter on high heat. Brown, then discard both. Drain meat. Stir fry meat on high heat until brown. Lower heat. Cover. Cook 3-5 min. Uncover. Raise heat. Add 5 c vegetables. Stir fry 3-5 minutes. Season with salt and ½ ts Accent. Add 2 c water, Snow peas or beansprouts and bring to boil. Combine cornstarch, cold water and sugar. Stir into pan. Stirring constantly, cook until mixture thickens. Serve over chow mein noodles. Garnish with butter fried almonds, slivered cooked ham and sliced green onions.

Butter Fried Almonds:
1 c almonds
2 Tb butter
Fry almonds in butter until golden brown. Toss pan to fry both sides. Drain well on paper towel. Cool. Serves 8.

OVEN KALUA PORK

6 lb pork butt
1 Tb Liquid Smoke
2½ Tb Hawiian salt
Preheat oven to 350°. Rub pork with liquid smoke and 1½ Tb salt. Wrap pork with foil, sealing completely. Place pork in roasting pan and bake for 5 hrs. After baking, shred pork; sprinkle with remaining salt. Serves 12.

FRUIT STUFFED PORK ROAST
(Norwegian)

½ ts salt
½ ts cinnamon
½ ts allspice
½ ts pepper
¼ ts cloves
¼ ts mace
3-3½ lb boned pork loin roast
12 pitted prunes, cut in half
2 med. apples, cored, pared and cut in wedges
2 Tb raisins
¼ ts cinnamon
¼ c apple juice
1½ ts currant jelly, melted
1 c fresh bread crumbs
¼ c melted butter

Combine first six spices and rub inside pork roast; refrigerate overnight. Combine prunes, apple wedges, raisins, ¼ ts cinnamon and apple juice; refrigerate overnight.

Open up the roast or cut a pocket in it; stuff with fruit. Roll and tie up with string. Baste roast with liquid left from fruit. Roast on rack in shallow roasting pan at 325° for 1 hr. Brush roast with melted jelly, then roll in bread crumbs. Baste with melted butter and roast for 1½ hrs more. Let stand for 15 min. before serving.

* * * *

You can always do more through push than you can do through pull.

To be born a gentle man is an accident. To die one is an achievement.

PAELLA

2-4 Tb olive oil or salad oil
4 lg onions, chopped
1 lb lean, boneless pork, cut in 3/4" cubes
3 lb broiler-fryer chicken, cut in about 2" pieces
About 2 ts salt
2 medium-sized chorizos, casings removed
1 lg peeled, seeded, and diced tomato
1½ c uncooked long grain rice
5½ to 6 c chicken broth
1/16 ts saffron
1-1½ lbs lg shrimp, deveined and unshelled
4 small (about ½ lb each) rock lobster tails, split lengthwise or 1 to 2 doz small clams in shells or use mussels when in season
1 can (4 oz) whole pimientos, thickly sliced
½ c minced parsley

Heat 2 Tb of oil in very wide frying pan (or 2 regular-sized pans) and add onions; cook over high heat, stirring until soft and lightly browned. Push onions to one side of pan. Sprinkle pork and chicken with about 1½ ts of the salt. Brown pork cubes on all sides over high heat, then push pork to one side of the pan. You will have to scrape free the accumulating browned particles continuously.

Add chicken to pan, a few pieces at a time to avoid crowding, and as pieces become well browned, remove to a small bowl. Pour remaining oil into pan if needed. Crumble chorizos in pan, add tomato and rice, and continue cooking over high heat, stirring, until rice is lightly toasted. Return chicken and pork to cooked mixture. (At this point you can cool the mixture and refrigerate, covered, overnight. Reheat to use.)

Mix 4 c of the chicken broth and saffron into the hot rice mixture. Cook rapidly, stirring for 10 min. Then add the shrimp and lobster or clams (thawed if frozen) and an additional 1½ c broth. Cook rapidly, uncovered and stirring frequently, for about 20 min more or until rice is tender (add more broth if needed to prevent sticking). Carefully fold in pimiento, ½ c parsley and salt to taste. If desired, keep the paella warm as long as 45 min in a 300° oven before serving. Arrange lobster, clams and shrimp over the rice and sprinkle with more parsley. Note: To devein shrimp without shelling, insert a thin wooden or metal skewer into the back of each shrimp.

LENTIL & SAUSAGE GOULASH

1½ c chopped onion
¼ c butter
1½ Tb sweet Hungarian paprika
1 lb smoked Polish sausage
1 c dried lentils
½ ts marjoram
salt
3 c water
2 Tb fresh parsley, chopped

In large saucepan saute onions in butter until soft. Remove from heat and stir in paprika. Add sausage, cut into ½" slices, and saute until browned. Stir in lentils that have been picked over and rinsed. Add marjoram and salt to taste, then add water. Bring water to boil over moderate high heat, reduce heat and simmer, covered for 45 min. Remove lid and cook 5 min longer until mixture is thickened and lentils are soft. Serve with minced parsley. Serves 4-6.

SAUSAGE & ZUCCHINI

2 lb small green zucchini cubed in 1" pieces
½ lb pork sausage
¼ c onion, diced
seasoning
2 eggs, slightly beaten
½ c cheese
½ c buttered crumbs

Parboil zucchini. Saute sausage and onions. Drain off fat. Combine zucchini, sausage, onion, spices and eggs in casserole. Top with bread crumbs and cheese. Bake in 350° oven for 30 min. Serves 4.

SAVORY SPARERIBS & SAUERKRAUT

2 lbs spareribs
1 ts salt
1 Tb shortening
¼ c water
1 lb 4-oz can sauerkraut
3 Tb chopped onions
1/8 ts caraway seed
1/8 ts salt
3 Tb sugar
3 Tb drippings

Cut ribs into serving pieces. Season. Brown in shortening in heavy skillet. Add water. Cover and cook slowly 1 hr. Empty kraut into a second kettle. Add remaining ingredients. Cover and cook slowly ½ hr. Pour off drippings from ribs. Save 3 Tb drippings and add along with kraut to ribs. Cook an additional hour.

HAM CASSEROLE

Prepare and set aside: 1 c raw rice cooked in boiling, salted water; 3 c ham diced into 1" cubes; 4 eggs, hard boiled and sliced.

Mix together: ½ ts curry powder, ½ c mayonnaise, ½ c sour cream, 1 can cream of mushroom soup, 3 ts lemon juice, 1 c grated cheddar cheese.

Layer in 9x13" casserole: rice, then ham, then eggs. Cover with soup mixture. Bake at 350° for 30 min. uncovered. Remove from oven and top with 1 can onion rings. Serves 10.

HAM IN SOUR CREAM

1 c cooked ham in strips
¼ c chopped onion
1 c sour cream
2 Tb butter or margarine
2 ts flour
1 6-oz can broiled sliced mushrooms (drained)

Cook ham and onion in butter until onion is tender, but not brown. Stir in sour cream; add mushrooms. Cook over low heat stirring constantly until mixture thickens, 2-3 min. Garnish with parsley and serve with fluffy rice or noodles. Add cream of celery or mushroom soup to increase quantity.

HOLIDAY HAM & TURKEY COMBO

Mix together: 1 (10 oz) frozen chopped cooked spinach, well drained
1 pt dry curd cottage cheese
½ c chopped green onion
½ ts dry mustard
salt to taste
2 slightly beaten eggs
½ pt sour cream

Match together in pairs with ham slices on bottom:
16 thin rectangular ham slices (luncheon meat or leftovers)
16 thin rectangular turkey slices (luncheon meat " ")
Fill each matched pair with small amount of spinach mixture
Roll up starting with smallest width of rectangle.
Place roll-ups with seamside down in large baking dish.
Blend 1 can cream of mushroom soup and ½ c sour cream.
Pour over roll-ups. Bake at 325° for 15 min or until heated through. Can be made in advance and kept 1-2 days

HAM LOAVES

Mix together:

2 lb ground ham	1 lb ground beef (lean)
1 can Spam, mashed	2 c bread crumbs
3 eggs	1 c canned milk

Shape into individual loaves (makes 15) and place close together in dripper pan. Baste with:

1 lb brown sugar	1 Tb mustard
½ c vinegar	

Heat to dissolve and pour over loaves. Bake 1 hr at 300°

Sauce

½ c sugar	4 ts dry mustard
1 ts salt	1 ts cornstarch

Mix and add:

2 beaten eggs	½ c milk
½ c vinegar (salad)	2 Tb butter

Cook 15 min in double boiler, stirring occasionally. Serve cold.

HAM HOCKS WITH LIMA BEANS

2 c dry lima beans	water & 1 Tb salt
4 ham hocks	2 bay leaves
1 large onion, chopped	½ green pepper, sliced in rounds
1 lb can tomatoes	
1 8 oz can tomato sauce	¼ ts each pepper and cloves

Soak the beans in water to cover overnight (or if your time is limited, cover with water, boil briskly 2 min, remove from heat, and soak only 1 hr.)

Without draining the beans, add ham hocks, bay leaves, and water--if needed to cover the beans again. Simmer about 1 hr or until beans are tender. Add onion, green pepper, tomatoes, tomato sauce, salt, pepper, and cloves. Mix until blended and pour into a large 4 qt casserole.

Cover and bake in a 350° oven about 1 hr, or until the meat is tender. Remove meat from beans; chop meat and return to soup before serving. Makes 6 servings.

SAUSAGE 'N APPLE BAKED STUFFED SQUASH

2 med-sized acorn squash
1 c chopped apples
1/3 c fine dry bread crumbs
½ ts ground sage
1 lb bulk pork sausage
½ c chopped onion
½ ts Accent
¼ ts black pepper

Cook squash as directed above, for about 4 min or until partly tender.

Cut in half and remove seeds. Sprinkle lightly with salt.

Combine remaining ingredients. Fill squash with sausage mixture. Arrange in shallow glass baking dish and microwave for about 6 min or until squash is tender and sausage mixture is no longer pink in center. Makes 4 servings.

Conventional method: Preheat oven to 375°. Combine all ingredients but squash. Cut acorn squash in half lengthwise; scoop out seeds and stringy portion.

Fill squash with sausage mixture. Place in baking dish; cover and bake 50-60 minutes. Makes 4 servings.

CORNPATCH SUPPER PLATE

2 cans corn
½ c celery
½ c green pepper
½ to 1 ts chili powder
1 lb bulk sausage
½ c onion
1 can tomato sauce

Fry meat until brown and drain. In drippings fry the diced celery, pepper and onion. Add cooked meat and tomato sauce and add corn. Heat thoroughly. Serve between cornmeal pancakes with tomato-cheese sauce and season to taste.

CUTLETS SUPREME

Brown 1-2 lb veal cutlet or minute steaks
Remove from frying pan. To the drippings
add: 1 can mushroom soup
1/3 c milk
Heat, but do not boil. Put rings of fresh onion on top of meat. Pour gravy over all. Cover and bake at 325° for 1 hr 15 min.

HEARTY MEAT FILLING

4 slices American cheese (¼ lb) cubed
1 c undiluted evaporated milk
2 c chopped cooked potatoes
¼ c chopped green onions and tops (or use dry onion)
2 Tb chopped green pepper or pimento, if desired
¼ to ½ ts salt, ¼ ts pepper
1 can Spam, cubed

Heat oven to 425°. Melt cheese in evaporated milk, stirring constantly. Mix with all remaining ingredients except Spam. Spread in pastry-lined pan. Top with cubed Spam. Trim bottom crust. Place top crust over, gently peel off paper. Turn upper crust under lower crust and seal by pressing edges together. Flute. Make 3 or 4 slashes near center. Bake 35-40 min. Serve hot, with sauce. Serves 6-8.

Easy Stir-n-roll Pastry

2 c sifted flour
½ c wesson oil
2 Tb water
1½ ts salt
2 Tb undiluted evaporated milk

Mix flour and salt. Measure oil, milk and water in same cup (but don't stir). Pour all at once into flour; stir until mixed. Press into smooth ball. Cut in half; flatten slightly. Place one half between 2 sheets of waxed paper, 12" square. Roll out gently to edges of paper. Dampen table top to prevent slipping. Peel off top paper. If dough tears, mend without moistening. Line paper and pastry by top corners. Place paper-side up in 9" pie pan. Peel off paper. Fit pastry into pan. Roll out top crust same way.

Sauce

Heat together 1 can undiluted soup (mushroom, tomato, chicken or celery) and ½ c undiluted evaporated milk.

* * * *

One thing about the speed of light--it gets here too early every morning.

SAVORY SAUSAGE CASSEROLE

1 lb bulk pork sausage
1 c uncooked rice
2 pkg (2 oz) chicken noodle soup
1¼ c finely chopped onion
1 c sliced celery
2½ c water
1 Tb soy sauce

Brown sausage, drain. Grease casserole dish, mix soup, sausage, rice and celery; add water and soy sauce. Bake 1 hr at 350°. Serve with applesauce as accompaniment.

"MOST REQUESTED LIVER"

(as defined by an Oregon restaurant chef who shared recipe with Sunset Magazine food editor.

6 strips bacon
All purpose flour
1½ lb baby beef liver, cut into serving size pieces
1 lg onion, sliced
1 envelope dry onion soup mix (for 4 servings)
salt and pepper
1 med-size green pepper, seeded & sliced
1 lb can stewed tomatoes
hot cooked noodles (optional)

In wide frying pan over medium heat, cook bacon until crisp. Remove bacon from pan, drain, and set aside. Pour off and reserve drippings; return 2 Tb of the drippings to pan.

Dust liver with flour, shaking off excess. Add liver to pan and cook, turning once, until lightly browned on both sides; add drippings to pan as needed. Arrange liver in a 9x13" baking dish.

Add onion and green pepper to pan and cook until onion is soft. Spoon vegetables evenly over liver, sprinkle with onion soup mix, and pour tomatoes over all. Season to taste with seasoned salt and pepper, and top with bacon.

Bake, covered, in 350° oven for 25 min or until heated through. Serve with noodles, if desired. Serves 6.

CHIMICHANGAS

1 deer or elk roast (beef may be used) 4-5 lbs
2 can (6-oz) tomato paste
3 c hot water
1 small garlic button, minced or mashed
¼ c salad oil
1½ ts salt
1 Tb crumbled oregano
¼ ts ground cumin
12 flour tortillas
shredded cheese
shredded lettuce
radishes, finely diced
green onion, finely diced
1 6-oz can California chilies (use more if desired)

Cook roast completely. (I usually pressure mine) and cut into bite-sized pieces. Add diced chilies, tomato paste, water, garlic, oil, salt, oregano and cumin. Blend well and simmer until flavors blend. Prepare tortillas.

Spoon 3 Tb filling down the center of each tortilla. Fold tortilla around the filling and fasten with wooden toothpicks. Assemble only two or three at a time, as the tortilla will absorb the liquid from the sauce.

Fry in 1" of hot oil over medium heat (about 350°) turning until golden. This takes about 1-2 min.

Lift from fat with a slotted spoon. Drain, then place on a thick layer of paper towels; keep in a warm place until all are cooked.

Serve garnished with 2-3 Tb each of shredded cheese, lettuce, radishes or green onion. Allow two or three Chimichangas for a main dish serving.

Note: Do not brown tortillas before filling.

Flour Tortillas

4 c all purpose flour
½ c lard or shortening
1½ ts salt
1/8 ts baking powder
1 c water, or more to make soft dough

Make soft dough by combining dry ingredients; cut in lard or shortening. Add water to make soft dough. Knead until smooth and well mixed. Shape into 12 balls; roll each very thin. Spoon filling down center of tortilla and proceed as directed above.

To use flour tortillas for other dishes, roll out as directed. Place each on hot grill; lightly brown on both sides. Use as desired.

IMPOSSIBLE TACO PIE

1 lb ground beef (lean)
½ c chopped onion
1 envelope taco seasoning mix
1 can (4 oz) chopped chilies (drain)
1¼ c milk 3 eggs
3/4 c bisquick 2 tomatoes (sliced)
1 c shredded monterey jack or cheddar cheese

Grease 10" quiche pan or pie plate. Cook beef & onions. Drain. Stir in seasoning mix and spread in plate. Sprinkle with chilies. Beat milk, bisquick and eggs until smooth. Pour into plate. Bake in 400° oven for 25 min. Top with tomatoes, sprinkle with cheese and bake 8-10 min. until knife comes clean. Cool 5 min and serve w/sour cream, chopped tomatoes and lettuce. Serves 6-8.

OLD FASHIONED KRAUT & FRANK STEW

1 lb frankfurters, cut in thirds crosswise
2 Tb salad oil 1 c chopped onions
1 can (16 oz) tomatoes, undrained
1 medium green pepper, diced
3 medium carrots, cut into 1/3" pieces
2 c drained sauerkraut (16 oz undrained weight)
3 medium potatoes, peeled and diced
2 c water 2 Tb brown sugar
1 ts salt ¼ ts pepper
2 ts basil leaves

Brown frankfurters in oil in large kettle. Remove with slotted spoon and set aside. Add onions to drippings in kettle; saute until lightly browned. Add tomatoes and liquid; break tomatoes into pieces with fork.

Add all remaining ingredients; cover and simmer 25 minutes, stirring occasionally. Stir in franks; simmer three minutes more.

* * * *

The Bible says, "Eat, drink, and be merry" but it does not say "Over-eat, over-drink, or over-marry."

SPICY PORK SKILLET

3/4 lb boneless pork, cut into thin strips and trimmed of fat
1 med. onion, thinly sliced
1 Tb cooking oil
1 8-oz can tomato sauce
½ c water
1½ ts chili powder
1 ts worcestershire sauce
¼ ts salt
¼ ts ground red pepper

1 12-oz can whole kernel corn, drained
1 lg green pepper, cut into strips (1 c)
1 2-oz jar sliced pimento, drained
¼ c shredded cheddar cheese (1-oz)

In 10" skillet, brown pork strips and sliced onion in hot cooking oil. Combine tomato sauce, water, chili powder, worcestershire sauce, salt, and red pepper; add to meat in skillet. Cover and simmer for 15 min or till meat is tender. Stir in the drained corn, green pepper strips, and drained pimento. Simmer, uncovered for 10 min, or until green pepper is tender and some of the liquid has evaporated. Sprinkle cheese atop before serving. Makes 4 servings.

* * * *

Oversleeping will never make one's dreams come true.

The best way to climb high is to remain on the level.

If you are right, take the humble side--you will help the other fellow. If you are wrong, take the humble side--and you will help yourself.

True Christian charity is not just giving a man a dime when he is hungry, but giving a man a dime when you are as hungry as he is, and need the dime just as much.

VENISON POT ROAST

6-8 lb venison pot roast
¼ lb bacon or salt pork, cut into strips
1 clove garlic, crushed
2 bay leaves
¼ c (½ stick) butter
3 med. onions, chopped
3 lg carrots, quartered lengthwise
2½ c vegetable stock or water
¼ ts allspice
4 Tb honey
2 Tb vinegar
salt & pepper
2 c sour cream

Rub roast with salt and pepper in large kettle, with lid; melt butter. Add roast, turning until all sides are brown. Place salt pork strips over top of roast. Add onions, bay leaves, garlic, carrots, hot stock, allspice, honey, vinegar, salt and pepper. Stir liquids and bring mixture to a boil. Reduce heat to simmer and cook 2-2½ hrs, covered. Remove to warm oven. Strain stock and return to kettle. Stir in sour cream blended with flour (about ¼ c). Bring to boil. Return roast to gravy and simmer 5 minutes. Serves 10-12.

BUFFALO MEATLOAF

1½ lb buffalo burger
½ c bread crumbs
1 egg
½ c milk
1 Tb flour
1 rounded ts salt
1 ts sage
¼ ts pepper
1 med size onion

Mix together in order given. Bake in a loaf pan at 325° for 30 min.

* * * *

Some of the most insecure things in the world are called securities.

A model wife is one who, when she spades the garden, picks up the fish worms and saves them for her husband.

LAMB SHANKS

Every Thursday for 59 years, this customers' favorite is served at Lamb's Grill Cafe, Utah's oldest surviving restaurant.

8 lamb shanks
2 med onions, chopped
4 cinnamon sticks
4 bay leaves
2 Tb pickling spices
½ ts paprika
¼ ts salt
¼ ts pepper
1 c water
1 can (8 oz) tomato sauce
1 can (6 oz) tomato paste
2 c water

Wash lamb shanks. Place in large pot. Add onions, cinnamon sticks, bay leaves, pickling spices, paprika, salt and pepper. Braise until brown over medium heat. Add one c water. Simmer 30 min. Stir in tomato sauce and paste. Gently simmer 20 min. Blend in 2 c water. Cover. Simmer 1½ to 2 hrs or until tender. Serves 8.

CURRIED LAMB CHOPS

4 shoulder lamb chops
salt and pepper
3/4 c apricot nectar
½ ts curry powder
¼ ts garlic salt

Preheat broiler; place chops on broiler rack. Season with salt and pepper. Combine remaining ingredients. Broil chops 2" from heat about 6-8 minutes. Turn and broil 3 minutes longer. Spoon curry glaze over chops. Broil 2 more minutes. Makes 4 servings. Serve with rice, green beans, cherry tomatoes and vanilla ice cream topped with honey and toasted slivered almonds.

* * * *

There's a difference between sound good reasons and reasons that sound good.

Even if the cost keeps going up indefinitely, education will never become as expensive as ignorance.

KOREAN BARBECUED SHORT RIBS

3 lb short ribs
2 Tb water
½ ts sesame oil
3 Tb brown sugar
¼ ts powdered ginger
1 Tb toasted sesame seed
3/4 c soy sauce
4 ts sherry or orange juice
2 cloves garlic, minced
2 Tb chopped green onions

Cut meat in ½" slices down to within ½" from bone. Combine remaining ingredients. Marinate short ribs 1 hr before broiling. Broil 5" from broiler unit for 10 min; turn and broil 10 more minutes. Makes 6 servings.

MARINATED BEEF & VEGETABLES

¼ c chopped onion
¼ c vinegar
1 ts ground pepper
2 lb lean beef chucks or round, cut in I-2" cubes
Quartered green peppers
Tomato chunks
Thick slices cucumber
½ c salad oil
1 ts salt
2 ts Worcestershire or steak sauce
Small, new potatoes, partially cooked
Whole fresh mushrooms
Small pearl onions or yellow onion, small

In deep dish, combine all ingredients except meat and mix well. Add beef cubes to marinade and stir to coat well. Let stand at room temperature 2-3 hrs or refrigerate overnight. Turn meat occasionally.

String on individual long skewers, alternating beef cubes with a variety of vegetables. Place about 5" away from heat. Cook about 25 minutes, turning often and basting with marinade.

Note: Save room on end of skewers, add tomatoes last few minutes of cooking. Serve with browned rice.

Variation: Use chunks of frankfurters instead of beef. Marinate approximately 3 hrs in sauce of soy sauce, catsup, salad oil, vinegar, and prepared mustard. String on skewers with choice of vegetables.

CHEROKEE CASSEROLE

1 lb beef browned in 1 Tb salad oil; then add:
3/4 c finely chopped onion and cook until tender; add
1½ ts salt
dash pepper
1/8 ts garlic powder
1/8 ts each thyme & oregano
½ small bay leaf
1 20-oz can tomatoes
1 can cream mushroom soup
1 c Minute Rice
3 stuffed olives, sliced

Bring to a boil, reduce heat, and simmer 5 min, stirring occasionally. Discard bay leaf. Spoon into a shallow 1½ qt baking dish. Arrange a lattice of cheese over top using 2-3 slices process cheese cut into ½" strips. Broil just until cheese melts. Garnish with additional slices of olives, if desired. Serves 4-6.

SEVEN LAYER CASSEROLE

½ c rice
½ pkg frozen corn
salt & pepper to taste
1 can tomato sauce plus 1 can water
½ c chopped onion
½ c chopped green pepper
1 lb hamburger crumbs
6-8 bacon strips

Arrange in pan in order given. Bake at 350° for 1 hr.

HAMBURGER CASSEROLE

8 oz noodles (medium size pkg)
1½ lb ground beef
2 8-oz cans tomato sauce
1/8 ts worcestershire sauce
8 oz cream cheese
1 c cottage cheese
½ c sour cream
1/3 c chopped green onion or chives
1 ts chopped green pepper
2 ts melted butter

Cook noodles and drain. Brown beef and add tomato sauce and worcestershire sauce. Combine cottage cheese, cream cheese and sour cream, onions and green pepper. Butter casserole and place ½ noodles in bottom. Cover with cheese and place remaining noodles on top. Pour in butter and top with meat mixture. Cook at 350° for 20 min., 45 if cold. Sprinkle with chopped parsley on top.

SWEET-SOUR FLANK STEAK

2 lb flank steak
¼ ts pepper
2 Tb shortening
3/4 c vinegar
1 can tomato soup
1 ts nutmeg
1 ts salt
¼ c flour
1 c sugar
¼ c soy sauce
1 ts allspice
1 ts cinnamon

Preheat oven to 350°. Score and pound steak; sprinkle with salt and pepper and coat with flour. Melt shortening in skillet and brown meat on both sides. Place meat in 13x9x2" baking pan. Combine ingredients in skillet. Bring to boil; pour over meat. Bake, covered, 1 hr. Serves 6.

SUKIYAKI

1½ lb beef sliced across the grain
3 Tb vegetable oil
½ lb fresh mushrooms, sliced
1 green pepper, cut in squares
3 stalks celery, bias cut
Accent seasoning
3 green onions
1 large onion, sliced
1 16-oz can water chestnuts, drained & sliced
Bamboo shoots (optional)
½ c soy sauce
1 bouillon cube dissolved in hot water
2 c hot rice

In hot skillet at 400° brown meat in oil. Add 3 Tb water, all the vegetables and rest of ingredients except rice. Sprinkle with Accent. Cover and lower heat and cook about 10 min. Vegetables should be crisp and retain their color. Serve with hot rice. Serves 4-6.

TERIYAKI STEAK

2 lb boneless beef steak
1½ c soy sauce
½ c sugar
½ ts crushed garlic
1 Tb grated fresh ginger root

Cut meat into 4 pieces and place in a bowl. In a pan, combine soy sauce, sugar, garlic and ginger. Heat just until sugar is dissolved; cool. Pour mixture over meat and marinate for 1 hr. Remove meat from marinate and grill over glowing coals or broil in oven until done. Slice into finger-size pieces. Serves 4.

SPAGHETTI PIE

8 oz spaghetti noodles, cooked; don't rinse
2 Tb butter
2 eggs, beaten
1/3 c Parmesan cheese
Put in buttered pie pan. Spread 1 c cottage cheese on top. Brown 1 lb sausage and add 1 chopped onion and 1 green pepper. Drain fat and add:
1 5-oz can tomato sauce
1 can mushrooms, drained
1 pkg Schilling spaghetti mix, dry
Simmer altogether. Top with 2 c grated cheddar cheese. Bake at 350° for 20 min. Then add mozzarella cheese (about ½ c) and put in oven again for 5 min.

MEATZA PIE

1 lb ground beef
½ c soft bread crumbs
2/3 c canned milk
1 ts garlic salt
1/3 c tomato paste
Mix together and shape in pie plate; then add:
2 Tb chili sauce and rest of tomato paste
¼ ts oregano
1 Tb instant onion
½ can mushrooms
Cover with mozarella cheese and 3 Tb Parmesan cheese. Bake at 400° about 20 min. or until cheese is melted.

CURRIED HAMBURGER

1 lb hamburger
2 lg onions, chopped
Brown the above ingredients, then add:
1 can tomato soup
1 can water
1-2 ts curry
pinch of chili powder
1 ts sugar
salt & pepper to taste
Add leftover vegetables, carrots, beans, etc. Simmer 1 hr and serve over rice.

* * * *

At the Barbershop: "Don't regard it as losing hair. Think of it as gaining face."

In certain parts of the world people still pray in the streets. In this country they are called pedestrians.

LASAGNE

1 pkg frozen spinach
10 oz lasagne noodles
2 lb ground beef
¼ lb sausage
1½ ts oregano
1½ ts salt
¼ ts pepper
1½ Tb Worcestershire sauce
1 lb Mozzarella or Monterey Jack cheese
½ lb mild cheddar cheese
2 cans mushroom soup
½ c milk
3 8-oz cans tomato sauce
½ c grated parmesan cheese

Cook and drain spinach; brown beef and sausage. Add seasonings and mix in spinach. Cook noodles, rinse and drain. Arrange half noodles in a buttered 9x13" dripper pan. Top with half of meat, cheese and soup mixed with milk. Repeat using all noodles, meat, cheese and soup. Top with tomato sauce and sprinkle with the parmesan cheese. Bake at 350° for 30 min. Serves 12-16.

ECONOMY CABBAGE CASSEROLE

1 lb ground beef
salt & pepper to taste
1 small head cabbage, cut up coarsely
1 medium onion, chopped
1 can tomato soup

Cook ground beef in skillet until lightly browned; season with salt and pepper. Drain off fat.

In 3 qt casserole dish or baking pan layer 1/3 of cabbage, ½ of the beef and ½ of the onion. Top with another 1/3 portion of the cabbage, the remaining beef and the remaining onion. Place remaining cabbage overall.

Pour tomato soup on top; do not mix or stir. Cover and bake at 350° for 40-50 minutes. Serves 6.

EASY CASSEROLE

Brown and drain 1 lb hamburger and 1 chopped onion. Layer in casserole dish: prepared meat (whatever you like, spam, ham, roast left-overs, etc.)
1 can green beans, drained 1 can tomato soup
Add recipe for 6 servings of instant mashed potatoes and spread on top. Sprinkle 1 c shredded cheese. Can be prepared ahead and refrigerated or frozen. Kids love it! Bake at 350° for 3-45 min.

MEATLOAF WELLINGTON

1 loaf frozen white bread dough
1½ lb ground extra lean beef
½ c tomato sauce
2 eggs
½ to 3/4 c chopped onions
1 c bread crumbs
1 Tb chopped parsley
2 ts salt
¼ ts pepper
garlic salt to taste
brown beef gravy or tomato soup

Start to thaw dough. Combine ground beef, bread crumbs, tomato sauce, 1 egg, onions, parsley, salt, pepper and garlic. Mix thoroughly. Place in a loaf pan 8½x4½x2½". Bake at 375° for about 1 hr. Remove from pan, drain and cool. Soften dough. Roll out to a 16 x 7" rectangle. Brush with one-half beaten egg. Place on greased baking dish or into a 9x5x3" loaf pan. Let rest for 30 min. Brush with remaining beaten egg and prick dough with fork around sides. Bake at 375° for 30 min or until golden brown. (If crust is over browning, turn oven down to 350° the last 10 min.) Slice and serve hot with favorite brown gravy or heated tomato soup with only one-half can of water added.

Hints:

If time is short, thaw the frozen bread dough and partially cook the meatloaf in a microwave oven, following microwave directions (before wrapping in dough) Finish in regular oven according to recipe directions.

If meatloaf is too dry for your taste, add ¼ c canned milk. If too moist, the bread may become soggy.

A dry bread dressing might be substituted, in the same amount for the bread crumbs.

* * * *

The way restaurants are cutting pies into smaller and smaller pieces, makes us want to lobby for a minimum wedge law.

The quickest way to become convinced that spanking is unnecessary is to become a grandparent.

QUEBEC MEAT LOAF

2 lb ground beef chuck
2 med potatoes, raw, grated
1 ts salt
½ ts pepper
6 link sausages
1 onion, finely chopped
2 eggs
1 ts powdered ginger
2 cans or 4 c baked beans
¼ c prepared mustard

Blend thoroughly ground beef, onion, potatoes, eggs, salt and pepper. Put mixture on large sheet of waxed paper and pat out to form a rectangle about 12x8". Place a double row of link sausages down middle of rectangle. Roll meat mixture to enclose sausages by lifting it up with waxed paper. Form a neat roll, lift with paper and slide into baking dish. Mix mustard and ginger and spread over meat roll. Bake 45 min at 350° then pour baked beans over and bake another 30 min. If beans are getting too dry on top during cooking, cover with foil, removing the last few minutes to give a nice baked appearance. If using canned pork and beans it is better to season them with molasses, brown sugar, dry mustard and a bit of vinegar to give them a real baked bean flavor. This serves 6-8.

FAVORITE MEAT LOAF

2/3 c fine cracker crumbs or bread cubes
1 c milk
2 beaten eggs
dash of pepper
¼ c catsup
1½ lb ground beef
1 ts salt
dash onion powder

Soak crumbs in milk, add meat, eggs and other seasonings. Shape in loaf. Bake in covered pan for 1 hr, then with lid off for 20 min. in 350° oven.

* * * *

Most of the folks I know are always dieting, (at least they tell me so). What's most disquieting is that it doesn't show.

Mother: "How did you get Tommy to mow the grass?"
Father: "I told him I lost the car keys somewhere in the yard."

GOURMET STUFFED MEAT LOAF

1½ lb ground beef
2 ts salt
1 egg
½ c milk
½ to 3/4 c rolled oats
¼ ts pepper
1 ts Worcestershire sauce
Evaporated milk

Combine all ingredients except evaporated milk thoroughly. Add a little evaporated milk if mixture is too dry. Place half of meat mixture in shallow baking pan. Shape to form an oval base. Down the center, lengthwise, make a shallow "well" for the stuffing. Spoon stuffing mixture over "well".

Shape remaining meat mixture over filling, making sure all filling is covered. Seal bottom and top meat mixtures together. Bake in preheated oven 350° about 1 hr. Let stand 5 min. before slicing

Stuffing:

2 Tb butter or margarine
½ c finely chopped onion
1/3 c dairy sour cream
1 c fresh or canned sliced mushrooms, drained

Melt butter in skillet. Lightly brown mushrooms and onion. Remove from heat and stir in sour cream. Set aside until ready to add to meat loaf above.

SWEDISH MEAT BALLS

2 lb ground beef
1 onion
2 eggs
3 ts baking powder
2 cans cream chicken soup
1 can mushroom soup
1 c canned milk
salt and pepper

Mix beef, onion, eggs, baking powder, seasonings and milk. Mix cream of chicken soup, mushroom soup and milk and pour over the first ingredients. Mix well and spoon into baking dish. Bake at 350° for 1 hr.

* * * *

Anytime you want to attract attention and can't afford a press agent, let your car stall on a busy street corner.

RAISED MEAT BALLS

Soak 4 slices of bread in ½ c milk and 2 beaten eggs for 10 minutes. Add:

1 lb ground beef
½ ts salt
¼ ts pepper
2 Tb minced onion
2 ts baking powder

Form into balls and brown. Place in baking dish and add:

1 can cream of chicken soup & 1 can cream mushroom soup
1½ c milk. Mix well and pour over meatballs. Bake for 1 hr at 325°. Do not salt meat while browning. Makes 30 meat balls.

ALSTON MEAT BALLS

1 lb ground beef
¼ c bread crumbs
¼ c chopped onion
1 egg

Mix together, form in balls and brown in 1 Tb shortening. Combine 1 can golden mushroom soup, ½ c chopped tomatoes

2 Tb vinegar
2 Tb brown sugar
2 ts soy sauce
salt & pepper

Cook slowly for 20 min. Stir often. Serve over rice, noodles or spaghetti.

SWEET & SOUR MEATBALLS

1 lb hamburger
¼ c fine dry bread crumbs
¼ c milk
1 egg
3/4 ts salt

Mix together and shape into balls. Bake on cookie sheet at 500° for 5 min until brown.

Sauce:

1 can pineapple chunks
3/4 c chicken broth
3 Tb brown sugar
¼ c vinegar
1 Tb soy sauce
1 Tb catsup
2 Tb cornstarch
½ onion & green pepper

Drain juice from pineapple and mix with remaining ingredients. Cook until thick. Add pineapple chunks and pour over meatballs.

HAWAIIAN BEEF JERKY

3 lb flank steak
¼ c Hawaiian salt
½ c soy sauce
¼ ts Accent

Trim all fat from meat and cut into long strips about 2" wide. Place in a medium rectangular dish. Combine remaining ingredients; pour over meat. Marinate meat 4 hrs. Preheat oven to 275°. Place meat on cooling racks set on baking sheets. Bake 3 hrs. Slice diagonally to serve. Makes 12 servings.

BARBEQUED BEEF SHORT RIBS

3 lb beef short ribs
1 large onion
2 cloves garlic
3 stalks celery
sprig parsley
1 bay leaf
2 ts salt
water

Spicy Baste

½ c white table wine
¼ c brown sugar or juice from sweet pickles
1 Tb wine vinegar
¼ ts garlic salt
1 ts soy sauce
¼ ts dry mustard

Have butcher crack bones and cut ribs into serving-size pieces. Peel onion and garlic; wash celery and parsley. Place beef, vegetables, bay leaf, and salt in large kettle. Add water to barely cover, and simmer until meat is tender. Remove meat, add to Spicy Baste. Marinate overnight. Drain beef; place on skewers or in wire broiler. Barbecue over charcoal until well browned, basting with drained marinade. Makes 5-6 servings.

* * * *

TV is an appliance which changes children from irresistable forces to immovable objects.

PORCUPINE BALLS

1 lb lean ground beef
¼ c chopped onion
1 ts salt
1 can condensed tomato soup
½ c water
1/3 c uncooked rice
¼ c water
dash pepper
½ ts chili powder

Combine beef, rice, onion, water, salt and pepper. Shape into about 15 one inch balls. Blend soup and chili powder; stir in ½ c water; bring to boil, and add meatballs. Cover and simmer gently for 1 hr, stirring occasionally, Makes about 6 servings.

MEATBALLS IN MARINARA SAUCE

Poaching the moist meatballs in the sauce rather than browning them is the easy technique used here.

¼ lb mild Italian pork sausage
2 cans (about 1 lb each) marinara sauce
1 c water
2 lb ground beef
1/3 c regular strength beef or chicken broth (or water)
1 ts each salt and oregano leaves
1 egg
¼ c flour
½ to ¼ lg spaghetti, hot, cooked and drained
Grated or shredded Parmesan cheese

Remove casings from sausage and crumble or chop the meat. Brown meat lightly in a saucepan, then add marinara sauce and 1 c water. Heat sauce to simmering.

Meanwhile, mix well the beef, broth, salt, oregano, egg, and flour. Shape beef into balls about 1" diameter and drop as they are formed into the simmering sauce; stir gently occasionally to prevent sticking. When all the meat is added to the sauce, continue to simmer for 15 min, skim off and discard fat (or chill, lift off fat, and reheat). Serve hot on spaghetti, top with cheese.

* * * *

Some people think that church is like a convention. They send delegates.

CORNED BEEF CASSEROLE

4 potatoes cooked and sliced
4 hard boiled eggs, sliced   1 med onion, sliced
1 lg can corned beef or 2 c left-over ham
2 c medium thick white sauce - 3/4 c grated cheese (cheddar)
Saute onion in butter or margarine, drain and use left-over butter to make white sauce, using flour and milk. To sauce, add sauteed onions, grated cheese. In greased casserole, alternate layers of corned beef, sliced eggs, sliced potatoes. Pour white sauce over all. Top with buttered bread crumbs. Bake 30 min. in 350° oven.

GOURMET CORNED BEEF

4-5 lb corned brisket or rump of beef
2½ qts water
2 c white table wine
½ c finely chopped raw onion
1/8 ts garlic powder
1 ts dried dill
2 stalks celery
2 bay leaves
1 small orange, sliced
1 stick cinnamon
3 whole cloves
2-3 drops Tabasco sauce

Cover corned beef completely with cold water; bring to a boil and simmer for ½ hr. Discard this cooking water. Add the 2½ quarts of water and all remaining ingredients. Cover and simmer until meat is tender, about 3 hrs. Allow beef to cool in liquid, if not to be served hot and immediately after cooking. Place weight on top of cooling beef for better conformity in slicing. Serves 10.

EASY CORNED BEEF & CABBAGE

1 can cream of celery soup
½ c chopped onion
1 ts dry mustard
1 c diced cooked corned beef
4 c coarsely shredded cabbage

Mix all ingredients in a 1½ qt casserole. Cover. Bake at 375° for 45 minutes.

MING'S BEEF

1½ lb flank steak
2 Tb cornstarch
2 Tb sugar
2 Tb sherry
2 Tb soy sauce
2 Tb vegetable oil
2 cloves garlic, minced
1 Tb fresh ginger, slivered
4 oz saifun
Deep fat for frying
2-3 Tb vegetable oil
¼ c oyster sauce
3 green onions, slivered
Toasted sesame seeds

Cut the flank steak against the grain into 3" long strips. Combine cornstarch, sugar, sherry, soy sauce, 2 Tb vegetable oil, garlic and fresh ginger root. Marinate the meat in this sauce for 15 min or longer. While meat is marinating, make "snow" by frying a little saifun at a time in 1" deep hot fat. When puffed, turn and fry other side. Keep as white as possible. Drain on paper towel. Set aside. Heat 2-3 Tb vegetable oil in skillet or wok. Add marinated meat and stir. Fry 2 min until meat changes color. Add oyster sauce and continue cooking another minute or two. Serve on bed of "snow". Garnish with green onion slivers and toasted sesame seeds. Serves 6-8.

BEEF KEBOB

1½ lb sirloin steak, cut thick
8 plum tomatoes
¼ c soy sauce
½ c salad oil
3/4 ts powdered ginger
1/8 ts garlic powder or 1 clove fresh garlic, minced
2 Tb instant minced onion or 1 med raw onion, chopped
pepper
2 green peppers
8 fresh mushrooms
3/4 c sweet sherry wine or fruit juice
1 ts salt
8 small boiling onions

Cut beef into 2" squares. Combine soy sauce, sherry, salad oil, ginger, garlic, minced onion, salt and pepper. Marinate beef squares in mixture for 2 hrs. Peel and parboil onions. Cut green pepper in 2" squares. Alternate beef squares, green pepper and onions on skewers. Broil, turning to brown sides. (Takes about 10 min, depending on doneness desired). Brush with marinade during cooking. About 3 min before ready to serve, put tomatoes and mushrooms on end of each skewer and finish broiling. Serves 4.

BEEF POT PIE

2 lb lean beef stew meat
½ ts dried dill
¼ ts ginger
2 Tb oil or drippings
½ c Sauterne wine or water
3 stalks celery
1 ts garlic salt
1 ts paprika
2 Tb flour
1 10½ oz can consomme
4 carrots
12 small white onions

Cut beef into generous chunks; combine salt, dill, paprika, ginger and flour. Sprinkle over beef and mix well. Brown meat slowly and well in heated oil. Add consomme, any remaining seasoned flour, and wine; cover and simmer about 45 min. Pare and slice carrots; slice celery in large pieces; peel onions. Parboil vegetables about 5 min. Add drained vegetables to meat; cover and simmer until meat and vegetables are almost tender. Turn into a 10x6" oblong baking dish or pan. Cover with pastry below:

Pastry

1½ c sifted flour
¼ ts rosemary
½ c shortening
3/4 ts salt
½ ts thyme
3-4 Tb cold milk or water

Sift flour, salt, rosemary and thyme into bowl; cut in shortening. Add liquid, mixing to stiff dough. Roll out on floured board to fit top of casserole. Seal edges to edge of dish; prick top crust or cut out crust in small pattern. Bake in hot oven (425°) until browned about 25 minutes. Serves 6.

ROULADEN (Beef Rolls)

1. Pound with wooden mallet until very thin, 6 thin slices round steak (2-3 lbs)
2. Rub each piece with salt and pepper.
3. Spread one side with Dijon-style mustard.
4. On each steak put 1 strip bacon, 1 slice onion, 1 strip dill pickle.
5. Roll the steaks up tightly and tie them with string.
6. Dredge rolls lightly in flour.
7. In skillet, saute until brown, beef rolls, 1 onion, sliced in 1½ Tb butter and 1½ Tb oil.
8. Add and cook over low heat for 1 hr, turning occasionally - 3/4 c water.
9. Remove rolls with slotted spoon to heated platter.
10. Add to pan juices, 1-2 Tb red wine or sherry or fruit juice.
11. Thicken sauce with 1 Tb flour, 1-2 ts catsup, salt and pepper to taste. Serves 4-6.

KUN KOKI (Korean Broiled Steak)

1½ lb flank steak
3 Tb salad oil
¼ c sliced green onions, with tops
1 clove garlic, mashed
1 slice fresh ginger root ¼" thick, slivered
2 Tb sugar
3 Tb toasted sesame seeds
¼ c soy sauce
¼ ts pepper

Cut meat into 1" cubes. Place meat in bowl with remain- ingredients to marinate for 1 hr at room temperature. Skewer meat on pre-soaked bamboo skewers. Broil 3" from source of heat for 4 min. Turn and broil 3 min. on other side. Serve hot. Serves 4-6. Wonderful!!!

PIONEER STEW

3 lb round steak, cut thick, then cubed
4 c cubed carrots
3 c onion, chopped
2 c water
6 Tb (level) dry tapioca
4 c new potatoes
3 cans tomato soup
1 ts salt, dash of pepper

Put all ingredients in roaster. Cook in oven at 250° for 6 hrs. Add to taste 2 Tb Worcestershire Sauce. Serve hot.

FANCY SWISS STEAK

4 lb beef round, top or bottom, cut about ½" thick
3/4 c flour
1 Tb salt
½ ts thyme
1 c chopped celery
4 c tomatoes
4-6 Tb shortening
¼ ts pepper
2 c water
1 c chopped green pepper
½ lb mozzarella cheese, thinly sliced

Cut meat into serving-size pieces. Dredge with ½ c flour. Brown in hot shortening. Remove meat to a large dutch oven or roasting pan. Blend remaining flour with hot drippings. Add seasonings. Gradually blend in water. Add vegetables. Cook and stir until slightly thickened.

Pour mixture over meat and bake at 325° for 2½-3 hrs, or until meat is tender. Top with slices of cheese. Return to oven just until cheese melts. Serve at once. Serves 8-10.

WINNER CASSEROLE

2 lb beef for stew
salt and pepper to taste
2 lg onions, sliced
2 Tb oil
1 4½ oz can whole mushrooms
4 med. potatoes
cracker or dry bread crumbs
1 can mushroom soup
3/4 c milk
3/4 c dairy sour cream
1 ts salt
¼ ts pepper
2 c shredded cheddar cheese

Cut meat into 1" cubes, season with salt and pepper. Cook and stir meat and onions in oil in large skillet over medium heat until meat is brown and onions are tender. Pour off oil. Drain mushrooms, reserving liquid. Add enough water to mushroom liquid to make 1 c. Stir mushrooms and liquid into meat and onions. Heat to boiling; reduce heat and cover. Simmer 2 hrs. Heat oven to 350°. Pour meat mixture into 9x13" baking dish. Pare and thinly slice potatoes and arrange over meat. Mix soup, milk, sour cream, salt and pepper; pour over potatoes. Sprinkle with cheese. Bake uncovered 1 hr. Sprinkle with cracker crumbs if desired. Bake uncovered until potatoes are tender and crumbs are brown, 20-30 minutes. Serves 6.

FESTIVE BEEF STIR-FRY

1 lb boneless beef chuck blade steak
1½ lb broccoli, separated into stalks
1 small sweet potato, peeled and cut into matchstick strips
2 Tb vegetable oil
2 c fresh bean sprouts or 1 can (16 oz) drained
2 green onions, cut in ¼" pieces
1 clove garlic, minced
½ c water
1 Tb cornstarch
¼ c soy sauce
¼ ts ground ginger
¼ c whole blanced almonds, optional

Partially freeze steak to firm it up for easier slicing. Cut across grain into very thin strips. Cut broccoli stalks into 1" pieces; cut top into flowerets. In large pan of boiling water, blanch broccoli & sweet potatoes 1½ min; drain. In large skillet heat oil over medium heat. Add steak strips, half at a time, and stir-fry 2-3 min. Remove from skillet. Add bean sprouts, broccoli & sweet potato; stir fry about 5 min.

BEEF & SEVEN VEGETABLES

1 Tb cooking oil
3 c sliced cooked roast beef (about 1½ x 2" strips)
or 1½ lb fresh lean beef, cut into strips
2½ c carrots, cut in thin circles
1½ c sliced green pepper
2½ c slant-cut celery
1½ c sliced onions
1 can (about 4 oz) bamboo shoots, drained
4 c beef stock or 4 beef bouillon cubes and 4 c water
½ to ¼ c soy sauce
3 Tb cornstarch in ¼ c cold water
15 cherry tomatoes or frozen snow peas (1 c)
Cooked rice or Chinese noodles

Heat oil in frying pan. Add beef and brown lightly. Remove meat; add carrots and green pepper and stir-fry for 1 min. Add onions and celery; stir-fry for 1 min. Add bamboo shoots. Remove vegetables and keep warm. Vegetables should remain crisp as in Chinese cooking.

In heavy skillet, add soup stock and soy sauce. Bring to a gentle boil; thicken with cornstarch-water mixture. Add tomatoes, snow peas, vegetables and meat, and heat gently. Serve in soup plates over boiled rice or Chinese noodles. Serves 8.

GROUND BEEF STROGANOFF

½ c chopped onion
1 Tb butter or margarine
1 lb ground beef
1 ts salt
¼ ts Accent
1 c sliced mushrooms
1 c sour cream
1 small clove garlic, minced
2 Tb flour
¼ ts pepper
¼ ts paprika
1 can cream mushroom soup
cooked rice or noodles

Saute onions and garlic in a little butter or margarine in a hot skillet. Stir in meat, flour, and seasonings, and saute about 5 min or until meat loses its color. Add mushrooms, then soup. Simmer about 10 min. Stir in sour cream and heat, but do not boil. Add a little milk if needed. Season to taste. Serve on hot rice or noodles. Makes 4-6 servings.

FIESTA BURGERS

3 lb ground beef
2 Tb salt
1½ Tb chili powder
1 Tb Worcestershire sauce
½ c chopped onion
1/3 c salad oil
3 eggs
¼ ts pepper
1/3 c catsup
2 lb cooked kidney beans
6 cloves garlic
25 round buns
1 lb 9 oz. cheese (25 1-oz slices)

Beat eggs and combine with meat. Add salt, pepper, chili powder, catsup, Worcestershire sauce and beans. Mix well. Saute onion and garlic in the oil until brown. Combine with meat mixture. Portion the mixture with a half cup measure and shape into patties. Bake at 350° until done, about 30 min. Place patties on lower halves of buns. Top each with a slice of cheese and cover with top of bun. Place on sheet pans and heat in the oven at 300° until cheese melts. Serve immediately.

* * * *

Nowadays some people expect the door of opportunity to be opened with an electric eye.

"Little shavers" we called them when their faces were smooth as a ball. And now that they have grown so tall most of them do not shave at all.

Some of the singers were off key, but it was such a jolly gang! How dreary this old world would be if none except good singers sang.

Liza Minnelli, actress: "I'd rather be a first-rate version of myself than a second-rate version of anybody."

TOSTADA GRANDE

1 lb ground beef — 3-4 drops Tabasco sauce
2 Tb seeded, chopped canned green chilies
1 can tomato sauce (8 oz)
½ to 1 pkg taco or chili seasoning mix
1 can (10 biscuits) refrigerated buttermilk biscuits
1 can (16 oz) refried beans
1 c (4 oz) shredded Mozzarella or Monterey Jack cheese
½ head iceburg lettuce, shredded
1 large tomato, chopped
1 small onion, chopped or sliced

Brown ground beef, drain. Stir in chilies, Tabasco sauce and seasoning mix; heat until hot and bubbly. Simmer, uncovered, 15 minutes or until thick.

Heat oven to 400°. Separate dough into 10 biscuits. Separate each biscuit into 2 layers; arrange in ungreased 12" pizza pan. Press over bottom and ½" up sides to form crust. Spread refried beans evenly over dough; top with meat mixture. Bake at 400° for 18-22 min, or until crust is golden brown. Sprinkle immediately with cheese. Cool slightly.

ENCHILADAS

1 lb lean ground beef — ½ ts salt
½ lb cheddar cheese, grated (save 1 c)
1 can chopped black olives (4½ oz)
1 doz tortillas

SAUCE:
2 c tomato sauce (8 oz) — 1 Tb chili powder
1 can tomato paste (6 oz) — ½ ts salt
1 can tomato soup (10½ oz) — ¼ c cooking oil
½ ts garlic powder

Brown ground beef. Add other ingredients. Dip tortillas in sauce and put meat mixture inside. (1 heaping Tb per tortilla.) Pour 1 c sauce over enchiladas arranged in baking dish. Bake 45 min in 350° oven. Add reserved cup cheese last 5 min and bake until it melts. Serve with remaining sauce.

MEXICAN SKILLET

1½ lb ground beef
½ c onion
½ c green pepper
1 pkg enchilada mix
1 6-oz can tomato paste
1 lg can pinto beans
3 c water, tomato juice or tomatoes

Simmer meat with chopped onion and pepper until brown. When done drain off the fat. Add other ingredients and cook slowly for 20 min. When ready to serve, shred lettuce, put on a plate and cover lettuce with fritoes. Cover with meat and bean mixture; sprinkle cheese on top and serve. Serves 8.

TACO PIE

1¼ lb ground beef
½ c water
1 pkg taco or chili seasoning
1/3 c sliced olives
1 can refrigerator crescent rolls
1½-2 c crushed corn chips
1 c dairy sour cream
6 slices cheese or 1 c shredded cheese

Press crescent rolls into pie plate to form crust. Layer corn chips, beef and seasoning, water and olives. Spread sour cream over meat. Top with cheese and rest of crushed chips. Bake at 375° for 20-25 min. To serve, top with shredded lettuce, tomatoes and avocado if desired.

Note: if seasoning pack is unavailable, make your own by mixing together:

¼ c catsup
1-2 Tb chili powder
1 Tb instant onion
½ ts minced garlic
dash of tabasco sauce

* * * *

Every survival kit should include a sense of humor.

People who tell you never to let little things bother you have never tried sleeping a room with a mosquito.

"MOST REQUESTED" CHILI

It's a far cry from any chili you've ever tasted. Along with the traditional ingredients, half of these are just for flavor. The result is an unforgettable meal-in-a-bowl. A favorite of many, its bound to become your favorite chili, too.

2 lb lean ground beef
1 lg onion, chopped
1 lg can (1 lb 12 oz) tomatoes
1 can (15 oz) tomato puree
2 cans (15½ oz each) beans, drained
3 Tb Worcestershire sauce
1½ c water
3 cloves garlic, minced or pressed
1 beef bouillon cube
1 ts crushed red pepper
2 bay leaves
1 Tb chili powder
1 ts each ground coriander and ground cumin; thyme leaves and oregano leaves, and dry basil
Shredded Cheddar cheese
Sour cream
Sliced green onion including tops

Crumble beef into a 5-6 qt kettle over medium heat; cook, stirring to break up, until browned. Add onion and cook until soft. Stir in tomatoes (break up with a spoon) and their liquid, tomato puree, beans, Worcestershire, water, garlic, bouillon cube, red pepper, bay, chili powder, coriander, cumin, thyme, oregano, and basil.

Bring to a boil; reduce heat and simmer, uncovered, stirring occasionally, until chili is thick and flavors are well blended (about 2 hrs). Skim and discard fat; remove bay leaves.

Pour into bowls and pass cheese, sour cream, and onions to spoon over individual servings. Makes 6-8 servings.

LAMB ZUCCHINI CASSEROLE

1 lb lean boneless lamb, cut into thin bite-size strips and trimmed of fat
3/4 c chopped onion
1 clove garlic, minced
1 Tb cooking oil
2 10-oz pkgs frozen chopped spinach, thawed & drained*
½ ts dried basil, crushed
1½ c shredded mozzarella cheese (6 oz)
½ ts salt
2/3 c cold water
1 ts instant chicken bouillon granules
1 ts cornstarch
2 small zucchini, thinly sliced
¼ c grated Parmesan cheese
¼ ts dried basil, crushed

In skillet brown the meat, onion, and garlic in hot oil. Drain off the fat. In large bowl combine spinach, ½ ts basil, and stir in drained meat mixture, mozarella cheese, and salt. Combine water, bouillon granules, and cornstarch; add to spinach mixture. Mix well; turn mixture into a 10x6x2" baking dish or other oblong baking dish. Arrange zucchini slices atop, overlapping as necessary. Sprinkle with Parmesan cheese and ¼ ts basil. Bake, covered, in a 350° oven for 30 min. or till zucchini is crisp-tender. Uncover and bake 5-10 min more or till golden. Makes 8 servings.

**Note: press out any excess liquid from the thawed and drained spinach.

* * * *

The hardest way to learn to drive a car is by accident.

If you eat fresh vegetables for 90 years you can be sure you won't die young.

Only one American in every two knows how to drive a car well--and she usually sits in the back seat.

MARINATED BEEF POT ROAST

3-4 lb beef pot roast
salt & pepper
1 8-oz bottle Italian salad dressing or 1 c homemade
1 large onion, sliced

Season meat with salt and pepper. Place in bowl. Add dressing. Cover and refrigerate overnight. Remove meat from marinade, place in roasting pan, brown on all sides on a top burner. Add onion and marinade. Cover and simmer on medium to low heat, 3½ to 5 hrs. Add water, if needed to keep from burning. Thicken liquid for gravy. Or roast in oven at 325° covered until tender.

BEEF POT ROAST WITH LIMA BEANS

1 beef chuck roast (about 4 lbs)
1 envelope dry onion soup mix (amount for 4 servings)
1 can (10½ oz) condensed Scotch broth or beef soup
with vegetables and barley
1½ c water
3 medium-size carrots
1 pkg (10 oz) frozen baby lima beans, thawed

Place beef in a 5 qt casserole. In large bowl, combine onion soup mix, broth, and water; pour over meat. Bake. covered, in a 425° oven for 1 hr.

Meanwhile, cut carrots into 1" chunks. Remove casserole from oven and stir carrots into cooking liquid. Return to oven and bake, covered, for 1¼ more hrs or until meat is tender when pierced; add more water if needed.

Skim and discard fat from juices. Stir lima beans into juices. Return casserole to oven and continue baking, covered, for 25 more minutes or until beans are tender. Serves 6-8.

HAM LOAF

3/4 lb ham
½ lb veal or beef
¼ lb fresh lean pork
2 eggs, beaten
3/4 c soft bread crumbs
3/4 c milk
dash of pepper
dash of onion salt
dash of seasoning salt
1-2 ts prepared mustard
¼ c brown sugar
1/3 c pineapple juice

Grind together the ham, veal or beef and pork. Mix in eggs, bread crumbs, milk, pepper, onion salt and seasoning salt. Pat mixture into a 9x5x3" loaf pan. Spread top of loaf with the mustard and brown sugar, mixed together. Pour pineapple juice over the loaf. Bake for one hour in 350° oven. Serves 8-10.

To serve a crowd: Make up into individual loaves, using ½ c mixture per person. Place in large baking pans; spread with topping, and bake for ½ hr or until done.

* * * *

Small boy to mother: "It was a fun party until her mom's tranquilizer wore off."

Man saying grace at dinner table: "And from whatever additives there are in same, make us truly immune."

Notes

Notes

Notes

Notes

fish

Notes

SEAFOOD FONDUE

Friends who like seafood should enjoy selecting from scallops, salmon, swordfish and shrimp. Bottled or homemade seafood cocktail sauce, a chutney sauce, and gaacamole or avocado sauces are good complements. You might also offer wedges of lemon, Caesar Salad, sourdough breads or rolls, and a fruit and cheese dessert could round out this meal.

Cut salmon and swordfish into 3/4" squares, discarding skin and bones. Peel and devein shrimp. Cut scallops into bite-sized pieces. Arrange in separate sections on a bed of lettuce or other greens.

Fill fondue pot 1/3 to ½ full with oil; heat to about 375° or use electric fondue pot as manufacturer directs. Oil should be hot enough so that fish sizzles and oil bubbles rather vigorously immediately upon contact. Place over table top heating element; adjust heat to keep oil at correct temperature. Arrange tray of fish and condiment sauces alongside the fondue pot.

Let each person spear a piece of fish with a fondue fork or bamboo skewer and dip it into the bubbling oil to cook. When fish takes on a tinge of brown on its edges (this takes about a minute depending upon temperature of fish and oil and size of pieces), it is usually done. Makes 4 servings

½ lb salmon steaks
½ lb swordfish steaks
3/4 lb medium-sized raw shrimp
½ lb scallops
About 2 c salad oil or half salad oil and half clarified butter

HALIBUT AU GRATIN

1 lb fresh or frozen halibut
2 bay leaves
¼ c flour
2 c cheddar cheese, shredded
grated pepper
1 Tb parsley, chopped
Paprika
4 slices onion
¼ c butter or margarine
2 c milk
½ ts salt
½ c buttered bread crumbs

Arrange halibut on rack in skillet with a little water; lay onion slices and bay leaves over halibut. Cover; steam for 30 min, adding water as needed. In meantime, melt butter, stir in flour and add milk. Stir and cook until sauce thickens and is smooth. Add cheese; stir until melted. Season to taste. Separate halibut into serving size pieces; place in buttered 1½ qt casserole. Pour over cheese sauce; sprinkle with buttered crumbs, then with parsley and paprika. Bake 30 min at 350° or til bubbling hot. Serves 4-6.

GOLDEN HADDOCK FILLET

Simple--and simply delicious!!

1½ lb skinless haddock fillet
3/4 c mayonnaise
1 ts garlic salt
butter or margarine
flour
3/4 c coarsely crushed unseasoned croutons
lemon wedges & parsley

Preheat oven to 425°; place large, shallow baking pan in oven. Wipe fish with damp cloth. Coat with flour; shake off excess. Lay on wax paper.

With a small spatula, spread half the mayonnaise over top and sides of fish. Combine crushed croutons and garlic salt. Sprinkle half the crouton mixture evenly over mayonnaise coating and pat lightly.

Remove pan from oven. Put butter in pan and swirl until melted (butter should be about 1/8" deep). Lay fish, mayonnaise side down in pan. Spread top with remaining mayonnaise and sprinkle evenly with remaining crumbs, patting lightly.

Return pan to oven and bake until fish flakes readily when prodded in thickest portion. (Allow 10 min for 1" thickness). Serve immediately, garnished with lemon wedges and parsley. Makes 4 servings.

BAKED CRAB IMPERIAL

¼ c butter or margarine
2 c milk
1/8 ts pepper
dash of cayenne
2 Tb sherry wine or fruit juice
1 lb crab flakes
1 ts minced onion
paprika
¼ c flour
1 ts salt
½ ts celery salt
1 egg yolk, beaten
1 c soft bread crumbs
1 ts minced parsley
¼ c buttered crumbs

Melt butter; add flour and blend. Gradually add milk and seasonings and cook over low heat, stirring constantly until thickened.

Gradually add egg yolk and cook 2 min more. Remove from heat and add sherry or fruit juice, soft bread crumbs, crab meat, parsley and onion; mix gently. Pour into well greased 1½ qt casserole. Top with buttered crumbs and sprinkle with paprika.

Bake at 400° for 20 to 25 minutes. Serves 6.

FISH & SPINACH QUICHE

1 pkg (1 lb) frozen white fish fillets
2 eggs lightly beaten
2 Tb Parmesan cheese
1 Tb frozen chives or frozen chopped green onion
1 Tb butter or margarine
Green Goddess dressing (optional)
1 10 oz pkg spinach, chopped & defrosted
salt & pepper to taste

In a saucepan simmer frozen fish in salt water for 10 min, or until fish flakes easily with fork. Drain fish on paper towel, flake fish into 9" pie plate.

Combine eggs, spinach and all seasonings. Pour over flaked fish then dot with butter or margarine. Bake in 400° oven for 20 minutes. Serve hot or cut into wedges and serve cold with Green Goddess dressing. Makes 4 servings.

HALIBUT OR TURBOT CASSEROLE

2 lb fish (frozen fillet)
1 bay leaf
1 sliced onion

Boil fish in salted water with bay leaf and onion until flaky. About 10 min. Break into pieces and place in casserole dish.

Make white sauce of:

2 Tb butter
1 c milk
2 Tb flour
½ c canned milk
1 ts onion juice

Cook until thickened. Pour sauce over fish. Top with layer of grated cheese. Pour 1 can undiluted cream of celery soup over top. Top with buttered bread crumbs. Bake 30 min at 325°.

FISH FANTASTIC

2 lbs fish fillets, frozen or fresh
½ c mushrooms, sliced
¼ c grated cheddar cheese
1 can cream of mushroom soup
½ onion, thinly sliced in rings
1 Tb parsley, fresh or dried
salt & pepper to taste
juice of 1 lemon

Spread fillets in a buttered dish. Sprinkle with lemon juice, salt and pepper. Layer with onions, then mushrooms, then cheese, and finally concentrated mushroom soup. Sprinkle with parsley. Bake at 350° for 25 min. Serves 6.

* * * *

Always try to drive so that your license will expire before you do.

The man who marries for money will earn it.

When an old man marries a young wife, he grows younger--but she gets older.

SEAFOOD & RICE CASSEROLE

1 can cream of mushroom soup
¼ c finely chopped onion
¼ ts salt
1 1/3 c minute rice
1 7-oz can salmon, drained
½ c grated cheddar cheese
1½ c water
1 ts lemon juice
dash of pepper
1 12-oz pkg green peas, partially thawed

Combine onion, water, lemon juice, salt and pepper in 1½ qt saucepan. Bring to boil over medium heat, stirring occasionally. Pour about half of the soup in mixture into a greased casserole dish. Then in layers, add 1 1/3 c rice, peas, salmon, drained and flaked. Pour on remaining soup mixture. Sprinkle with ½ c grated cheese. Cover and bake at 375° for 10 min; stir, cover and bake 10 minutes longer. Serves 4.

WILD RICE CASSEROLE WITH TUNA

2 hard cooked eggs, chopped
3 Tb parsley chopped
½ c cream
½ c bread crumbs
½ c almonds
1 can tuna
1 can mushroom soup
1/8 ts pepper
3 Tb melted butter
2 c cooked wild rice

Wash rice. Place 4 c water in pan, 1 ts salt and rice. Cover, bring to boil, then simmer and let steam for about 40 min. Drain rice. Add all ingredients except buttered crumbs and nuts. Sprinkle crumbs and nuts on top. Bake at 350° for 30 minutes. Serves 6.

TUNA ALMOND CRISP

½ ts salt
1/8 ts pepper
1/8 ts marjoram
½ ts dry mustard
1 2/3 c undiluted canned milk
1 Tb lemon juice
½ c sliced almonds
3 c slightly crushed potato chips
1 3/4 c (10-oz) cooked green beans
1 c (6½-7 oz can) well drained chunk tuna
1 c (4-oz) grated cheese

Combine salt, pepper, marjoram, dry mustard and canned milk. Slowly add lemon juice, stirring constantly. Place 2 c of potato chips in 8" baking dish. Arrange green beans, tuna, almonds and grated cheese in alternate layers. Pour milk on top. Add cheese. Bake at 350° 20-25 min. Serves 4.

SEAFOOD NEWBURG

¼ c minced onion
1 c butter or margarine
1 ts salt
¼ ts white pepper (optional)
4 c milk, heated
2 Tb lemon juice
1 green pepper, finely chopped
1 c flour
¼ c chopped pimiento
dash of cayenne
4 c cooked seafood and fish*
pastry shells, cooked rice or hot buttered toast

Saute onion and green pepper in butter until soft but not brown. Blend in flour and seasonings. Add hot milk and stir on medium heat until mixture thickens. Add seafood, fish and lemon juice. Taste to correct seasonings. Heat thoroughly. Keep warm, if necessary, over hot water.

Serve in pastry shells or over hot cooked rice or buttered toast. Makes about 2 quarts or 10 servings.

Note: The Newburg sauce (without seafood) may be prepared and frozen up to a month in advance. Thaw overnight in refrigerator and reheat over boiling water, stirring frequently. If necessary, blend with a whip or rotary beater until smooth. Then add seafood and remaining ingredients as directed.

*Use at least 2 c shrimp, crabmeat, lobster; the remainder may be flaked drained white tuna, salmon, cod, haddock, halibut, sole, or other fish.

SPICED SHRIMP

Wash 2 lbs shrimp
1 lg glass of water (Iced tea glass)
2 Tb salt
1½ Tb whole allspice
1 small bay leaf
1 ts pepper
½ Tb thyme
2 cloves garlic

Pour over shrimp and cook 20 minutes with lid on. Turn off heat and let stand 10 min; then drain.

* * * *

If you must beat a child, use a string.

It is better that a child should cry than its parents should.

Better to be embarrassed than ashamed.

BROILED FISH STEAKS OR FILLETS

8 fish steaks or fillets, washed well in cold running water

Salt
½ c lemon juice
¼ c chopped parsley
paprika
½ c melted butter or margarine

Place fillets or steaks on well-greased baking sheet. Sprinkle with salt and paprika. Drip lemon juice and butter generously over fish. Broil about 6" from heat for approximately 10 min for each 1" of thickness, basting once with lemon juice and butter. When fish is firm and flakes easily, remove from broiler. Baste again with lemon and butter; garnish with parsley and serve immediately. Makes 8 servings.

Lemon Sauce

1 Tb cornstarch
1½ c water
1 Tb butter or margarine
¼ c lemon juice

Make a paste of cornstarch and butter. Bring water and lemon juice to a boil. Stir in cornstarch paste and cook until thickened. Use about 2 Tb sauce on each fillet.

CREAMY BAKED HALIBUT STEAKS

4 halibut steaks, about ¼" thick
salt and pepper
¼ c dry bread crumbs
3/4 c sour cream
¼ ts garlic salt
1½ ts chopped chives, fresh or frozen
1/3 c grated Parmesan cheese
1 ts paprika

Place steaks, close fitting, in a shallow buttered dish. Sprinkle with salt and pepper. Mix together sour cream, bread crumbs, garlic salt and chives, and spread over steaks. Sprinkle with Parmesan cheese and paprika. Bake, uncovered, at 400° for 15-20 min, or until fish flakes with a fork. Makes 4 large or 8 small servings.

SHRIMP CREOLE WITH RICE

2½ Tb butter or margarine ½ c chopped green pepper
1/3 c chopped green onions (use some green tops)
1 c chopped celery 2 Tb flour
1/8 ts paprika 1 small bay leaf
1 can (1 lb 12-oz) whole tomatoes, drained
2 c reserved tomato liquid, heated
2 cans (about 5 oz each) shrimp, drained (or use 1½ lb fresh shrimp, cooked)
1 Tb chopped parsley (or use ¼ ts dry parsley flakes)
salt to taste cooked rice

Melt butter in large frying pan or dutch oven. Saute green pepper, onions, and celery until soft but not brown (5-10 min on low heat). Add flour and paprika; blend well. Add hot tomato liquid; cook and stir until smooth and thick. Add whole tomatoes and bay leaf. Cover and simmer 30 min. Add shrimp and continue cooking until shrimp is heated (about 5 min). Add parsley. Taste to correct seasonings. Serve immediately over hot cooked rice. Makes 6 servings.

SHRIMP DELIGHTS

3/4 c mayonnaise ½ c chopped celery
¼ c chopped black olives ½ c grated Colby or Cheddar cheese
1 5-oz can shrimp, drained and rinsed
4 English muffin halves Parmesan cheese

Gently mix together mayonnaise, celery, olives, cheese and shrimp in small bowl. Place English muffin, cut-side up, on a flat cookie sheet. Spoon shrimp mixture on muffins, dividing equally.

Sprinkle with Parmesan cheese Broil for 3-4 minutes or until lightly browned. Serve with soup or salad. Serves 4.

* * * *

If you don't grow, you'll grow smaller.

Don't add to the truth; if you do, you will subtract from it.

TROUT WITH SUGAR SNAPS

2 whole, portion-sized trout, cleaned
5 Tb corn oil
5 med. mushrooms, sliced
1 med. onion, peeled and sliced
1 Tb powdered chicken bouillon
¼ lb Sugar Snaps

Preheat oven to 375°. Rub trout with 2 Tb of the corn oil and place in casserole or foil. Cover casserole tightly or seal foil for baking to steam. Bake 15 min or until fish tests flaky with fork.

While fish are cooking, heat remaining 3 Tb corn oil in skillet. Add sliced mushrooms, sliced onion, and sprinkle with powdered bouillon. Cover and let simmer 6-8 min.

String Sugar Snaps and when fish are almost done, add whole peas to skillet and cover to cook just 2 min and no longer. Remove vegetables from heat and fish from oven. Arrange fish on warm platter and garnish with sauteed vegetables and juices. Serves 2.

For Micro-Wave: In 12x8x2" dish, arrange trout. Rub trout with oil and cover with vented plastic wrap (vent it yourself). Microwave on HIGH POWER for 8-9 min, or until fish flakes done. Set fish aside in warm spot.

In another microwaveproof dish, combine oil. mushrooms, onion and bouillon. Cover and microwave on HIGH POWER for 4 min, stirring after 2 min. Add strung Sugar Snaps and cover again. Cook 2 min longer. Serve vegetables over fish after letting them stand a minute.

* * * *

The first sign of old age is when you hear "snap, crackle and pop" in the morning and it isn't your cereal.

One sign that we are no longer a rural nation is that hailstones, which used to be classified as the size of hen's eggs, are now compared to golf balls and baseballs.

OYSTER STEW

2 jars (10-oz ea) Pacific oysters
4 Tb butter or margarine
1 small onion, chopped
½ c thinly sliced celery
1 can (14 oz) regular-strenth chicken broth
1 pt (2 c) half and half (light cream) or milk
salt, pepper and ground nutmeg
About 1 c unseasoned croutons
1 Tb all-purpose flour

Pour oysters and their liquid into a wide frying pan over medium-high heat; cook just until edges curl. Cut oysters into bite-size pieces, then set aside with their liquid.

In a 3 qt pan over medium heat, melt butter. Spread croutons in a shallow baking pan; drizzle croutons with about half the butter and toast in a 350° oven for about 10 min.

Meanwhile, add onions and celery to remaining butter in pan and cook, stirring, until onion is soft. Stir in flour and continue cooking and stirring for 1 min. Gradually pour in broth and cream and continue cooking and stirring until bubbly.

Add oysters and their liquid to onion mixture; season to taste with salt, pepper and nutmeg. Pass croutons to spoon over individual servings. Serves 6-8.

OYSTER CRISP

1 pt (1 lb) shucked oysters, with their juices
¼ ts salt
1/8 ts papper
1/8 ts ground or freshly grated nutmeg
6 strips bacon, cooked until crisp, then crumbled
1 c shredded Swiss cheese
1 c whipping cream
½ c coarsely crushed saltine crackers
2 Tb butter or margarine

Preheat oven to 400°. Grease a shallow 1½ qt baking dish. Arrange oysters evenly in dish; pour their juices over them. Sprinkle salt, pepper and nutmeg evenly over oysters. Scatter crumbled bacon over oysters; then top with cheese. Pour cream evenly over all; then cover evenly with cracker crumbs and dot with butter. Bake, uncovered for 20 min. Serves 4.

TROUT AMANDINE

2 lbs trout fillets (or fillet of sole)
salt and papper to taste
1 egg
1 c milk
flour
½ c butter
1/3 c slivered almonds
2 Tb Worcestershire sauce
juice of 2 lemons
1 Tb parsley, chopped
lemon and tomato wedges

Season fillets with salt and pepper. Beat egg and milk. Dip trout in egg mixture. Drain. Dredge in flour. Saute fillets until golden brown in butter (about 6 min). Remove to warm platter. Add almonds to frying pan. Brown lightly. Stir in lemon juice, worcestershire sauce and parsley. Heat through. Pour over fish. Garnish with lemon and tomato wedges. Serves 6.

TROUT & MUSHROOMS IN CREAM

1/3 c butter or margarine
½ lb small whole mushrooms (or large mushroom, sliced)
2 Tb finely chopped parsley
4 whole dressed trout (each about ½ lb)
all-purpose flour
¼ ts salt
2 Tb lemon juice
1/3 c whipping cream

In a wide frying pan, melt butter over medium-high heat; add mushrooms and saute, stirring frequently until golden brown (about 5 min). Stir in parsley, then remove pan from heat and lift mushrooms from pan with slotted spoon. Arrange evenly to cover bottom of large warm serving platter; keep warm. Set pan aside.

Wipe fish with damp cloth, inside and out. Coat fish with flour; shake off excess. Arrange in single layer on wax paper. Return pan to medium heat; add salt to remaining butter.

Place in pan as many fish as will fit without crowding. Cook, turning once, until fish is lightly browned and flakes when prodded in thickest portion with fork. When fish is done, remove from pan and arrange on top of mushrooms. Keep warm and repeat process with remaining fish. After removing last fish, add lemon juice and cream to pan; bring to boil, stirring and scraping to blend with pan drippings. Spoon immediately over fish and mushrooms, and serve. Serves 4.

TEMPURA

Delicious "French Fries of the Far East

Select large raw shrimp, scallops, or white fish, cut in strips, and any four or five vegetables.
fresh mushrooms, small, whole or halved
green pepper squares
onion rings
eggplant strips
shredded carrots, fry in clusters
squash or zucchini blossoms
sweet potato slices
broccoli flowerets
parsley sprigs
zucchini strips
green onions, cut in 1" lengths
cucumber slices
bamboo shoots
cauliflowerets
pea pods

<u>Tempura Batter</u> (4 servings)

1 egg	1 c ice water
1 c flour	½ ts sugar
½ ts oil	½ ts salt
pinch soda	2-2½ c oil for frying

<u>Ready</u>: Prepare fish and vegetables, pat dry, and arrange on platter or tray. Refrigerate. Combine batter ingredients with wire whip or fork. Do not overmix. Use promptly.

<u>Set</u>: Wok on high heat. Add oil and heat to medium high 375°.

<u>Go</u>: Dip shrimp and vegetables one at a time into batter. Allow excess to drip off, then slide into hot oil. Fry until light brown and crispy on both sides. Drain on rack or paper towels. Serve immediately with Tempura Sauce. (Or keep warm in 200° oven).

<u>Tempura Dipping Sauce</u>:
½ c Japanese soy sauce
½ c chicken broth
1 Tb brown sugar
¼ ts Accent (optional)
finely minced white radish, green onion sweet green
Combine ingredients and serve in individual dishes. Let each add minced vegetables as desired.

INDIAN SHRIMP CURRY

1 lg onion
1½ ts curry powder
1 ts salt
1½ lb shrimp
1 lg can tomatoes
1 can whole green beans
2 Tb fat
1 Tb sugar
2 Tb flour
2 small cans tomato paste
OR 1 can tomato soup

Brown onion in fat. Mix together curry powder, sugar, salt, and flour. Add shrimp; stir to coat shrimp. Place the coated shrimp in a skillet with tomato soup and canned tomatoes. Simmer for 1 hr over very low heat, stirring frequently. During last 15 minutes of cooking add the drained green beans. Serve on a platter with the curry in the center of a rice ring. Serves 6.

SHRIMP NEWBURG

1 lb frozen cleaned and deveined shrimp
1 can cream of shrimp soup
½ c milk
½ ts salt
¼ ts ground nutmeg
2 egg yolks
¼ c apple cider
hot cooked rice

Cook shrimp, following directions. Combine soup, milk, salt and nutmeg in medium size saucepan, boil.

Beat egg yolks with cider slightly in a small bowl; blend in about 1 c hot shrimp sauce; slowly stir into remaining mixture in saucepan. Cook, stirring constantly, over low heat for 1 min, or until slightly thickened. Add drained shrimp. Serve with rice; garnish with parsley and lemon wedges, if desired.

* * * *

Wife: "You look tired, dear. Did you have a hard day at the office?"
Husband: "I'll say. I took a personal interest inventory, and believe me, it's a good thing I own the company!"

sh

ORANGE POACHED FISH

1 c orange juice
2 Tb dry sherry or bouillon
1 Tb soy sauce
¼ ts salt
dash of pepper
4 med. carrots, thin sliced
1 med. onion, sliced and separated into rings
1 med. green pepper, cut into strips (3/4 c)
1 lb frozen flounder or sole fillets, thawed
2 ts cornstarch
1 med. tomato, cut into 8 wedges

In a 12" skillet combine orange juice, sherry or bouillon, soy sauce, salt, and pepper. Add sliced carrots and onion rings; bring to boiling. Reduce heat; simmer, covered, for 8 min. or till vegetables are crisp-tender. Stir in green pepper. Push vegetables to edge of skillet.

Season the fish with salt; arrange in center of the skillet. Bring to boiling; reduce heat and simmer, covered 2 to 3 minutes or till fish flakes easily when tested with a fork. Remove fish from the skillet; set aside.

Combine cornstarch and ¼ c cold water; stir into mixture in skillet. Cook and stir till thickened and bubbly; cook and stir 2 min. more. Return fish to skillet; arrange tomato wedges atop. Heat through; serve immediately. Garnish with green onion brushes, if desired. Serves 4.

CHILLED SALMON WITH CUCUMBERS

4 frozen or fresh salmon steaks, cut 3/4" thick
1 small onion, quartered
½ c white wine vinegar
2 Tb sugar
½ ts marjoram, crushed
1 small tomato, chopped
1 small cucumber, coarsely shredded
¼ c sliced green onion
1 Tb snipped parsley
shredded lettuce

Place the salmon in a greased 10" skillet. Add boiling water to cover. Add onion and ½ ts salt. Cover; simmer 5 to 10 min. or till fish flakes easily. Place fish in baking dish. Mix vinegar, sugar, marjoram, ¼ c water, and ½ ts salt. Stir in tomato, cucumber, green onion, and parsley. Pour atop fish. Cover and refrigerate 3 to 24 hrs. Before serving, line plates with shredded lettuce. With slotted spoon remove salmon and vegetables from liquid and place atop lettuce. Drizzle with some of liquid. Makes 4 servings.

CREAMED SHRIMP

1 lg onion, diced
1 c celery, diced
1 Tb butter
1 can (4 oz) sliced mushrooms, drained
1 8-oz can water chestnuts, drained
1 can sliced bamboo shoots, drained
¼ c water
white sauce
4 oz slivered almonds
½ lb fresh small shrimp
Rice, noodles or pastry shells

Brown onion and celery in butter. Add mushrooms and bamboo shoots with ¼ c water. Steam 2 min.

Stir in white sauce, almonds and shrimp. A little orange juice may be added for flavor. Serve over rice, noodles or in pastry shell. Serves 4.

White Sauce :
1 stick butter (½ c) ½ c flour 2 c half and half

Melt butter; add flour, blending well. Gradually add half and half over high heat, stirring constantly, until smooth and thickened.

SHRIMP PARMESANO

1½ lb fresh shrimp, peeled and deveined
½ c butter, melted
1 clove garlic, pressed
1 Tb fresh parsley, finely chopped
1 Tb Italian seasoning
¼ ts fresh ground pepper
1 c fine bread crumbs
½ c Parmesan cheese, grated
3 Tb fresh lemon juice

Prepare the shrimp as indicated, then lay the shrimp on a medium-size baking sheet or dish. In a small saucepan combine the butter, garlic, parsley, Italian seasoning, pepper and capers. Heat this mixture through, then slowly drizzle over the shrimp. Sprinkle the crumbs and Parmesan cheese over all. Place in a preheated 350° oven and bake for 15 min. Set the heat temperature to broil. Remove the sheet from the oven and sprinkle the lemon juice over the shrimp. Place under the broiler and broil for 3 min. Serve immediately. Serves 4-6.

SEAFOOD STEW

1 lg fresh or frozen fish fillets
12 oz fresh or frozen shelled shrimp
3/4 c chopped onion
2 Tb olive or salad oil
4 oz package dru orzo (2/3 c)
2 ts dry oregano, crushed
2 cloves garlic, minced
2 16-oz cans tomatoes, cut
½ c dry wine or bouillon
1 9-oz pkg green artichoke hearts, thawed

Thaw frozen fish and shrimp. Cut fish into 1½" pieces, removing any skin; set aside. In Dutch oven cook onion and garlic in oil till tender but not brown. Stir in undrained tomatoes, orzo, wine, and oregano. Heat to boiling. Stir in fish pieces and artichoke hearts. Reduce heat; simmer, uncovered for 5 min. Stir in shrimp and green pepper. Simmer, uncovered, 1 to 3 min. more or till shrimp turn pink; stir occasionally Serves 8.

SALMON LOAF

1 7 3/4-oz can salmon
1 beaten egg
3/4 c soft bread crumbs (1 slice)
2 Tb thinly sliced green onion
1 Tb butter or margarine
2 ts flour
¼ ts dry mustard
½ c milk
½ ts Worcestershire sauce

Drain salmon, reserving 2 Tb liquid. Flake salmon, discarding skin and bones. Combine reserved liquid, egg, bread crumbs, half of the green onion, ¼ ts salt, and 1/8 ts pepper. Add salmon; mix well. Spoon into a well greased 6 x 3 x 2" loaf pan. Bake in a 350° oven 35 minutes or till done.

Cook remaining green onion in butter till tender but not browned. Blend in flour, mustard, ¼ ts salt, and dash of pepper. Add milk and Worchestershire sauce all at once. Cook and stir till thickened and bubbly. Cook and stir 1 minute. Spoon some sauce atop salmon; pass remaining. Makes 2 servings.

COQUILLES ST. JACQUES au GRATIN

2 lb scallops (thawed if frozen) cut in bite-size pcs.
About 1 c regular-strength chicken broth

¼ c butter or margarine	3/4 lb mushrooms, sliced
1 Tb lemon juice	1 lg onion, finely chopped
6 Tb flour, unsifted	½ c whipping cream
1/8 ts ground nutmeg	1½ c shredded Swiss cheese
¼ c lightly packed minced parsley	salt

Combine scallops and 1 c of the broth and bring to a boil; reduce heat, cover and simmer gently for about 5 min. or until scallops are just opaque. Remove from heat; let scallops cool in liquid. Drain cooled liquid into a pint measuring cup. Add broth, if necessary, to make 2 c liquid; reserve. Cover scallops and chill.

In a wide frying pan, melt 2 Tb of the butter over medium-high heat and add mushrooms and lemon juice. Cook, stirring, until mushrooms are golden brown and all liquid is evaporated. Pour into a small bowl and set aside.

To frying pan, add remaining 2 Tb butter and onion. Cook over medium-high heat, stirring, until onion is soft but not browned. Stir in flour and cook until bubbly. Remove pan from heat and using a wire whip, gradually stir in reserved scallop liquid. Return to heat and bring to a boil, stirring; cook until thickened (about 10 min). Add mushroom mixture, cream, nutmeg, and ½ c of the cheese; stir until blended. Cover sauce and chill.

When sauce is cold, stir in scallops along with parsley and salt to taste. Divide scallop mixture equally among 4 to 6 individual 2-c ramekins (or use scallop shells, commercially prepared for baking) and sprinkle remaining 1 c cheese evenly over top, dividing equally among ramekins. Cover and chill until ready to bake (up to 24 hrs).

Preheat oven to 400°. Bake, uncovered, until bubbling and edges are beginning to brown (about 12-15 min). Serves 4-6.

BAKED FISH HAWIIAN

2 lb mahimahi fillets (any type of fish may be used)
1 ts salt
dash of pepper
2 Tb lemon juice
¼ c mayonnaise
1 ts soy sauce
3/4 c cornflake crumbs
3/4 c chopped macadamia nuts or slivered almonds

Sprinkle salt and pepper on fish; baste with lemon juice. Let fish stand for 15 minutes. Preheat oven to 350°. Grease a shallow baking pan. Mix together mayonnaise and soy sauce; spread over fish. Combine corn flake crumbs and macadamia nuts; roll fish in crumb mixture. Place in prepared pan and bake for 25-30 min. Serves 6.

TUNA-CORN BAKE

1 can cream of chicken soup
1 can (9¼ oz) tuna, drained and flaked
1 can (8 oz) stewed tomatoes (reserve 3 tomato pieces)
1 c coarsely crumbled corn chips
½ small green pepper, chopped (about ¼ c)
2 ts instant minced onion
½ ts chili powder
Dash of garlic salt
1 c shredded cheddar cheese (about 4 oz)
1 c coarsely crumbled corn chips
Chili sauce (optional)

Heat oven to 352°. Mix tuna, soup, tomatoes, 1 c corn chips, green pepper, onion, chili powder and garlic salt in greased 1½ qt casserole. Sprinkle with cheese and arrange reserved tomato pieces in center. Sprinkle 1 c corn chips around tomatoes. Bake uncovered until bubbly, about 30 min. Serve with chili sauce. Serves 8.

* * * *

After a certain age, the candles on a woman's birthday cake probably represent the number of years she has been married.

CREAMED SCALLOPS WITH GRAPES

1½ lb scallops (thawed if frozen) cut in bite-size pcs.
¼ c butter or margarine — 1 med. onion, chopped
¼ c flour, unsifted — 1 Tb curry powder
1¼ c half and half (light cream) — 1 ts lemon juice
4 hard-cooked eggs, diced — 1 c seedless green grapes
salt & pepper — dash nutmeg
6 baked patty shells or hot cooked rice

Prepare court bouillon. Bring to a boil, add scallops and simmer, uncovered, for about 5 min or until scallops are just opaque. Lift scallops and seasonings from bouillon with a slotted spoon; set scallops aside and discard seasonings. Pour bouillon through a wire strainer; return to pan and boil rapidly, uncovered, until reduced to about 1 c; reserve.

In a frying pan, melt butter over medium heat; add onion and cook until soft. Stir in flour and curry powder and cook until bubbly. Remove from heat; using a wire whip, gradually stir in reserved court bouillon and the cream. Return to heat and cook, stirring, until bubbly and thickened. Remove from heat and stir in lemon juice, scallops, eggs, and grapes; season to taste with salt, pepper, and the dash of nutmeg. Return to medium heat and cook, stirring, just until heated through.

To serve spoon mixture into patty shells, dividing equally; pass any remaining scallop mixture in a serving bowl. Or serve scallop mixture over rice. Serves 6.

Court bouillon:

In a pan combine 1 bottle (8 oz) clam juice, 1 can (about 14 oz) regular-strength chicken broth, 1 bay leaf, 4 whole cloves, 6 whole black peppers and ½ ts crumbled thyme leaves. Bring to a boil, reduce heat and simmer 5 min.

SHRIMP & CLAM SAUCE

Drain juice from 1 can (6½ oz) chopped clams into a pint measuring cup; set clams aside. Add enough whipping cream or half and half (light cream) to clam juice to make 1½ c; set aside.

In a small pan over medium heat, melt 2 Tb butter or margarine. Stir in 2 Tb flour and cook until bubbly. Gradually stir in clam juice mixture. Reduce heat to medium-low and cook, stirring until sauce thickens.

Add dash of nutmeg; stir in chopped clams and ½ lb shrimp; season to taste with salt. Let cool.

SEVEN SEAS CASSEROLE

1 6½ oz can drained crab
1 4½ oz can shrimp, drained
1 c mayonnaise
1/3 c onion, chopped
1 c celery, diced
1/3 c green pepper, chopped

Combine ingredients and pour into 1½ qt baking dish. Top with 1½ c buttered bread crumbs. Bake in 350° oven for 5 minutes. Serves 8.

CRAB CASSEROLE

1 can crab meat marinated in juice of ½ lemon
1 c homogenized milk
1½ c Best Foods mayonnaise
1¼ c fresh bread crumbs (3-4 slices) broken in pieces
1 T parsley
1 Tb minced onion
4 hard-boiled eggs, chopped
½ c buttered crumbs

Mix together and bake in buttered casserole 20-30 min at 350°. Place buttered crumbs on top. Serves 7.

FANCY FISH DISH

1½ lb fish filets
½ c Romano or Parmesan cheese
1 green pepper chopped
½ onion chopped
Parsley
3 stalks celery, chopped fine
½ c slivered almonds
1½ c sour cream
1 c seedless grapes
½ c Mandarin oranges
½ c peach slices
1 apple sliced
Pimientos

Place fish in buttered baking pan; sprinkle with cheese. Saute pepper, onion, parsley, celery, then add pimiento and seasonings and almonds. Stir in sour cream, pour over fish and bake 50 min until all moisture is gone. Arrange grapes and fruit slices all around and bake 15 min more. Put on platter and sprinkle with paprika.

EASY SALMON THERMIDOR

4 salmon steaks (about 1¼ lb)
½ c milk — 2 Tb sherry or bouillon
¼ ts salt — 2 hard-cooked eggs, sliced
1/8 ts pepper — ½ c grated Swiss cheese
1 10-oz can cream of mushroom soup, undiluted
paprika

About 40 min. before dinner: Start heating oven to 350°. Place salmon in shallow baking dish; pour on milk, sprinkle with salt, pepper. Bake 30 min. or until salmon flakes, but is still moist, when tested with fork.

Meanwhile, in saucepan, stir soup till smooth; add sherry or bouillon; heat till boiling. When salmon is done, arrange sliced eggs around fish; pour on sauce. Sprinkle with cheese, paprika. Place low under broiler until bubbling hot, about 5 min. Makes 4 servings.

OVEN FRIED FISH

It's hard to believe--but it's true. With this method there's no pot watching, no turning, and no odor. Try it.

1. Choose fillets, steaks, or dressed small fish.
2. Mix ¼ c milk or evaporated milk, and 2 ts salt with a bit of dried thyme, tarragon, dill, or rosemary, or minced onion or garlic or Tabasco in shallow dish.
3. In second dish, combine ½ c packaged dried bread crumbs or crushed corn or wheat flakes with ½ ts paprika and a little dry mustard, grated cheese, chili powder, or snipped parsley.
4. Start heating oven to 500°. Now, with one hand, dip each piece of fish into milk, then with the other hand roll it in crumbs, arranging, side by side, in greased shallow baking dish, lined with foil, if desired.
5. Drizzle a little salad oil or melted butter or margarine onto fish. Then bake 12-15 minutes or until golden and easily flaked with a fork--but still moist.
6. Serve on heated platter "as is" or with one of the sauces of your choice.

BAKED RED SNAPPER

2 lbs fresh or frozen red snapper fillets or other fish fillets
2½ Tb lemon juice
3/4 c vegetable juice cocktail
½ c chopped celery
½ c chopped onion
¼ c chopped green pepper

Thaw fish, if frozen. Place fish in greased baking dish. Season with salt and pepper. Drizzle lemon juice over fish. Bake fish in a 350° oven for 10 min. Meanwhile, in saucepan combine remaining ingredients. Simmer, uncovered, 10 minutes. Remove fish from oven. Drain off all excess liquid. Pour simmered vegetable sauce over fish. Return to oven; bake 15 minutes more or till fish flakes easily when tested with a fork, basting with vegetable sauce occasionally. Makes 6 servings.

* * * *

If I were to list the ten smartest people in town, who would be the other nine?

Drive-in banks were established so that the cars could see their real owners.

Teachers are never fully appreciated by parents until it rains all day Saturday.

The man of few words doesn't have to take so many of them back.

QUICK SALMON PLATTER

1 1-lb can salmon
1 c milk
½ c grated Cheddar cheese
¼ ts dry mustard
1/8 ts salt
1/8 ts Tabasco
2 Tb butter or margarine
2 Tb flour
Hot cooked, seasoned broccoli, green beans or asparagus

Heat salmon gently in its own liquid. Meanwhile, melt butter; add flour, mustard, salt, Tabasco; stir until smooth. Add milk; cook, stirring, until mixture thickens and comes to boil. Remove from heat. Add cheese; stir until melted. Arrange salmon, in large pieces, on hot platter, with broccoli around it. Serve with sauce. Serves 4.

SALMON SCALLOP DIVAN

1 10-oz pkg frozen broccoli, thawed
3 Tb butter or margarine
3 Tb flour
½ ts salt
1/8 ts pepper
2 c liquefied non-fat dry milk
1 1-lb 4 oz can tomatoes, drained
½ c grated process sharp Cheddar cheese
1½ c day-old bread crumbs
1 1-lb can Chum salmon, in large chunks
2 hard cooked eggs, sliced lengthwise

Start heating oven to 375°. Place broccoli in 2 qt casserole; cover; then put in oven to bake while preparing rest of fish--about 10 min. In saucepan, melt butter; blend in flour, salt & pepper, then milk. Cook, stirring until thickened and smooth; remove from heat. Carefully fold in tomatoes, cheese, and bread crumbs. Remove casserole from oven; arrange salmon over broccoli; then pour on tomato mixture. Arrange egg slices on top, pressing them down into sauce. Bake 25 min. Makes 4 servings.

* * * *

Tis better to remain silent, and be thought a fool, than to open your mouth and remove all doubt of it.

FISH A LA CANADIENNE

Fish is the basic protein for many a delicious dish. All fish need not have a sauce to be tasty, but it does have to be fresh and correctly cooked. Most kinds of fish have delicate flesh and need very little cooking. In fact, the Japanese "sushi" is not cooked at all. By and large, most cooks overcook fish.

The so-called Canadian method for cooking fish gives the home cook an adequate guide. A little experience helps one to develop that inner sense of timing to the exact point. We don't know where the Canadian method came from--but we assume it came from Canada! It is found in print in various publications. But here it is:

Measure fish at thickest point; allow 10 minutes cooking time per inch. If fish is sauced or in foil, allow 5 minutes per pound extra. If fish is frozen, double cooking time.

Broiling or baking: Use greased broiler and baste with butter or basting sauce. Bake at 450° F or broil 2-4" from heat. Fish should not be more than 3/4" thick for broiling.

Pan frying: Use oil or clarified butter. Dip fish in seasoned flour for crispness. Turn half-way through cooking period.

Poaching: Bring to a boil water to cover fish. Add fish, and cover. Reduce heat; simmer gently. Begin timing when fish "shivers."

A high temperature is usually best for cooking fish by any method. Have oven, broiler pan, or frying pan hot before adding fish, so that surface is sealed and juices kept in. Fine, unsalted cracker crumbs are better for coating fish than bread crumbs since they burn less easily.

* * *

Today there are millions of Americans who are suffering from respiratory problems. It comes from standing at supermarket checkout counters holding their breath.

Church sign: "Think Metric. Observe the Ten Commandments."

Notes

Notes

Notes

Notes

poultry

Notes

NESTED CHICKEN

1 c cooked rice
1 Tb butter
1 Tb onion soup mix
1 Tb dry onion soup mix
1-3 pieces seasoned raw chicken
2 Tb canned milk

On each piece of 12" foil (heavy duty or doubled regular), butter 5" in center. Place in order listed above. Drugstore wrap and place in a shallow baking pan. Bake in a 350° oven for 1 hr. Serve package on each plate. Have each one open their package by slitting with a knife or unfolding the wrap. This main dish will wait for anyone and still be good to serve anytime. Just keep warm in the oven with the heat turned off. Use Lowry Seasoned Salt for seasoning.

ALMOST KENTUCKY FRIED CHICKEN

3 lb fryer
1 Tb paprika
2 pkg Good Seasons Italian dressing
1 ts seasoned salt
3 c self rising flour
2 Lipton Tomato cup of soup

Shake and mix dry ingredients. Wash chicken under cold water and drain. Coat, 1 piece at a time and place on large greased cookie sheet not touching. Melt margarine. Let coating dry and brush on margarine. Bake 1 hr at 350°.

* * * *

Every woman has a secret desire to write--checks that is.

There's nothing like a dish towel for wiping that contented look off a married man's face.

June is the month when girls look on the bride side of life.

Some people get lost in thought because it is such unfamiliar territory to them.

SOUR CREAM ENCHILADAS

12 corn tortillas
1 chopped green pepper
1 chopped onion
1 cooked boned chicken
1 lb grated cheese
1 can evaporated milk
1 sm can green chilies chopped
2 cans cream of chicken soup
8 oz carton sour cream

Soften tortillas by dipping briefly in hot grease. Drain between paper napkins. Combine soup, green pepper, chilies onion and milk. Heat until bubbly. Turn off heat, stir in sour cream. Put small amt of sauce in bottom of 9 x 13 pan. Line dish with half of tortillas. Lay ½ of chicken over tortillas, half of sauce and half of cheese. Repeat, ending with cheese. Bake covered for 30 min at 350°. Let stand 20 min. before serving.

CHICKEN TACOS WITH AVOCADO AND CHEESE

1 small avocado
½ ts salt
1 can (4 oz) chopped green chilies, drained
1 sm onion, sliced
2 Tb vegetable oil
2 c shredded Monterey Jack cheese
1/3 c sliced pimiento-stuffed olives
1 c shredded lettuce
Dairy sour cream
lemon juice
2 c chopped cooked chicken
3/4 ts salt
10 taco shells
taco sauce

Cut avocado into halves; cut halves into slices. Sprinkle with lemon juice and ½ ts salt. Cook and stir chicken, chilies, onion and 3/4 ts salt in oil in 10" skillet until chicken is hot. Heat taco shells as directed on pkg. Spoon about ¼ c chicken mixture into each shell. Top with cheese, olives, lettuce and avocado. Serve with taco sauce and sour cream. Makes 4-6 servings.

* * * *

Bishop Fulton J. Sheen: "Knowledge is as necessary as light. In fact, it is like light; it is in itself devoid of color, taste, and odor, and it should be kept pure and without admixture. If it comes through to us through the medium of prejudice, hate, or uncontrolled passions, it is discolored and adulterated."

OLD FASHIONED CHICKEN & VEGETABLES

2 lb fryer parts
2 Tb shortening
1 can (10½ oz) condensed cream of chicken soup
½ soup can milk
1 pkg (10 oz) frozen lima beans
dash pepper
6 sm yellow onions (whole, remove skins)
4 med carrots, cut lengthwise
¼ ts salt (or to taste)
¼ ts poultry seasoning

Brown fryer parts in shortening in a skillet. Place in 2 qt casserole. Discard drippings. Stir soup, milk and seasonings together in the skillet or a saucepan. Add onions and carrots. Cover and cook over low heat on top burner for 10 min, stirring often. Add lima beans; cook till they are separated, stirring often. Pour soup mixture over chicken in casserole. Cover; and bake approx. 45 min in a 375° oven; then uncover and bake 15 min more or until chicken is tender. This recipe may be prepared just to the oven stage and immediately refrigerated, several hours earlier the same day. Then increase the covered baking time 15 min.

TRIPLE DIVAN

2 pkg (10 oz) each frozen broccoli spears
2 c cooked, diced chicken or turkey
2 c cooked, diced ham
1 c cooked shrimp
2 cans (10 3/4 oz ea) cream of mushroom soup
1½ c milk
1 ts curry powder
2 c shredded cheddar cheese
2 c bread crumbs
2 c mayonnaise
2 ts lemon juice
4 Tb butter, melted

Cook broccoli according to package directions; drain. Arrange spears in lightly greased 11x7x1½" baking pan. Top with turkey or chicken, ham and shrimp. Blend soup, mayonnaise, lemon juice, milk and curry powder. Pour soup mixture over broccoli topped with chicken, ham and shrimp. Sprinkle with cheese. Combine melted butter and crumbs and sprinkle over all. Bake at 350° for about 30 min.

CHICKEN & VEGETABLE CREPES

Filling

5 Tb butter
1 sm onion, chopped
¼ lb mushrooms (sliced)
3 Tb flour
2/3 c chicken stock
½ c milk
2 c cooked chicken, turkey or ham (shredded or cut in strips)
1/3 c Parmesan cheese, grated
½ ts dry rosemary (crushed)
salt to taste
12-16 spears asparagus, lightly cooked or 1 pkg frozen peas
1 c shredded Swiss cheese

Melt butter and saute onions and mushrooms. Cook, stirring until vegetables are limp. Add flour and cook until bubbly, and remove from heat and gradually stir in chicken stock and milk. Cook while stirring until thick. Stir in meat. Remove from heat and add cheese and rosemary. Cool slightly.

TO ASSEMBLE CASSEROLE: Have ready asparagus lightly cooked or frozen asparagus thawed, or frozen peas thawed. If you use peas, stir them into the filling. Spoon filling down the center of each. Add an asparagus spear (if used) to each roll. Arrange seam side down in casserole. (Can freeze at this point.)

TO SERVE: Cover with foil and bake in 385° oven for 20 min. (35-40 if frozen) or until hot. Uncover and sprinkle with Swiss cheese. Bake uncovered until cheese melts. Serves 6 to 8.

*See basic Crepe recipe in Eggs & Cheese section.

* * * *

Housework is something you do that nobody notices unless you don't do it.

Blessed are the hard of hearing for they miss much small talk.

Inflation is bringing us true democracy. For the first time in history, luxuries and necessities are selling for the same price.

CRUNCHY CHICKEN CASSEROLE

2 lg chicken breasts, cooked, cut into small pieces
2 Tb minced onion
1 sm pkg sliced almonds
1 can water chestnuts, sliced
1 can cream of chicken soup
1 c finely chopped celery
1 Tb lemon juice
2 Tb mayonnaise
salt & pepper to taste

Mix ingredients in order given. Place in casserole, top with crushed potato chips. Bake at 425° for 20 min. Serves 4.

MEXI-CHICKEN

1 lb grated sharp cheese
4 breasts chicken
12 corn tortillas
1 can mushrooms
1 can chicken soup
1 grated onion
1 can salsa sauce
1 can diced green pepper

Let stand for an hour. Bake 1-1½ hr at 300°. Mix sauce, diced pepper and soup together with onion. Cut tortillas and criss cross

CHICKEN CACCIATORA

¼ c oil
1 2-3 lb fryer, brown in oil
2 med onions cut in ¼" slices
2 cloves garlic, minced

Remove chicken and cook onions and garlic until tender, but not brown.

Combine:
1 1 lb can (2 c) tomatoes
1 8 oz can seasoned tomato sauce
1 t salt
¼ ts pepper
½ ts celery seed
1 ts crushed oregano or basil
2 bay leaves

Serve on platter over home made noodles.

* * * *

It's pretty hard to tell about prosperity--when the hog's the fattest it goes to the butcher.

It's too bad that success makes failures out of so many men.

CHICKEN-APRICOT BARBECUE

1 lb apricots, fresh or canned
¼ c onion, chopped
½ ts dry mustard
¼ c brown sugar, packed
3½ lb chicken parts
3 Tb butter
1 clove garlic, crushed
¼ ts salt
1 ts lemon juice
1 Tb soy sauce

Pit seven of the apricots; puree in electric blender or food mill. Set remaining apricots aside.

To prepare barbecue sauce, melt butter in small saucepan; add onion and garlic and saute until light brown. Stir mustard, soy sauce, salt, sugar, lemon juice and pureed apricots into onion mixture and cook, stirring constantly, until it simmers. Remove from heat.

Wash chicken pieces and pat dry. Broil on both sides until almost done, 10 to 15 min on each side. Cut reserved apricots into halves; remove pits and place on broiler pan with chicken. Brush skin side of chicken and cut side of apricot halves with barbecue sauce. Continue broiling just until chicken and apricot halves begin to brown. Heap in center of serving platter and surround with apricots. Makes 6 servings.

BAKED CHICKEN

6-8 chicken breasts, skinned, boned and cut in half
Marinate in 3 beaten eggs for 1 hr
Roll in fine bread crumbs. Brown in butter. Place in baking dish; top with sauted mushroom slices and 1 pkg Mozarella cheese. Slice cheese over the top. In baking dish place half cup chicken broth in bottom. Bake at 350° for 10 min covered and 20 min uncovered. Serve with rice.

* * * *

At a Singles Club: "Polite? He won't open an oyster without knocking first."

In an elevator: "He has a waterproof voice--no one can drown it out."

CHICKEN DUMPLINGS

2/3 c herb seasoned bread stuffing mix, crushed
(Pepperidge Farm)
½ c finely chopped walnuts
Put bread stuffing crumbs in a bowl and set aside.
Cream: 2 3 oz pkg creamed cheese with chives
4 Tb softened butter
½ c chopped mushrooms
½ ts pepper
Mix with: 2 c cooked cubed chicken
4 cans Crescent rolls and 6 Tb butter, melted.
Separate rolls into triangles. Put about ¼ c chicken mixture on each roll and beginning with small end, roll and seal ends. Dip each roll into melted butter, then into crumb mixture. Place on ungreased cookie sheet and bake 15 to 20 min at 370°. Serves 8.
Make chicken stock gravy to serve over rolls, or use Lowry chicken gravy mix.

REUBEN CHICKEN

12 pcs or 8 breasts (skinned)
1 big can saur kraut (drained & rinsed)
slice of Swiss cheese for each piece chicken
8 oz Thousand Island dressing.
Put half kraut on bottom of casserole dish;
layer chicken and cheese, then reaminder of kraut.
Pour dressing overall. Bake 1 hr at 350°.

* * * *

Lukewarm water will not take a locomotive anywhere, nor will lukewarm purpose lift a man to any noticeable height of achievement.

The successful man lengthens his stride when he discovers that the signpost has deceived him; the failure looks for a place to sit down and grumble.

He who trusts men will make fewer mistakes than he who distrusts them.

CHICKEN CASSEROLE

6 c bread crumbs (day-old hamburger buns, etc.)
3-4 celery sticks, chopped
½ c margarine — 1 med chopped onion
½ ts salt — 1 ts sage
¼ ts pepper & some parsley

Brown celery with tops in margarine. Add onion and seasonings. Put in buttered baking dish. Prepare chicken breasts beforehand and place in lg. pieces on top of dressing. Make gravy with 1 c chicken fat or butter, 1 c flour, 1 c milk, 4 c chicken broth, 1 ts salt or less. Beat 1 egg and add to slightly cooled gravy. Pour over chicken. Bake at 325° for 1 hr.

DELIGHTFUL CHICKEN

1 lg chicken (boned & stewed) save broth
6 c bread stuffing (1½ slices per cut approximately)
1½ c chopped celery (tops included)
1 lg onion, chopped — ½ ts salt
1 ts sage — ¼ ts pepper
4 Tb chopped parsley — 1 sq margarine

Saute chopped celery & onion in 1 sq margarine until clear. Add salt, sage, pepper and parsley to bread stuffing and mix lightly. Then combine with sauted mixture. Place in bottom of 9 x 11" pan. Cover dressing with boned chicken meat. Then pour gravy over chicken.

Gravy:
1 sq margarine — 1 c flour
1 c milk — 4 c chicken broth
½ ts salt

Beat 1 egg and add to slightly cooled gravy. Bake at 325° for 1 hr. Serves 10.

* * * *

Wife to husband looking at garden tools: "Don't buy anything we can borrow."

CHICKEN BROCCOLI

4 lb chicken cooked (large pieces)
2 pkg frozen broccoli cooked
2 8-oz pkg cream cheese
1 ts garlic salt
2 c milk
1 c parmesan cheese
Make sauce using ½ cheese. Place broccoli on bottom of 2 qt casserole and top with sauces. Add large pieces of chicken and remainder of sauce. Top with ½ c Parmesan cheese. Bake 20-30 min at 350°. Serves 8.

EASY CHICKEN BAKE

Brown 10-12 pieces of chicken
1 can each of cream of chicken, celery soup
1 can chicken broth or bouillon cubes
Add ½ can chopped ortega green chilies
½ c chopped onion
1 small diced tomato
After soup mix is heated, add about 1 c shredded cheese until it melts. Pour over chicken and bake 2 hrs at 325°. Pour the gravy over rice.

ONE PAN TURKEY & STUFFING

1 c bisquick mix — 1 1/4 c milk
3 eggs — 1 ts parsley flakes
1 ts dried sage or 3/4 ts ground sage
3/4 ts thyme — ½ ts salt
½ ts poultry seasoning
1/8 ts pepper — 2 c cut-up turkey
1 c chopped celery — ½ c finely chopped onion

Heat oven to 400°. Grease rectangular dish (9x13"). Mix baking mix, milk, eggs, parsley, sage, thyme, salt, poultry seasoning and pepper in dish with fork until batter is of uniform color (batter will be lumpy). Stir in remaining ingredients. Bake until golden brown and knife inserted comes out clean, 35-40 min. Serves 6.

CHICKEN ROYALE

4 whole chicken breasts, halved
2 Tb butter
¼ c chopped onion
¼ lb fresh mushrooms
2 Tb flour
1 c light cream
1 c sour cream
1 ts lemon juice
8 slices cooked ham
½ of a small pkg of stuffing mix, made up by directions (or make your own, using any favorite recipe for about 2 c stuffing)

Skin and bone each chicken breast half. Flatten each piece, skinned side down, between pieces of plastic wrap to about 1/8" thickness, using a meat mallet or rolling pin.

In large frying pan, melt butter, then cook onions and mushrooms, covered, until soft but not brown, about 10 min. Remove from pan and reserve.

In same pan, brown flattened chicken breasts. Add a little more butter, or cooking oil, if needed. Remove chicken pieces from pan and reserve.

Add flour to pan drippings and blend well. Gradually add the light cream and sour cream. Heat well but do not boil, stirring constantly until mixture thickens. Add reserved onions and mushrooms, and lemon juice. Taste to correct seasonings.

Grease a 9x13x2" baking dish. Cut ham slices to fit chicken breasts and place each ham slice in baking pan. Top ham slices with about ¼ c stuffing; then cover with chicken breast.

Pour sauce mix over all. Heat in 325° oven for about one-half hour, or until hot and bubbly and chicken is fork tender. Makes 8 servings.

PARMESAN CHICKEN BAKE

1 c butter or margarine
1 clove garlic, crushed
1 c bread crumbs
salt & pepper to taste
½ c Parmesan cheese
1 whole chicken, disjointed or 6 chicken breasts

Melt butter. Set aside. Combine bread crumbs, cheese, garlic, salt and pepper. Dip chicken into butter then bread mixture. Put in 9x13" baking pan. Bake at 350° for 55 min. Serves 4.

CREAMY LEMON CHICKEN

3 whole broiler-fryer chicken breasts, halved
½ c flour
½ ts paprika
½ ts salt
½ ts pepper
1 egg, beaten
1½ c seasoned crouton crumbs
½ c butter
¼ c chicken consomme
½ c slivered almonds
3 Tb chopped chives
3/4 c whipping cream, whipped, salted to taste
1 lemon, sliced thin

In shallow dish mix together flour, paprika, salt and pepper. In another shallow dish place egg; and in third shallow dish place crumbs.

Add chicken one piece at a time to flour mixture, dredging to coat. Then dip chicken in egg and roll in crumbs. Place butter in heavy frypan and melt over med. heat. Add chicken and cook, turning, about 10 min or until brown on all sides. Add consomme and almonds; cover and simmer about 25 min or until fork can be inserted in chicken with ease.

Fold chives into salted whipped cream and chill until time to serve. When chicken is done, remove to warm serving platter and place a lemon slice on each piece of chicken and then top with a spoonful of cream. Makes 6 servings.

BAKED CHICKEN

2 pkg (3 oz each) chipped beef
2 c sour cream
16 slices bacon
2 cans cream of mushroom soup
8 chicken breasts, halved, boned and skinned

Put chipped beef in 9 x 13 pan. Roll strip of bacon around each breast half. Fasten with toothpick. Layer over chipped beef. Cover with sour cream and concentrated soup. Cover. Refrigerate overnight. Next day, bake at 250° for 3-4 hrs. Serves 8.

* * * *

Probably nothing in the world arouses more false hopes than the first four hours of a diet.

Show me a litter of cats, and I'll show you a kitten caboodle.

BAKED CHICKEN SUPREME

4 whole chicken breasts, halved*
¼ c shortening
1/3 c chopped onion
1 ts sugar
¼ c flour
1 can (10½ oz) tomato soup
¼ c milk
Hot cooked rice
1 sm. clove garlic
1¼ ts salt
½ ts oregano (optional)
1 c tomato juice
1 c sour cream
2 Tb grated Parmesan cheese

Brown chicken breasts in shortening. Use more shortening if needed. Remove from frying pan and place in 9x9x2" baking dish. Pour off all but 2 Tb of the drippings. Add garlic and onion to skillet; cover and cook until soft brown (about 5 min.) Blend in salt, sugar, oregano and flour. Add tomato juice and tomato soup; heat to boiling, stirring constantly. Remove from heat and blend in sour cream. Stir vigorously. Add milk to thin sauce a bit (add a little more if needed). Add Parmesan cheese. Pour over chicken in baking dish. Cover and bake at 325° for about 45 min or until meat is fork tender. Serve with cooked rice. Makes 8 servings.

*Skinned and boned breasts are a little nicer, but unskinned, unboned pieces may be used. Or use all the pieces from one chicken, or the pieces desired from two chickens.

APRICOT CHICKEN

2 frying chickens, cut up
1 bottle (8 oz) Russian salad dressing
1 c apricot jam
2 ts curry powder (opt.)
1 pkg (1 1/8 oz) dry onion soup mix

Wash chicken. Pat dry. Mix the dressing, jam, curry powder and onion soup mix. Pour over chicken. Bake at 350° for 1 hr 15 min. Serves 8.

CHICKEN ASPARAGUS SUPREME

4 c soft bread cubes
2 c shredded cheddar cheese
1 stick butter or margarine, melted
2 c cooked asparagus
¼ c butter
½ c flour
1 ts salt
¼ ts pepper
1 c chicken broth
2 c milk
2 ts lemon juice
½ ts curry powder
1 chicken, cooked, boned, skinned and cut into bite-size pieces

Mix bread cubes with cheese and melted butter. Toss. Place half of this mixture in 9x13" baking pan. Cook asparagus and set aside.

Melt the ¼ c butter and add flour, salt and pepper. Stir in chicken broth and milk and cook until thickened and smooth, stirring constantly. Add lemon juice and curry powder. Stir in chicken.

Place cooked, drained asparagus over bread cube mixture. Top with cream sauce and sprinkle with remaining bread cub mixture. Bake at 350° for 30 min, or until brown. Serves 8.

CHICKEN BROCCOLI BAKE

8 chicken breasts, with skins
3 c water
2 bay leaves
1 ts celery salt
2 pkg (10 oz ea) broccoli spears
2 c milk
2 pkg (8 oz ea) cream cheese, softened
1 ts salt
½ ts garlic salt
1/3 c grated Parmesan cheese
2/3 c grated Parmesan cheese

Put chicken breasts, water, bay leaves and celery salt in large pot. Simmer 1 hr. Cool. Discard liquid. Skin and bone chicken. Cool broccoli spears following pkg. directions. Drain. Set aside. In a saucepan, mix milk, soft cream cheese, salt, garlic salt and 1/3 c Parmesan cheese. Stir and cook until thick. Put broccoli in bottom of greased 9x9" baking dish. Pour in 1 c sauce. Put in chicken breasts. Pour in remaining sauce. Sprinkle 2/3 c Parmesan cheese on top. Bake at 350° for 25 min. Serves 6-8.

CHICKEN SUEY

¼ c chopped onion
2 Tb butter
2/3 c chicken broth
2 Tb soy sauce
4 c diced chicken
2/3 c cashew nuts
1 c diced celery
2 cans cream mushroom soup
1 can bean sprouts
6 drops Tobasco sauce
1 can chow mein noodles
pepper to taste

Saute onions and celery in butter. Add soup and broth. Blend thoroughly. Add seasoning, diced chicken and bean sprouts. Simmer a few min and pour a little of mix into casserole. Add layer of chow noodles and nuts. Alternate layers ending with nuts. Bake 20 min in 350° oven. Serves 8-12.

ORIENTAL CHICKEN WINGS

5 lbs chicken wings (5 or 6 to a lb) Have butcher cut into 3 pieces. Use small part to make stock.
2/3 c soy sauce
2 Tb chicken stock
2 Tb sugar
2 cloves garlic or 1¼ Tb garlic powder

Boil chicken until done and marinate in above sauce. Bake at 350° until warmed through or longer if crispiness is desired.

CHICKEN-BEAN SPROUTS & OYSTER SAUCE

2 chicken breasts, cubed
4 green onions
1 garlic clove, minced
4 Tb oyster sauce
2 Tb fresh ginger, minced
1 Tb soy sauce
½ c chicken broth or stock
2 ts sugar
1½ lb bean sprouts
1 ts salt
4 Tb oil

Skin, bone & cube raw chicken. Peel onions & cut into 1" lengths. Mince garlic. Peel and mince fresh ginger. Heat pan. Add oil, salt, ginger and garlic. Cook stirring constantly until slightly brown. Add chicken and stir fry for 2 more min. Combine oyster sauce, soy sauce, stock & sugar. Pour over chicken. Add onions and bean sprouts. Heat through. Serve at once over cooked rice or noodles.

BREAST OF CHICKEN SUPREME

6 chicken breast halves
¼ c flour
1 ts paprika
1/8 ts pepper
½ ts salt
1/3 c shortening
¼ c butter
4 oz can mushroom pieces

¼ c flour
1 ts salt
¼ ts pepper
1½ c chicken stock
½ c light cream
1 egg yolk, slightly beaten
2 ts lemon juice

Dredge chicken in mixture of flour, paprika, salt and pepper. Saute in shortening until tender. Saute mushrooms in butter. Blend in flour, salt, pepper. Add stock and cream, cook until thickened. Add some of hot sauce to egg and blend. Add to sauce and cook 2-3 min. Remove from heat and add lemon juice. Place chicken on serving platter and top with sauce. Sauce and chicken may be cooled and frozen separately. To reheat from frozen state: Place frozen chicken breasts in baking dish in 350° oven 30-40 min. Thaw and heat sauce over low heat.

CHICKEN CORDON BLEU

4 whole chicken breasts, halved
8 thin slices cooked ham (baked or boiled ham slices)
4 slices Swiss cheese, cut into fingers about 1½" long and ½" thick
salt and pepper
Thyme or rosemary
¼ c melted butter or margarine
½ c cornflake crumbs

Skin and bone chicken breast halves. Place each half between sheets of plastic wrap, skinned side down, and pound with meat mallet to about 1/8" thickness.

On each ham slice place a finger of cheese. Sprinkle lightly with seasonings. Roll ham and cheese jelly-roll style, then roll each chicken breast with ham and cheese inside. Tuck in ends and seal well. (Tie rolls if necessary, or fasten with toothpicks). Dip each roll in cornflake crumbs, turning to thoroughly coat each roll.

Place rolls on 9x13x2" baking dish. Bake, uncovered in 400° oven for about 40 min, or until golden brown. Serve with Cordon Bleu Sauce, p. 411. Serves 6-8.

try

HAWAIIAN CHICKEN

8 half chicken breasts--season with pepper and dredge in flour and place in shallow casserole. Combine:

½ c melted butter
¼ ts ground ginger
1/16 ts cardamon
2 ts instant minced onion
2 ts soy sauce
2 Tb pineapple juice
¼ ts salt

Spoon over chicken. Cover with tight fitting lid or tightly sealed aluminum foil. Bake 1 hr and 30 min at 350°. Serves 8.

BANANA CURRY CHICKEN

½ c butter
4 ts curry powder
½ ts pepper
½ c flour
1 ts salt
4 c chicken broth or 2 c broth & 2 c coconut milk

4 c diced cooked chicken
Cooked rice
Chopped hard-cooked eggs
Crumbled crisp cooked bacon
5-6 bananas
Shredded coconut
Chopped peanuts or almond slivers
Mango or peach chutney (homemade, please)

Melt butter; add flour, curry powder, salt and pepper. Stir until smooth.

Gradually add chicken broth and cook, stirring constantly, until smooth and thickened. Add diced chicken; heat thoroughly, 15-20 min.

Before serving, add bananas, cut in 1" lengths. Serve over cooked rice with condiments of shredded coconut, chopped hard-cooked eggs, chopped peanuts or almond slivers, crumbled bacon and Mango or peach chutney (homemade). Serves 6-8.

*This is so popular you will be requested to double or triple it each time!

* * * *

Show me a lazy butcher and I'll show you a meat loafer.

Show me someone shopping for a sweater and I'll show you a knit picker.

ALMOND CHICKEN

3 Tb oil (peanut oil, if possible)
½ c slivered almonds
1 onion thinly cut in rings
1 c diagonally sliced celery
3/4 c sliced pea pods
1 can chicken broth
3-6 Tb soy sauce
2 c bean sprouts
1 lg sliced tomato
¼ to ½ ts ginger
2 c raw chicken breasts, diced
½ c sliced mushrooms
1 Tb sugar
1 Tb cornstarch
1 can waterchestnuts, sliced
Optional ingredients: spinach, asparagus, carrots, zucchini or summer squash.

In lg. skillet, heat oil and saute almonds til brown. Remove and drain. Cook chichen in remaining oil til done (3-5 min). Remove chicken and stir fry onion, celery, mushrooms & pea pods. You may need to add a bit more oil. Add 3/4 c chicken broth and simmer until onions are clear. Mix soy sauce, sugar, cornstarch & remaining chicken broth. Add to onion. Cook until thickened. Add beansprouts, spinach, etc., everything but tomato, almonds, chicken. Cook til warmed. Add tomatoes just before serving, heated through. Serve over rice. Serves 6-9.

CHICKEN MONTEREY WITH PECAN PILAF

2 3½ lb fryers
3/4 c flour
2 ts salt
3/4 ts tarragon
6 Tb butter
1 lb mushrooms (2 cans)
2 c chicken broth or cubes
1 bouillon cube
1 Tb curacoa (non-alcoholic)
6 c hot cooked rice
1 c coarsley chopped pecans
1 c mandarin orange slices) add to the rice
green grapes and parsley) use as garnish as desired

Mix flour with salt and tarragon and coat chicken (reserve remaining flour mixture for later). Melt 3 Tb butter. Brown chicken well & place in large roaster.

Drain mushrooms and fry until brown. Place in roaster over chicken. Add remaining 3 Tb butter and stir in ¼ c seasoned flour. Add chicken broth bouillon cube. Stir until thick. Add curacoa. Pour sauce over chicken. Cover and bake 1 hr at 350°. Serves 18.

TURKEY TETRAZZINI

1. Cook in boiling salted water for 9 min. or until tender — 5 oz egg noodles
2. Drain noodles.
3. Add — 2 Tbs melted butter
4. Combine — 1 can cream of chicken soup
   1 can cream of mushroom soup
   ¼ c milk
5. Fold into soup mixture 3½ c diced turkey
6. In a greased 2 qt casserole place alternate layers of noodles and turkey mixture, starting with noodles and ending with turkey.
7. Sprinkle over the top ½ c grated cheddar cheese
8. Bake at 350° for 30 min. Serves 4-6

May be garnished with chopped ripe olives or sliced green olives just before serving.

SWISS-TURKEY-HAM BAKE

1. Saute in large skillet ½ c chopped onion, 2 Tb butter
2. Blend in 3 Tb flour, ½ ts salt, ¼ ts pepper
3. Add 1 can (3 oz) sliced mushrooms & liquid
   1½ c light cream
4. Cook and stir until thickened.
5. Add to cream mixture 2 c cubed cooked turkey
   1 c cubed cooked ham
   1 can (5 oz) water chestnuts, drained and sliced
6. Pour into 1½ qt casserole dish.
7. Top with ½ c shredded Swiss cheese.
8. Mix together and sprinkle around edge of casserole
   3 Tb melted butter, 1 c bread crumbs
9. Bake at 400° for 20-25 min. Serves 6.

* * * *

We often have reason to believe the weather bureau is a non-prophet agency.

Where there's a will, there's a crowd of relatives.

Mama Bear to Papa Bear: "This is POSITIVELY my last year as a den mother!"

CHICKEN & CASHEWS

4 chicken breast halves
4 Tb cornstarch
¼ c soy sauce
1 ts Worcestershire sauce
2 c hot chicken stock*
½ c cashews
1 ts sugar
½ ts salt
1 ts vinegar
3 Tb salad oil
2 ts lemon juice
Cooked rice

Bone and skin the chicken breasts. Cover chicken bones and skin with cold water. Bring to a boil slowly and simmer for ½ hr or more. (The addition of a few slices of onion, carrot, and celery will improve flavor of stock). Strain and cool stock. Remove fat from surface.

Cut raw chicken into bite-size pieces. Combine sugar, 2 Tb cornstarch, salt, soy sauce, vinegar, and Worcestershire sauce. Dredge chicken pieces in this mixture. Drain and save dredge; then stir-fry chicken in hot oil in frying pan or wok until chicken is lightly brown and tender, about 10 min. Remove chicken from oil and drain excess oil from pan. Add remaining cornstarch and the dredge drained from the chicken. Blend well, then add chicken stock to the pan and bring to a boil, stirring constantly. Cook until thickened. Add lemon juice; add chicken pieces and reheat. Do not boil. Taste to correct seasonings. Add cashews. Serve over hot rice.

*Chicken soup base or canned chicken stock may be used. Add water to make the desired consistency, if needed.

* * * *

The world is like a jigsaw puzzle with a "peace" missing.

We've made a lot of medical progress in the last generation. What used to be merely an itch is now an allergy.

To keep snow from sticking to the snow shovel, move to Panama.

To improve the flavor of salt, sprinkle on watermelon.

CRUNCHY TURKEY CASSEROLE

6 c diced cooked turkey or chicken
3 c chopped celery
3 5-oz cans water chestnuts, sliced & drained
1½ c diced cheddar cheese
1½ ts salt
1½ c Best Foods mayonnaise
1½ c sour cream
2 c crushed shredded whole wheat flakes, about
 12 triscuits

Lightly mix together turkey, celery, chestnuts, cheese and salt. Blend mayonnaise and sour cream. Toss lightly with turkey mix. Turn half the mixture into 9x13 casserole. Top with 2/3 of the crushed crackers. Top with remaining turkey mixture and crackers. Bake uncovered in 375° oven 30 min or until heated. Serves 12.

QUICK TURKEY OR CHICKEN PIE

2 c cooked turkey, diced
½ ts salt
1½ c milk
3 eggs
2 Tb chopped onion
1 c Swiss cheese, shredded
3/4 c bisquick

Preheat oven to 400°. Grease a 10" pie plate. Sprinkle turkey, onions, salt & cheese into pie plate. In a medium bowl combine milk, bisquick and eggs. Beat until smooth, 15 secs. with blender on high, or 1 min with hand beater. Pour into pie plate. Bake 400° for 30-35 min or until knife comes out clean. Cool 5 min before serving. Serves 6-8.

* * * *

Some folks are not paid what they are worth--and they should be glad.

Some men dream of being something; others stay awake and are.

It's great to have your children home from school; it takes your mind off your other troubles.

Notes

Notes

eggs & cheese

Notes

DEVILED EGGS

6 hard cooked eggs
¼ ts salt
3/4 ts prepared mustard
2 Tb mayonnaise
dash onion powder
dash of pepper
2-3 drops Worcestershire sauce
Paprika, parsley or chives

Cut hard-cooked eggs in half, lengthwise. Remove yolks carefully and force through a coarse sieve. Add next 6 ingredients and beat until smooth and fluffy. (Add more mayonnaise if necessary, as amount will depend on size of yolks.) Heap into egg whites. Do not pack or pat surface smooth. Sprinkle with paprika, parsley or chives. Keep in cool place until ready to serve. Makes 12 halves.

*If you like an egg "with a bite" add some commercial horseradish or horsey sauce.

QUICHE SALSALITO SUPREME

1 unbaked 9" pastry shell
8 strips bacon
1 onion, chopped
1 ts bacon fat
pinch of salt
2 egg yolks
2 whole eggs
½ c heavy cream
½ ts salt
¼ ts nutmeg
dash of cayenne
1½ c grated Swiss cheese

Prepare a 9" pastry shell. Set aside. Fry bacon until crisp. Saving 1 ts fat, drain off remainder. Crumble bacon. Set aside. Saute onion in bacon fat with salt until golden brown. Remove. Drain on paper towels. Beat egg yolks, whole eggs, cream, salt, nutmeg and cayenne. In unbaked pastry shell, layer cheese, crumbled bacon and onion. Pour egg mixture on top. Bake at 375° for 35-40 min (until set). Cut into narrow wedges. Serve hot or cold. Can be made ahead and frozen. Defrost before baking. Makes 24 wedges.

* * * *

Icicle: eavesdripper.

Hibernating: living on burrowed time.

Icy path: slidewalk.

SCRAMBLE EGG CASSEROLE

2 Tb margarine, melted
2 Tb flour
2 c milk
½ ts salt
½ ts pepper
1 c American cheese, grated
½ c chopped onion
1 c chopped ham or Canadian bacon
3 Tb margarine
1 dozen eggs, beaten
1 c sliced fresh mushrooms
1 c buttered crumbs
1/8 ts paprika

Combine melted margarine and flour; blend until smooth. Cook over low heat until bubbly. Gradually add milk. Cook until smooth and thickened, stirring constantly. Add salt, pepper and cheese. Stir until cheese melts; set aside.

Saute bacon and onion in 3 Tb margarine until onion is tender. Add eggs. Cook until set, stirring occasionally to scramble. Fold in mushrooms and cheese sauce.

Spoon egg mixture into lightly greased 12x7x2" baking dish. Top with bread crumbs and sprinkle with paprika. Bake at 350° for 30 min. May be prepared ahead of time. Serves 8.

EGGS HUSSARDE

2 lg thin slices ham, grilled
2 Holland rusks
2 sliced tomatoes, grilled
3/4 c Hollandaise sauce*
¼ c Marchand de Vin Sauce*
2 eggs, soft poached

Lay a large slice ham across each rusk and cover with Marchand de Vin Sauce. Cover next with tomato and then egg. Top with Hollandaise Sauce. Garnish with sprinkling of paprika. 1 serving.

*Recipe for sauce in sauce section.

* * * *

When young, you adjust your hair to the existing hair style; when old, you adjust your hair style to the existing hair.

BROCCOLI CHEESE QUICHE

1 pastry shell, 10"
1 beaten egg yolk
6 eggs
1 pkg (3 oz) cream cheese, softened
½ c almonds
¼ c grated sharp Cheddar cheese
3 green onions, finely chopped (include some tops)
2 Tb finely chopped parsley
½ ts salt
2 Tb grated Parmesan cheese
1 Tb grated Parmesan cheese
1 10-oz pkg frozen chopped broccoli
dash of pepper
1 lg tomato, cut in wedges

Bake pastry shell partially in 425° oven for about 15 min. Lightly brush with beaten egg yolk. Return to oven for 2 min.

Cook broccoli according to package directions. Drain out all liquid. Leave no moisture in the broccoli.

Combine beaten eggs, cream cheese and Cheddar cheese. Stir in broccoli, almonds, green onions, parsley, salt and pepper. Pour into pastry shell. Sprinkle with 2 Tb Parmesan cheese.

Bake at 425° for 15 min or until edges are set. Top with tomato wedges and the 1 Tb Parmesan cheese. Return to oven for 4 min. (For more quiche see pp. 126, 203, 228, 245, 252, 261.)

FRESH MUSHROOM QUICHE

Pastry for 1 crust
2 c shredded Swiss cheese
2 Tb flour
2 eggs beaten
3/4 c milk
½ ts dried summer savory, crumbled
½ ts salt
¼ ts pepper
2 c fresh mushrooms, sliced

Roll out pastry and fit into a 9" pan; flute edges. Toss shredded cheese with flour. Add beaten eggs, milk and seasonings. Fold in sliced mushrooms. Turn mixture into a pastry-lined pan. Bake in a 350° oven for about 1 hr. Serves 6.

* * * *

Pres. Reagan was asked if he ever watched any of his old movies on TV. "No," said the President. "When one of my pictures comes on, I know it's past my bedtime."

EGG SAUSAGE CASSEROLE

1 lb link sausage
2 Tb sliced green onion
2 Tb chopped green pepper
8 slices bread, or enough to cover bottom of baking dish
1 c grated sharp cheese
12 eggs
3/4 ts dry mustard
1½ c milk
1 can cream of mushroom soup
1 can cream of chicken soup
¼ c milk
1 4 oz can sliced mushrooms drained

Brown sausage and cut into 1" pieces. Chop onion and pepper. Remove crusts from bread.

Butter 2½-3 qt 4" deep dish; line with bread. Cover with cheese and sausage.

Beat eggs; add mustard, milk, onion and green pepper. Pour over bread, cheese and sausage. Cover tightly and place in refrigerator overnight.

Just before baking, dilute can of soup with ¼ c milk. Add mushrooms to soup mixture and pour on top of casserole. Bake at 300° for 1½ hrs or until set. Serves 6-8.

DANISH SANDWICH-PUFF

12 slices day-old bread
6 slices Cheddar cheese
2 6½ oz cans tuna
2/3 c mayonnaise
4 eggs
2½ c milk
½ ts prepared mustard
¼ ts hot pepper sauce
1 Tb minced onion
½ ts salt

Remove crusts from bread and arrange six slices in 8½x14" casserole. Cover with cheese slices. Blend tuna and mayonnaise in small bowl, spread mixture over cheese slices. Cover with remaining bread slices. Beat eggs, blend in milk and remaining ingredients; pour over bread. Refrigerate one hour. Bake, uncovered at 325° for about 50 min or until puffy and brown. Garnish with lime slices and twists, pimiento, capers and dill. Serve immediately. Makes 6 servings.

* * * *

The driver of an elderly, battered jalopy rattled into a gasoline station and filled his tank. The charge was almost $20. "How about that?"the man murmured. "One tank of gas and I have doubled the value of my car."

COUNTRY OMELET

4 strips bacon
1 small skinned potato, cut into ¼ " cubes
¼ c finely chopped onions
3-4 eggs, lightly beaten
2 Tb shredded Swiss cheese
¼ c sour cream
8 walnut halves
2 Tb margarine or butter
¼ c Swiss cheese
1 Tb minced parsley
salt

In a wide frying pan over medium heat, cook bacon until crisp. Remove bacon from pan, drain, and crumble; set aside.

Add walnuts to drippings; cook, stirring, until light brown (1-2 min)--they scorch easily. Lift out and set aside.

Discard all but 2 Tb drippings. Add potato and onion to pan, reduce heat to medium low and cook, stirring, until potato is soft but only lightly browned (about 10 min). Remove potato mixture from pan and keep warm.

Wipe pan clean, then melt butter over medium low heat. Pour in eggs and cook, gently lifting cooked portion to let uncooked egg flow underneath, until eggs are set but top still looks moist and creamy. Sprinkle evenly with bacon, potato mixture, diced cheese, shredded cheese and parsley.

Mould sour cream in center of omelet and garnish with walnuts. Season with salt to taste. Cut into wedges and serve from pan. Makes 2-4 servings.

* * * *

The older a man gets, the farther he had to walk to school as a boy.

An absent-minded man is one who helps his wife out of the car when no one is looking.

"What are you smiling at?" asked Noah.
"I was just thinking," replied his wife, "how lucky it was we could go ahead and build this ark without waiting for an appropriation from Congress."

SWEET CORN OMELET

1½ c corn kernels (cut from 2-3 med. ears)
½ c chopped green pepper
¼ c water
8 eggs
½ to 1 ts dry mustard
4 Tb butter, divided
cherry tomatoes, optional
Parsley sprigs, optional
½ c chopped onion
3/4 ts salt, divided
½ c water
1/8 ts pepper
1 c shredded Cheddar cheese, divided

In med. saucepan combine corn, green pepper, onion, ¼ c water and ¼ ts salt. Bring to boiling. Cover, reduce heat and simmer until corn is tender, about 5 min. Keep warm while preparing omelet. Drain before filling omelets.

Mix eggs, ½ c water, remaining salt, mustard and pepper until blended. For each omelet, in 7 or 10" omelet pan or skillet, over medium high heat, melt 1 Tb of butter until just hot enough to sizzle a drop of water.

Pour in ½ c of the egg mixture. Mixture should immediately set at edges. With an inverted pancake turner, carefully push cooked portions at edges toward center so uncooked portions can reach hot pan surface, tilting pan and moving cooked portions as necessary.

While top is still moist and creamy looking, place about ½ c of the corn mixture on half of the omelet. Sprinkle ¼ c of the cheese over corn mixture. With pancake turner, fold omelet in half and invert onto plate. Keep warm while preparing remaining omelets. Garnish with tomatoes and parsley if desired. Serves 4. Note: It is better to fill the omelet when it is slightly underdone. Heat retained in eggs completes the cooking.

* * * *

Another reason for unhappy marriages is that men can't fool their wives like they could their mothers.

At middle age, your tripping becomes less light and more fantastic!

SOUTH-OF-THE-BORDER BRUNCH EGGS

6 corn tortillas
1 can (4 oz) whole green chiles, seeded & chopped
1 c milk
2 Tb salad oil
½ c thinly sliced green onion including tops
1 can (6 oz) white sauce
8 eggs
4 Tb butter or margarine
3 med. size tomatoes, peeled, seeded & chopped
1 can (2¼ oz) sliced ripe olives, drained
2 c (8 oz) shredded jack cheese

With scissors, snip tortillas into short strips and set aside. In a large bowl, mix onions, chiles, white sauce, and milk; beat in eggs and set aside.

Heat oil and 2 Tb of the butter in an electric frying pan set at 350° (or use a wide frying pan over med. heat). When hot, add tortilla strips and cook, stirring often, until crisp. Reduce temperature to 250° (or med. low).

In pan, melt remaining 2 Tb butter, then pour the egg mixture and cook, gently lifting cooked portion to let uncooked egg flow underneath until eggs are set to your liking.

Evenly distribute tomatoes, olives, and cheese over eggs. Cover, turn off heat, and let stand until cheese is melted. Makes 6-8 servings.

EGG FOO YUNG WITH HAM

½ c bean sprouts
½ c green pepper, diced
½ c onions, shredded
½ c bamboo shoots, diced
2 ts soy sauce
2 Tb oil
1 c ham, diced (or Spam)
5 eggs

Stir, do not beat, eggs, soysauce, bean sprouts, green pepper, onions, bamboo shoots & ham.

Heat pan with small amount of oil. Spoon 2-3 Tb egg mixture into pan. Cook until eggs have browned on one side, turn over and brown the other side. Repeat until egg mixture is used up, adding more oil as needed.

Sauce

1 Tb cornstarch
¼ ts sugar
2 Tb soy sauce
1½ c stock

Combine ingredients, cook over medium heat until thickened. Serve over cooked egg foo yung.

GREEN BEAN SCRAMBLE

½ lb fresh green beans, cut into 1" pieces
½ c water
½ c milk
½ ts seasoned salt
1/8 ts pepper
2 Tb butter
8 eggs
1 Tb instant minced onion
½ ts tarragon, rosemary or savory leaves, crushed
½ c shredded Swiss cheese

In medium saucepan, combine beans and water. Bring to boiling. Cover, reduce heat, simmer until beans are crisp-tender, 10-15 min. Drain and set aside.

Mix eggs, milk and seasonings until blended. In 10" omelet pan or skillet over medium heat, melt butter until just hot enough to sizzle a drop of water. Pour in egg mixture. Stir in reserved green beans and cheese. As mixture begins to set, gently draw an inverted pancake turner completely across the bottom and sides of pan, forming large soft curds. Continue until eggs are thickened but still moist. Do not stir constantly. Makes 4 servings.

OVEN OMELET (QUICHE)

10 small slices of bacon (can omit)
¼ c milk
1 Tb dried minced onion
1 can cream of chicken soup
6 eggs
¼ lb Monterey Jack cheese
½ ts salt
1/8 ts sugar
1/16 ts cayenne
1/8 ts pepper

Set oven at 425°. Grate cheese, combine milk and minced onion. Fry bacon until crisp and drain. Crumble bacon, stir eggs with soup, salt, sugar, cayenne and pepper. Add milk and onions, bacon and cheese; stir well to blend. Pour into oiled 2 qt casserole. Place casserole in lg pan of water (about 1"). Bake 15 min at 425°. Reduce oven temp to 300 or 325° and bake 40 min longer, or until knife comes out clean.

CHILE RELLENO CASSEROLE

4 slices firm bread (white)   2 Tb butter
2 c shredded sharp cheddar cheese
2 c shredded Jack cheese
1 can (4 oz) green chiles minced (seeds removed)
6 eggs   2 c milk
2 ts paprika   1 ts salt
½ ts each crumbled oregano leaves & pepper
¼ ts garlic powder   ¼ ts dry mustard

Trim crusts from bread and spread one side each with butter. Arrange buttered side down in a 7½ x 11½" baking pan. Sprinkle cheddar over bread and then Jack over the cheddar. Distribute green chiles over cheese layers evenly. Beat eggs in a bowl with milk adding paprika, salt, oregano leaves, pepper, garlic powder and dry mustard. Beat well until blended. Pour egg mixture over the cheese. Cover and chill overnight or at least 4 hrs. Bake uncovered in a 325° oven about 50 min. or until top is lightly browned. Let stand 10 min. before serving.

PECAN CHEESE LOG

1. Blend together in a medium sized bowl:
   2 glasses Old English Cheese
   1 glass Blue Roka cheese
   1 8-oz pkg cream cheese
   1 Tb worcestershire sauce
   ½ c chopped parsley
   1 small onion, grated
2. Chill until firm enough to handle.
3. Shape into an 8" long log and roll in
   ½ c chopped pecans
4. Wrap in foil and place in refrigerator overnight.
5. Garnish with parsley and serve with assorted crackers.

* * * *

It's a small town if . . . it's easier to resist temptation than to find it.
. . . no social event can be scheduled when the school gym floor is being varnished. . . or friends, neighbors and relatives are all the same people.

FLUFFY-PUFFY OMELET

1. Beat egg white until stiff.
2. Beat egg yolk until thick and lemon colored, beat in 1 Tb milk or cream per egg. Salt and pepper to taste.
3. Fold a small amount of whites into yolks. Then yolks into remaining whites.
4. Pour into sizzling butter in a heavy skillet, ½ Tb butter per egg.
5. Turn to low heat. Cook slowly until bottom is light brown. About 10 min. (Bubbles will still appear through the uncooked puffy top and mixture will look moist.)
6. Place skillet in preheated 350° oven. Bake until light and brown on top. When touched lightly with finger, no imprints remains (about 10-15 min.)
7. Make a ½ inch deep crease across omelet-halfway between handle and opposite side, slip turn under, tip skillet to loosen omelet, and fold in half without breaking.
8. Roll omelet topside down onto hot platter.
9. Garnish with hot sauce and serve at once.
10. Plan on 2 eggs per person.

VARIATIONS: Add about ½ c chopped cooked meats, fish, or vegetables in fold of omelet before serving, if desired. Or sprinkle on top of half-cooked omelet before slipping into oven to bake (step #6). Or sprinkle ¼ to ½ c grated cheese on top of fold before serving. Or spread the same amount of jam or jelly for a change.

* * * *

DEMOCRACY is based upon the conviction that there are extraordinary possibilities in ordinary people.

Strike from mankind the principle of faith, and men would have not more history than a flock of sheep.

CHEESE BALL

2 c grated cheddar cheese
1 jar Kraft Roka Blue
1 pkg cream cheese (8 oz)
½ ts garlic powder

Blend in food processor or blender. Shape into ball and roll in crushed walnuts.

VEGGIE-CHEESE BALL

2 8 oz-pkg cream cheese
1 8-oz Cracker Barrel sharp cheese, shredded
1 Tb chopped pimiento*
1 ts chopped onion
1 ts lemon juice
2 ts Worcestershire sauce
1 Tb chopped green pepper*

*Optional

Mix all ingredients together and shape into 2 small balls. Chill at least 12 hrs. Roll in chopped nuts or fresh chopped parsley, if desired. Serve with crackers or vegetable sticks.

CREAM CHEESE ROLL

Remove crusts from bread and cut in half. Spread with cream cheese; roll up. Wrap ½ slice bacon around each roll and secure with toothpick. Broil.

* * * *

Are Pat Boone's and Richard Boone's physicians called the Boone Docs?

A reckless driver is one who passes you on the road despite anything you can do.

Little girl's essay on parents: "The trouble with parents is that they are so old when we get them, it's hard to change their habits."

SPANISH OMELET

1. Heat in skillet 1 Tb butter
2. Beat with fork 2 eggs
3. Stir in 1-2 Tb each chopped tomatoes, green onions
   1 Tb chopped canned green chilies
   1-2 Tb butter cooked mushrooms, sliced
   2-4 Tb small diced mozzarella cheese
   ¼ ts salt
4. Pour mixture into hot butter. Lower heat to medium low. Cook until bottom is set. Place a plate to fit pan and hold in place with a hot pad. Over sink turn out omelet. Slip omelet back into pan and cook until other side is set.
5. Slip omelet half-way onto serving dish and flip in half to fold.
6. Serve plain or with a sauce. Serves 1.

NOTE: Make only 1 omelet at a time with not more than 2 eggs for a successful omelet. A small heavy cast iron skillet #5 works well.
Garnish with strawberries and/or avocado.

* * * *

President Theodore Roosevelt, in 1906, threatened to ban football by executive edict unless some of the roughness was taken out of the game!

The common food flavoring, vanilla, is extracted from the pods of the exotic orchid.

Dr. Norman Vincent Peale: "All of us are surrounded by people who need understanding and love. When you give that, you will receive it in return. The two most powerful healing forces in human relations are understanding and love. They work wonders."

CHEESE FONDUE

You can melt the cheese in an earthenware fondue pot or heatproof dish directly over a denatured-alcohol or canned-heat flame. If you use a metal pan, place it in simmering water. (Use the water bath with a chafing dish, or a double boiler.) The heating unit should be designed so you can regulate the heat--a candle warmer won't do.

Only imported cheese will melt properly. Don't substitute domestic cheese.

1 clove garlic, cut in half
2 c chicken bouillon
½ lb imported Swiss cheese (Emmental) shredded
½ lb imported Swiss or Danish Gruyere (Samsoe) shredded
1 Tb cornstarch
1 ts dry mustard (opt)
3 Tb light cream
freshly ground nutmeg and pepper to taste
1 small loaf French bread, cut in 1" cubes with some crust on each.

Rub fondue pot with garlic. Add bouillon and heat slowly until bubbles form and slowly rise to the surface. Combine the cheeses, cornstarch and mustard. Add cheese mixture, a spoonful at a time; stir slowly and continuously until blended into a smooth sauce. It should bubble very slowly; if it gets too hot, cheese will separate.

Stir in light cream a tablespoon at a time, and again bring to a slow boil. Sprinkle with nutmeg and pepper, to taste. Take to the table with the bread cubes and adjust heat so fondue keeps bubbling slowly. If fondue gets too thick, thin with a little cream. To eat: each person spears bread with a fork, swirls it in the cheese. Makes 12-16 appetizer servings, or serves 4 as a main dish.

* * * * * * * *

We cannot compel love to come to us. We simply invite it. When it comes, let us give thanks for it and see what we can do to attract still more. We should express affection, even if all we do is pat dogs. The more love we give away, the greater love we have to share.

--Thomas Dreier

SPICED EGGS

1. Heat in saucepan for 5 min on moderate heat:
   - 1 T mixed pickling spices
   - 1 ts salt
   - 1¼ c cider vinegar
   - ¼ c sugar
   - 1 ts fresh ground pepper
2. Place in qt jar 6 hard cooked eggs, shelled
3. Remove saucepan from heat and add ¼ to ½ ts food coloring, of your choice, if desired. Pour over eggs. Allow liquid to cool before screwing on jar lid. Age 2 days to weeks in the frig.
4. To serve slice on egg cutter, quarter, halve or serve whole.
5. Yields 6 spiced eggs.

HAM & CHEESE CASSEROLE
(Mock Souffle)

8 slices of bread
6 slices ham, in small pieces
2 c grated med or mild cheddar cheese
4 eggs, slightly beaten
2½ c milk
1 ts salt
3/4 ts dry mustard
1 can cream of mushroom soup & ½ c milk

Remove crusts, butter bread and cube. Put in bottom of buttered 9 x 13" casserole. Cover with ham. Top with grated cheese. Beat eggs with 2½ c milk, salt, and dry mustard. Pour over ham. Refrigerate overnight. In morning dilute soup with ½ c milk. Pour over casserole. Bake at 300° for 1½ hrs. It should be firmly set. Ham may be replaced by link sausage that has been browned, drained and cut into thirds. Serves 6-8.

CHILI RELLENO CASSEROLE

4 4-oz cans Ortego whole chiles
1 lb Jack cheese
1 lg can evaporated milk
1 ts salt
1 lb Tillamook cheese
4 eggs
3 Tb flour

Wash chiles, remove all seeds, drain well. In 9x13 pan, place layer of chiles flat, layer of grated Tillamook cheese, then layer of chiles, then Jack cheese. Separate eggs. Beat yolks, add milk, flour and salt. Beat whites and fold into yolk mixture. Pour over chiles and cheese. Bake at 325° for 1 hr. Serves 12.

HEAVENLY EGG CASSEROLE

Devil eggs and place around bottom of buttered pan.

Prepare sauce by browning 1 lg chopped onion in 4 Tb butter, add 3 Tb flour, mixing well, then 1 can evaporated milk plus ¼ c whole milk and 1 4-oz can parmesan cheese. Stir until sauce thickens.

Pour over eggs, garnish with buttered bread crumbs and bake at 350° until bubbly.

(This is good for brunch, however, if you'd like it a delicious luncheon dish, add shrimp or crab).

RINKTUM TIDDY ON TOAST SNIPPETS

1 35-oz tomatoes, drained, about 2 cups
1 ts salt
1 ts sugar
1/8 ts pepper
1 Tb chopped onion
½ lb mild Cheddar cheese, cut into bits
1 Tb butter
1 egg
Hot buttered toast (4-6 slices)

Chop tomatoes coarsley, then heat in saucepan. Add seasonings and onion. When hot, melt in cheese over low heat, stirring constantly. When smooth, add butter, then egg, stirring well.

On each plate, cut toast into small pieces and rearrange neatly to resemble an uncut piece of toast.

Pour Tiddy over toast snippets and serve.

*This is a recipe a half-century old found in an old, old Good Housekeeping magazine, which is still delicious and worth reviving.

Connie's father, Harry E. Edwards, declares that he was raised on "Tinktum Tiddy" back in Ohio. It was a customary Sunday night meal, and so enjoyed!

BRAZILIAN OMELET CON CARNE

Sauce

1 c left over ground cooked beef
1 Tb fat or salad oil
1½ c canned tomatoes
½ ts salt
½ ts chili powder
½ green pepper, cut in strips

Omelet

6 egg yolks
1 ts salt
6 stiff-beaten egg whites
3 Tb tomato juice
dash of pepper
3 Tb fat or salad oil

Brown meat in 1 Tb fat; add tomatoes, salt, chili powder, and green pepper; cook 10 min. stirring frequently.

Beat egg yolks until light-colored and thick; add tomato juice and seasonings. Fold in whites.

Heat 3 Tb fat in skillet; pour in egg mixture; cover; cook over very low heat till mixture puffs, about 8 min. Uncover, bake in slow oven (325°) 15 minutes, or brown under broiler. Fold. Pour sauce over. Serve with fried rice. Serves 6.

EGGS PIQUANT

1 clove garlic, minced
1½ c water
1 ts Worcestershire sauce
¼ ts paprika
2 Tb salad oil
¼ c chili sauce
½ ts salt
6 eggs

Simmer garlic in hot salad oil 10 min; remove garlic; add water, chili sauce, Worcestershire sauce, and seasonings. Bring to a boil; reduce heat and slip eggs into sauce; poach till eggs are set, about 4 minutes.

Remove eggs to hot buttered toast slices; pour 1 Tb hot sauce over each egg. Serves 6.

* * * *

A letter from a college student: "Please send food packages! All they serve here is breakfast, lunch and dinner."

Nothing annoys a woman more than to have friends drop in unexpectedly and find the house looking as it usually does.

WELSH RAREBIT

1½ Tb butter or margarine
1½ Tb enriched flour
1½ c milk
1 c grated American or nippy, spreading cheese
½ ts salt
½ ts dry mustard
Dash paprika
Melt butter; add flour; blend. Add milk; stir over low heat till thick; add cheese; stir till melted. Add seasonings. Serve hot over buttered toast or crackers, or pour over slice of tomato on toast; garnish with bacon slices. Serves 6.

GARDEN FRESH QUICHE

1 3/4 c chopped broccoli
½ c grated onion
1/3 c chopped green pepper
1½ c grated cheese
10 slices crumbled cooked bacon

3/4 c bisquick)
3 eggs)
1½ c milk)
1 ts salt)
1/4 ts pepper)

Blend dry bisquick ingredients. Heat oven to 400°. Lightly grease pie pan. Cook broccoli for 7 min. and drain. Mix broccoli, onion, bacon, green pepper and cheese in pie plate. Beat remaining ingredients until smooth. Pour into pie plate. Bake until knife comes out clean. (30-40 min.) Let stand 5 min. before serving. Can also be baked in muffin tins for individual servings.

* * * *

If the grass on the other side is greener, your own grass may need a good watering.

No man's head aches while he is comforting another.

Our kiddies just can't buy enough dry cereals, all sizes. Of course, they never eat the stuff, they only want the prizes!--Nova Timple Ashley

TACO SCRAMBLED EGGS

6 beaten eggs
½ c reconstituted nonfat dry milk
½ c shredded cheddar cheese (2-oz)
½ ts salt
Few dashes bottled hot pepper sauce
½ c chopped onion
¼ c chopped canned green chili peppers
2 Tb butter or margarine
2 med. tomatoes, peeled, seeded & chopped
shredded lettuce (optional)
2 ts chili powder 2/3 c plain yogurt

In bowl combine eggs, milk, cheese, salt, & hot pepper sauce. In skillet cook onion and green chili peppers in butter or margarine till onion is tender, but not browned. Add the egg mixture. Cook without stirring till egg mixture begins to set on bottom and around edges. Lift and fold the partially cooked eggs with a spatula so uncooked portion flows underneath. Continue cooking 5-8 min. or till eggs are cooked throughout but still glossy and moist. Add the chopped tomato. Cover and cook 1 min. Serve eggs on shredded lettuce, if desired. Combine yogurt and chili powder; pass to dollop atop eggs and lettuce. Serve eggs immediately. Makes 4 servings.

* * * *

Mother and Father were getting ready for a party, and their young boy and girl watched attentively from the doorway. First, Mom fastened Dad's cuffs, then Dad zipped up the back of Mom's dress. Mom knotted his bow tie, and he fastened her pearls.

The young daughter was quiet for a moment, then turned to her brother and asked, "I wonder why they expect us to dress ourselves?"

Tommorrow: The day that comes before you have finished solving all of today's problems.

Missing baggage: flight plight.

Prognosticators: hunch bunch.

MUSHROOM SOUFFLE

2 Tb fat
3 Tb flour
½ c milk
1 c canned mushroom pcs.
½ c mushroom liquid
½ ts salt
3 beaten egg yolks
3 stiff-beaten egg whites

Make white sauce of fat, flour, liquids, and salt. Blend slowly into egg yolks. Add mushrooms. Fold in egg whites.

Pour into ungreased 1½ qt casserole. Bake in pan of hot water in moderate oven (350°) 45 minutes or until mixture doesn't adhere to knife. Serve with shrimp sauce or salsa. Serves 4.

ASPARAGUS SOUFFLE

1 10½ or 11-oz can condensed asparagus soup
3/4 c grated sharp American cheese
4 well-beaten egg yolks
4 stiff-beaten egg whites

Heat soup and cheese over hot water, stirring till cheese is melted. Remove from heat.

Add a little soup mixture to beaten egg yolks; stir into remaining soup mixture.

Carefully fold in egg whites. Pour into 1½ qt. casserole. Place in shallow pan; pour water into pan till 1" deep. Bake in slow oven (300°) for 1 hr. Serves 4.

PIZZA BUNS

1 c tomato sauce
1 can mushrooms, stems & pcs.
1 lb cheddar cheese, shredded
½ c vegetable oil
1 small onion, chopped
1 ts oregano
1 ts garlic salt
1 c black olives
salt & pepper to taste

Mix all of the above. Spread on buns and broil until brown.

BASIC CREPE

3 eggs)
1 c milk)
3/4 c flour)
1 Tb sugar)
¼ ts salt)

In a blender, combine milk and eggs. Cover and whirl smooth. Set aside in a cool place for at least 1 hr. Pour about 2 Tb batter for each crepe onto a lightly buttered, 6-8" pan over medium heat. Turn once, baking until golden brown on both sides. Makes 16 or more crepes.

To freeze: Make stacks of from 6-12 crepes. Wrap together tightly in foil or in plastic bags and freeze. To thaw, set in a warm place over a wire rack for 2-3 hrs or place the foil wrapped crepes in a 175° oven for 15-20 min. (For more crepes see pp. 117, 118, 120, 228, 281 & 288.)

CHEESE & MUSHROOM FILLING FOR CREPES

1 c cottage cheese or
8 oz cream cheese
1 c minced mushrooms
1 Tb butter

1 egg
salt & pepper
1 Tb minced green onions
½ Tb oil

Forming the mound:
3 Tb grated cheese
½ Tb butter

9" baking dish

Mash cheese in a bowl with seasonings. Beat in raw egg. Saute mushrooms and green onions in butter and oil for 5-6 min. Stir into the cheese mixture.

Butter cooking dish and center crepe in bottom. Spread it with a layer of cheese and mushroom filling. Press a crepe on top and spread with spinach filling. Continue with alternating layers of crepes and fillings ending with a crepe. Pour over remaining cheese sauce. Sprinkle with 3 Tb cheese and dot with butter.

Bake 25 to 30 min. in preheated 350° oven. Heat through thoroughly and brown the top lightly. To serve cut in pie-shaped wedges.

* * * *

Soft drink company: fizz biz.

Rubber tree: limber timber.

Inept acrobat: bumbler tumbler.

Notes

Notes

dessert

Notes

ICE CREAM

3½ c sugar
2 cans canned milk
1½ pt whipping cream
juice of 4 lemons
(4 Tb per lemon)
1 lg can crushed pineapple

Place sugar, lemon juice and fruit together. Add canned milk, cream and milk. Takes about ½ gallon milk. Makes 6 qts.

STRAWBERRY ICE CREAM

2 4-oz pkg strawberry jello
2 pkg frozen strawberries in syrup
2 c sugar
2 c water (hot to dissolve sugar)
2 cans canned milk
2 pts frozen coffee rich (thawed)

Mix jello with hot water. Add all ingredients and freeze. Makes 4 qt.

RASPBERRY ICE CREAM
(No Cook)

3 pkg frozen raspberries
3 bananas, mashed
3 oz lemon juice
½ pt whipping cream
3 c sugar
1 c orange juice
2½ pts half and half

Pour into tub of 6 quart freezer and freeze according to manufacturer's directions.

VANILLA ICE CREAM

6 eggs beaten
4 ts salt
1 can canned milk
3 c sugar
2 Tb vanilla
1 qt whipped cream

Fill 6 qt freezer to within 2½" of the top with milk. Freeze.

EGG NOG ICE CREAM

Substitute 1½ to 2 Tb rum flavoring for the vanilla in any vanilla ice cream recipe. Add 1¼ ts nutmeg and freeze as directed.

BURNT ALMOND FUDGE

6 eggs
4 c sugar
1 pt whip cream
½ ts salt
4 squares semi-sweet chocolate
3 cans canned milk
1 c almonds cut in half

Beat sugar and eggs together. Melt chocolate and pour very slowly into egg mixture. Mix altogether. Freeze until mush. Add almonds that have been baked 1 hr in 2 Tb oil in 200° oven. Roll in towel to remove grease before adding to icecream. Add milk enough to almost fill 4 qt freezer.

EASY SHERBET

1 can apricot pie filling
1 can crushed pineapple
2 c sugar
4 c cream
vanilla
4 med. bananas, crushed

Mix pineapple and apricot pie filling together. Add cream, vanilla and bananas. Freeze.

FUDGESICLES

1 pkg (3 oz) chocolate pudding
1/3 c sugar
3 c milk
1 c whipping cream

Cook chocolate pudding according to directions, adding the sugar and additional milk. Remove from heat and add whipping cream. Pour into molds and freeze.

POPSICLES

1 small pkg jello dissolved in 1 c hot water
1 pkg presweetened Kool Aid
OR
1 regular Kool Aid plus sugar

Mix in ½ gallon container. Fill to top with cold water. Shake before freezing. Pour into Tupperware popsicle forms.

CANADIAN VANILLA ICE CREAM

6 large eggs
1 qt heavy cream, whipped
¼ ts salt
3 c sugar
2 Tb vanilla
2 qts milk (approximately)

Beat eggs to a foam. Add sugar gradually, beating until mixture is thick as cake batter. Fold in whipped cream vanilla and milk. Freeze in 6 qt freezer. When to desired freeze, remove dasher, pack and allow to ripen 2-3 hrs before serving. Serves 20.

EASY MINT CHOCOLATE CHIP ICE CREAM

1 can sweetened condensed milk
2 ts peppermint extract
3-4 drops green food coloring
2 Tb water
2 c heavy whipped cream
1 c small chocolate baking chips

In large bowl combine sweetened condensed milk, peppermint extract, green food coloring and water. Mix well. Fold in whipped cream and chocolate chips. Pour into foil-lined 9x5" loaf pan. Freeze in freezer compartment of refrigerator for 6 hrs or until firm. Makes about 1½ qts.

PEPPERMINT CANDY ICE CREAM

Prepare any vanilla ice cream recipe. Churn for about 15 min. or until the ice cream has frozen to a mushy consistency. Add 1½ c crushed peppermint stick candy and continue freezing as directed.

NUT BRITTLE ICE CREAM

Prepare any vanilla ice cream recipe. Churn for about 15 min. or until the icecream has frozen to a mushy consistency. Add 2 c crushed nut brittle and continue freezing as directed.

RHUBARB ICE CREAM

4 c fine diced red rhubarb
½ c water
1 c light corn syrup
4 eggs, well beaten
2 c whipping cream
4 c sugar
4 Tb lemon juice (1 lemon)
½ ts salt
4 c milk

Combine rhubarb, sugar and water in medium saucepan and simmer 5 min. or until sauce is formed. Add lemon juice, syrup and salt. Cool. Add milk and cream to beaten eggs. Pour into 4 qt freezer along with rhubarb mixture. Freeze according to manufacturer's directions.

PINEAPPLE SHERBET

8 c milk
2 c whipping cream
3 c sugar

Mix above ingredients together and place in freezer, freezing until mushy. Then add juice of 3 lemons and 3 oranges. Add one No. 2 can crushed pineapple. Fill can with milk.

FRESH APRICOT ICE CREAM

2 lbs fresh apricots
2 c light cream
1 c milk
1 ts vanilla
1¼ c sugar
2 c heavy cream
¼ ts salt

Dip apricots, a few at a time, in boiling water for about 30 seconds until skins will slip off easily when peeled. Plunge into cold water and remove skins. Cut apricots in half and remove pits; place in electric blender or puree in food mill. Blend until smooth. Combine pureed apricots and remaining ingredients in 4 qt freezer. Cover container and place in ice cream maker. Pack ice cream maker with crushed ice and coarse salt using about 1 c salt per 3 qts crushed ice. If ice cream is not to be eaten immediately, repack with fresh ice and salt or transfer to metal pan and place in freezer until serving. Makes 2 qts.

CHOCOLATE FONDUE

1 pkg (12 oz) chocolate morsels)
1 8-oz bar milk chocolate)
¼ c light cream ½ c water)
½ ts ground cinnamon)
Small pieces of angel food cake or sponge cake
chunks of apple, banana, pineapple
Large marshmallows
Chopped nuts

Combine ingredients in a fondue pot or top of double boiler. Stir over low heat until mixture is melted and smooth. Dip pieces of cake or fruit pieces or marshmallows into chocolate then into chopped nuts, if desired. Makes about 3 c.

CARAMEL FONDUE

50 light caramels 1/3 c water

Melt caramels with water in top of double boiler or in saucepan over low heat. Stir occasionally. Place in fondue pot. Keep warm while serving. Spear fruit (listed above) or marshmallows and dip in caramel sauce. Roll in chopped nuts.

MINI CHEESECAKES

18-20 vanilla wafers
3/4 c sugar
2 eggs
2 8-oz pkg cream cheese softened
2 ts lemon juice
Cherry pie filling
1 ts vanilla

Use cupcake liners in cupcake tins. Put one vanilla wafer in the bottom of each liner, round side up.

Combine sugar, eggs, cream cheese, lemon juice and vanilla. Beat until very smooth.

Spoon filling on vanilla wafers in cupcake tins about half-way full. Bake at 350° for 20 min. Let cakes cool completely before removing papers carefully. They will sink a little in the center.

Top with cherry pie filling or the pie filling of your choice. Fresh fruit in season may also be used. Makes about 18-20 cheesecakes.

CHOCOLATE ANGEL DESSERT

1 pkg angel food cake mix
1 pt heavy cream
½ lb crushed English toffee
1/8 ts nutmeg
2/3 c fudge or chocolate sauce

Make 10" angel food cake as directed on pkg, adding nutmeg to batter; cool. Cut cake crosswise into two even layers. Whip cream till almost stiff; fold in fudge sauce. Frost lower layer of cake with some of cream mixture; sprinkle with some of toffee. Set top layer in place. Frost top and sides with cream mixture; sprinkle with remaining toffee. Refrigerate at least 8 hrs. May be kept frozen for one week.

CHOCOLATE DESSERT

20 lg marshmallows
1 lg Hershey bar
1/3 c milk
2 c whipping cream

Melt 3/4 of chocolate bar with milk. Cool. Fold in whipping cream. Pour into graham cracker crust pie tin (or use 9 x 13" pan with graham cracker bottom). Grate rest of chocolate bar on top and chill. Serves 24.

CHOCOLATE REFRIGERATOR DESSERT

¼ lb butter , melted
2 squares melted chocolate
3/4 c sugar
4 eggs, one at a time

Crush vanilla wafers and line pan. Combine above ingredients and pour over crushed vanilla wafers and chill.

CHERRY CHOCOLATE DESSERT

1 pkg chocolate cake mix
½ pt whipping cream
3 Tb sugar
2 cans cherry pie filling
1 small sweet chocolate bar

Bake cake according to directions on package, in wax paper lined 9½x13" pan. Remove from pan and allow to cool. Split cake through center, lengthwise. Fill bottom layer with cherry pie filling. Replace upper layer. Whip the cream, adding 3 Tb sugar and cover the top with the sweetened whipped cream and shaved sweet chocolate. Cut & serve.

RHUBARB CRISP

1 c flour
½ c rolled oats, uncooked
1 c brown sugar, firm packed
½ c butter or margarine, melted
4 c cut rhubarb (½" pcs)
1 c sugar ½ c water
¼ c flour
½ ts cinnamon

Preheat oven to 375°. Make topping by combining the flour, oats and brown sugar and mixing well. With a fork, stir in butter to make a crumbly mixture. Set aside.

To make filling, combine rhubarb, sugar, the ¼ c flour. cinnamon and ½ c water. Mix well. Place in 9x9x2" greased baking pan.

Sprinkle topping evenly over filling. Bake, uncovered for 35 min. or until topping is golden and rhubarb is tender in 375° oven. Serve with light cream or ice cream, if desired. Makes 6-8 servings.

FRUIT COCKTAIL DESSERT

1 c sugar
1 c flour
1 ts soda
½ ts salt
1 egg beaten
2 c fruit cocktail
½ c nuts
½ c brown sugar

Combine sugar, flour, soda and salt. Add egg, 1 ts vanilla and stir in fruit cocktail. Put in well greased 8x13 pan. Sprinkle with brown sugar and nuts. Bake 40 minutes at 325°. Serve with whipped cream.

EASY APPLE CRISP

2 squares margarine melted
2 cans prepared apple pie filling
1 pkg white or yellow cake mix

Grease 9x13" pan. Place 2 cans of pie filling in bottom. Sprinkle dry cake mix over filling. Pour melted margarine over dry cake mix. Bake at 375° for 40 min.

* * * *

Old gardeners never die. They just spade away and then throw in the trowel.

BEST EVER APPLE PUDDING

1 c sugar
¼ c soft butter
1 egg
2 lg unpeeled apples shredded
1 c sifted flour
1 ts soda
1 ts cinnamon
½ ts nutmeg
¼ ts salt
½ c chopped walnuts

Gradually add sugar to butter creaming well. Add egg beaten hard. Shred apples medium fine. Add at once to creamed mixture. Stir in sifted dry ingredients. Add walnuts. Bake in greased 8 or 9" pan at 350° for about 45 min. Cut in squares. Serve hot with Best Ever pudding sauce or whipped cream. Makes 8-9 servings. Can be doubled for 9x13" pan.

BEST EVER PUDDING SAUCE

½ c butter
1 c sugar
½ c light cream
1½ ts vanilla
dash nutmeg

Heat butter, sugar and cream together over very low heat 10-15 minutes. Stir occasionally until blended and slightly thickened. Don't let sauce boil. Add vanilla and nutmeg. Serve hot on hot pudding cake or plain cake. Makes 1½ c.

CHOCOLATE SOUR CREAM DESSERT

1 pkg (6 serving size) chocolate pudding & pie filling
¼ c sugar
¼ ts salt
1½ c water
1 c sour cream

Combine pudding mix, sugar, salt and water in saucepan, blend well. Cook and stir over medium heat until mixture comes to full boil. Cool 5 min. Stir once or twice. Stir in sour cream, blending well. Pour into a bowl or individual serving dishes. Garnish with prepared whipped topping, if desired. Chill.

CHOCOLATE REFRIGERATOR DESSERT

1 lb vanilla wafers
2 pkgs semi-sweet chocolate chips
1 c walnuts
3 eggs
¼ ts salt
1 c whipping cream
1½ Tb sugar
½ c hot water

Dissolve chips in water. Add sugar, salt and egg (yolks beaten). Cool thoroughly. Add whipped cream and beat egg whites and nuts. Place in layers with crumbs on top and bottom. Let stand 8 hrs.

CHOCOLATE ICE CREAM DESSERT

Crush as many Oreo chocolate cookies as you desire. Spread in 9x13" pan. Save same for top. Spread ½ gallon pink peppermint ice cream on cookie crumbs then more crumbs on top. Freeze. Cut in squares, top with warm chocolate sauce.

FESTIVE CHRISTMAS ICE CREAM

To a half gallon of ice cream add chopped almonds (blanched & toasted) and crumbled macaroons. Add some chopped red and green candied cherries. Stir ice cream thoroughly to remove air. Rechill ice cream mixture before serving.

FRENCH MINT DESSERT

1½ c crushed pecans (use half) in bottom of 9 x 13" pan. Melt 1½ c butter & 3 c powdered sugar. Beat 15 min. Melt 6 squares Baker's chocolate. Beat into other mixture for 5 min. Add 1½ ts peppermint. Add 6 eggs, one at a time. Add 3 ts vanilla and mix well. Add pecans on top and freeze. Serve with whipped cream. Serves 30.

* * * *

A good name is rather to be chosen than great riches. It's tax-free too.

Whoever said "easy as taking candy from a baby" obviously never tried it.

SACHERTORTE

A recipe of the famous restaurant keeper, Frau Sacher, who fed the impoverished Austrian nobility long after they had ceased to pay.

Preheat oven to 325°. Need a 9" removable rim pan
Melt in double boiler, over hot water:
5 oz semi-sweet chocolate (not chips)
Cream until fluffy:
3/4 c sugar and 3/4 c butter
Beat in gradually until light in color:
5 egg yolks and add the melted cooled chocolate. Sift and add gradually: 3/4 c flour. Beat until stiff but not dry, 5-6 egg whites. Gently fold the whites into the chocolate mixture. Bake in an ungreased pan 50 min. to one hour. When cool, slice the Torte horizontally and insert a filling of: Pureed Apricot Jam. Cover the torte with: European Chocolate Icing using strong coffee (Sanka) instead of the cream. If you are really Viennese you put on a great gob of "Schlag" or whipped cream. (And if you are really Mormon, skip the Sanka!)

European Chocolate Icing
Melt in a double boiler, over hot water:
1 Tb butter and 4 oz semi-sweet chocolate
When melted, add and beat well:
6 Tb whipping cream (or the coffee)
Sift and add, until the desired sweetness is reached and the icing is smooth, about 1½ c confectioner's sugar
2 ts vanilla. Spread while warm.

* * * *

It's funny but almost anyone can prescribe a sure-fire cure for a cold, except the doctor.

Always put off until tomorrow what you shouldn't do at all.

CHOCOLATE MINT DESSERT

Filling:
2 sq (1 oz each) unsweetened baking chocolate
1 c vanilla wafers, crushed
3 egg whites
1 c powdered sugar
½ c butter, softened
3 egg yolks, beaten
½ c walnuts, chopped

Topping:
1 c heavy cream
½ c peppermint candy, finely crushed
10 lg (or 40 miniature) marshmallows (cut up)
2 drops red food color

Melt chocolate over very low heat. Cool. Lightly butter 8" square pan. Line bottom with crushed vanilla wafers. Set aside. Beat egg whites until stiff peaks form. Set aside. In another bowl, cream powdered sugar and softened butter. Thoroughly stir in beaten egg yolks. Blend in melted chocolate and chopped walnuts. Fold in beaten egg whites. Pour over wafers. Chill 3 hrs. Whip cream. Stir in peppermint candy, marshmallows and food coloring. Pour on top of chocolate layer. Freeze. To serve, cut in squares. Serves 9.

COCONUT TORTE

1 c graham cracker crumbs
½ c coconut flakes, chopped
½ c walnuts, chopped
4 egg whites
1 ts vanilla
¼ ts salt
1 c sugar
coffee ice cream
caramel sauce

Combine the cracker crumbs, coconut and walnuts. Set aside. Beat the egg whites, vanilla and salt until soft peaks form. Gradually beat in the sugar until stiff peaks form. Fold graham crackers into egg whites. Spread in greased 9" pie pan. Bake at 350° for 30 min. To serve, top with coffee ice cream and caramel sauce. Serves 6.

* * * *

When adults act like children, they're silly; when children act like adults, they're delinquent.

Business conditions may slip, but a mother's business is always picking up!

CHOCOLATE ECLAIRS

Cream Puffs

1 c water ½ c butter or margarine	In saucepan, heat to rolling boil

Stir in 1 c flour and cook over low heat for about 1 min. or until mixture forms a ball. Remove from heat. Beat in 4 eggs, one at a time, beating until smooth. Shape dough by ½ cupsful into "fingers", 4½" long by 1¼" wide. Place on greased cookie sheet. Bake in 400° oven for 35-40 min. or until puffed and golden. Cool away from draft. Cut off tops. Pull out any filaments of soft dough. Carefully fill puffs with vanilla cream pudding. Frost.

Vanilla cream pudding

1/3 c sugar	1/8 ts salt	2 Tb butter or margarine, softened
2 Tb cornstarch	2 c milk	
2 ts vanilla	2 egg yolks, slightly beaten	

Blend sugar, cornstarch and salt in 2 qt saucepan. Combine egg yolks and milk; gradually stir into sugar mixture. Cook over medium heat, stirring constantly, until mixture thickens and boils. Boil for 1 min., stirring. Remove from heat; stir in butter and vanilla. Pour into dessert dishes. Cool slightly, then chill.

Chocolate Icing

1 oz unsweetened chocolate	1 ts butter
1 c powdered sugar	2 Tb hot water

Melt 1 oz unsweetened chocolate and 1 ts butter over low heat. Remove from heat; stir in 1 c confectioners' sugar and about 2 Tb hot water. Beat until smooth. Frost and refrigerate eclairs until serving time. Makes 12.

* * * *

I don't mind the sleet and snow, nor winter's dreary haze; 'cause sleet and snow're the only things that're coming down these days!

HOLIDAY MERINGUE TORTE

For Two-Layer Torte

8 egg whites
1½ ts vanilla
1 ts vinegar
2 c sifted sugar
2 c heavy cream, whipped
1 c crushed pineapple, drained
3/4 c maraschino cherries, drained & cut into fourths

Bring egg whites to room temperature. Add vanilla and vinegar and beat till mixture forms peaks. Add sugar, 1 Tb at a time. Beat until mixture is stiff and all sugar is dissolved. This makes two layers.

Spread mixture gently into two 9" round cake pans. Use the pan with a blade scraper or line pans with brown paper. Bake at 300° for 1 hr and 15 min. Cool well in pans. Meringue will be delicately crusty on the outside, tender and still a little moist on the inside. They're all ready now for the filling.

Run scraper around edge of pan. Turn first meringue onto serving plate. Lay any crumbs or broken pieces of meringue atop layer. Fold pineapple and cherries into whipped cream. Spread mixture generously over meringue with a narrow spatula. Top with second meringue. Frost with rest of whipped cream. Chill 8 hrs or overnight. Garnish with cherries.

For Three-Layer Torte

12 egg whites
2 ts vanilla
1½ ts vinegar
3 c sifted sugar
1 No. 2 can (2½ c) crushed pineapple, drained
1 c maraschino cherries, cut in fourths
3 c heavy cream, whipped

Prepare as for above, using three 9" round cake pans and assembling torte three layers high.

* * * *

A book about pita, a staple of many Mediterranean cultures, is called Pita the Great.

A Chinese cooking course offered on a Princess Lines cruise: "Wokking on Water."

There is a manual on beekeeping called The Queen and I.

SCHAUM TORTE

1 c of egg whites (have egg whites cold)
1 ts vinegar
½ ts cream of tartar
Combine above ingredients and beat until very stiff at high speed. Then add 2 c of sugar slowly keeping mixer at high speed. Put into 2 well-buttered pyrex pie dishes and bake at 300° for 10 minutes and at 250° for 30 minutes. Turn oven off and let cool in the oven.

When serving take out of pie dish and put on serving platter. Lift off top crust (it will break but don't worry). Fill with whipped cream.

Whip 1 pt cream with 1 Tb sugar and 1 ts vanilla. (This amount will fill both tortes). Then on the cream put fresh strawberries, raspberries or peaches. Cooked sour cherries, canned or frozen strawberries or raspberries can also be used. Now put the top back on and serve.

RICE CUSTARD PUDDING

1 c cooked rice
2 c milk, scalded
2 eggs , slightly beaten
1 c raisins
½ c sugar
vanilla
nutmeg
cinnamon

Mix altogether, putting cinnamon and bits of butter on top. Set pan in water and bake at 350° for 45-60 minutes.

Cream Sauce for Pudding

2 Tb margarine
3/4 c sugar
2 c milk
1 ts vanilla
¼ c cornstarch
½ ts salt
2 egg yolks, slightly beaten

Melt butter; blend in cornstarch, sugar and starch. Gradually add milk. Heat to boiling over direct heat. Stir into egg yolks. Cook 2 min. stirring constantly. Add vanilla. Cool thoroughly. Makes 2 c. Can be used for Boston Cream pies or Coconut Cream pies. If used with rice, add 2 c cooked rice and raisins if desired.

CHOCOLATE CINNAMON TORTE

2 3/4 c flour
2 Tb cinnamon
1½ c butter
2 c sugar
2 eggs, unbeaten
12 walnut halves
1 sq unsweetened chocolate
2 sq semi-sweet chocolate
4 c heavy cream
2 Tb cocoa
12 candied cherries

Several days ahead, make these "cookies":

1. Start heating oven to 375°. Grease, line bottom with wax paper, then grease again, two or three 9" layer cake pans. Sift flour with cinnamon.
2. In large bowl, with mixer at medium speed, mix butter with sugar, then with eggs, until very light and fluffy. Then at low speed, mix in flour mixture, a little at a time, until smooth.
3. With spatula, spread 1/3 c "cookie" dough in a very thin layer in each layer-cake pan. Bake, at one time (place on two racks, making sure pans are not directly over one another), about 8-12 min. or until golden brown.
4. Then immediately and carefully remove each "cookie" from pan to wire rack, and cool. Continue baking "cookies" until all dough is used, making at least 12. Store carefully stacked, in tight container.

About 1 hr before serving:

1. Grate unsweetened chocolate medium fine; with vegetable parer, shred semisweet chocolate with curls; whip cream.
2. Place one "cookie" on flat cake plate; then spread with ¼ to 1/3 c whipped cream. Continue building the layers in same way until you have a 12 layer torte.
3. Now fold cocoa and unsweetened chocolate with left over whipped cream; heap over top of torte.
4. As a finishing touch, decorate top edge of torte with cherries and walnuts; then heap chocolate curls in center.
5. Refrigerate torte for about ½ hr before serving, so it will be easy to cut into 12 wedges.

**Weight-watchers, beware!

HAWAIIAN FIVE-O TORTE

1 c sifted flour
½ c margarine or butter
1/3 c finely ground pecans or hickory nuts
1/3 c coconut
1 envelope unflavored gelatin
¼ c cold water
3/4 c sugar
3 egg yolks
Meringue
1 (1 lb 4 oz) can crushed pineapple
1 (4 3/4 oz) pkg lemon pie filling
1 c dairy sour cream
powdered sugar

Preheat oven to moderate (350°). Combine flour, butter nuts and coconut and blend to crumb consistency. Press in even layer in bottom of 8" square baking pan. Bake in preheated oven 20 min., until very lightly browned. Cool.

Drain juice from pineapple and add water to measure 2 c. Soften gelatin in ¼ c water. Prepare lemon pie filling with sugar and egg yolks, reducing liquid to the 2 c pineapple juice and water. Cook until smooth and thick, stirring constantly.

Remove from heat, add softened gelatin, and stir until dissolved. Fold in the drained pineapple. Cool 10 minutes, stirring occasionally.

Preheat oven to very hot (500°). Fold sour cream into pudding mixture and turn into cooled crust. Prepare Meringue (recipe below) and spread over filling.

Place in very hot oven, turn off heat and allow torte to remain in oven for several hours, until it is completely cold.

Remove torte from oven, and sift powdered sugar over top Chill several hrs before serving.

Meringue

Beat 3 egg whites with ¼ ts cream of tartar to a fine foam. Gradually beat in 1¼ c sifted powdered sugar, continuing to beat at very high speed until very stiff and shiny.

****A $25,000 winner in the recent National Pineapple Cooking Classic!

MEXICAN SWEET

Home economists suggest this mouth-watering Mexican sweet for dessert fare. Fry 8, 5" flour tortillas in hot oil until crisp and puffy; drain on absorbent paper. Brush each "tostada" with melted butter. Mix ¼ c sugar and 1 ts cinnamon together. Sprinkle mixture over tostada. Top with scoop of vanilla icecream. Sprinkle with grated chocolate and top with sliced toasted almonds. Makes 8 servings.

BLINTZES (Crepes)

Filling
2 lg pkg cream cheese
1 egg
½ ts vanilla
2 Tb sugar

Blintz
2 eggs
2 Tb salad oil
1 c milk
2 Tb sugar
½ ts salt
3/4 c sifted flour

Warm cheese at room temperature and cream until smooth. Put 3 Tb on edge of crepe, fold edge over and roll in buttered pan and fry to a golden brown. Serve warm with fruit sauce or jam on top of sour cream. (See p. 264 for detailed instructions on preparation of crepes.)

* * * *

The younger generation has no faults that being a parent and taxpayer will not eliminate.

Grade School Teacher: "What was George Washington most noted for?"
Johnny: "His memory."
Teacher: "Why do you think his memory was so great?"
Johnnie: "Well, they erected a monument to it."

A canny Maine farmer was approached by a stranger one day and asked, "How much is your prize Jersey heifer worth?"

The farmer thought for a moment, then asked, "Are you the tax assessor, or has she been killed by a train?"

LEMON ANGEL FOOD DESSERT

3/4 c lemon juice ½ c sugar
1 can sweetened condensed milk
1 pt whipped cream 1 large angel food cake

Combine juice, sugar and milk and fold into whipped cream. Break cake into bite-size pieces. Put ½ cake into 9x13" pan and spoon over half of the sauce. Repeat. Sprinkle with coconut and refrigerate 24 hrs.

LEMON MERINGUE DESSERT

1 12 oz box vanilla crushed wafers
2/3 c melted margarine

Mix and press into 9x13" glass pan and 1 9x9" pan. Beat 6 egg yolks. Add 2 cans sweetened condensed milk and 1 12-oz can frozen lemonade. Beat till thick. Fold in one carton dessert mix or large cool whip or 2 c whipped cream. Pour over crumb crust. Beat 6 egg whites with 3/4 c sugar till stiff. Spread over dessert. Put under broiler until lightly brown. Freeze. Serves 25-30.

LEMON FLUFF

8 eggs, separated 3/4 c sugar
½ c lemon juice 1 envelope Knox gelatin
2/3 c water vanilla wafers

Separate eggs and beat yolks till fluffy. Add 3/4 c sugar and lemon juice. Cook in double boiler till thickened. Soften gelatin in 2/3 c cold water. Add to cooked mixture while hot. Let cool. Roll vanilla wafers into crumbs, line buttered pans. Beat egg whites till stiff. Gradually add ½ c sugar. Fold lemon mixture into egg whites and pour into pans. Sprinkle crumbs on top. Set in frig. May be made the night before needed.

BAKLAVA

1 lb shelled walnuts, coarsely ground
1 lb shelled almonds, coarsely ground
2 Tb cinnamon
½ ts allspice
½ ts nutmeg
½ ts ground cloves
½ ts mace
1 c granulated sugar
1 lb Fillo
1 lb butter
whole cloves
honey syrup

Mix nuts in large bowl with sugar and spices. Brush bottom of pan with melted butter. Place 6 buttered sheets of Fillo to form the bottom layer. Sprinkle a thin layer of nut mixture on top of the 6 buttered sheets. Layer Fillo, butter and nuts until all nuts are used. Finish dessert with 6-8 Fillo, placing one on top of the other and brushing each with butter. Cut with serrated knife into 1" wide pieces, cut on the bias. Position whole clove in center of each. Bake in slow oven at 300° for 1 hr 15 min. Immediately after taking out of oven, pour boiling hot syrup over it slowly. Reserve 3/4 c syrup and return to heat and boil 5 min longer. Then return Boklava to oven for 5 min at 400°. Remove from oven and finish glazing with remaining syrup. Cool 6 hrs before serving.

Honey Syrup

In saucepan, combine 3 c sugar, 3 c water, 1 ts lemon juice, 1½ c honey. Boil 20-25 min. Add vanilla last with grated peel of whole orange.

BERRY DESSERT

Step 1

½ lb butter
2 Tb sugar
1½ c flour

Cream together and spread in 9x13 pan. Bake at 350° for 20 min. and let cool.

Step 2

1 sq butter
2 3-oz pkg cream cheese
2 c powdered sugar
1 c nuts

Cream together the above and spread on the cooled crust.

Step 3

1 c boiling water
1 small pkg raspberry or strawberry jello
2 pkg frozen berries; raspberry or strawberry

Cool step 3 mixture till almost set and spread on top of step 2 mixture & refrigerate. Serve with whipped cream.

PISTACHIO DESSERT

1½ c flour
1½ sq margarine
2/3 c crushed pecans
2 boxes pistachio pudding
8 oz cream cheese
1 c sifted powdered sugar
9 oz tub Dream whip
3 c milk

Mix flour, margarine and pecans together and spread in 9x13" pan. Bake at 350° for 30 min. Beat well with electric mixer cream cheese, powdered sugar and half whipped topping. Pour over cooled crust; let set 30 min. Mix pudding and milk with blender for 1 min. Pour over second layer. Cover. Let set for 2 hrs. or overnight. Spread with remaining whipped topping. Chill until ready to serve.

Variations: chocolate or vanilla pudding are also used with this recipe. However, the pistachio is the favorite at our household, and quite different.

DATE REFRIGERATOR DESSERT

½ lb graham cracker crumbs
1 c chopped nuts
½ pt whipping cream
1 c chopped dates
½ lb small marshmallows

Save half crumbs. Mix together well. Whip cream and add to mixture. Mold into roll, and roll in ½ c crumbs. Cover with wax paper and leave in refrigerator over night.

HEAVENLY HASH

3/4 lb graham cracker crumbs
32 marshmallows (1 large package)
½ to 3/4 lb maraschino cherries, cut up
1 or 2 c chopped nuts
1 can sweetened condensed milk

With hands, mix above ingredients together, kneading until well blended. Press firmly together and roll in powdered sugar. Chill 24 hrs and serve with dallop of whipped cream. Very colorful and impressive for special occasions. It is a Christmas tradition at the Horman household, but is good any time of year!

ORANGE DREAM DESSERT

JELLO MIXTURE
1 6 oz package orange jello
2 c hot water
1 6 oz can frozen orange juice
1 slim 13¼ oz can crushed pineapple with juice
2 11 oz cans Mandarin oranges with juice
TOPPING
1 pkg Lemon Instant Pudding (3½ oz)
2 c milk
1 c heavy cream for whipping or 1 pkg
Dream Whip topping and ½ c milk (Whip following pkg directions)
Dissolve jello in hot water. Add orange juice, pineapple and juice, mandarin oranges and juice. Mix together in bowl. Pour into large sized rectangular shallow baking dish. Chill to set.

JELLO PINEAPPLE FLUFF

Put one large can canned milk in the freezer. Meanwhile, set 1 lg pkg jello (whatever color you want the dessert to be.) Let it set up, but not firm. Whip the canned milk until about triple in bulk. Drain 1 small can crushed pineapple. Fold it into a large bowl with the canned milk mixture and beaten jello mix.

Meanwhile, crush graham crackers or vanilla wafers and line 9x13" pan. Save half crumbs for top of dessert. Pour the fluff into the pan and sprinkle generously with crumbs. Inexpensive and elegant to serve. (I often serve it for showers and it is always a hit!) You may want to add whipped cream dallop on top.

RASPBERRY ANGEL CAKE

1 6 oz pkg raspberry jello
1 c boiling water
3 10-oz each frozen raspberries
1 pint heavy cream, whipped
1 small angel food cake

Dissolve gelatin in boiling water. Let stand in frig until partially firm. Stir in raspberries and whipped cream.

Break angel food cake into large pieces, fold into raspberry mixture, Place in refrigerator in 9 x 13" pan. To serve, top with some of whipped cream and raspberries, if desired. Serves 4-6.

FROZEN STRAWBERRY DESSERT

1 c flour
1 sq butter
2 egg whites
¼ c brown sugar, packed
½ c pecans or walnuts, broken
1 10-oz pkg frozen strawberries, partially defrosted
1 c sugar
2 Tb lemon juice
1 c heavy cream, whipped

Combine flour and brown sugar. Cut in butter as for pastry until mixture forms crumbs; stir in nuts. Spread in large shallow pan. Bake 15 min., stirring 3 or 4 times to keep from burning. Remove from oven. Cool and crush into crumbs. In large bowl combine egg whites, strawberries and sugar; beat until stiff and thick--about 5 min. Stir in lemon juice. Fold in whipped cream. In bottom of 9x13x2" baking pan, spread all but 1 c of crumbs. Pour strawberry filling evenly over crumbs. Sprinkle remaining crumb mixture over top, cover with foil or plastic wrap and freeze for several hrs. Will not freeze hard. Cut into squares to serve. If desired, each piece may be garnished with dollop of whipped cream and a fresh strawberry with its stem.

* * * *   * * * *

Small boy at piano to mother: "Gee, Mommy, I wish you hadn't been deprived of so many things as a child."

PINEAPPLE SNOW BALLS

½ c sugar
6 Tb butter or margarine
1 c drained crushed pineapple - 1 well beaten egg yolk
½ pt whipping cream
2 c coconut
¼ c chopped nuts
1 egg white stiffly beaten
Pinch salt
60 vanilla wafers

Cream butter and sugar until light. Add egg yolk, pineapple and nuts. Add beaten egg white with pinch of salt, and fold in lightly. For each snow ball take 3 wafers, spread mix between wafers but not on top, stacking together. Let stand in refrigerator 3 hrs or over night. Whip cream and sweeten and add vanilla. Spread over each snow ball. Sprinkle with coconut. Let stand again for 3 hrs.

FANCY SUMMER DESSERT

1 egg
2 Tb sugar
½ c heavy cream, whipped
2 Tb lemon juice
pinch of salt
1 c diced orange
6 fancy crests (cookies with coconut and marshmallow tops, quartered)
1 c drained, canned pineapple tidbits
1 c seedless grapes
1 banana sliced
8 maraschino cherries, quartered
½ c slivered toasted almonds

In top of double boiler, beat egg with fork. Stir in lemon juice, sugar and salt. Cook over hot water, stirring constantly for 5 min. or until mixture thickens. Remove from heat, cool. Fold in cream, fancy crests, and fruit. Cover and chill overnight. To serve, fold in almonds.

* * * *

If he can remember so many jokes, with all the details that mold them, why can't he recall, with equal skill, all the times he's told them!

Each gives pleasure his own way, of that there is no doubt. Some do it coming in a room; while others, going out.

VANILLA REFRIGERATOR PUDDING

3 eggs
1 med. can crushed pineapple
1 7 oz pkg crushed vanilla wafers
¼ lb butter
1 ts vanilla
sliced strawberries
2 c powdered sugar

Place half crushed vanilla wafers on bottom of 8" pan. Cream sugar and butter; add eggs beaten smooth. Pour mixture over vanilla wafers. Drain pineapple and sprinkle on top of above. Slice strawberries on top of all. Beat ¼ pt cream with vanilla and sugar and spread over fruit. Sprinkle remaining crumbs on top. Place in refrigerator for several hours before serving.

RASPBERRY ICEBOX DESSERT

1st layer: 1 c graham cracker crumbs
2nd layer: Cream together 1 c sugar, ½ c butter, 2 eggs
3rd layer: 2 cups raspberries (fresh)
4th layer: 1 c whipped cream sweetened, with vanilla
5th layer: 1 c graham cracker crumbs
Chill thoroughly and serve cut in squares.

STRAWBERRY CREPES

1 8-oz pkg cream cheese
2 Tb sugar
12 crepes
6 Tb sugar
3/4 c dairy sour cream
2 ts grated lemon rind
¼ c butter
3 c fresh strawberries, sliced
½ c whole berries

Combine cream cheese, sour cream and 2 Tb sugar; beat until smooth and fluffy. Stir in lemon rind. Spoon mixture onto crepes and roll up. Place on platter and keep warm.

Combine butter with remaining sugar and cook in small saucepan until sugar is dissolved. Stir in sliced strawberries. Transfer to chafing dish and heat. Spoon sauce over crepes. Garnish with whole berries. Makes 6 servings, allowing 2 crepes per serving.

*For basic crepe recipe see p. 264 .

STEAMED GUM DROP PUDDING

½ c dry bread crumbs
1½ ts baking powder
1/3 c brown sugar
½ c quartered red & green gum drops
2/3 c broken walnuts
1 egg, beaten
1 c flour
½ ts salt
1/3 c shortening
1/3 c chopped prunes
1/3 c chopped dates
1/3 c raisins
1/3 c water

Combine bread crumbs, flour, baking powder, salt and brown sugar. Cut shortening into flour mixture until the size of peas. Add remaining ingredients and mix well. Pour into greased 1 qt mold or pudding pan.

Cover mold with double thickness of waxed paper, securely tied, or aluminum foil. Steam for 3 hrs. Or steam in pressure saucepan for 20 min. without pressure, then 60 minutes with 10 pounds pressure. Serve hot with Creamy Sauce or any other desired sauce. Garnish with bits of green and red gum drops, if desired. Makes 6 servings.

Creamy Sauce: Beat 1 egg until foamy. Add 2½ Tb butter and 3/4 c powdered sugar and mix well. Blend in ½ c heavy cream that's been whipped, a pinch of salt and ½ ts vanilla. Makes 1½ c.

DATE PUDDING

4 eggs well beaten
1 ts vanilla
½ ts nutmeg
2 c seedless raisins or dates
1 c walnuts
1½ c sugar
1 heaping ts cinnamon
2 heaping c graham cracker crumbs

Mix together and add 2 ts soda dissolved in 1 c hot water. Steam 1½ hrs.

* * * *

Never try to guess your wife's size. Just buy her anything marked "PETITE" and hold on to the receipt.

Remember, the Christmas presents of today are the garage sales of tomorrow.

Stop believing in Santa Claus and you get underwear.

OLD FASHIONED APRICOT COBBLER

1 sq butter or margarine	2 c flour
1 Tb baking powder	1½ c sugar
1½ c milk	1 qt bottled apricots

In 9 x 13" baking pan, melt butter or margarine. Stir or sift together dry ingredients and stir into melted butter, along with milk, until blended. Spread evenly in pan. Empty 1 quart canned apricots, including juice, over top of batter and bake at 350° until deep brown, about 45 min.

PEACH COBBLER

1 qt sliced peaches	1 c sugar
1½ Tbs flour	1½ c flour
1 ts baking powder	¼ c butter or margarine
1/3 c milk	

Place peaches into buttered 2 qt baking dish. Mix sugar with 1½ Tb flour and fold into peaches. Combine 1½ c flour, 1 ts baking powder. Cut in with a pastry blender ¼ c butter or margarine. Add 1/3 c milk mixing lightly with fork. Turn on a well-floured board and roll to fit the top of the baking dish. Lay on top of fruit, making several incisions. Bake at 350° for about 45 min. Serve with cream, dairy topping or ice cream.

* * * *

Some parents spend half their time wondering how their kids will turn out and the other half wondering when they will turn in.

One thing to be said for children: they never bore you with pictures of their parents.

Very few men have been able to learn a business from the top down.

PLUM PUDDING

1 1/3 c raisins	½ ts salt
1 1/3 c sugar	1 ts baking powder
1 1/3 c currants	3/4 c orange juice
2 c ground beef suet	1 ts cinnamon
1 1/3 c flour	¼ ts nutmeg
2 2/3 c soft bread crumbs	3 eggs
1 lg bottle maraschino cherries (cut in half)	1 c cherry juice (if not enough add water)

Mix dry ingredients, then cherries. Add eggs slightly beaten, orange juice, and cherry juice. Batter is thinner than fruitcake. Steam for 6 hrs. When serving use favorite sauce or Plum Pudding Sauce below.

Sauce for Plum Pudding

2 sq butter	3 c sugar
3 heaping Tb flour	1½ qts water

Brown butter, sugar, and flour in heavy pan and then add water stirring constantly. When it is thick remove from stove and add 2 ts brandy extract, or flavoring of your choice. Makes 20 servings.

STEAMED HOLIDAY PUDDING

½ c grated peeled raw carrot)
½ c grated peeled raw potato) Mix together
½ c chopped suet)

½ c raisins	½ c dry currants
½ c chopped dates	½ c sugar
½ c flour	½ ts soda
1 ts baking powder	¼ ts salt
1 ts ground cinnamon	½ ts each cloves & nutmeg

Pack into greased 1 qt mold. Cover, put on rack in kettle, and add boiling water to come halfway up sides of mold. Steam, covered, for 2 hrs. Cover with hard sauce.

Hard sauce. 1/3 c butter, 1 c powdered sugar, ½ ts vanilla ¼ c heavy cream. Cream well and spoon over pudding.

NORWEGIAN RICE IN CREAM

2¼ c boiling water	1 ts salt
1 c long grain rice	2/3 c milk (approximately)
1/3 c sugar (approximately)	½ ts almond extract
2 c heavy cream, whipped	

Bring water to boil in 1½ qt saucepan; add salt. Stir in rice slowly so water keeps boiling. Cover; turn heat to simmer; allow rice to cook 30 min. or until just tender. Add enough milk to barely fill in rice and be level with top of rice. Cover pan; simmer another 30 minutes or until all milk is absorbed. Stir in sugar to taste and almond extract. Chill. Just before serving, fold in whipped cream. Served with fruit sauce of your choosing.

NOTE: In Scandinavia during the holidays it is traditional to stir one whole blanched almond into pudding. The one who gets the almond is given a marzipan candy in the shape of a Christmas pig.

BREAD PUDDING

4 c milk	2 ts cinnamon
4 c broken bread	½ ts nutmeg
½ ts allspice	½ c raisins/nuts
4 eggs, beaten	1 c solid pack brown sugar

Heat milk. Butter a 4 qt casserole and pour hot milk over bread. Beat eggs and add sugar and spices to same. Pour over all. Bake at 300° for 45-50 min. Serves 6-8.

ORANGE RAISIN RICE

1 c cooked rice	1/4 c orange juice
1/4 c raisins	2 Tb sugar
1 Tb butter or margarine	

Simmer over medium heat to blend flavors. Serves 2.

ENGLISH TRIFLE

2 pkg (3½ oz each) tapioca jello pudding or vanilla jello pudding
2 pkg (3 oz each) strawberry raspberry gelatin jello
3 c boiling water
1 c vanilla ice cream
2 pkg (10 oz each) frozen raspberries
2 pkg (10 oz each) frozen strawberries
3 bananas, sliced
½ lb pecans whole (optional)
1 angel food cake, broken in chunks

whipped cream

Make tapioca pudding according to package directions. Refrigerate. Dissolve gelatin in boiling water. Stir in vanilla ice cream, raspberries, strawberries, sliced bananas and pecans. Pour equally into a mixing bowl and a glass punch bowl. Refrigerate. When partially set, layer half of angel food cake chunks in the glass punch bowl. Spread one-half of the tapioca pudding over this. Pour other partially set gelatin from mixing bowl over tapioca. Add remaining cake chunks and finally, a tapioca layer. Refrigerate. To serve, top with whipped cream.
Serves 12.

REFRESHING FRUIT PIZZA

A beautiful sight to behold!

1 (15 oz) can pineapple chunks
1 (15 oz) pkg sugar cookie mix
1 (10½ oz) can mandarin oranged, drained
2 c sliced fresh strawberries
1 kiwi fruit
3 bananas
8 8-oz whipped topping
½ c cherry pie-filling

Drain juice from pineapple chunks into a small bowl. Slice bananas into juice; set aside. Preheat oven to 375°. Prepare cookie dough according to package directions. Lightly grease a 12" pizza pan. Press dough into pizza pan, about 1/8" thick. Bake 12-15 min. or until edges begin to brown. Cool on rack.

Spread whipped topping over cooled cookie dough crust. Drain juice from bananas. Arrange fruit in circles on topping, working from outside toward center. Arrange strawberries around outside of pan, then bananas, cherry-pie filling, pineapple chunks and mandarin oranges. Place a whole strawberry in center. Refrigerate until served. Create your own fresh-fruit combinations.
Serves 8.

FROZEN PUMPKIN SQUARES

1 c flour
1½ ts ginger
1 pkg coconut pecan or coconut almond frosting mix
½ c softened butter

Combine in large bowl until crumbly, using a pastry blender. Pour into ungreased 9x9" pan and bake 15 min. at 350°.

Stir mixture and bake another 5-10 min. or until light brown. Crumble crumb mixture and remove 1½ c from pan. Pat remaining crumbs evenly in pan and cool.

Filling :

1-2 ts cinnamon
½ ts salt
3 c miniature or 27 large marshmallows
1 16-oz can or 1¾ c canned pumpkin

In large heavy saucepan, over low heat, combine above ingredients. Heat stirring frequently, until marshmallows are melted. Cool to lukewarm. Spoon in 1 qt vanilla or butter-brickle icecream, softened, into pumpkin mixture and stir until slightly marbled; pour over crumbs. Top with remaining crumb mixture. Freeze 3-6 hrs or until firm. Store in freezer. Makes 9-12 servings. *Absolutely out-of-this-world!

* * * *

There is an identity crisis everywhere. Americans are seeking to find out who they are, where they're coming from, what they're made of--and how they can lose 10 or 20 pounds of it.

Minister to member of congregation: "I'm sorry you're moving. You've been excellent sermon material."

Nothing in life prepares you for your first raw oyster.

FRESH FRUIT PIZZA

1 roll (17 oz) ready-to-slice sugar cookie dough
1 pkg (8 oz) cream cheese, softened
1/3 c sugar ½ ts vanilla extract
3 fresh peaches, halved and pitted
9 strawberries, halved
20 fresh or frozen blueberries, thawed
¼ c orange marmalade
1 Tb water

Preheat oven to 375°. Cover a 14" pizza pan or 15½x10½" jelly roll pan with foil. Slice cookie dough into 1/8" slices. Arrange slices, slightly overlapping, in bottom of pan. Bake 10 to 12 min. or until golden brown. Cool. Remove from foil. In small bowl, combine cream cheese, sugar and vanilla, mixing well. Spread mixture over cookie crust. Arrange fruit over cream cheese. In small bowl, combine orange marmalade and water, mixing well. Spoon over fruit. Chill about 1 hr. Cut into wedges and serve.

Cooking Tip: To remove foil from crust, place wire rack or cookie sheet over crust. Hold rack in place and invert pan. Peel off foil. Replace baking pan or serving dish and turn crust right side up. Serves 8-12.

CHEESECAKE

1 graham cracker crust & 1 pkg Danish dessert
½ c icing sugar
4 oz pkg cream cheese
1 c whipping cream
1 ts vanilla 1 basket of fresh raspberries

Whip cream. Add cream cheese, vanilla and sugar. Line crust with the cream cheese mixture. Prepare Danish dessert as per directions. Let cool. Put raspberries atop the cheese mixture. Pour Danish dessert over. Chill thoroughly before serving. (Can use fruit juice thickened in lieu of Danish dessert if desired, adding 1 c sugar for fresh berries.) Serves 12-14.

BROWNIE PIZZA

"Pizza" actually is a brownie. It is especially attractive using various fruits such as blueberries, strawberries, raspberries, kiwi, peaches or sliced bananas.

3/4 c shortening
1 c light brown sugar, packed
1 egg
2¼ c unsifted flour
¼ ts soda
¼ ts cinnamon
¼ ts salt
½ c (5.5 oz can chocolate flavored syrup)
1 qt ice cream (any flavor)
chocolate-carmel sauce & fresh fruit

Cream shortening and brown sugar in large bowl. Add egg and blend well. Combine flour, soda, cinnamon and add alternately to syrup and blend well. Pat dough evenly into 12" pizza pan, forming a thicker 1" wide edge against rim of pan. Bake at 375° for 10-12 min or until top springs back. Cool completely. Cut in 10-12 wedges but do not remove from pan. Place small scoops of icecream around edge. (Can be frozen at this point). When ready to serve, prepare chocolate-carmel sauce, p. 415. Arrange assorted fruit on pizza and pour warm sauce over ice cream. Serve immediately. Makes 10-12 servings.

* * * *

A watched pot often causes one to join Weight Watchers.

Progress is the mother of problems.

Imitation is the sincerest form of television.

Woman in restaurant, staring at another diner, to companion: "I wish I had her figure and she had my cottage cheese."

cake & icings

Notes

DREAM CAKE

½ c sugar
½ c butter
2 egg yolks beaten well
1½ c flour
1 ts baking powder
Press into cake pan like short bread and add:
2 egg whites, beaten stiff
1 c brown sugar
1 c shopped nuts
1 ts vanilla
Spread on 1st mixture. Bake in moderate oven for 25 min.

PUMPKIN ROLL CAKE

3 eggs
1 c sugar
2/3 c pumpkin
1 ts lemon juice
3/4 c flour
1 ts baking powder
1 ts ginger
½ ts salt
½ ts nutmeg
1 c finely chopped walnuts
powdered sugar, as needed
2 ts cinnamon

Beat the eggs on high speed of the mixer for 5 min. Gradually beat in the sugar. Stir in the pumpkin and lemon juice. Stir together the flour, baking powder, spices and salt. Fold into the pumpkin mixture. Spread in a greased and floured jelly roll pan. Top with the chopped nuts. Bake at 375° for 15 min. Turn onto a towel sprinkled with powdered sugar. Starting at the narrow end, roll the towel and cake together. Cool. Unmold.

Filling:
1 c powdered sugar
6 oz cream cheese
4 Tb butter
½ ts vanilla

Combine all the ingredients and beat until smooth. Spread over the cake, and roll back up. Chill. Serves 8.

* * * *

Something every home could use during the holidays is a bathroom scale that's seasonally adjusted.

Santa Claus is that jolly old gent who goes "Ho! Ho! Ho!" Then again, if you had to work only one day a year you'd laugh too.

BOILED RAISIN CAKE

3 3/4 c water | 2 c sugar
½ lb butter | 1 lb raisins

Boil the above mixture for 20 min.
Sift together the following:
4 c flour (half whole wheat is very good)
1 ts cinnamon | ½ ts cloves
¼ ts pumpkin spice | ½ ts salt
1 ts nutmeg | 1 c chopped nuts
2 ts soda

Add 2 beaten eggs to raisin mixture when it is cool. Add wet mixture to dry. Bake in 2 greased and floured loaf tins 1½ hr at 350°.

POUND CAKE

1 c shortening (butter is best) | 2 c sugar (scant)
3/4 ts salt | 1 Tb vanilla
1 Tb lemon extract | 4 eggs, one at a time
1 c buttermilk + 2 Tb | 3 c sifted flour
½ ts soda (scant) | ½ ts baking powder (scant)

Mix in order given until mixture is smooth and creamy. Bake at 350° an hour or until it pulls from sides. Makes 1 large loaf and one small one.

EASY ORANGE CAKE

Use Betty Crocker white cake mix. Use 2/3 c orange juice and 1/3 c milk in liquid requirements. Add grated orange rind from oranges before juice is extracted. Put in mixer and beat on fairly high speed for about 10 min. Bake and ice with orange icing. Powdered sugar, orange juice, rind, butter and/or cream make the icing. Sprinkle with coconut for variety.

* * * *

Many an old hen makes a goose of herself trying to look like a chicken.

ORANGE-COCONUT POUND CAKE

2 3/4 c sugar
5 eggs
3 c flour
¼ ts salt
3½ ounces flaked coconut
1¼ c butter or margarine, soft
1 ts vanilla
1 ts baking powder
1 c evaporated milk
2-3 Tb shredded orange peel

Heat oven to 350°. Grease and flour tube pan or 12-c bundt cake pan. Blend sugar, butter, eggs and vanilla in large mixer bowl ½ min on low speed, scraping bowl constantly. Beat 5 min on high speed, scraping bowl occasionally. On low speed, mix in flour, baking powder and salt alternately with milk. Fold in coconut and orange peel. Pour into pan. Bake until wooden pick inserted in center comes out clean, 1-1½ hrs. Cool 20 min; remove from pan. Cool completely. Wrap and refrigerate or freeze. Store in refrigerator up to 1 week, in freezer up to 4 months. 2 hrs before serving, remove cake from freezer and loosen wrapper so that it does not touch cake. Thaw at room temperature.

Almond Pound Cake: Substitute almond extract for vanilla and sprinkle sliced almonds on batter before baking; omit coconut.

Lemon Pound Cake: Substitute lemon extract for vanilla & 2-3 ts grated lemon rind.

SPONGE CAKE

6 eggs (separated)
1 ts salt
¼ c milk or juice
1 ts cream of tartar
1 c sugar
1 c sifted flour
1 ts vanilla

Beat egg whites with cream of tartar and salt, until stiff holding a peak. Add sugar to beaten egg yolks alternately with ¼ c milk or juice. Beat until thick and lemon colored. Add flour alternately with egg yolk mixture to the egg whites, stirring with a whisk until whites are mixed well with yolks. Bake 1 hr at 310° in tube pan.

* * * *

Why do latecomers to the theater always have seats in the middle of the row?

Why is it listeners always know when the speaker should stop and he seldom does?

ORANGE PECAN CAKE

1 c butter or margarine
2 c sugar
4 eggs
1 1/3 c buttermilk
1 ts soda
4 c flour
2 Tb grated orange rind
1 lb chopped dates
1 c broken pecans

Cream butter and sugar, beat in eggs one at a time. Dissolve soda in buttermilk. Add flour in about three parts to cream mixture alternately with buttermilk. Beat until smooth after each addition. Add orange rind, dates and nuts. Bake in tube pan at 350° for 1½ hrs. When cake is done pour following sauce over and allow to cool in pan:

2 c sugar
2 Tb grated orange rind
3/4 c orange juice

Stir and heat above until sugar is dissolved.

CHERRY CAKE

1 c sugar
1½ c cherries
4 Tb sour cream
½ ts cinnamon
½ ts nutmeg
1 ts cocoa
2 ts vanilla
3/4 c margarine
3 eggs
2½ c flour
½ ts cloves
1 ts soda dissolved in water
2/3 c cherry juice

Cream sugar and margarine; add eggs. Sift dry ingredients and add alternately with cherry juice and other wet ingredients. Add vanilla. Bake at 350° for about 45 min. or until tooth pick comes out clean.

* * * *

Generally speaking, a woman is generally speaking.

CARROT CAKE

1 c cooking oil 2 c sugar
3 eggs well beaten 2 c shredded carrots
1 sm can crushed pineapple (drained)
3 c flour 1 ts salt
2 ts soda 1 ts cinnamon
2 ts vanilla 1 c chopped nuts
1 c raisins 1 c cocoanut (optional)

Mix oil and sugar together. Add eggs, carrots and pineapple. Mix in dry ingredients and blend well. Add nuts and raisins. Bake in 2 greased and floured tins. Bake 40-45 min. at 350°.

Icing

1 8-oz pkg cream cheese
½ stick butter or ¼ c margarine
2 ts vanilla 1 box powdered sugar

Mix altogether and blend until smooth. Put on cool cake.

CRANBERRY PUFF CAKE

1. Combine in small bowl, ½ c whole cranberry sauce and ½ c orange marmalade
2. Spread sauce in bottom of greased 8" baking pan or divide evenly between 9 greased muffin cups.
3. Combine in a medium bowl, 1 c biscuit mix and ¼ c sugar
4. Blend together and add to biscuit mix, stirring until dry ingredients are moistened, 1/3 c milk and 1 egg, slightly beaten
5. Spread over sauce.
6. Bake in a 400° oven for 20-25 min., or until light brown.
7. Invert on cake plate immediately. Serve warm with butter sauce, below:

Heat to boiling in med. saucepan, stirring constantly:
½ c sugar ¼ c light cream
Turn off heat and beat in:
¼ c butter or margarine ½ ts vanilla
Heat to boiling. Stir until sugar is dissolved.

CHOCOLATE SHEET CAKE

1 cube butter)
1 c water) Boil together, then add:
½ c shortening)
3 Tb cocoa)

2 c flour
½ ts salt
½ c buttermilk or sour milk
1 ts soda
2 ts cinnamon
2 c sugar
2 eggs
1 ts vanilla

Mix well altogehter. Bake in 9 x 13" pan at 350° for 25-30 min. Frost while hot with the following:
1 stick butter, 1/3 c milk, 4 Tb cocoa. Boil, then add 1 lb powdered sugar. Add nuts if desired.

CHOCOLATE POUND CAKE

1 c soft butter or margarine
1 ts vanilla
5 eggs
3 sq unsweetened chocolate, melted
2 c sifted flour
½ ts salt
¼ to ½ c finely chopped nuts
1½ c sugar
¼ ts mace
1 grated orange rind
1 ts baking powder
¼ c orange juice

Cream butter, sugar, vanilla, mace and eggs for 5 min at high speed of mixer. Blend in cooled chocolate and orange rind. Sift together flour, baking powder and salt; add alternately with orange juice. Fold in chopped nuts which have been mixed with a little of the flour. Turn into heavily greased and lightly-floured 9 x 5 x 3" loaf pan. Bake at 300° for 1 hr plus 25-30 min. Cool on rack. Cool cake for about 15 min before removing from pan to finish cooling. If possible, allow cake to season for a day to blend flavors. Note: Coarsely ground filberts give an unusual flavor.

* * * *

Why must the phrase, "it's none of my business" always be followed by the word "but"?

Psychiatrist to patient: "I'd say you're coming along fine--already you've progressed from 'everybody's out to get me' to 'nobody cares about me."

ITALIAN CREAM CAKE

5 egg whites, beat in soft peaks and set aside
Cream together:

2 c sugar	1 cube butter
½ c crisco	1 ts vanilla
Add:	5 egg yolks
Mix:	1 c milk
1 Tb vinegar	2 c sifted flour
1 ts soda	½ ts salt

Add alternately with the sugar mixture then add:

2 c coconut	2 c nuts

Fold in egg whites. Makes 3 to 4 eight-inch cake pans full. Grease and flour pans and then put in wax paper and grease and flour wax paper. Bake 30-40 min at 350°. When cool spread with cream cheese frosting.

FOURTEEN KARAT CAKE

1½ c sugar	2¼ c flour
2 ts baking powder	1½ ts soda
2 ts cinnamon	1½ c oil
4 eggs	1 ts salt
2 c finely shredded carrots	8½ oz can crushed pineapple
3/4 c coarsley chopped pecans	(well drained)

Stir dry ingredients together. Add oil, eggs and beat well. Fold in carrots and pineapple and nuts. Bake between 35-40 min at 375°.

FRENCH BANANA CAKE WITH MIX

1 pkg white cake mix	2 eggs
2/3 c water	1 Tb vinegar
1 ts soda	1¼ c mashed bananas
2/3 c chopped walnuts	

Combine water, vinegar & soda. Blend cake mix and eggs until moistened. Add mashed bananas and blend. Beat 2 min on medium speed. Pour into two 9" pans or one 9½ x 13" pan and bake at 350° for 25-30 min.

TEXAS PECAN CAKE

In bowl mix:

2 c sugar	1 ts baking soda
2 c flour, sifted	2 eggs
½ ts salt	½ c sour cream

In saucepan mix:

2 sticks margarine	1 c cold water
½ c cocoa	

Bring in bubbling, add at once to first mixture. Beat well. Pour into greased jelly roll pan. Bake at 350° for 20 min. While baking, mix icing:

1 pkg powdered sugar, sifted
1 ts vanilla
1 c chopped pecans

In saucepan, bring to boil:

4 Tb cocoa	1 stick margarine
6 Tb milk	

Pour over powdered sugar mixture and beat well. Pour over cake immediately after removing it from oven. Serves 20.

QUICK ORANGE REFRIGERATOR CAKE

1 can (6 oz) frozen orange juice
1 pkg vanilla pudding
1 c whipped cream
2 sponge cake layers

Dilute orange juice concentrate with water to make 1½ c (1 6-oz can water). Use as liquid with vanilla pudding and cook according to package directions. When pudding is chilled, fold in whipped cream. Cut each sponge cake layer in half crosswise to make 4 thin layers. Use orange pudding as filling and frosting. Place in refrigerator several hours or overnight. If desired, decorate with flaked coconut or orange sections.

* * * *

How come vices are more habit-forming than virtues?

Mechanic to customer: "I'm afraid you have more of a problem than I anticipated. Your battery needs a new car."

TWINKIE CUPCAKES

1 c margarine 1 c water 6 Tb cocoa
Put ingredients in pan and bring to boil. Add:
2 c sugar
2 beaten eggs
1 ts vanilla
2 c flour
½ c buttermilk
1 ts soda
Beat together and pour into oblong pan or about 28 cup cakes. Bake at 400° 20-25 min.

Filling

Stir together and cook one c milk & 4 Tbs flour. (Make a thick whitesauce). Let cool. Add 1 c sugar, ½ c crisco. Beat 5 min at highest speed. Put in pastry tube (use #9 tip). Poke down into top of cupcakes and squeeze in filling. Use favorite frosting for the top.

BOTTOMS-UP GINGERBREAD

2 Tb butter
½ c chopped nuts
1 can (lb 5 oz) apple pie filling
1 pkg gingerbread mix
Melt butter in a 10" skillet and brush sides of skillet with butter. Sprinkle over melted butter the chopped nuts, spread over the nuts the apple pie filling. Prepare gingerbread mix according to directions adding 2 Tb water for altitude adjustment. Pour gingerbread mix over apples. Cover with tight fitting lid and place large burner set on med. heat for 30 minutes. Remove lid last 5 min. Cool 5 min. and turn upside down on serving plate. Serve with whipped cream or whipped topping.

* * * *

"Your mother has been with us for 20 years," said John. "Isn't it time she got a place of her own?" "My mother?" replied Helen. "I thought she was your mother."

POPPY SEED CAKE

3/4 c poppy seed
1½ c milk
1½ c sugar
½ c butter
2 c flour
2½ ts baking powder
4 egg whites beaten stiff
1 ts vanilla

Heat 1 c milk, pour over poppy seeds and allow to stand overnight. Cream butter and sugar; add poppy seed mixture. Add remainder of milk, flour and baking powder. Fold in egg whites last, and vanilla. Bake at 350° for 45 min. Frost with 1 box caramel cake frosting mix.

PEACH CAKE SUPREME

Prepare filling and set aside.

Filling: In small bowl of electric mixer combine:

1/3 c sugar
¼ ts salt
1 3-oz pkg cream cheese, softened
½ c dairy sour cream
1 egg

Beat at med. speed 3 min or until smooth and creamy.

Cake:

1 29-oz can sliced peaches
1 c sifted flour
2/3 c sugar
1 ts baking powder
¼ ts salt
½ c butter softened
1 ts vanilla
2 eggs

Drain peaches, reserving 1 Tb syrup. In large bowl of electric mixer combine syrup and remaining ingredients. Blend, then beat at med. heat 3 min. Spread evenly on bottom and sides of greased 10" pie pan (fluted edge, kind for berry pies). Pour in filling and bake at 350° 25 min or until crust is light golden brown. Top with drained peach slices. Prepare topping and spoon over peaches. Bake 5 min longer, then chill. Serves 8.

Topping: Mix well 1 c dairy sour cream and ¼ c packed brown sugar.

* * * *

The average number of times a man says "no" to tempation is once weakly.

EASY CHOCOLATE LOG

The old-fashioned French Yule log made modern, convenient, practical. If you make nothing else for the holidays, make this one.

1. Line a 15 x 10" jelly roll pan with foil.
2. Melt in pan — ¼ c butter or margarine
3. Sprinkle over butter — 1 c chopped pecans; 1 1/3 c flaked coconut; 1 15⅓ oz can sweetened condensed milk
4. In mixing bowl, beat at high speed 2 min until fluffy — 3 eggs
5. Gradually add and continue beating 2 min. 1 c sugar
6. Add to mixture, blend one minute at low speed
   - 3/4 c unsifted flour
   - 1/3 c cocoa
   - 1/3 c water
   - 1 ts vanilla
   - ¼ ts salt
   - ¼ ts soda
7. Pour cake evenly in pan and bake in 375° oven for 15-20 min.
8. Sprinkle cake in pan with powdered sugar (1/3 c)
9. Cover with towel. Place cookie sheet over towel; invert.
10. Remove pan and foil.
11. Start with 10" side, roll up jelly-roll fashion using towel to roll cake. Do not roll towel in cake. Leave wrapped until serving time. Makes 8-10 servings.

CHOCOLATE CHIFFON CAKE

1 pkg milk chocolate or Swiss chocolate cake mix. Prepare as directed using two 9" round pans. Cool and cut each layer in half. Frost with chocolate fluff frosting as follows: Mix in chilled bowl 2 c whipping cream, 1 c sifted powdered sugar, ½ to 1/3 c cocoa (or less) and a dash of salt. Beat until stiff enough to hold peaks.
*This delightful whip-cream cake is a birthday tradition at the Fairbanks home.

* * * *

Woman to date: "Tell me, Donald, do you think I'm too aggressive? I want a straight answer, and I want it now."

DEVIL'S FOOD CAKE

2¼ c sifted flour
1 ts baking powder
1 ts baking soda
½ ts salt
1½ c sugar
1/3 c water (hot)
1 c sour milk
2 eggs well beaten
½ c shortening
1 ts vanilla
½ c cocoa

Combine shortening and sugar. Beat until fluffy. Add beaten eggs and vanilla. Sift flour and soda, baking powder and salt together. Alternately add dry ingredients with milk, beginning and ending with flour. Mix cocoa and water and blend in cake. Pour into greased baking pans (two 9" or one 13 x 9 x 2). Bake for 30-35 minutes at 350°.

SPOOF RAISIN CAKE

When guests arrive and you want something out-of-this world in a hurry, you'll love this one!

1 golden cake mix
1 can raisin pie filling
3 eggs
1 ts cinnamon
½ ts each of cloves, nutmeg and allspice

Beat 3 min until smooth. Pour in bundt pan at 350° for 1 hr. Delicious alone, or with icecream.

OATMEAL CAKE

Pour 1½ c boiling water over 1 c oats and 1 cube margarine. Mix:

2 eggs
1 c brown sugar
1 c white sugar

Add:

1½ c flour
½ ts nutmeg
1 ts soda
1 c nuts
½ ts cinnamon

Add oatmeal mixture, bake in 9 x 12 pan for 40 min. at 350°.

Topping:

1 c sugar
1/3 c canned milk
¼ c brown sugar
5 Tb margarine

Melt over low heat and add 1 c cocoanut. Spread on cake and put under broiler till bubbly and brown. Let topping cool and thicken

FRUIT COCKTAIL CAKE

3 c sugar | 3 c flour
3 ts salt | 3 ts soda

Mix well together. Beat 4 eggs and add to the above.
1 28-oz can fruit cocktail and
1 15 oz can fruit cocktail. Save juice, discarding one third. Add rest (2/3) to flour and egg mixture. Bake 1-1½ hrs at 325°. Sprinkle batter with 1½ c brown sugar and 1½ c walnuts.

LUNAR RHUBARB CAKE

½ c butter
1½ c white sugar
1 egg
1 ts vanilla
2 c flour
1 ts soda
½ ts salt
1 c buttermilk
2 c chopped rhubarb (½" pieces)
1 Tb flour

Cream butter and sugar until smooth and creamy, beat in egg and vanilla. Sift together 2 c flour, soda and salt. Add to creamed mixture alternately with buttermilk, making 3 dry and 2 liquid additions. Toss rhubarb with 1 Tb flour and mix gently into batter. Spoon into buttered 9 x 13" pan and smooth the surface.

Topping:
¼ c butter
2 ts cinnamon
1 c firmly packed brown sugar

Blend all ingredients together and sprinkle evenly over batter. Bake at 350° for 45 min or until cake has risen and browned and come away from edges, or until skewer tests clean. Makes about 18 servings.

* * * *

A man walked into a credit office to pay the final installment on a baby crib. "Thank you," the manager said, "And how is the baby today?"
"Oh," the man replied. "I'm fine."

PENNSYLVANIA DUTCH APPLE CAKE

½ c firmly packed br. sugar	1 c granulated sugar
½ c soft shortening	2 eggs
2 ts grated orange rind	2 c sifted flour
1½ ts baking powder	½ ts soda
½ ts cinnamon	1 ts salt
1 c undiluted evaporated milk	
2 c finely chopped peeled apples	
½ c chopped pecans	2 Tb sugar

Mix shortening, sugar, eggs and orange rind until smooth and creamy. Sift flour, baking powder, soda, cinnamon and salt together. Add to sugar mixture alternately with evaporated milk, beginning and ending with dry ingredients. Stir in apples. Pour into buttered 8 x 12" pan and spread evenly over bottom of pan. Sprinkle pecans and 2 Tb sugar over top of cake batter. Bake at 350° for about 45 min. Makes 12 servings.

OLD FASHIONED JAM CAKE

1. Cream together: ½ c butter, 1¼ c sugar, 3 egg yolks
2. Dissolve: 1 ts soda in 1 c buttermilk
3. Sift together: 2¼ c flour, ¼ ts salt & ¼ ts cloves, ½ ts each cinnamon & allspice
   Add to first mixture:
4. Gently mix together and stir in 1 c strawberry or blackberry jam
5. Beat 3 egg whites stiff and fold in last. Pour into loaf pans and bake at 375° 35-40 min. Frost with butter cream icing.

* * * *

The main trouble with the future is that it keeps getting shorter and shorter.

Autumn is when an unwatched boy, raking, leaves.

PRUNE CAKE

3/4 c shortening
1 c sugar
2 eggs
2 cans baby food
(prunes & tapioca)
1½ c cake flour
1½ ts soda
½ ts salt
3/4 ts cinnamon
3/4 ts cloves
½ c milk
½ c nuts

Put together as you would a cake and bake at 350° for 30 min. Put icing on cake while hot.

Icing:

6 Tb melted butter
3/4 c brown sugar
¼ c cream or canned milk
½ ts vanilla
1 c chopped nuts

*Also very good with commercial butter brickle icing.

WHOLE PRUNE CAKE

Beat 4 eggs, add 2 c sugar and 1 c oil in that order. Add 1 ts soda to 1 c buttermilk (or soured sweet milk) and add: 2½ c flour sifted with 1 ts each cloves, nutmeg and cinnamon and ¼ ts salt. Add 1 c cooked prunes, chopped. Grease and flour one 10" tube pan. Bake at 350° for 1 hr. As cake is removed from oven, pour over the following sauce: ½ c sugar, ¼ sq butter, 1/8 ts salt and ¼ c buttermilk to which ¼ ts soda is added. Boil sauce 2 min.

APPLESAUCE WEDDING CAKE

1½ c applesauce
½ c shortening
1 egg
¼ ts salt
½ ts cloves
1 c raisins
1 c boiling water
2 ts soda
2 c sugar
2 1/8 c flour
½ ts cinnamon
½ ts allspice
1 c nuts (chopped)

Combine applesauce and soda. Cream together shortening and sugar. Add egg and blend well. Add dry inredients and mix well. Add boiling water last. Bake at 350° for 35-40 min in small loaf tins.

TOASTED SPICE CAKE

2 1/3 c flour
½ ts cloves
3/4 ts salt
1 c brown sugar
1 ts soda
1 ts vanilla
1 ts baking powder
1 ts cinnamon
3/4 c shortening
2 eggs (yolks)
1¼ c sour milk

Sift together several times flour, baking powder spices and salt. Cream shortening and gradually add 1 c brown sugar and egg yolks in one brisk beating. Dissolve the soda in sour milk and add alternately with flour mixture.

Icing:

Beat 2 egg whites until stiff and gradually add 1 c brown sugar which has been sifted. Beat until mixture forms in peaks. Then spread over raw batter and sprinkle with ½ c finely chopped nuts. Bake at 350° for 25-30 min. or until toothpick comes clean.

*This is an old pioneer recipe and won first prize during the Deseret News recipe contest staged during the Centennial year, 1947.

APPLE CAKE

4 c diced apples
½ c oil
1 c raisins
2 ts vanilla
2 ts soda
1 ts salt
2 c sugar
2 unbeaten eggs
1 c nuts
2 c plus 2 Tb flour
2 ts cinnamon

Cream wet ingredients and mix well. Add sifted dry ingredients and blend, adding nuts and raisins last. Bake in 9 x 12" cake pan at 350° for 1 hr.

* * * *

A neck is something if you don't stick out you won't get in trouble up to.

Only a light globe can go out every night and still be bright the next day.

CINNAMON BUTTER BUNDT CAKE

1 yellow cake mix
3/4 c cooking oil
4 eggs
1 ts butter flavoring
1 pkg Instant Vanilla Pudding
3/4 c water
1 ts vanilla

<u>Filling</u>

¼ c sugar
2 Tb cinnamon

1. Beat cake ingredients together for 6-8 min.
2. Grease bundt pan or angel food pan.
3. Put 3/4 of batter in pan.
4. Sprinkle filling on top then add the rest of the batter on top of filling.
5. Bake 45 min at 350° or until done. Let stand for 15 min then remove from pan.
6. While warm pour glaze over top of cake.

<u>Glaze</u>

powdered sugar, milk, vanilla, butter flavoring

ANGEL CLOUDS

1 pkg angel food mix
1 c slivered almonds (chopped, not too fine)
Line muffin tins with paper bake cups. Prepare cake batter according to pkg directions. Put 1 heaping Tb of batter into each paper cup. Sprinkle 1 ts of almonds over each portion of batter. Bake at 375° for 15 min.

* * * *

If we'd all drive right, more people would be left.

An optimistic gardener is one who believes that what goes down must come up.

MONTERO'S CALIFORNIA FRUIT NUT LOAF

1. Place in large containter: 1 3/4 c flour
   1¼ c sugar 1 3/4 ts baking powder
   ½ ts salt 1 c orange tang
2. Add and stir to coat well: 2 c dried fruits cut in large pieces
   (10 ea peaches, pears, figs, and pitted dates or other fruits of your choice)
   ½ c each dried apple slices and golden raisins
   3/4 c mixed nuts, whole or halves or pieces
3. Beat well and stir in: 4 large eggs
   ¼ c water ½ ts ea vanilla & almond
4. Divide mixture in greased and floured pans, size of your choice.
5. Bake in preheated 300° oven until golden brown and toothpick comes out clean. Cover all pans with foil to prevent top being too crusty.
6. When cool, wrap in plastic and refrigerate.

LITTLE FRUIT CAKE

½ c butter or margarine
1 c sugar
1 lb fruit mix
1 c dates chopped
2 c flour
¼ ts cloves
2 eggs
1½ c applesauce
1 c raisins
1 c nuts
2 ts soda
1 ts cinnamon

Mix as cake, add applesauce alternately with dry ingredients. Put fruit and nuts in bowl with ½ c extra flour. Toss until well coated. Grease and flour loaf tin or miniature cupcake pans. Fill almost full. Bake at 325° for 20 min. Do not cook dark.

* * * *

Man's body is remarkably sensitive. Pat him on the back and his head swells.

If a buttercup is yellow, what color is a hiccup? Burple.

WALNUT RAISIN SPICE CAKE

1. Combine in blender: 1½ c seedless raisins
   1 c walnuts
   1½ c hot water
2. Blend until raisins are finely chopped, then add:
   1½ ts baking soda
3. In large bowl, cream together until light and fluffy:
   3/4 c butter or margarine & 1½ c sugar, little at a time
4. Add one at a time, beating after each addition:
   2 eggs 2 egg yolks
5. Add: 1½ ts lemon juice 1½ ts vanilla extract
6. Add raisin and nut mixture alternately with:
   2¼ c flour 1½ ts cinnamon
   ¼ ts salt
7. Pour into greased and floured pans, either a bundt pan, a tube pan, 3 8" layer pans, 9 x 13" pan or 2 loaf pans.
8. Bake at 375° for 25-30 min for layers, 35-50 min for other sizes.
9. Let cool and frost with cream cheese icing or serve either warm or cold with lemon sauce.

LEMON SAUCE

1. Combine and mix well: 2½ Tb cornstarch
   1 c sugar ½ ts salt
2. Add and cook 10 min, stirring constantly:
   1½ c boiling water
3. Remove from heat and add:
   2 Tb butter 2 beaten egg yolks
   2 Tb water juice & rind of 1 lg lemon

* * * *

Best way to make a speech: Have a good beginning and a good ending, and keep them as close together as possible.

UNBAKED FRUIT CAKE

This is so good and so easy, you may never bake another

Bake a honey spice cake (Betty Crocker Cake mix)
Cool and crumble into a large bowl.
Add to crumbled cake:
2-4 c candied fruit mix
½ c red candied cherries
½ c green candied cherries
3/4 c raisins
4½c pecan halves
1 c dates (chopped)
Now make up a pkg of Betty Crocker fluffy frosting mix according to box directions. Mix altogether with hands and press into foil-lined pan and refrigerate at least 24 hrs before cutting. Keep refrigerated. Put in tiny loaf containers for Christmas presents, if desired. Has a flavor they'll remember all year long!

ALMOND WHITE FRUIT CAKE

1 lb butter
4 c flour
9 eggs
½ ts almond extract
1 lb white sultana raisins
½ lb cherries, candied
½ lb pineapple, candied
2 c sugar
2 ts baking powder
½ lb figs (white)
½ lb citron thinly sliced
½ lb orange & lemon peel cut in strips
½ lb cocoanut, shredded
½ lb almonds, blanched and sliced

Proceed as for regular cake. Fruit should not be cut too fine and some large pieces reserved for top decoration. Makes three 2-lb cakes. Use instructions for baking according to size of pan. Do not overcook, or it will dry out. Store in an airtight tin.

* * * *

Restlessness is discontent. And discontent is the first necessity of progress. Show me a thoroughly satisfied man and I will show you a failure.--Thomas Edison

LIGHT FRUIT CAKE

1. Sift together: 4 c flour, 1½ ts cinnamon, 1½ ts salt, 1 ts nutmeg, ½ ts baking powder
2. Add, mixing until all fruit and nuts are coated: 8 c whole pecans, 1 3/4 c candied pineapple, chopped, 1 lb golden raisins, 1 3/4 c candied cherries, chopped
3. Cream together 2¼ c sugar & 1 c butter
4. Add, one at a time 6 eggs
5. Blend in 3 Tbs brandy flavoring
6. Add to fruit mixture, mixing well.
7. Turn into one 10" tube pan or two 9 x 5 x 3" loaf pans, filling 2/3 full.
8. Bake at 275° for 2½ hrs.
9. About ½ hr before cake is done, brush top with honey or light corn syrup. Decorate with fruit and nuts and return to oven.
10. Cool cake completely.
11. Wrap tightly in cheese cloth soaked with apple cider or brandy before wrapping in aluminum foil.
12. Keep in cool, dry place dampening cheese cloth often.

Delicious for any festive occasion!

SNOW PEAK FROSTING

1¼ c white corn syrup
pinch salt
2 egg whites
1 ts vanilla

In small saucepan, heat corn syrup till boiling. With electric mixer at high speed or with hand beater, beat egg whites until they form soft peaks when beater is raised. Add salt. Slowly pour in syrup; contine to beat until frosting is fluffy and forms peaks when beater is raised. Fold in vanilla. Frosts two 8 or 9" layers.

* * * *

A lot of novels have one common failing--their covers are too far apart.

A man found he really had insomnia when he couldn't even sleep after the alarm rang.

EASY CHOCOLATE ALMOND ROLL

¼ c butter
1 c flaked coconut
2/3 c sweetened condensed milk
3/4 c sugar
½ ts baking powder
3 Tb water
¼ ts baking soda
1 c diced roasted almonds
1 c semi-sweet chocolate pieces
4 eggs
½ c flour
¼ ts salt
1 ts vanilla
powdered sugar
Sweetened whipped cream, optional

Line a 10x16x1" jelly roll pan with foil. Melt butter in pan, spread evenly. Combine almonds, coconut and ½ c chocolate pieces, sprinkle over butter. Drizzle with sweetened condensed milk, set aside.

Melt remaining ½ c chocolate pieces over warm, not hot, water. Remove from heat. In large bowl beat eggs with sugar until thick and light, about 10 min. Add flour, baking powder and salt; blend well. Fold into flour mixture. Spread evenly into prepared pan. Bake at 375° for 20 min.

Sift powdered sugar over cake and cover with cloth towel. Turn out and roll up jelly-roll fashion starting from short side. Chill until filling is set, at least 1 hr. Serve with whipped cream if desired. Makes 1 10-inch roll.

* * * *

The hardest thing for a young father to learn is that other people have perfect children too.

A tearful woman phoned a reducing salon to wail that her husband had just given her a lovely present and she couldn't get into it. The operator gave her an appointment and added: "Don't you worry, Madam. We'll have you wearing that dress in no time."
"Dress?" the matron sobbed. "It's a porsche!"

GERMAN CHOCOLATE CAKE FROSTING

Combine 1 c evaporated milk with 1 c sugar, 3 egg yolks, ¼ lb margarine and 1 ts vanilla. Cook and stir over med. heat until thickened, about 12 minutes. Add 1 1/3 c flaked cocoanut, 1c chopped pecans and beat until thick enough to spread. Makes 2 2/3 c.

SEA FOAM FROSTING

Combine in saucepan 1/3 c sugar, 1/3 c firmly packed brown sugar, 1/3 c water and 1 Tb corn syrup. Cook until a little syrup dropped in cold water forms a soft ball (236°). Meanwhile, beat 1 egg white with ¼ ts cream of tartar until stiff peaks form. Add syrup to egg white in slow, steady stream, beating constantly until thick enough to spread. **Grand Prize Winner in Pillsbury Bake Contest.

FRENCH BUTTER ICING

5 Tb sifted flour | 1 c milk

Cook until mixture coats spoon then cool. Blend if not smooth. Cream ½ c sugar, ½ c butter & 1 c powdered sugar Add to pudding mixture. Can add egg yolk to thicken icing.

CARAMEL ICING

2 c brown sugar | pinch salt
3/4 c rich milk | flavoring

Cook to soft ball stage. Add pinch of salt and flavoring. Let cool, then beat to spreading consistency.

EASY PENUCHE FROSTING

½ c butter | 1 c brown sugar
¼ c milk | 2 c powdered sugar

Melt butter in saucepan; stir in sugar. Bring to boil, and cook and stir over low head for 2 min. Stir in milk; return to boiling, stirring constantly. Remove from heat and cool to lukewarm (120°). Gradually beat in powdered sugar. Add more milk if necessary to make of spreading consistency.

BOILED FROSTING

1½ c sugar
2 c boiling water
1 ts vanilla
½ ts light corn syrup
2 egg whites, stiffly beaten

Combine sugar, corn syrup and boiling water in saucepan. Cook until mixture spins a long thread. Pour syrup slowly over beaten egg whites, beating constantly. Add vanilla and beat until the frosting is cool and stiff enough to hold its shape. Makes enough to cover tops and sides of two 9" layers.

CANDY CARNIVAL FROSTING

1½ c light brown sugar
1½ c white sugar
2 Tb light corn syrup
3/4 c milk
¼ c shortening
¼ c butter
1 ts orange extract
1 c pecans, chopped

Place both sugars, corn syrup, milk, shortening, butter and salt in saucepan. Bring to full rolling boil, stirring constantly. Boil for 2 min. Cool to lukewarm. Add orange extract and beat until thick enough to spread. Add nuts and mix. If frosting becomes too thick, add a little cream or canned milk. Makes enough to frost sides and tops of two 9" layers.

MINT FROSTING

1. Beat together
   2 Tb cream
   1 ts mint extract
   3 Tb butter
   1 c powdered sugar
   3-4 drops green food coloring
2. Spread over baked cake or cookies and allow time to firm up.
3. Brush with slightly cooled glaze.

<u>Glaze</u>

1. Melt together 1 oz bittersweet chocolate, 1 Tb butter
2. When slightly cooled, brush lightly over first layer.
3. Sprinkle top with nuts if desired.

CHOCOLATE ROLL

5 egg yolks
¼ c flour
3 Tb cocoa
1 c sifted powdered sugar
½ ts salt
1 ts vanilla
5 egg whites, stiffly beaten
1 c heavy cream
8-12 large marshmallows, cut up
½ c nuts, chopped

In small bowl beat egg yolks until thick and lemon-colored. Sift together powdered sugar, flour, salt and cocoa 3 times; beat into egg yolks until well blended. Add vanilla. Fold in stiffly beaten egg whites. Bake 15 to 20 minutes in jelly roll pan (10x15x1") that's been greased, lined with wax paper and greased again. Turn out onto towel sprinkled with powdered sugar. Remove waxed paper. Roll chocolate sponge and towel up together to cool. Unroll. Whip cream and sweeten slightly. Fold in marshmallows. Spread over chocolate sponge. Roll as for jelly roll. Frost top with Chocolate Butter Cream frosting; sprinkle with chopped nuts. Chill. Slice to serve.

Chocolate Butter Cream Frosting

2 Tb butter or margarine, softened
2 c powdered sugar
1/8 ts salt
1 sq (1 oz) unsweetened chocolate, melted
1 ts vanilla
2 Tb warm cream or evaporated milk

In small mixing bowl cream butter. Add powdered sugar, salt, melted chocolate, vanilla and enough warm cream to make of spreadable consistency.

NOTE: For rich, more satiny icing increase butter to ¼ c.

* * * *

A taxpayer is one who doesn't have to pass a civil service examination to work for the Government.

READY FROSTED CAKES

1 small pkg chocolate pudding
1 Swiss chocolate cake mix
1 c chocolate bits
2 c milk
2 well-beaten eggs
1 c walnuts or pecans

Mix pudding with milk and cook like pudding as directed. Cool slightly and add cake mix and eggs. Stir until smooth. Put in 9 x 12 greased pan. Cover with chocolate bits and nuts. Bake at 350° 25-30 min. Serves 12.

* * * *

Football season must be upon us. You hear talk about tight ends without mention of designer jeans.

The nice thing about a vacation is that it fills so much of that year. If you take your vacation in August, you get your slides back in September; your bills back in October; your health back in November; and your luggage back in December.

When asked how birds know they should fly south, one third-grader replied, "It's a family tradition."

* * * *

Home cooking: Something that most contemporary women are not.

Wife (cleaning fish) to husband: "Why can't you be like other men and not catch anything?"

Businessman" "We're a nonprofit organization. We didn't mean to be, but we are."

CHERRY CHOCOLATE ROLL-UP

4 eggs
1 ts vanilla
¼ c cocoa
¼ ts salt
3/4 c sugar
½ c flour
1 ts baking powder
Powdered sugar
1 3-oz pkg cream cheese, softened
1 can (21 oz) cherry pie filling
½ pint whipping cream, whipped

Butter a 15x10x1" baking pan; line with foil or waxed paper; butter foil. Beat eggs until thick and lemon colored. Gradually beat in sugar and vanilla. Sift together flour, cocoa, baking powder, and salt. Sift dry ingredients over egg mixture; fold in.

Spread butter evenly in prepared pan. Bake at 375° about 12 min. or until top springs back when lightly touched. Loosen edges and immediately turn upside down on towel sprinkled with sifted powdered sugar. Carefully remove foil.

Trim away any stiff edges. While cake is still warm, roll cake and towel from narrow end. Cool on wire rack.

Beat cream cheese until smooth. Gradually stir in cherry pie filling. Whip cream until soft peaks form. Fold about half whipped cream into cherry mixture. Refrigerate remaining cream in tightly covered container in refrigerator.

Unroll cake and spread with cherry mixture. Roll again. Chill. Garnish with remaining whipped cream and, if you wish, dust topping lightly with sifted cocoa. Serves 8-10.

* * * *

Time that is wasted "getting even" can never be used in getting ahead.

The typewriter makes it easy to write, but it's just as hard to think as ever.

ZUCCHINI CHOCOLATE CAKE DELUXE

½ c margarine
1 3/4 c sugar
2 eggs
2½ c flour
1 ts soda
½ ts cloves
2 c grated zucchini
½ c oil
½ c sour milk
1 ts vanilla
½ ts baking powder
½ ts cinnamon
6 Tb cocoa
¼ c chocolate chips

Blend wet ingredients together. Add dry ingredients, blend well. Add chocolate chips last. Pour in a bundt pan at 325° for 40-50 minutes. Serves 12.

RHUBARB CAKE

5 c chopped rhubarb
1 pkg (3 oz) strawberry jello
1 c sugar
3 c miniature marshmallows
1 pkg yellow or white cake mix

Place rhubarb in the bottom of a greased 9x13 baking dish. Sprinkle gelatin over rhubarb. Top with sugar, then the marshmallows. Prepare cake mix according to directions. Pour batter over marshmallows and bake at 350° for 1 hr. or until cake pulls from sides of pan. Turn out onto a piece of foil large enough to fold over cake. Turn edges of foil up to form a rim. Cool. To serve, top with whipped cream. Makes 12-16 servings.

* * * *

It seems the hardest thing to give is in.

America has more TV's than bathtubs. Guess commercials aren't quite long enough to permit taking a bath.

To err is a privilege of human beings. But if you want things really fouled up, install a computer.

Criticizing an egg is easier than laying one.

Notes

Notes

cookies

Notes

TERZEL TARTS

2 c flour)
2 ts baking powder) Sift together
dash salt)
1 c butter)
1 c brown sugar) With pastry blender or fingers, work in until like corn meal

Add 1 egg and blend. Roll in balls size of walnuts and put in tiny chocolate cups. Indent each with finger or thumb and fill with jam. Place on cookie sheet. Bake at 375° for 15 min. Will freeze well.

TEA TIME TASSIES

1 (3 oz) cream cheese
½ c butter
1 c sifted flour

Let cream cheese and butter soften to room temperature. Blend it, stir in flour, chill about 1 hr. Shape into 2 doz 1" balls. Place in tiny ungreased muffin cups. Shape dough around sides and bottom to leave hole in center.

Pecan Filling

Beat 1 egg together with 3/4 c brown sugar, 1 Tb butter, 1 ts vanilla, dash salt, 2/3 c chopped pecans. Put a little in each cup, few more nuts on top. Bake at 325° for 25 min or until filling is set. Let cool before removing from pan.

DAD'S COOKIES

1 c white sugar
1 c butter
Pinch of salt
2 c flour
½ ts soda
1½ c coconut
1 c brown sugar
2 eggs, beaten well
Vanilla flavoring
1 ts baking powder
2 c oatmeal

Mix flour with oatmeal, soda and baking powder. Blend butter, sugar and eggs; then mix altogether and roll in small balls. Bake at 350 until light brown 8-10 min.

ENGLISH TOFFEE COOKIES

1 c butter
1 c brown sugar
1 egg
1 ts vanilla
2 c flour

Cream sugar and butter. Stir remainder until blended and pat into 10 x 15 jelly roll pan. Bake at 350° 15-25 min until barely brown. Remove from oven. Break up large Hershey bar and put pieces on hot cookies and spread around as the chocolate melts. Sprinkle with chopped slivered almonds.

COCONUT BUTTER CHEWS

3/4 c butter
3 Tb sugar
1 3/4 c flour

Mix as for pie crust and put in bottom of 9 x 12 pan and bake 15 min at 375°. If using pyrex, bake at 325°. Remove from oven and spread with the following mixture:

3 beaten egg yolks
2 c brown sugar
3/4 c shredded coconut
½ c chopped nuts

Mix together and fold in 3 stiffly beaten egg whites. Spread over first mixture and bake at 375° for 20 min.

CHOCOLATE MINT COOKIES

3¼ c sifted flour
1 ts baking soda
½ ts salt
1 c soft butter or marg.
1 c granulated sugar
½ c brown sugar, packed
2 eggs
1½ ts vanilla
1½ c seedless raisins
4 doz sm chocolate mints

Sift dry ingredients together. Cream butter with both kinds of sugar, eggs and vanilla. Mix in raisins. Chill dough. Shape small balls around chocolate mints. Bake at 375° 10-12 min. Makes 4 doz.

NO BAKE SKEDATTLES

1 6-oz pkg chocolate chips	
2 c chow mein noodles 1 c miniature marshmallows 1 c unsalted, shelled peanuts	Mix in large bowl
3/4 c sugar ½ c canned milk 2 Tb butter	Combine in saucepan

Bring to a full boil over high heat, stirring constantly. Remove from heat and add chocolate chips. Stir to melt. Let stand 15 minutes. Pour over noodle mixture and stir. Drop by spoonsful onto waxed paper. Chill until set.

BUTTERSCOTCH COOKIES

1 c shortening
2 eggs, unbeaten
½ c glace cherries
½ c raisins
½ ts salt
1 ts soda
2 c brown sugar
1 ts vanilla
½ c walnuts
¼ c candied ginger (if desired)
½ ts baking powder
3-4 c flour

Sift soda, baking powder, salt with flour. Cream shortening adding sugar gradually, beating between additions. Add eggs and mix well. Gradually add dry ingredients. Form dough into 2-3 cookie size rolls and wrap in heavy wax paper. Chill overnight. Cut and bake when desired. Bake in 375-400 oven until light brown. Best when not quite done.

SESAME SEED COOKIES

1 c butter, marg. or shortening
1 c sugar
1 egg beaten
1 ts vanilla
2 c flour
½ ts soda
¼ ts salt
3/4 to 1 c toasted sesame seeds

Cream butter and sugar. Add beaten eggs and vanilla. Sift dry ingredients together and add to creamed mixture. Chill about 1 hr. Form into small balls, roll in sesame seeds. Place on greased cookie sheet and flatten with bottom of a water glass. Bake 375° for 10-15 min. *Can add ½ c toasted sesame seeds to dough and use remainder for rolling before baking. (Toast in heavy skillet over high heat, shaking until brown).

CORN FLAKE MACAROONS

2 egg whites
1 c sugar
2 c cornflakes
½ c broken nut meats
½ ts vanilla
1 c shredded coconut

Beat egg whites until they are stiff enough to hold a peak. Fold in sugar carefully. Add vanilla. Next fold in all the remaining ingredients. Drop on a well greased baking sheet, spacing about ½" apart. Bake at 350° about 20 min. Makes 1½ doz.

HONEY SCOTCH COOKIES

¼ lb butter
yolk of 1 egg
1¼ c flour
½ c sugar
¼ ts salt

Roll in balls. Place on cookie sheet & flatten with bottom of glass. Beat egg white and brush on top of dough. Sprinkle with sugar and cinnamon. Bake at 375° for 10 min.

SUGAR COOKIES

4½ c flour
1 ts salt
3 eggs
2 ts vanilla
¼ ts soda
1½ c sugar
1 ts almond extract
½ lb butter

Blend sugar, butter and eggs; then add dry ingredients. Roll out thin, cut and bake at 350°.

SOFT COOKIES

½ c sugar and 1 egg
¼ c milk
1 3/4 c flour
½ ts soda
½ c oil
2 ts vanilla
¼ ts salt
2 ts baking powder

Beat sugar and egg until light. Add oil and milk. Mix and sift dry ingredients. Combine. Chill 45 min. in frig. Cut cookies and press with fork. Bake 10 min at 400°.

HELLO DOLLY COOKIES

¼ c melted butter
1 c chocolate chips
1 c chopped nuts
1 c crushed graham crackers
1 c coconut
1 c sweetened condensed milk

Melt butter in 8 x 8" baking pan. Crush graham crackers and press down into melted butter. Top with chocolate chips, coconut and chopped nuts. Pour sweetened condensed milk over all and bake for 25 min. at 350°. Cut into squares while warm.

FRUIT REFRIGERATOR COOKIES

½ c flour
1 lb candied cherries
1 lb pecans, chopped
½ lb raisins
1 lb green & red pineapple

Dredge fruit and nuts with ½ c flour.

4 c flour
1 lb butter
½ ts cinnamon
1 ts baking powder
½ ts almond extract
2 c sugar
3 eggs
1 ts soda
1 ts vanilla

Beat well sugar, shortening, eggs and flavoring. Sift 4 c flour with dry ingredients and gradually add to the first mixture. Mix with hands and form into small rolls. Store in freezer. When ready to make slice ¼" thick and bake at 375° for 10 min or until light brown.

THE GREAT PUMPKIN SQUARE

1 can Libby's Pie filling (29 oz) (Just plain pumpkin)
1 Jiffy cake mix
¼ c margarine or butter

Prepare pumpkin filling as if making a pie. In separate bowl add the Jiffy cake mix and cut in the margarine as if making pie crust. Pour on top of pumpkin mixture which has been placed in a 13 x 9 x 2 greased pan. Bake at 350° for one hr.

DREAM BARS

½ c margarine
½ c brown sugar, packed
½ ts salt
1 c sifted flour

Cream the first three ingredients together and add flour. Mixture will be dry. Sometimes add an extra Tb of margarine to make it spread easier. Pat into a greased 9 x 12 cake pan. Bake at 325° for 15 min.

2 well beaten eggs
1 c brown sugar, packed
1 ts vanilla
2 Tb flour
½ ts baking powder
1½ c coconut
1 c chopped nuts

Spread over the first mixture as soon as it comes from oven. (Second mixture is runny.) Put back into oven immediately and bake another 20 min. Be careful not to over-bake.

* * * *

The world stands aside to let anyone pass who knows where he is going.

If a man does not know his port, no wind will be favorable.

Today's mighty oak is merely yesterday's little nut that managed to hold its ground.

Old age is like everything else. To make a success of it you've got to start young.

Never insult an alligator until after you've crossed the river.

Improvement begins with "I".

ORANGE DATE BARS

Filling:

20 candy orange slices, cut up)
1 c dates, cut up)
3/4 c water)
2 Tb flour)
pinch salt)
1 ts vanilla)

Cook until thick, stirring constantly

Dough

1 c brown sugar
3/4 c margarine
2 eggs
1½ c flour
½ ts soda

Spread half the dough on botton of 8 x 12" pan. Drop filling by Tbs and spread around lightly. Cover with other half of dough. Bake at 350° for 35 min. Cool and cut in bars. This is one of our very favorites, thanks to Joan!

SPICY RAISIN BARS

1 c raisins
1 3/4 c water
1 ts soda
1½ c sugar
3/4 c shortening
½ ts salt
2 eggs beaten
1 c raisin liquid
2½ c flour
1 ts cinnamon
1 Tb cocoa

Bring to a boil raisins and water. Save 1 c liquid. To this add 1 ts soda. Cool. Sift dry ingredients together; add to creamed sugar, shortening and egg mixture. Add raisin liquid containing soda and raisins. ½ c nuts may be added if desired. Bake in greased, shallow jelly roll type pan, about 11 x 17" for 25 min at 375°. Cool in pan. Frost with sugar glaze. Cut in squares.

REFRIGERATOR OATMEAL COOKIES

1 c shortening
1 c white sugar
1 ts vanilla
1 ts salt
3 c quick cooking oats
1 c brown sugar
2 well beaten eggs
1½ c flour
1 ts soda
½ c chopped walnuts

Cream shortening and sugars; add eggs and vanilla; beat well. Add sifted dry ingredients. Add oatmeal and nuts. Mix well. Shape in rolls, wrap in waxed paper, chill thoroughly overnight. Slice ¼" thick, bake at 350° for 10-12 min. Makes about 5 doz.

PEANUT BUTTER OATMEAL COOKIES

1½ c peanut butter
3/4 c butter or margarine
3/4 c shortening
3 3/4 c packed br. sugar
3 eggs
1 c chocolate chips
3 ts vanilla
3 c whole wheat flour
3 ts baking powder
1½ ts salt
3 c rolled oats

Mix together peanut butter, butter, shortening and sugar till creamy. Add eggs and vanilla and mix well. Add flour, baking powder and salt to creamed mixture, blending well. Stir in oats. Drop cookies onto ungreased cookie sheet. Bake 14 min at 350°. Makes 12 doz.

PINEAPPLE CHERRY SQUARES

1 c flour
½ c margarine or butter
pinch salt
1⅓ Tb sugar
½ ts almond extract

Mix and pat in 6 x 9¼" pan. Bake for 20 min until brown.

Filling

1 c crushed pineapple
½ c sugar
½ ts almond extract
3/4 c chopped maraschino cherries
2 Tb corn starch

Cook until thick, stirring constantly. Spread on first mixture. Beat 2 egg whites, 2 Tb sugar until stiff. Spread on second mixture. Sprinkle with coconut and brown in oven.

PINEAPPLE BARS

1 c butter or margarine
3/4 c sugar
3 c flour
1 ts vanilla
½ ts salt

Combine and mix well until mixture resembles fine crumbs. Firmly press 2/3 of crumb mixture into bottom of an ungreased 15 x 9 pan. Then mix:

3½ c undrained crushed pineapple
3/4 c sugar
3 Tb corn starch
¼ ts salt
1 ts lemon juice

Combine all ingredients in saucepan and cook over medium heat stirring constantly until thick . Pour over pressed crumbs and sprinkle remaining 1/3 of crumb mixture over the pineapple and bake 50 min. at 325°.

MARZIPAN BARS

1. Cream together ½ c butter, ½ c brown sugar
2. Add: 1 egg yolk, 1 ts vanilla
3. Sift together: 2 c flour, ½ ts soda, ¼ ts salt
4. Add to creamed mixture, alternately, ¼ c milk
5. Pat dough into thin layer in the bottom of greased 10 x 15" pan.
6. Spread over top of butter mixture, 1 c raspberry jam
7. Break into small pieces, 1 8-oz can almond paste
8. Add, mix until smooth: 1 egg white, ½ c sugar, 3 Tb softened butter
9. Beat in, one at a time, 3 eggs
10. Tint mixture light green with 2-3 drops food coloring.
11. Pour over jam.
12. Bake at 350° for 35-40 min. Spread with chocolate frosting. Makes 96 squares which freeze well.

DATE CRUMBLES

Batter

½ lb butter or 1 c shortening | 1 c brown sugar
1 c flour | 1 ts baking powder
3 c oatmeal
1 ts soda in 2 ts boiling water | 2 ts vanilla

Mix ingredients well and put half of mixture into cake pan.

Make filling as follows:

2 c pitted cut dates | 1 c brown sugar
2/3 c water | 1 Tb lemon juice
1 ts grated lemon rind | 2 Tb butter

Boil above for 15 min. Cool and add to batter mix in pan. Put remaining crumbs on top and bake 25 min in 350°. (Also called Matrimonial Cake because it is so special!)

DATE CHERRY SQUARES

2 c flour)
1 c butter)
3/4 c brown sugar)
Mix well together and press in cake pan evenly

Filling:

1 lb sliced dates)
1 lb cherries, candied, any color)
1 pkg slivered almonds)
Layer in pan

Pour 1 can Eagle Brand Sweetened Condensed milk over and bake at 325 for 35 min. Slice warm.

NOTE: See Pot Pourri section, p. 448 for recipe on how to make your own sweetened condensed milk. A real money saver and just as effective in any recipe.

* * * *

Ever notice . . . that when your arms are filled with packages, the sign on the door says "Pull"?

I found out how completely my children were geared to television the morning my four-year-old awoke with her first case of laryngitis. She rushed up to me and excitedly whispered, "Mommy, someone's turned my volume down!"

FRUIT COCKTAIL COOKIES

4 c flour
1 ts soda
½ c sugar
3 eggs
1 ts salt
1½ c chopped nuts
1 c shortening
½ c brown sugar
1 ts cloves
1 c raisins
1 ts vanilla
2 c drained fruit cocktail

Sift flour, soda, baking powder and spices. Add raisins and fruit cocktail. Add nuts to dry ingredients. Cream shortening, sugar, eggs and vanilla. Drop by teaspoon on cookie sheet. Bake at 350° until light brown.

FINNISH ALMOND BARS

2 c flour
1 c butter
½ c sugar
1 Tb almond extract

Combine flour, sugar and butter. Add almond extract. Press evenly in 8½ x 13" pan. Sprinkle with 2 Tb sugar and ½ c slivered blanched almonds. Bake at 375° for 15 min. or until light golden brown. Cool slightly and cut into bars. Cool completely before removing from pan.

* * * *

My child once said to me: "Mother, are we hundredaires, or thousandaires."

Inscription on the tombstone of a hypochondriac: "Now will you believe I'm sick?"

CASHEW CARMEL YUMMIES

3/4 c sifted flour
½ ts baking powder
¼ ts salt
2 eggs
½ c sugar
½ c brown sugar, packed
½ c chopped salted cashews

Sift together flour, baking powder and salt. Beat eggs until blended. Gradually add sugars and mix until blended.

Stir in dry ingredients along with chopped nuts. Spread in well-greased and lightly floured 9 x 9 x 2" pan. Bake at 350° for 20-25 minutes or until it springs back when touched. Remove from oven immediately and spread with cashew topping, covering the cookies completely. Place under broiler until bubbles form on topping and it becomes light brown 1-3 min. Cut into bars while still warm, then allow to cool thoroughly in pan.

Cashew Topping:
Melt 2 Tb butter. Add ¼ c brown sugar, 1½ Tb cream, and 1/3 c chopped salted cashews.

FRESH ORANGE CHEWIES

2 med oranges
2 eggs
1 pkg Pillsbury's Buttercream Vanilla Frosting Mix (regular size)
1 c sifted flour
3/4 ts baking powder
½ ts salt
1/3 c butter or margarine
2/3 c chopped walnuts
2 Tb butter
1-2 Tbs water

Grate oranges to obtain 1 Tb orange rind; set aside. Peel and section oranges; chop, combine with rind and set aside. Beat eggs in large mixer bowl at high speed for 2 min. Add 1½ c firmly packed dry frosting mix, flour, baking powder, salt and 1/3 c butter.Blend at low speed. Add nuts and oranges; beat at low speed until blended.

Spread batter in greased and floured 13 x 9" pan. Bake at 350° for 30-35 min until golden brown.
In saucepan, heat remaining dry frosting mix, 2 Tb butter, and water. Stir over med heat until smooth. Drizzle over cool bars. Makes 24 lg bars, or 48 tea-size bars.

LEMON BARS

Crust:
1 c softened butter or margarine
½ c powdered sugar
2 c flour
dash of salt

Combine all ingredients. Mix well and press well into 9 x 13" pan. Bake at 350° for 15-20 min, until nicely browned.

Filling:
4 well beaten eggs
2 c sugar
6 Tb lemon juice or juice & rind of 2 lemons
4 Tb flour
¼ scant ts salt
¼ ts nutmeg

Pour second mixture over slightly cooled crust and bake at 350° for 25 min. Cool slightly; sprinkle with powdered sugar. Cool and cut.

* * * *

A wise school teacher sends this note to all parents on the first day of school: If you promise not to believe everything your child says happens at school, I'll promise not to believe everything he says happens at home.

A lady was entertaining the small son of a friend. "Are you sure you can cut your own meat, Tommy? she inquired.
"Oh, yes, thanks, I've often had it as tough as this at home."

OATMEAL CARMELITAS

3/4 c brown sugar
1 c oatmeal
½ ts salt
3/4 c butter, melted
1 ts baking soda
1 c flour

Combine and press ½ mixture in bottom 9 x 9" pan. Bake at 350° for 10 min.

Filling

3/4 c caramel topping with 2 Tb flour
1 c semi-sweet chocolate pieces
3/4 c chopped pecans

Place filling on warm oatmeal mixture. Spread remaining oatmeal mixture on top. Bake at 350° for 15-20 min. Cool before cutting. Freezes well.

BROWNIES

½ c butter
3/4 c flour
½ ts baking powder
2 sq melted chocolate
½ c nuts
1 c sugar
2 eggs
¼ ts salt
1 ts vanilla

Melt butter and chocolate and mix with all other ingredients. Bake at 350° until pulls away from sides. Do not overbake. Ice with chocolate icing.

CHOCO-MARSHMALLOW BROWNIES

1 c butter
2 c sugar
1½ c flour
1½ c chopped nuts
½ c cocoa
4 eggs (one at a time)
2 ts vanilla
½ ts salt

Cream butter, cocoa and sugar. Add remaining ingredients and put in 11 x 17 x 3/4" pan. Bake 20-25 min at 350°. Remove from oven and sprinkle with 1 pkg miniature marshmallows. Spread to all surface areas. Return to oven for exactly 3 min till they puff and flow together. Remove from oven and cool before icing with:

½ c butter
1 2/3 c powdered sugar
1/3 c cocoa
1/3 c canned milk

FRUIT-NUT SQUARES

2 c sifted flour
1 c brown sugar, packed
½ c soft butter
2 ts baking powder
1 Tb grated orange rind
3/4 c chopped walnuts
1 egg
1 ts soda
½ ts salt
1 c buttermilk or sour milk
3/4 c dates chopped
3/4 c maraschino cherries

Beat sugar, butter and egg until fluffy. Sift flour, baking powder, soda and salt together. Mix together with dates, nuts, cherries and rind with 2 Tb flour. Mix dry ingredients into creamed mixture alternately with buttermilk. Add fruit and nuts, stir to blend. Pour into greased pan 9 x 13" (or a little larger). Bake in 375° oven for 30-35 min.

When cool it may be iced with the following: Juice of half an orange, a little grated orange rind, butter and icing sugar with enough boiling water to make an icing easy to spread.

THE BISHOP'S SQUARES

½ c sugar
½ c shortening
1¼ c flour
vanilla
yolks of 2 eggs
2 Tb water
1 ts baking powder

Mix and put dough on greased sheet. Beat 2 egg whites stiff and add 1 c brown sugar. Stir well together and spread over cookie mixture. Sprinkle with chopped nuts. Bake 30-35 minutes at 350°. Cut in squares while still warm. Deliciously different!

* * * *

Women are trying to get mens' wages now, but then they always have.

Middle age is when you know all the answers and nobody asks you the questions.

ALMOND BROWNIES

4 sq (1 oz ea) unsweetened chocolate
2/3 c shortening — 2 c sugar
4 eggs — 1¼ c all purpose flour
1 ts baking powder — 1 ts salt
1 c chopped nuts — 1 c chopped almond paste

Heat oven to 350°. Grease baking pan 13 x 9 x 2". Heat chocolate and shortening in 3 qt saucepan over low heat until melted; remove from heat. Stir in remaining ingredients. Spread in pan.
Bake until brownies begin to pull away from sides of pan, about 30 min. Do not overbake. Cool slightly, cut into bars, about 2x1½". About 3 doz bars.

SESAME BARS

4 pkg (2½ oz ea) sesame seed — 1 c butter or margarine softened
2 c br. sugar packed — 1 c flour
2 eggs, beaten — 3/4 ts salt
2 Tb hot water

Heat oven to 325°. Mix all ingredients. Spread in greased jelly roll pan 15½ x 10½ x 1". Bake until center is set, 45 min. Cool; cut into bars 2 x 1" Makes 6 doz.

BUTTERSCOTCH BROWNIES

¼ c butter — 1 c brown sugar
1 ts vanilla — ½ c flour
½ ts baking powder — 1 egg
½ ts salt — ½ c chopped nuts
3/4 c shredded coconut

Melt together butter, brown sugar. Cool slightly. Beat in egg and vanilla. Sift flour, salt and baking powder together. Add to butter mixture. Mix well. Add nuts and coconut. Bake ½ hr at 350°.

Icing

1½ c brown sugar — ¼ c butter
¼ c milk — 1 Tb flour
1 ts vanilla

Mix and bring to boil. Stir for 1 min and beat until thick. Put over cake before it comes too stiff to spread.

THUMBPRINT COOKIES

¼ c butter or margarine softened
¼ c shortening
¼ c brown sugar packed
1 egg, separated
½ ts vanilla
1 c flour
¼ ts salt
3/4 c finely chopped nuts
Jelly

Heat oven to 350°. Mix thoroughly butter, shortening, sugar, egg yolk and vanilla. Work in flour and salt until dough holds together. Shape dough by teaspoonsful into 1" balls. Beat egg white slightly. Dip each dough ball into egg white; roll in nuts. Place 1" apart on ungreased baking sheet; press thumb deep into center of each. Bake about 10 min or until light brown. Immediately, remove from baking sheet. Cool; fill thumbprint with jelly. Makes 3 doz. Using various kinds of jelly makes a very colorful and tasty treat!

GUM DROP COOKIES

1½ c margarine
1½ c white sugar
2 ts vanilla
1⅓ ts salt
4 c oatmeal (quick)
1⅓ c brown sugar
4 eggs
3 c flour
2 ts soda
2 pkg gumdrops
nuts optional

Cream shortening, sugars, eggs and vanilla. Add dry ingredients. Mix well and add gumdrops. Drop on greased baking sheet. Bake at 350° for 10-12 min. If you can keep the kids out of 'em long enough, they freeze well!

* * * * * * * * * * *

It was a wild week on television. One channel showed The Ten Commandments, and the other channels were breaking six of them.

An optimist is someone who says he's going to watch the first 15 minutes of the late late show.

ORANGE FROSTED CARROT DROPS

2 lg carrots, cut in chunks
3/4 c sugar
2½ c flour
3/4 ts baking soda
orange frosting
1 c butter or margarine
2 eggs
2 ts baking powder
½ ts vanilla
grated orange peel, opt.

Preheat oven to 350°. Cook carrots in small amount of boiling water 20 min or until very tender. Drain and mash well, then measure 1 c. Set aside to cool.

Cream butter, sugar and eggs together until well blended. Stir in carrots. Mix flour, baking powder, soda and salt. Stir into first mixture and add vanilla.

Drop by dessert spoonsful about 2" apart onto ungreased baking sheets. Batter will spread slightly.

Bake 15 min or until golden brown. Remove to wire racks to cool. Spread with frosting and if desired, sprinkle with grated orange peel.

Frosting

3 Tb soft butter or margarine
1 Tb lemon juice
2 Tb orange juice
2-2¼ c confectioners' sugar

Combine butter with juices and gradually stir in the sugar, mixing until smooth and of spreading consistency.

PEANUT BUTTER CRISSCROSSES

1 c shortening
1 c sugar
1 c brown sugar
1 ts vanilla
2 beaten eggs
1 c peanut butter
3 c sifted flour
2 ts soda
dash of salt

Preheat oven to 375°. Cream shortening, sugar and vanilla. Add eggs, beat; stir in peanut butter. Sift dry ingredients; stir into mixture. Form into small balls; place on ungreased cookie sheet. Press with back of fork to make crisscross. Bake 10 min. Makes 8 doz.

JIM DANDY COOKIES

1½ c flour
½ ts salt
½ c cherry juice
¼ c maraschino cherries
2 sq (1 oz ea) unsweetened chocolate, melted
½ c chopped nuts
chocolate frosting
½ ts soda
2/3 c brown sugar
1 egg
2 Tb milk
marshmallows

Sift flour, soda and salt together. Set aside. Cream brown sugar, shortening and eggs until fluffy. Add dry ingredients alternately with cherry juice and milk. Stir in melted chocolate, cherries and chopped nuts. Drop by teaspoonsful onto greased baking sheet and bake at 350° for 12-15 min. Remove from oven and immediately place a cut marshmallow on top of each cookie, cut side down. Cool and frost with chocolate frosting.

Chocolate Frosting

2 c confectioners' sugar
2 Tb light cream or evaporated milk
½ ts vanilla
3 Tb butter
1 sq (1 oz) unsweetened chocolate melted

Combine all ingredients and beat until smooth. Spread on cooled cookies.

LEMONADE COOKIES

1 c margarine
2 eggs
1 ts soda
1 c sugar
3 c flour
1 6-oz can lemonade

Use half lemonade in batter. Blend all ingredients together and drop on cookie sheet. Brush rest of lemonade on top of cookies. Bake at 350° until light brown.

* * * *

Do you realize that before television no one really knew what a headache looked like?

In real-estate section: "Beautiful home overlooking the mortgage."

Allergy doctor: antisneezeologist.

THE BEST OF ALL CHOCOLATE CHIP COOKIES

1 c solid shortening
½ c butter or margarine
1 1/3 c sugar & 1 c br. sugar
4 eggs
1 Tb vanilla
1 ts lemon juice
2 ts soda
1½ ts salt
1 ts cinnamon
½ c rolled oats
3 c flour
2 lg pkg (12 oz ea) semi-sweet chocolate chips
2 c walnuts, chopped

In large bowl beat shortening, butter and sugars at high speed until light and fluffy (about 5 min). Add eggs, one at a time, beating well after each addition. Beat in vanilla and lemon juice.

In another bowl, stir together baking soda, salt, cinnamon, oats and flour. Beat into creamed mixture until well combined; stir in chocolate chips and nuts.

For each cookie, drop a scant ¼ c dough on a lightly greased baking sheet, spacing cookies about 3" apart. Bake in a 350° oven for 16-18 min or until golden brown. Transfer to racks and let cool. Makes about 3 doz large cookies.

PEANUT BLOSSOMS

1 3/4 c flour
1 ts soda
½ ts salt
½ c sugar
½ c brown sugar packed
½ c shortening
½ c peanut butter
1 egg
2 Tb milk
1 ts vanilla
48 milk chocolate candy kisses

Combine all ingredients except candy in large mixer bowl. Mix on lowest speed of mixer until dough forms. Shape dough into balls, using a rounded teaspoonful for each. Roll balls in sugar; place on ungreased cookie sheets. Bake at 375° for 10-12 min. Top each cookie immediately with a candy kiss; press down firmly so cookie cracks around edges.

OLD FASHIONED OATMEAL COOKIES

1 c raisins
1 c water
3/4 c shortening
1½ c sugar
2 eggs
1 ts vanilla
2½ c flour
1 ts soda
1 ts salt
1 ts cinnamon
½ ts baking powder
½ ts cloves
2 c oats
½ c chopped nuts

Simmer raisins and water over med. heat until raisins are plump, about 15 min. Drain raisins, reserving the liquid. Add enough water to reserved liquid to measure ½ c.

Heat oven to 400°. Mix thoroughly shortening, sugar, eggs, and vanilla. Stir in reserved liquid. Blend in remaining ingredients. Drop dough by rounded teaspoonsful about 2" apart onto ungreased baking sheet. Bake 8 to 10 min or until light brown. Makes 6½ doz.

"BETTER THAN ROBERT REDFORD" SQUARES

1 c flour ½ c butter
1 c pecans (finely chopped)
1 8-oz pkg cream cheese
1 c icing sugar
1 lg container Cool Whip
1 lg pkg instant vanilla pudding mix
1 lg pkg instant chocolate pudding mix
3 c cold milk
1 grated milk chocolate bar

Mix first three ingredients until crumbly. Press into 9x13 pan. Bake 350 ° for 15-20 min or until golden. Mix cream cheese, icing sugar and ½ Cool Whip. Spread over cooled crust.

Mix both pudding mixes with milk until smooth and thickened. Spread remaining Cool Whip over the top. Cool. Sprinkle with grated chocolate bar. Refrigerate.

PARGAS GINGER COOKIES

1.	Cream until fluffy	1 c butter
		7/8 c sugar (1 c less 2 Tb)
2.	Beat in	1 egg
3.	Add boiled and cooled	1/3 c molasses
		1 ts ginger
		1 ts ground cloves
		1 ts cinnamon
		2 ts grated orange rind
4.	Combine and stir in	3½ c flour, sifted
		2 ts baking soda

5. Chill dough until thoroughly cold.
6. Roll as thin as possible. Cut out desired shapes.
7. Place on baking sheet. Bake in preheated oven at 400° for 3-5 min or until light brown.
8. Cool thoroughly on rack. Store in airtight container. Container had better be kid-proof! Makes 6-10 doz.

* * * *

TV weather forecast: "Fair today--and grossly unfair tomorrow."

Husband to wife: "It's a deal! I'll stop quoting Ronald Reagan if you'll stop quoting Erma Bombeck."

In a radio interview marking the grand opening of a new supermarket, the store manager praised the long service record of an employee: "The meat head's been with us 28 years."

Lawrence Welk, reading directly from a cue card: "And now the boys in the band will play a medley from World War Eye Eye."

CHOCOLATE DROPS

½ c butter or margarine
1 c sugar
1 egg
½ ts salt
1/3 c buttermilk
1 c chopped nuts
1 ts vanilla
1 3/4 c flour
½ ts soda
2 oz melted unsweetened chocolate (cool)
Vanilla Butter icing

Mix thoroughly butter, sugar, egg, chocolate, buttermilk, and vanilla. Stir in flour, soda, salt and nuts. Cover; chill 1 hr. Heat oven to 400°. Drop dough by rounded teaspoonsful 2" apart on ungreased baking sheet. Bake 8-10 min or until almost no imprint remains when touched. Immediately remove from baking sheet; cool. Frost with the following icing:

Blend ¼ c soft butter or margarine and 2 c confectioners' sugar. Stir in 1 ts vanilla and about 2 Tb light cream. Makes 4½ doz cookies.

CHOCOLATE MACAROONS

4 egg whites, beaten till soft peaks

Add 1 c sugar very gradually, ½ ts salt and beat until stiff. Add 1 ts vanilla. Fold in lg pkg chocolate chips (12 oz). Line cookie sheet with brown paper and drop by spoonsful on to paper. Bake at 325° about 20 min. Cool on paper before removing. Can use mint chocolate chips and/or 1½ c shredded coconut.

DOUBLE CHOCOLATE COOKIES

2 eggs beaten
½ c soft butter
1 c sour cream
2 c packaged biscuit mix
2 3 5/8-oz pkg instant chocolate pudding mix
1 6-oz package semi-sweet chocolate chips
½ c nuts

In mixing bowl stir together eggs, sour cream, butter, biscuit mix and pudding mix. Stir in chocolate chips and nuts. Drop by spoonsful onto ungreased cookie sheet. Bake at 350° about 12 min. Makes 6 doz.

OATMEAL MACAROONS

½ c sugar
½ c melted shortening
½ ts salt
1 ts vanilla
½ ts soda
2 c rolled oats
½ c brown sugar
1 egg, beaten
½ c coconut
1 banana mashed
1 c sifted flour

Combine the ingredients in the order given. Drop from teaspoon on greased baking sheet. Press down with fork. Bake in a moderate oven of 350° for 12-15 minutes. Makes 3½ doz.

FRUIT PINWHEEL COOKIES

2¼ c sifted flour
½ ts salt
½ c butter
½ c sugar
½ c brown sugar
1 ts vanilla
1 egg

Filling

½ lb dates, chopped
½ c sugar
½ c nuts
6 oz figs, chopped
½ c water

Boil filling ingredients about 5 min. or until thickened. Add nuts and cool. Chill dough for 30 min. then divide into 4ths and roll each into oblong piece. Spread on filling and roll. Bake at 375° for 8-10 min.

GINGER SNAPS

3/4 c oil (no substitute)
1 lg egg
1 ts cloves
1½ ts ginger
2 c unsifted flour
½ c molasses
2 ts soda
1 ts cinnamon
¼ ts salt
1 c sugar

Beat egg, add sugar, molasses and oil. Beat well. Sift together flour, spices, soda, salt and add to oil mixture. Make into balls size of nickle (no larger). Dip in sugar and lay with sugar side up on oiled cookie sheet. Bake at 350° about 10-12 min.

Notes

Notes

pies

Notes

NEVER FAIL PIE CRUST

1 lb lard
5 c flour
1 ts salt
½ ts baking powder
2 ts brown sugar

Combine above and add 1 egg slightly beaten plus 2 Tb vinegar. Put in cup and fill with water to make 8 oz. Mix together with pastry blender. Roll in three balls to be used instantly or frozen and used later. Makes at least 4 crusts.

GRAHAM CRACKER CRUST

1½ c graham cracker crumbs
3 Tb sugar
1/3 c butter, melted

Heat oven to 350°. Mix mixture together in a 9" pie tin. Reserve ¼ c cracker crumbs for top covering over pie filling if desired. Mix mixture firmly into even layer on bottom and sides of pan. Bake 1 min. Cool and fill. Never serve it hot.

BLACK BOTTOM CRUST

22 ginger snaps (finely rolled)
¼ c softened butter or margarine
¼ c sugar

Thoroughly blend together ginger snap crumbs, softened butter or margarine and sugar. Pour mixture into 9" pie plate. Firmly press into an even layer against bottom and sides of plate.

CRUNCHY COOKY CRUST

1 c flour
½ c margarine
¼ c finely chopped nuts
¼ c powdered sugar

Mix above until mixture forms a ball. Press firmly and evenly against bottom and sides of pie pan. Bake in hot oven about 12 min or until light brown. Cool and fill as desired.

PUMPKIN CHEESE PIE

1/3 c margarine
1/3 c sugar
1 egg
1¼ c flour
2 pkg (8 oz) cream cheese

3/4 c sugar
1 can (16 oz) pumpkin
1 ts cinnamon
¼ ts ginger
2 eggs
dash of salt

Cream together the margarine and sugar until light and fluffy. Blend in 1 egg. Add the flour and mix well. Press the dough on the bottom and 2" high around the sides of a 9" springform pan. Bake at 400° for 5 min. Reduce oven temperature to 350° and remove the pan.

Combine the softened cream cheese and sugar, mixing at medium speed until well blended. Blend in the pumpkin, spices and a dash of salt. Mix well. Add the eggs, one at a time, mixing well after each addition. Pour mixture into pastry lined pan; smooth the surface to the edge of crust. Bake at 350° for 50 min. Loosen the cake from the rim of the pan; cool before removing the rim of the pan. Chill. Garnish with whipped cream just before serving, if desired.

CHEESECAKE

Mix the following in a blender:

1 c cottage cheese
3/4 c sugar
1 egg

1 8-oz pkg cream cheese
1 ts vanilla

Pour into graham cracker crust and bake at 325° for 25 min. Mix and spread over the top of hot pie: 1 c sour cream, 3 Tb sugar, 1 ts vanilla. Put pie in 400° oven for 7 min. After pie has cooled, put in refrigerator for 24 hrs before serving. Top with favorite topping.

FLAKY PIECRUST

2 c flour
1 ts salt

½ c salad oil) measure to-
¼ c milk) gether but do not stir.

Pour ingredients into flour and stir. Gather together in two balls. Roll between wax paper. Peel off paper and press into pie tin. Prick bottom of shell if being used for single crust pie. Makes one two-crust pie or two single crust pies. Never a failure and always flaky!

CIDER CUSTARD PIE

Simmer 4 c cider until reduced to 1 c. Meanwhile, beat 3 eggs until thick and lemony. Gradually add 2 Tb cooking oil, 2 Tb flour, 1 c sugar, and 1 c milk blended with the cider. Pour into pastry lined pan and bake at 400° for 10 min, then at 350° about 25 min or until knife blade comes out clean.

LIP SMACKIN' CHERRY PIE

1 can sweetened condensed milk
1/3 c lemon juice
½ ts almond
1 ts vanilla
Mix together

<u>Topping</u>

2 c drained cherries (pie)
2/3 c juice
¼ c sugar
1 Tb cornstarch & red food coloring

Mix and bring to boil. Cool before putting on pie.

THREE-MINUTE PIE SHELL

1½ c flour
1½ ts sugar
1 ts salt
2 Tb cold milk
½ c oil

Put into pie pan. Stir and press into pan. Add slivered almonds and put into dough. Serve with whipped cream.

* * * *

Remember the days when "blush" was put on naturally instead of with a brush?

The Texas oil millionaire went to his dentist one day and learned that his teeth were in perfect shape. "You don't need a thing done to them" the dentist said.

"I feel lucky today," countered the millionaire. "Drill anyway."

CHEESE CAKE

Crust
20 single graham crackers, rolled fine. (I use blender to get them even.)
3 Tb sugar ½ c melted butter
Mix altogether and press into pie pan. Save a few for top if you wish.

Filling
Mix very smooth in mixer in this order:
1 lg pkg cream cheese 2 eggs
½ c sugar ½ pt sour cream
1 t vanilla
Pour into crust. Bake at 350° for 25 min. Put into refrigerator immediately for 15 min. Add topping.

Topping
3 ts sugar ½ pt sour cream
1 ts vanilla
Beat and spread evenly and carefully on top. Bake 500° for 5 min. Remove from oven, sprinkle with remaining crumbs and let cool. Put in refrigerator at least 6 hrs before serving. You can eliminate topping and spread a can of cherry or blueberry pie filling on top.

CHOCOLATE CHEESE CAKE

Crust 2 c chocolate cookies, crushed
½ ts cinnamon 3 Tb butter, melted
Filling 1 c sugar 4 eggs
1½ lb cream cheese, room temperature
12 oz semi-sweet chocolate, melted
1 Tb vanilla 3 Tb cocoa
3 c sour cream ¼ c butter, melted

Prepare the cookies as indicated (scrape and discard any filling on cookies). Combine cookies, cinnamon and butter, then press mixture over bottom and side of a 9" springform pan, chill. In a mixing bowl, beat the sugar and eggs until light and fluffy. Add cream cheese gradually, beating until mixture is thick and smooth. Melt the chocolate and add to the cream cheese mixture. Beat in vanilla, cocoa, sour cream and butter, beating after each addition. Pour this into the chilled shell. Bake at 350° for 45-50 min or until cake has "set". Remove from oven, let cool and chill several hours. Serve in thin wedges.

JELLO CHEESECAKE

1. Dissolve 1 pkg lemon jello in 1 c hot water
2. Mix 2 c graham cracker or vanilla wafer crumbs with ¼ lb melted butter and 2 Tb icing sugar
3. Mix together and cream well, 1 8-oz cream cheese
   1 c sugar   2 ts vanilla
4. 1 large can chilled condensed milk
   Beat well and add 1 Tb lemon juice

Mix items 1, 3 & 4 together. Put wafers in 9 x 13" pan, reserving ½ c crumbs for top. Cut creamed mixture over crumbs. Top with reserved crumbs. Set overnight or 8 hrs. Serve with pineapple or cherries and/or whipped cream.

CHOCOLATE CREAM CHEESE PIE

1½ c finely crushed chocolate wafers
1/3 c butter or margarine, melted
Combine chocolate wafers with melted margarine. Press into bottom of 10" spring-form pan. Bake at 325° for 10 min. Cool completely.

Filling (or can use prepared chocolate pudding)
1 pkg (8 oz) cream cheese, softened
¼ c sugar
1 ts vanilla
2 beaten egg yolks
1 pkg (6 oz) semi-sweet chocolate chips, melted
2 egg whites
½ c sugar
1 c heavy cream
3/4 c chopped pecans

Combine softened cream cheese with the ¼ c sugar, vanilla, mixing until well blended. Stir in beaten egg yolks, melted chocolate; blend well.

Beat egg whites until soft peaks form. Gradually beat in the ½ c sugar, beating until very stiff. Fold into chocolate mixture with whipped cream and pecans.

Pour over cooled crust and freeze. To serve, decorate with additional whipped cream and top with chocolate curls. Serves 8-10.

Note: This is not a Weight Watcher recipe!

LEMON MERINGUE PIE

1 c sugar | 1¼ c water
1 Tb butter | ¼ c cornstarch
3 Tb cold water | 6 Tb lemon juice (1½ lemon)
1 ts grated lemon rind (½ lemon)
3 egg yolks | 2 Tb milk
1 9" baked pastry shell

Before making the pie filling, assemble all ingredients. Combine sugar, water and butter in medium saucepan; heat until sugar is dissolved. Add cornstarch that has been dissolved in cold water. Cook, stirring, over medium heat until mixture thickens and becomes quite clear, about 8 min. Add lemon juice and peel; cook, stirring for 2 more minutes. Remove from heat. Combine egg yolks with milk; beat thoroughly. Very slowly add egg yolk mixture to lemon sauce, stirring constantly. Return to heat; bring mixture just to boil. Remove from heat; cool and pour into baked 9" pastry shell. Spread meringue over pie filling, sealing it to edges of pastry shell on all sides. Bake 13 to 15 min or until meringue is slightly browned. Cool in draft-free spot for 2-3 hrs.

<u>Meringue</u>
3 egg whites 6 Tb sugar 1 ts lemon juice
Beat egg whites until stiff. Add sugar gradually; beat until sugar granules are dissolved. Add lemon juice; mix well.

CHESS PIE

¼ c butter, softened | ½ c whipping cream
1 c firmly packed brown sugar | 2 Tb flour
½ c sugar | 1 ts vanilla
¼ ts salt | 1 9" pie shell, unbaked
3 eggs | whipped cream, optional

In large mixing bowl beat together butter, sugars and salt at medium speed until creamy and fluffy. Beat in eggs, one at a time, until well blended. Mix in cream, flour, and vanilla. Pour into pie shell.

Bake in preheated 375° oven until knife inserted in center comes out clean, 25-30 min. Cool completely on wire rack. Garnish with whipped cream, if desired.

ORANGE-MARSHMALLOW CRACKER PIE

3 egg whites, beaten stiff   1 c sugar
12 soda crackers, finely crumbled
1 c chopped nuts
Place in well greased 10" pie pan. Bake at 300° for about 25-30 min. Turn heat down a little after 25 min. and cook another 10-15 min.

Melt 30 marshmallows (½ lb) in ½ c orange juice. After melted, place pan in cold water until partially set. Add 1 c heavy cream whipped and 1 pkg frozen raspberries well drained (save juice). Put in shell and refrigerate several hours. If desired, heat juice with a little more water and sugar to taste. Thicken slightly with cornstarch and spoon over pie when served. Garnish with whipped cream.

ORANGE CHIFFON PIE

4 eggs, separated
1 envelope unflavored gelatin
3/4 c sugar, divided
½ c orange juice
¼ ts salt
2 Tb lemon juice
2 ts grated orange peel
¼ ts cream of tartar
1 c whipping cream, whipped
1 9" graham cracker crumb crust
Orange slices, optional

In small mixing bowl beat egg yolks at high speed until thick and lemon-colored, about 5 min.

In medium saucepan combine gelatin, ¼ c sugar, orange juice and salt. Let stand 1 min. Gradually stir in beaten yolks. Cook, stirring constantly, over med. heat until mixture thickens slightly, about 5 min. Remove from heat and stir in lemon juice and orange peel. Chill, stirring occasionally, until mixture mounds slightly when dropped from a spoon, 30-45 min.

Wash and dry beaters. In large mixing bowl beat egg whites and cream of tartar at high speed until foamy. Add remaining ½ c sugar, 1 Tb at a time, beating constantly until sugar is dissolved* and whites are glossy & stand in soft peaks. Fold chilled yolk mixture and whipped cream into egg whites. Pile mixture into crust. Chill until firm, at least 3 hrs. Garnish with orange slices if desired. *Rub just a bit of meringue between thumb & forefinger to feel if sugar has dissolved.

ANGEL PIE

4 egg whites
¼ ts cream of tartar
1 c sugar

Beat egg whites until stiff. Add cream of tartar and beat 1 min.longer. Add sugar gradually beating until stiff again. Grease and flour pie tin well. Spread evenly in pie tin. (Spread straight across.) Bake at 275° for 20 min, then at 300° for 40 min. Take out of oven and let cool.

Filling

4 egg yolks
4 Tb sugar
1 Tb cornstarch
1 pinch salt
1 c milk
1 ts vanilla

Combine and cook over low heat until thick. Add 1 ts vanilla and cool. Spread in pie shell. Serve with ½ pt whipped cream adding sugar and vanilla to taste.

HEAVENLY LEMON PIE

1 can sweetened condensed milk
½ lemon juice & grated rind
1 ctn cool whip
1 can frozen lemonade mix (6 oz)
1 baked pie shell

Mix milk, lemonade, juice and rind together thoroughly. Fold in whipped topping. Pile high into baked pie shell and top with graham cracker crumbs. Serves 8.

Note: This can be made in orange, strawberry or banana flavor.

RITZ CRACKER PIE

Beat 3 egg whites slowly; add 1 c sugar and ½ ts baking powder. Beat until stiff. Fold in 2/3 c nuts and 14 ritz crackers coarsely broken. Grease a 9" pie plate. Bake at 325° for 30 min. Cool. Top with 1 c whipped cream. Place in refrigerator for at least 2 hrs before serving.

SODA CRACKER PIE

3 egg whites
1 c chopped nuts
1 c sugar
12 soda crackers (rolled)
1 ts vanilla
1 ts baking powder

Beat egg whites stiff. Add sugar and vanilla. Mix nuts, crackers, and baking powder together. Fold nut mixture into egg white mixture. Bake in well greased pie tin for 30 min at 350°. Top with whipped cream.

DREAM PIE

4½ Tb cornstarch
1½ c boiling water
3 egg whites
1½ ts vanilla
3/4 c sugar
¼ ts salt
3 Tb sugar
1 baked 9" pie shell
1 c caramel sauce (see sauces) p. 412.
1 c heavy cream, whipped and slightly sweetened
½ square (½ oz) unsweetened chocolate shaved into chocolate curls

In medium saucepan combine cornstarch and sugar; blend thoroughly. Add boiling water, stirring constantly. Cook and stir until thick and clear, 10-12 min. In large clean glass or stainless bowl combine salt and egg whites. Beat until stiff, gradually adding sugar and vanilla. Pour hot cornstarch mixture over egg whites, beating constantly. Cool mixture slightly; pour into pastry shell. Chill. Shortly before serving, pour enough Caramel Sauce in thin layer to cover entire filling. Cover with whipped cream; garnish with chocolate curls. Note: Caramel Sauce should be thin enough that when pie is cut, sauce slightly runs down sides of cut pieces.

MARSHMALLOW PUMPKIN PIE

32 large marshmallows
1 c pumpkin
¼ ts salt
½ ts cinnamon
¼ ts ginger
1 c whipping cream

Cook marshmallows, pumpkin, salt, ginger, and cinnamon over boiling water in double boiler until marshmallows are melted. Cool about 1 hr. Whip 1 c cream. Add ½ of the cream to pumpkin, mix then add the rest of the cream. Pour into pie shell. Let stand in refrigerator until ready to serve. Garnish with whipped cream, or crushed peanut brittle. Can be put in a graham cracker crust.

* * * *

There ought to be a course in school that teaches people to read the handwriting on the wall.

BANANA OR COCONUT CREAM PIE

1/3 c flour
2/3 c sugar
¼ ts salt
2 c milk
3 slightly beaten egg yolks
2 Tb butter
½ ts vanilla
1 9" baked pie shell
3 stiff beaten egg whites

Mix flour, 2/3 c sugar and salt. Gradually add milk. Cook in double boiler until thick, stirring constantly. Slowly add small amount of hot mixture to egg yolks; stir into remaining hot mixture. Cook 2 min. Cool; add butter and vanilla. Pour into baked pie shell and spread with meringue.

Meringue

¼ ts salt
3 egg whites
½ ts vanilla extract, opt.
6 Tb sugar

Add salt and extract to egg whites, beat to stiff foam. Add sugar a Tb at a time and beat until it forms peaks. Spread, sealing to edge of pastry. Bake 350° 12-15 min.
Banana - slice 2-3 bananas in shell and add filling.
Coconut- add 1 c coconut to filling. Sprinkle ½ c on meringue before baking.

FRENCH SILK CHOCOLATE PIE

1 9" baked pastry shell
½ c butter
3/4 c sugar
1 sq (1 oz) unsweetened chocolate, melted & cooled
1 ts vanilla
2 eggs
whipped cream, chopped nuts if desired

Cream butter in small bowl until fluffy. Add sugar gradually, creaming well. Blend in melted and cooled chocolate and vanilla. Add eggs, one at a time, beating 5 min after each addition, using medium speed on mixer. Spoon into cooled, baked pastry shell. Chill 1-2 hrs.

* * * *

What looks like mountains ahead of you, lots of times turns out to be just a mass of clouds.

They say swimming develops poise and grace, but did you ever take a good look at a duck?

PUMPKIN CHIFFON PIE

1 envelope gelatin
1¼ c pumpkin
1 c sugar
½ ts ginger
½ ts nutmeg
¼ c cold water
½ c canned milk
3 eggs
½ ts salt
½ ts cinnamon

To double, use 3 c pumpkin

To slightly beaten egg yolks, add ½ c sugar. Add pumpkin, milk, salt and spices. Cook in double boiler until thick. Soften gelatin in cold water. Add to hot pumpkin mixture. Cool in refrigerator. When thickened fold in thickly beaten egg whites to which remaining sugar has been added. Makes one 9" pie.

LIBBY'S MOST FAMOUS PIE OF ALL

Double this recipe for two pies

2 eggs, slightly beaten
3/4 c sugar
1 ts cinnamon
¼ ts cloves
1 9" unbaked pie shell
with fluted edge
1½ c solid pack pumpkin
½ ts salt
½ ts ginger
1 2/3 c evaporated milk
or light cream

Mix filling ingredients in order given. Pour into pie shell. Bake at 425° for 15 min. Reduce to 350° and con tinue baking for 45 min or until knife comes out clean. Cool. Garnish with whipped cream if desired.

For Pumpkin Pecan Pie

Bake above pie and cool. Combine 3 Tb soft butter or margarine, 2/3 c brown sugar and 2/3 c coarsely chopped pecans. Gently drop by spoonsful over cooled pie to cover top. Broil 5" below heat until mixture begins to bubble, about 3 min. Watch carefully, for if cooked too long it will turn syrupy. Cool on rack.

* * * *

August is when you finally realize what you saved for a rainy day--your vacation.

Travel is broadening, especially if you stop at all those recommended restaurants.

PUMPKIN ICE CREAM PIE

The filling for this pie is a pumpkin mousse; you freeze it inside an icecream "crust". Make it days ahead, if you wish.

1½ pts vanilla icecream
1 c canned pumpkin
3/4 c brown sugar, packed
½ ts each ground ginger and cinnamon
3/4 c whipping cream
3 ts rum flavoring and ¼ c orange juice
1/3 c candied orange peel or mixed candied fruit, finely chopped, optional
pecan halves for garnish

Put in 9" pie pan into the freezer when you remove the icecream; allow icecream to stand at room temperature a few minutes, until slightly softened. Then spread icecream evenly over the bottom and sides of the pie pan; set back in freezer if it gets too soft. Keep in freezer while you prepare the filling.
Filling: Combine pumpkin, sugar and spices in saucepan. Stir over medium heat until the mixture is just below simmering point. Stir in the candied fruit, flavoring & orange juice. Refrigerate to chill well. Whip cream and fold into chilled pumpkin mixture. Pour into icecream lined pie pan and freeze. Garnish with pecan halves just before serving.

ROYAL COCONUT PIE

Pastry for 9", 2 crust pie
3 c shredded coconut, packed
1¼ c sugar
3/4 c milk
¼ c cornstarch
¼ ts salt
½ c water
¼ ts vanilla

Line a 9" pie plate with pastry. Combine remaining ingredients; mix well. Let stand for 15 min. Preheat oven to 375°. Spoon coconut mixture into prepared pie plate and cover with top crust. Brush lightly with milk or cream. Bake for 45 min. Makes 8 servings.

* * * *

Department store ad: "Artificial plants, so lifelike they're unreal!"

EASY PINEAPPLE PIE

1 pt sour cream
1 can crushed pineapple with juice (15¼ oz)
1 pkg instant vanilla pudding (4 oz)
Place in 9" baked pie shell. Chill and serve. Top with whipped cream if desired.

RHUBARB STRAWBERRY PIE

1 beaten egg
1 Tb flour
3 c diced rhubarb
1 unbaked 9" pie shell
1 c sugar
1 ts vanilla
1 c fresh strawberries
topping

Combine egg, sugar, flour and vanilla. Add diced rhubarb and strawberries. Toss lightly to blend well. Spoon into unbaked pie crust. Sprinkle with topping. Bake at 425° for 10 min. Reduce heat to 350° for 40 min or until done. Delicious!

Topping

¼ c flour
1/3 c butter, softened
½ c brown sugar, well packed

Blend flour with brown sugar and cut in softened butter. Sprinkle over rhubarb-strawberry mixture.

RHUBARB CREAM PIE

Mix together 3 Tb flour
3 c diced rhubarb
2 ts grated lemon rind
1¼ c sugar
2 Tb water
1 egg

Put rhubarb in pie shell. Beat the egg and combine with remaining ingredients. Pour over rhubarb. Put on top crust. Bake at 450° for 15 min., reduce heat to 375° for 30 min. A scoop of icecream on top makes it magnificent!

* * * *

College freshman: "I just got a check from home!"
Pal: "Then pay me the five dollars you owe me."
Freshman: "Wait till I tell you the rest of my dream."

FRESH APRICOT-PEACH PIE

Pastry for a 9"-2 crust pie
1½ c fresh apricot halves
1½ c fresh sliced peaches
¼ ts cinnamon
1 ts lemon juice
1 c sugar
¼ c flour
2 Tb butter or margarine

Heat oven to 425°. Roll out half the pastry and fit into pie pan. Mix fruit with lemon juice. Stir together sugar, flour and cinnamon; mix with fruit. Turn into pastry-lined pan; dot with butter.

Roll out remaining pastry and cut slits in top crust; arrange over fruit. Seal and flute edges. Cover edge with strip of foil to prevent excessive browning; remove foil last 15 min of baking. Bake in preheated oven 35 to 45 min or until crust is golden brown and juices begin to bubble through slits in crust.

Excellent served with vanilla ice cream!

STRAWBERRY MALLOW PIE

Chilled graham cracker crust (9")
2/3 c evaporated milk
1/3 c evaporated milk
¼ c lemon juice
1 qt sliced, fresh strawberries
32 marshmallows
1 ts lemon rind
¼ c water

Put 2/3 c evaporated milk into an ice tray of refrigerator. Chill milk until ice crystals begin to form around edges. In meantime, put into quart saucepan marshmallows and 1/3 c evaporated milk. Cook and stir over low heat until marshmallows are just melted. Remove from heat and stir in lemon rind, lemon juice and water. Chill until slightly thicker than unbeaten egg whites. Put cold milk into a cold quart bowl. Whip with cold rotary beater by hand or with electric beater at high speed, until stiff. Fold into marshmallow mixture. Fold in fresh strawberries. Pour into chilled graham cracker crust. Chill until firm, about 3 hrs.

* * * *

The trouble with trying to get away from it all nowadays is that most of it is portable.

TRADITIONAL LEMON-LIME PIE

1 (8-9") graham cracker crust
2 eggs, separated
1 14-oz can sweetened condensed milk
½ c lemon juice
2 ts grated lime rind (or lemon)
green food coloring,

In medium bowl, combine egg yolks, sweetened condensed milk, lemon juice and rind. Set aside. In small bowl, stiffly beat egg whites; fold into sweetened condensed milk mixture. Add food coloring to desired shade of green. Mound filling lightly into prepared crust. Chill 3 hrs or until set. If desired, garnish with whipped cream and lemon and lime slices. Refrigerate any leftover filling and serve as pudding.

CHERRY-RHUBARB PIE

1 pkg (5 oz) refrigerated all-ready pie crusts (9" pie)
1 pkg (16 oz) frozen rhubarb, thawed & drained
1 can (16 oz) tart red pitted cherries, drained
1½ c sugar
2 Tb quick cooking tapioca

Preheat oven to 400°. Prepare pie crusts following package directions for 2 crust 9" pie.

In large bowl, mix rhubarb, cherries, sugar and tapioca. Pour into prepared pie pan. Top with second crust; flute edges and slit crust in several places. Place pie pan on cookie sheet (to catch any run-over during baking) and bake for 35-40 min or until crust is golden brown. Cover edge of pie crust with strip of foil during last 10 min of baking, if necessary, to prevent excessive browning.

Cooking Tip: 3 c fresh rhubarb can be substituted for frozen. For a different flavor, a 10 oz pkg frozen raspberries can be substituted for cherries; use only 1/3 c sugar.

* * * *

HUCKLEBERRY PIE

2 c fresh huckleberries
1½ Tb tapioca
3/4 c packed brown sugar
¼ ts salt
1½ ts lemon juice
1 Tb butter

Put in pie shell and bake at 450° for 10 min, 350° for 35 min. Makes 1 pie.

CHERRY PIE SUPREME

Two all-time American favorites--cherry pie and cheese-cake--are subtly mingled in this applause-winning recipe. The result is a delightfully different dessert that is as elegant and exciting as it is easy to make.

9" unbaked pie shell
1 can (1 lb 5 oz) cherry pie filling
4 pkg (3 oz) soft cream cheese
2 eggs
1 c dairy sour cream
½ c sugar
½ ts vanilla

Preheat oven to 425°. Prepare pie shell. Spread half cherry pie filling in bottom; set rest of filling inside. Bake shell 15 min, or just until crust is golden brown. Remove from oven. Reduce oven temperature to 350°.

Meanwhile, in small bowl, with portable electric mixer, beat cheese with sugar, eggs, and vanilla until smooth. Pour over hot cherry pie filling; bake 25 min. (Filling will be slightly soft in the center.) Cool completely on wire rack.

To serve, spoon sour cream around edge of pie. Fill center with remaining cherry pie filling.

Note: for Blueberry Pie Supreme, substitute 1 can (1 lb 5 oz) blueberry pie filling for cherry pie filling.

* * * *

Divorce: eliminate.

That important date you forgot: anniversorry.

ICECREAM PIE

1 c chocolate chips) Melt and pour over 6 c Rice
4 Tb butter) Krispies

Press into pie tin and freeze. When frozen, soften icecream (1 gal) and put in crust. Very good with peppermint or icecream of your choice. Makes 3 pies.

COCONUT CUSTARD PIE

1½ c milk
¼ c sugar
¼ ts cinnamon
1/8 ts salt
½ c flaked coconut
½ c half and half
¼ ts nutmeg
¼ ts vanilla
3 eggs, slightly beaten
9" unbaked pie shell

Combine all ingredients except coconut. Blend well. Cook over low heat or in double boiler until the mixture boils, stirring constantly. Place coconut in pie shell. Pour mixture over coconut until shell is full. Bake at 400° for 1 hr or until knife inserted in center comes out clean.

FROZEN FRUIT PIES

1. Combine 4 qts fresh strawberries
   4 c sugar
   3/4 c quick tapioca
   ¼ c lemon juice
   1 ts salt
2. Mix well.
3. Line four 8" pie pans with aluminum foil, letting it extend 5" beyond rims. Pour filling into pans. Fold foil loosely over filling. Freeze until firm. Put in shells and add top crust. Bake at 425° for 1 hr.

* * * *

Wouldn't it be nice if the Christmas spirit lasted at least as long as the quills in the carpet?

SIMPLE -FRESH PEACH OR STRAWBERRY PIE

Cut up enough fresh peaches or strawberries to fill one baked pie shell. In saucepan put ½ c sugar, 3 Tb corn starch and 1 c water. Bring to boil and remove from heat and add 3 Tb jello powder (either strawberry or peach) and dash of salt. Mix in with the cut-up fruit and put in pie shall. Refrigerate and top with whipped cream.

SWISS APPLE-CHERRY PIE

4 tart apples
1 c sugar
2 ts cinnamon
6 Tb butter or margarine
2 Tb flour
½ ts nutmeg
1 can (2½ size can) pitted sour red cherries, drained
Pastry for 9" two-crust pie

Pare apples; core and slice. Melt 2 Tb butter and brush on bottom of pastry shell. Arrange a layer of sliced apples on bottom of shell. Mix dry ingredients and sprinkle about ¼ over layer of apples. Arrange layer of cherries and sprinkle with ¼ of dry ingredients--then apples, dry ingredients, then cherries, dry ingredients, and end with layer of apples. Top with dots of remaining butter. After top crust is placed on pie, brush crust with cream or evaporated milk and sprinkle ½ ts sugar mixed with ¼ ts cinnamon over top. Cut vents in top crust. Bake at 425° for 30-40 min. Serve with a scoop of ice cream. They'll be back for more!

*In Thayne, Wyoming there is a cheese factory where we always stop enroute to Jackson. Our favorite thing is to stop and have a piece of this pie with some of their excellent cheese.

SOUR CREAM LEMON PIE

1 baked 9" crust
1 c white sugar)
3 Tb cornstarch)
1 Tb flour)
1 Tb grated lemon peel) Bring slowly to boil, stirring.
1/3 c fresh lemon juice)
1 c light cream)
1/4 c butter
1 c sour cream

Add butter and cook. Cool and add sour cream. Pour into shell. (See p. 367 for sour cream topping)

BAKED ALASKA PIE

1 8" baked pie shell
1 qt peppermint, chocolate chip, or vanilla icecream
2-3 Tb chocolate syrup
5 egg whites
2/3 c sugar
1 ts vanilla
½ ts cream of tartar

Spoon ice cream into pie shell. Drizzle with chocolate syrup. Place in freezer until ready to use.

Heat oven to 500°. Beat egg whites, vanilla and cream of tartar until foamy. Gradually beat in sugar until mixture is stiff and glossy. Completely cover ice cream in pie shell with meringue, sealing well to edge of crust and piling high. (If desired, pie may be frozen up to 24 hrs at this point.) When ready to serve, bake pie on lowest rack for 3 to 5 min or until meringue is light brown. Serve immediately. Or again return to freezer until ready to serve. Makes 6-8 servings.

IMPOSSIBLE PIE

1 c coconut
4 eggs
2 ts vanilla
½ c bisquick
2 c milk
½ c butter or margarine
3/4 c sugar

Butter 9" pie tin. Spread coconut in bottom. Stir sugar and flour together. Put milk, eggs, butter and vanilla in blender. Add the flour mixture. Carefully add blender mixture to pie plate so as not to move coconut. Place in unheated oven. Turn to 350° for 45 min. Remove and cool. Pie separates to produce coconut crust, custard and coconut on top.

* * *

<u>Sour Cream Topping</u> (for Sour Cream Lemon Pie)

1 c whipped cream
2 Tb icing sugar, folded in.
½ ts almond extract, folded in. Sprinkle with lemon peel and garnish with lemon slices.

RASPBERRY PIE

"A husband pleaser, for sure!"

1 pkg (10 oz) frozen raspberries, thawed
1 pkg (3 oz) raspberry flavored gelatin
3/4 c boiling water
½ c heavy cream, whipped
2 egg whites
baked pie shell
2 Tb lemon juice
dash of salt
¼ c sugar

Drain raspberries; add water to syrup from berries to make 2/3 c. Dissolve gelatin in boiling water; add lemon juice and raspberry syrup-water mixture. Blend well; chill until partially set. Beat until soft peaks form. Fold in raspberries and whipped cream.

Add salt to egg whites; beat until soft peaks form. Add sugar gradually;beat to stiff peaks. Fold into raspberry mixture. Pile into cooled pie shell. Chill. Top with whipped cream, raspberries.

CANNED PEACH PIE

1 qt canned peaches
½ c sugar
2 Tb quick-cooking tapioca
Pastry for double 9" crust
1 Tb lemon juice
½ ts salt
2 Tb butter

Drain peaches, reserving syrup and slice. Combine peaches and syrup with tapioca, lemon juice and salt. Place the fruit mixture into 9" pastry lined pie plate. Dot with butter and cover with top crust that has slits in it. Trim pastry edges, seal and flute. Bake at 400° for 50 min.

If crust edges darken, cover with strips of aluminum foil to prevent further browning.

Note: Pie may be seasoned with ½ ts cinnamon and ¼ ts nutmeg. Or it may be flavored with ½ ts almond extract. Also, for a fuller pie, use double the amount of peaches.

APPLE PIE
(The All-American Favorite)

Pastry for 9" two-crust pie
4-5 cups tart apples, peeled, cored and sliced

¼ to ½ c water	1-2 Tb flour	
½ to 1 ts cinnamon	1/8 ts salt	1 c sugar
1 Tb lemon juice	2 Tb butter or margarine	

Steam or simmer apples gently in water until they wilt and begin to become transparent. (This is a partial cooking only so that apples will cook thoroughly in the pie.)

Combine the sugar and other dry ingredients. Mix well. Spread half over the pastry-lined pie pan. Lift apples from cooking liquid into crust. Add ¼ c of the cooking liquid. Sprinkle with remaining sugar mixture. Sprinkle pie filling with lemon juice and dot with butter. Roll, fit, and seal top crust. Brush with milk and sprinkle with sugar, if desired.

Bake on lower shelf of oven at 425° for 30-40 minutes, or until nicely browned.

Note: Apple pie is only as good as the apples it contains. Tart, juicy apples are desirable, and some judgment is necessary as to amounts of sugar and thickening when sweeter, less juicy apples are used.

*The two compilers of this book differed dramatically as to whether apple pie should be made with white or brown sugar. Both are delicious, but try them yourself to see the delightful difference--but don't forget the luxury of a bite of cheese to go with the apple pie!

* * * *

Teenager to friend: "My mother gained weight because of shame--it's a shame to throw this out; it's a shame to throw that out."

Customer to TV salesman: "I don't need remote control. With four kids, my chances of controlling it are already remote!"

Mother to child at supper table: "Howard, on occasion you're going to find a lump in your mashed potatoes. Life is like that."

PINEAPPLE PECAN PIE

3 Tb sugar
3 Tb flour
1/8 ts salt
3 egg yolks, well beaten
2/3 c pineapple syrup
1 c crushed pineapple
2 c miniature marshmallows
1 c whipping cream
1 Tb sugar

Drain juice from pineapple. Mix sugar, flour and salt. Add syrup and egg yolks. Blend well. Cook over low heat until thick, stirring constantly. Remove from heat, add marshmallows and stir until melted and mixture is fluffy. Stir in pineapple and chill 2 hrs. Whip cream and add 1 Tb sugar. Reserve half of cream for topping. Fold remaining cream into chilled mixture.

<u>Crust</u>

3 egg whites
1 c sugar
¼ ts cream of tartar
3/4 c chopped pecans or walnuts
½ c salted cracker crumbs
1 ts vanilla

Beat egg whites until stiff; gradually add sugar. Mix cracker crumbs and cream of tartar. Fold in egg whites. Add ½ c nuts and vanilla. Turn into deep buttered pie plate (10") pyrex. Bake 30-35 min at 325°. Cool. Pour filling into crust. Top with whipped cream and sprinkle with remaining nuts. Serves 12. *A special dessert for special times!

BLACK BOTTOM PIE

1. Make Ginger Cookie crust (see Crust p. 349)
2. Soften 1 Tb gelatin in ¼ c cold water.
3. Mix in saucepan ½ c sugar, 1¼ ts cornstarch ½ ts salt and 2 c milk
4. Cook over low heat, stirring constantly until scalded. Remove from heat. Stir a little of the hot mixture into 4 egg yolks, slightly beaten.
5. Blend into hot mixture in saucepan. Cook over low heat, stirring until it begins to boil. Immediately remove from heat.
6. Pour out 1 c of this mixture and add to it 1½ sq. unsweetened chocolate, melted.
7. Beat well. Pour into cooled crust and chill. AND ENJOY!

MINCE-CHIFFON PIE

Baked 9" pie shell or graham cracker crust
1 envelope unflavored gelatin
½ c water
1½ c Mincemeat
¼ c water or substitute fruit juice
3 eggs
1/8 ts salt
½ c powdered sugar
1 c heavy cream
Soften gelatin in ½ c cold water on top of double boiler. Place over rapidly boiling water and heat until dissolved, stirring often. Remove from heat; add mincemeat and cold water. Chill, stirring occasionally, until slightly thickened. Beat egg whites with salt until stiff but not dry. Gradually beat in sugar, beating well after each addition. Whip cream. Fold egg whites, then whipped cream into mincemeat mixture. Pile high in shell. Chill until firm. Garnish with additional whipped cream if desired and a sprinkling of chopped nuts.

LEMONY MINCE MERINGUE PIE

3 c prepared mincemeat
3 slightly beaten egg yolks
1/3 c apple juice
¼ c sugar
2 ts grated lemon peel

1 unbaked 9" pie shell

3 egg whites
¼ ts cream of tartar
6 Tb sugar

Combine the first 4 ingredients; pour into pastry shell. Bake in hot oven (400°) for 40 min. Cool 15 min. Meanwhile, beat egg whites with cream of tartar to soft peaks; gradually add the 6 Tb sugar and the lemon peel, beating to stiff peaks. Spread over filling, sealing to pastry. Bake at 350° for 12-15 min, or until golden brown. Cool.

* * * *

Church-goer to pastor: "Your sermon reminded me of the mercies of God. I thought it would endure forever."

Boy to friend: "It's hard to take my father seriously when he's wearing Bermuda shorts."

RAISIN PIE

1½ c raisins
¼ c pineapple juice (or use ¼ c more water)
½ ts vanilla
¼ c cornstarch
¼ c lemon juice
1½ c water
1 c sugar
½ ts salt
pastry for 8" two-crust pie

In a small saucepan combine raisins, water, pineapple juice and vanilla. Bring to a boil and cook 5 min. Pour mixture through strainer. Set raisins aside and reserve the liquid.

Mix together sugar, cornstarch and salt; add hot raisin liquid, beating all together with a wire whip. Continue cooking and stirring until thick, about 5 min. Add raisins and lemon juice and pour into unbaked pie shell.

Roll out top crust and cut two 2" slits near center, then snip with scissors at sides and between slits. Or make any fancy cut-out design desired. Moisten edge of bottom crust rim. To adjust top crust, fold in half or roll loosely on rolling pin; center on filling. Pull slits apart slightly if necessary with a knife. (Steam must escape during baking.) Trim top crust, allowing it to extend ½" over rim. To seal, press top and bottom crusts together on rim. Then fold edge of top crust under bottom and flute. Bake at 400° for about 45 min or to the desired brownness. Good plain, but scrumptious with icecream!

SOUTHERN PECAN PIE

1/3 c butter
dash of salt
1 c pecan halves
1 c dark corn syrup
2/3 c sugar
3 eggs, well beaten
1 ts vanilla

Cream together butter, sugar and salt; stir in remaining ingredients. Turn into plain pastry lined 9" pie plate and bake in 350° oven for 50 minutes, or until knife inserted in center comes out clean. Serve with whipped cream if desired.

candy

Notes

WATER FONDANT

2 c sugar
2/3 c water
1 Tb white Karo
Wipe crystals down. Cook to 225°. Stir very little. Completely cool and beat until it sets up. Refrigerate in tupperware and form in balls when ready to dip.

BASIC CREAM FONDANT

4 c sugar	2 Tb butter
1 c milk	2 Tb white Karo
½ c cream	pinch of salt

Combine all ingredients in heavy pan. Stir constantly until boil cannot be stirred down. Bring to soft ball stage. Cool thoroughly and knead until it sets up. Refrigerate and when ready to use, flavor and form in balls.

FONDANT

2 c sugar	2 Tb white corn syrup
pinch of salt	1 c cream

Stir continually (in one direction) over high heat until rolling boil. Turn off heat and cover with lid 2-3 min to dissolve sugar crystals. Start heat again and cook until forms soft ball (237° on candy thermometer. Cool thoroughly before beating on platter.

BROWN SUGAR FONDANT

2 c brown sugar	2 Tb white Karo
2 c white sugar	4 Tb butter
3/4 c milk	vanilla
3/4 c cream	pinch salt

Follow instructions for basic cream fondant. When making this fondant as well as the basic cream fondant the richness of the milk can vary; however, because brown sugar has a tendency to curdle, it is advisable to use a rich liquid.

BAVARIAN MINTS

1. Melt in heavy saucepan over low heat until smooth and creamy:
   - 2 c milk chocolate chips
   - 1 sq (1 oz) unsweetened chocolate
   - 2 Tb butter or margarine
   - 1 can (14 oz) sweetened condensed milk
2. Stir in: 6-8 drops peppermint oil
3. Pour into buttered pan or drop by teaspoonsful onto waxed paper.

BROWN SUGAR NUT ROLL

2 c sugar
1 c brown sugar
1 c evaporated milk
¼ c light Karo
1 c chopped pecans

Butter sides of heavy two qt. saucepan. In it combine sugars, milk, corn syrup and dash of salt. Stir over med. heat until sugars dissolve and mixture boils. Cook to soft ball stage (228°) stirring frequently. Immediately remove from heat, cool to lukewarm; do not stir.

Beat until candy begins to hold its shape. Turn out on buttered surface. Knead until it can be shaped, keeping hands well buttered.

Shape in two seven inch rolls; roll immediately in chopped nuts, pressing to coat well. Wrap and chill. Cut in ½ inch slices. Makes about 28 pcs. candy.

Note: Mixture will curdle while cooking, but becomes smooth when beaten.

SEA FOAM

1 3/4 c light brown sugar
3/4 c white sugar
¼ c light corn syrup
¼ ts salt
2 egg whites
1 ts vanilla
½ c broken pecans (optional)

Butter sides of heavy two qt. saucepan. Combine sugars, corn syrup, salt and ½ c water. Cook, stirring constantly, until sugars dissolve and mixture comes to boiling.

Cook to hard ball stage (252°) without stirring. Remove from heat.

Immediately beat egg whites until stiff peaks form. Pour hot syrup in a thin stream over beaten egg whites, beating constantly, at high speed on electric mixer. Stir until loses gloss. Stir in nuts and drop from spoon.

PINEAPPLE FONDANT

4 c white Karo
3/4 c pineapple juice
3/4 c heavy cream
3-4 Tb crushed pineapple
2 Tb butter
1/8 ts cream of tartar
1/8 ts baking soda
Pinch of salt

Mix all ingredients except pineapple. Set it aside to drain. Place over heat and stir until sugar is dissolved and mixture comes to a boil. (Don't let it boil until the sugar is dissolved). Cook to a firm soft ball stage, 234-260° F. Cool and beat. After the fondant turns add crushed pineapple from which all juice has been drained and pressed.

OLYMPIAN CREMES

4½ c sugar
3/4 c milk
3/4 c cream
vanilla
¼ c white Karo
½ c hot water
4 Tb butter
pinch salt

In heavy saucepan or frying pan melt ½ c sugar. Let brown, add hot water and let simmer until a caramel syrup is formed. While syrup is simmering, mix remaining 4 c sugar, salt, syrup and milk and cream and butter. Heat stirring constantly until mixture is just about ready to boil. Add hot carmelized sugar and continue stirring until it boils. Remove spoon and boil rapidly until reaches soft ball stage. Cool. Beat until it sets up. (Takes a little longer than basic fondant recipe.) Vanilla, brown sugar and Olympian cream centers may be dipped plain with nut on top or dipped in chocolate, or rolled in chopped nuts or toasted cocoanut.

FONDANT

2 lb powdered sugar
2 cubes butter
1 can Eagle Brand milk
1 ts vanilla

Mix well and cool. Form in balls with buttered hands and dip, or use in making pecan rolls for centers.

2 c sugar
1½ c white Karo
1 can Eagle Brand
pinch salt
1 c butter

Cook to firm ball, 235° stirring constantly so as not to burn. Add 1 ts anise flavoring OR 3/4 ts anise oil. Add 3/4 ts black food coloring. Pour in dripper pan and cool. Cut in squares and wrap in wax paper or plastic wrap. Excellent for mailing.

PENUCHE

1. Combine in a heavy 3 qt suacepan:
   - 2 c brown sugar
   - 1 c white sugar
   - 1 c cream
   - 1 Tb corn syrup
2. Bring to a boil over med. heat, stirring constantly.
3. Cover and cook about 3 min. until the steam has washed down any crystals on sides of pan.
4. Remove cover and continue cooking, stirring just enough to keep from sticking, until candy registers 228° F.
5. Remove from heat and add 1 Tb butter or margarine
6. Pour onto greased platter or marble slab and allow to cool to lukewarm without stirring.
7. Beat until candy is thick and creamy and has lost its gloss.
8. Stir in 1 c chopped nuts.
9. Spread penuche in a well buttered 8 x 8 x 2" pan and allow to stand until firm. Cut into 1¼" squares. Makes 36 pieces.

* * * *

A Russian was convicted by a Soviet court for calling the Minister of Culture a fool. He got 20 years -- five years for slander and 15 years for revealing a state secret.

PECAN ROLL

1 jar (7½ oz) marshmallow creme
1 lb powdered sugar
1 t vanilla
¼ ts almond extract
Combine all ingredients, kneading sugar in gradually. Roll into rolls. Wrap in wax paper and freeze. Dip rolls into carmel and roll in pecans.

ENGLISH TOFFEE

1 c white sugar
1 c brown sugar
1 c corn syrup
1 c butter
1 can Eagle Brand milk
pinch of salt

Place all ingredients in large heavy kettle and boil, stirring constantly. Stir and cook until candy forms semi-hard ball when dropped in cold water (245-248° F). Pour into buttered pan and mark into squares when nearly cold. If a harder toffee is desired, cook longer. Dip or wrap in wax paper.

HONEY TAFFY

2 c sugar
2 c honey
2/3 c cold water
1/8 ts salt

Boil to brittle until it will crack in cold water.

TAFFY

1½ c sugar
¼ c water
1/8 ts salt
½ c light corn syrup
3 Tb butter or margarine
½ ts vanilla

In heavy saucepan combine all ingredients. Cook to soft-crack stage (270°). Pour into buttered platter. As candy cools, lift edges toward center, add vanilla and pull, using fingertips and stretching taffy until it becomes white. Pull into long rope and cut with scissors while soft or crack into pieces after it hardens. Makes 3/4 lb.

SIMPLE SIMON FUDGE

A simple no-cook candy that tastes like it took you hours to make!

1. Combine and melt over hot (not boiling) water:
   1 6 oz. pkg (1 c) milk choc. chips
   1 3 oz. pkg cream cheese
2. Blend in: ¼ c sifted powdered sugar
   ¼ c honey
   ½ ts vanilla
   1/8 ts salt
3. Add and mix well: 2 c finely crushed vanilla wafers (approx. 60 small wafers) and ½ c chopped nuts.
4. Form into 1 inch balls, using one level tablespoon for each. Roll balls in finely chopped nuts or press a walnut half into top of each. Chill until firm. Makes 3 doz. balls.

Candy can also be made into rolls, wrapped, and sliced.

CHOCOLATE CARMELS

1. Combine in 1½ qt pan and cook over med. heat to 226° F (soft ball) 1/3 c sweetened condensed milk
   1 c light corn syrup
   1 Tb butter
   ½ ts salt
2. Gradually add 1 c sweetened condensed milk
3. Stir in, one piece at a time, and cook to 226°, 2 sq (2 oz) unsweetened chocolate
4. Remove from heat and add 1 ts vanilla.
5. Pour into 8 x 8 x 2" buttered pan. Cool.
6. Cut with sharp knife into ½" squares. Makes 1 lb.

MAGIC FUDGE

20 oz white chocolate — ¼ ts salt
1 can Eagle Brand sweetened condensed milk — 1 ts vanilla

Melt chocolate in electric frypan slowly, or in double boiler or microwave. (Don't let any steam get in it). Add milk, vanilla and salt. Stir (don't beat) until blended. Add 1 c slivered toasted almonds and cut-up-well drained maraschino cherries.

BUCKEYES

1 lb butter
2 lb peanut butter
3 lb powdered sugar

Cream above well and make into balls. Refrigerate. Dip 3/4 up side in melted mixture of 1 lb package of chocolate chips (milk) and 2/3 slab of parowax. Keep cool until hard.

DIVINITY

3 c sugar
3/4 c water
½ c cocoanut
3/4 c white Karo
1 c nuts

Boil sugar, karo and water until reaches 252° over med. heat. Meanwhile, beat 2 egg whites until frothy. Gradually add 1 pkg jello any flavor. Add hot candy syrup gradually to egg-jello mix. Beat until thick about 5 min. Add nuts and cocoanut and few maraschino cherries. Place in buttered glass dish. Cut into squares.

DIVINITY

2 c sugar
½ c water
2 egg whites beaten stiff
½ c light Karo
pinch salt
vanilla

Cook until thread breaks in ice water (252°) Have egg whites beaten stiff. Add slowly while beating eggs and beat until will stand without melting down. Drop on waxed paper with a teaspoon.

KRAFT BALLS

Melt 1 pkg Kraft Caramels over double boiler with ½ c butter and 6½ Tb cream or canned milk. Add:

2 c corn flakes
1 c shredded cocoanut
3 c rice krispies
1 c nuts

Form in small balls, as it is very rich.

WHITE CHRISTMAS FUDGE

1. In 3 qt saucepan combine:
   3 c sugar
   1½ c whipping cream
   1 c light corn syrup
   1 ts salt
2. Stir until sugar is dissolved. Cover pan and bring mixture to a boil. Boil 1 min. or until all sugar crystals on sides of pan have dissolved. Remove cover from pan.
3. Continue cooking, stirring occasionally until a little of the mixture forms a soft ball in cold water (234° F.)
4. Remove from heat and add 2 ts vanilla.
5. Beat with mixture at med. speed (or with a spoon) until fudge loses its shine and becomes satiny, about 10 min.
6. Mix in:
   2 c pecan halves
   1½ c halved Brazil nuts
   1½ c broken walnuts
   1 c diced candied pineapple
   1 c halved candied cherries
7. Press into two greased 9 x 9 x 2" pans.
8. Chill until firm enough to cut. Best after 24 hrs. refrigeration. Makes about 4 lbs.

CREAMY WHITE FUDGE

3 c sugar — 1 c dairy sour cream
1/3 c light corn syrup — ¼ ts salt
2 Tb butter — 2 ts vanilla
1½ c chopped walnuts or pecans

Combine sugar, sour cream, corn syrup, salt and butter in heavy sauce pan. Stir over med. heat until sugar is dissolved and mixture boils. Cover and cook slowly for 5 min. Uncover and boil rapidly to soft ball stage, 228°. Let stand until cold. Add vanilla and beat until candy loses its gloss and begins to hold its shape. Stir in nuts and turn into buttered pan. Cut in squares when set. Makes about 2¼ lbs.

CHOCOLATE FUDGE

2 c sugar
3/4 c water
1 ts vanilla
6 Tb cocoa
1 stick (½ c) butter
1 c walnuts or pecans, chopped

Combine sugar, cocoa and water; stir over med. heat until sugar is dissolved. Cover and boil slowly for 5 min.

Add butter and cook, without stirring (uncovered) to soft ball stage, 228°. Remove from heat and pour into dry container without scraping sides of kettle. Let stand until completely cold. Add vanilla and beat until candy loses its gloss. Quickly stir in nuts. Cut into squares when set. Makes about 1 3/4 lb.

FUDGE

3 c sugar
2 sq baking chocolate
2 Tb Karo
1 ts vanilla
1 c thin cream (half whipping half homo)
1/8 ts salt
3/4 c nuts
2 Tb butter

Shave chocolate into heavy pan. Add ½ c cream. Heat over low heat until chocolate is melted. Add rest of cream. Then stir in salt, sugar and syrup. Stir until starts to boil. DO NOT STIR AGAIN. Cook to 228°. Remove from stove, add butter and vanilla and stir gently until butter is melted. Pour onto marble slab or cookie sheet. Do not scrape pan. Let cool until center is luke warm. Beat with spatula until thick enough to pour on plate or keep beating until it crumbles, then mold with hands until it softens. Divide into 4 parts and form into rolls. (If properly cooked, should only require 8 min. beating).

* * * *

Junior executive to friend" My boss and I never clash. He goes his way, and I go his."

You cannot train a horse with shouts and expect it to obey a whisper.

Patience often gets the credit that belongs to fatigue.

PEANUT BRITTLE

1. Combine over med. heat: 1½ c sugar
   ½ c light corn syrup
   ½ c water
2. Bring to boil, stirring constantly.
3. Place lid on pan for 1 min. to wash down sugar crystals
4. Cook without stirring to 262° F.
5. Add 1 c raw Spanish peanuts
6. Cook, stirring constantly to 302° F.
7. Remove from flame and quickly add:
   1 Tb butter
   ½ ts vanilla
   1/8 ts salt
   1½ ts soda
8. Pour onto a buttered cookie sheet.
9. As the candy cools, stretch it thin by lifting and pulling from the edges, using two forks. Loosen from cookie sheet as soon as possible and break into pieces.

ELEGANT CHOCOLATE CANDY

2 lb chunk of milk chocolate
1 pt soft mint icecream
chopped nuts
¼ ts peppermint extract

Melt together over low heat the chocolate and soft icecream. Pour into greased pan. Chill several hours and cut into squares and roll into small balls and then into chopped nuts.

* * * *

If it were up to me, all children would be born with fur. It would thicken in winter, thin in summer, and then fall off when they were old enough to shop for their own clothes.

Daffynition time:

Area code--sinus condition.

Bathing beauty--girl worth wading for.

Cartoon--song you hear on the car radio.

Incongruous--where laws are made.

NUTTY FUDGE

1. Mix together and bring to a boil on high, stirring constantly: 2/3 c undiluted evaporated milk
   1 1/3 c sugar
   ¼ ts salt
   ¼ c butter
   2 c small marshmallows
2. Turn to simmer and cook for 5 min.
3. Remove from heat and add, stirring until melted:
   1 ½ c semi-sweet chocolate pieces
4. Stir in: 1 ts vanilla
5. Spread in buttered 8" square pan.
6. Cool until firm.

MILLION DOLLAR FUDGE

3 4-oz. plain Hershey bars
1 12-oz pkg Hershey Dainties
1 jar marshmallow cream
1 Tb butter or margarine
12 oz or more pecans
1 ts vanilla
4½ c sugar
1 lg can evaporated milk

Mix the following ingredients in 6-8 qt saucepan:
4½ c sugar
1 can evaporated milk

Let sugar and milk come to boil. Cook 6 min. Pour over remaining ingredients and blend until smooth and creamy. After mixture is completely blended, add chopped pecans. Fold in pecans, then drop balls of the mixture onto waxed paper with a tablespoon or pour mixture into greased pans. Let stand 4-6 hrs until completely chilled. Makes 6 lb. of the best fudge ever.

CREAM CHEESE FUDGE

3 oz. cream cheese
1 ts vanilla
½ c cocoa or less
1 cube butter or margarine
4 c powdered sugar (enough to make mixture firm)

Cream together. Chill after making into rolls. May be rolled in chopped nuts.

* * * *

There are no rules of architecture for a castle in the clouds.

ALMOND BRITTLE

1. Place in skillet and melt over med. heat. Stir constantly: 2 c sugar
   ¼ c butter (½ cube)
2. When sugar is melted and light brown, stir in:
   ¼ ts plus 1/8 ts baking soda (3/8)
   1 c chopped almonds
3. Pour onto large greased cookie sheet or marble slab. With greased rolling pin roll ¼" thick or pull thin with gloved hands.
4. Allow to cool completely. When cold drop brittle on cookie sheet or slab and it will break into serving pieces.
5. Store in closed container.

Makes about 1¼ lb.

ALMOND TOFFEE

1. Melt together slowly in large skillet:
   1 c butter (2 cubes)
2. Add, stirring gently and cook until color of brown paper bag (about 8 min) 1 c sugar, 2 Tb water
3. Add 1 c almonds, slivered, chopped, etc.
4. Spread on cookie sheet or marble slab.
5. Sprinkle over top 1 c semi-sweet chocolate chips Allow to melt completely. When melted spread evenly over toffee with spatula.
6. Sprinkle chocolate with 1 c finely chopped almonds. Place a piece of wax paper over nuts and roll with rolling pin to press nuts into chocolate.
7. Allow to cool. When cold break into bite-size pieces by dropping toffee onto cookie sheet or slab.

Makes about 1½ lb.

* * * *

Culture is what your butcher would have if he were a surgeon.

Pay no attention to what the critics say. A statue has never been erected in honor of a critic.

ROCKY ROAD CANDY

½ stick (¼ c) butter or margarine
1 pkg (6 oz) semi-sweet chocolate pieces
3 c miniature marshmallows
½ c chopped nuts

In saucepan melt butter and chocolate over low heat. Remove from heat; stir in marshmallows and nuts just until coated with chocolate. Spoon onto wax paper or into buttered pan. Chill until set, about 30 min. Makes about 24 pieces.

CARAMELS

4 c white sugar
1 pt whipping cream
½ lb butter
1 c light corn syrup
1 lg can condensed milk

Mix sugar and karo and bring to hard boil. Add condensed milk. Stir well. Add whipping cream and stir. Add butter. Cook to hard ball stage (firm) then add vanilla. Pour into buttered pan. Sprinkle with nuts.

CARAMELS

2 sticks butter (1 c)
2¼ c brown sugar
Dash of salt
1 c light corn syrup
1 can sweetened condensed milk
1 ts vanilla

Melt butter in heavy 3 qt pan. Add sugar and salt; stir thoroughly. Stir in corn syrup; mix well. Gradually add sweetened condensed milk, stirring constantly. Cook and stir over med. heat to firm ball stage (327°) 12 to 15 min. Remove from heat; stir in vanilla. Pour into buttered 9 x 9 x 2" pan. Cool and cut into squares. Makes about 2½ lbs.

* * * *

FRUIT CHEWS

1 pkg (11 oz) dried apricots
1½ c raisins 1 c flaked cocoanut
¼ c toasted sesame seeds or finely chopped nuts
Put apricots and raisins through med. blade of food grinder. Mix with cocoanut and sesame seeds. Press into eight inch square pan or form to balls. Makes about 24 pieces.

TORRONE (NOUGAT)

1. Spread on cookie sheet, and toast in 350° oven for 10 min. or until golden: 1 c blanched filberts and 2 cans (4½ oz each) blanched whole almonds
2. In heavy, straight sided 3 qt. saucepan combine:
   2 c sugar 1 c light corn syrup
   ½ c honey ¼ ts salt
   ¼ c water
3. Stir over med. heat, until sugar is dissolved. Continue cooking, without stirring, to 252°, or until a small amount in cold water forms a hard ball.
4. In large bowl beat at high speed, until stiff peaks form: 2 egg whites
5. Using about ¼ of the prepared hot syrup, pour a thin stream over the egg whites, beating constantly at high speed.
6. Continue beating 5 additional minutes, until mixture holds its shape.
7. Heat remaining syrup to 315-318°, or until a small amount in cold water forms brittle threads.
8. Pour the hot syrup in a thin stream over the meringue beating constantly, at high speed until stiff enough to hold its shape.
9. Add and beat until thickened about 5 min.:
   2 ts vanilla, ¼ c butter or margarine softened
10. With wooden spoon, stir in reserved toasted nuts.
11. Turn mixture into buttered dish. Smooth with spatula. Refrigerate.
12. Loosen candy around edges; turn out in large block. Cut in pieces with sharp knife.
13. Wrap each piece in waxed paper. Refrigerate.

Makes 2½ lbs.

CARAMELS

4 c sugar
2 sq butter
2 c white corn syrup
2 cans evap. milk
1 ts vanilla
1 c nuts (optional)

Stir sugar, syrup and butter in heavy pan over med. heat until it boils in high roll. Add milk, little at a time, so mixture never stops boiling. Stir constantly with wooden spoon. Cook to firm ball stage. (Caramel is slightly chewy). Add vanilla and nuts. Pour into buttered 8 x 12" dish. Cool before cutting.

BUTTERSCOTCH DROPS

1. In small saucepan combine and cook over low heat, stirring until sugar dissolves: 1 c sugar
½ c light corn syrup
½ c water
2. Cover and cook about 3 min. until the steam has washed down any crystals on the sides of the pan.
3. Remove cover and continue cooking without stirring, until candy reaches 250° (hard ball).
4. Add and cook until candy registers 280° (hard crack)
2 Tb butter or margarine
5. Remove from heat and add 1 ts vanilla
6. Drop by teaspoonsful onto a greased baking sheet, working fast. When cool, remove with spatula. Makes about 3 doz. drops.

CREME DE MENTHE SQUARES

1. Blend together in bowl: ½ c butter or margarine melted
½ c cocoa
½ c sifted powdered sugar
1 egg, beaten
1 ts vanilla
2. Stir in: 2 c graham cracker crumbs
3. Press into bottom of ungreased 13 x 9 x 2" baking pan.
4. Combine in medium mixing bowl: ½ c butter or marg.
1/3 c green creme de menthe
5. Beat in until smooth: 3 c sifted powdered sugar
6. Spread creme de menthe mixture over crumbs. Chill 1 hr.
7. Melt in small saucepan over warm heat, 1 pkg (12 oz) semi-sweet chocolate pieces and ¼ c butter or marg.
8. Spread chocolate mixture over mint layer. Chill 1 hr. Cut immediately into small squares. Store in frig.

LITTLE ANGEL MARSHMALLOWS

1. In mixing bowl, soften 1½ Tb gelatin in 1 c cold water
2. Combine in heavy saucepan 3 c sugar
   pinch of salt
   1 c water
3. Cook and stir until mixture comes to a boil.
4. Place lid on pan for 3 min. to dissolve sugar.
5. Cook without stirring to 260°.
6. Pour sugar syrup over gelatin mixture and allow to cool for 5 min.
7. Beat until mixture becomes white, fluffy and stiff enough to form soft peaks, 10-15 min.
8. Add: 2 ts vanilla
9. Pour into a 9 x 9 x 2" buttered pan and refrigerate for two hours.
10. Immediately cut into six strips and remove from pan. Roll each strip in mixture of:
    2 2/3 c flaked cocoanut
    ½ c toasted flaked cocoanut
    1 c chopped salted peanuts
11. Cut each strip into 8-10 pieces and roll again in above mixture.

Store in tightly covered container in cool place.
Makes 4 doz. marshmallows.

CANDY CHEWS

3 Tb cocoa
2 c sugar
¼ ts salt
2 c quick Quaker oats
½ c milk
1 c cooked wheat (drained)
1 ts vanilla
½ c cocoanut

Bring to boil slowly, cocoa, milk, sugar, salt and vanilla. Remove from heat and add oats, wheat, cocoanut. Drop on waxed paper with teaspoon. Add nuts if desired. For variation use 1 c brown sugar and no cocoa. Put in tupperware to keep candy soft.

PEANUT BUTTER CUPS

¼ lb butter or margarine
1 8-oz. bar Hershey's Milk Chocolate
½ c peanut butter
Melt ingredients in double boiler . Put 1 Tb mixture in bottom of cup. Add dob of peanut butter (which has been heated by putting jar in hot water). Cool cup in frig. Put melted chocolate on top to finish.

BUTTER MINTS

1 c boiling water
¼ lb butter (no substitute!)
1/8 ts salt
3 c sugar
Place above in saucepan and cover, being careful not to stir until boiling and sugar crystals on sides have melted down. Remove lid and continue cooking until hard boil stage. Pour on large buttered slab or platter. Pick up with buttered hands as soon as you can stand the heat and pull. (Wear rubber gloves for the job.) Add 4 drops of oil of peppermint and continue pulling until creamy and candy has lost its shiny appearance and looks dull. Form into ropes and place on wax paper. Cut immediately into bite size pieces. Place in airtight container for 24 hrs and candy will mellow and melt in your mouth.

* * * *

One worm to another: "I saw my first robin today--and just in time, too!"

Old lawyers never die--they just lose their appeal.

Old comedians never die--they just go to the old jokes home.

QUICK MICRO FUDGE

3½ c milk chocolate pieces *
¼ ts salt
1 ts vanilla flavoring
1 can sweetened condensed milk
Chopped nuts

Place chocolate pieces, salt, flavoring and sweetened condensed milk in large glass bowl. Place in microwave for 1½ min. Remove from microwave and quickly stir until smooth. Stir in nuts and pour on buttered plate or in glass cake pan. Refrigerate until set. Cut into pieces and serve.

*This recipe has been tested with Hershey milk chocolate pieces.

One (12 oz) package chocolate pieces is not quite 2 c.

A variation:

MICRO BUTTERSCOTCH CASHEW CRUNCH

4 c (or 2 12-oz pkg butterscotch morsels)
1 ts vanilla (optional)
1 can sweetened condensed milk
Salted cashews (halves or chopped)

Place butterscotch pieces, flavoring and sweetened condensed milk in large glass bowl. Place in microwave oven for 1½ min. Remove from microwave and quickly stir until smooth. Stir in nuts and pour on buttered plate or in glass cake pan. Refrigerate until set. Cut into pieces and serve.

* * * *

As unadventurous as a windshield wiper's path.

As much expression on his face as an egg.

As empty as the Kremlin's suggestion box.

All the tension of a broken tennis racket.

MARSHMALLOWS

2 c sugar
1 c water
Cook to soft ball stage. Meanwhile, place 2 envelopes Knox gelatin in ½ c cold water. After syrup is to soft ball stage add pinch of cream of tartar. Mix in gelatin. Gently pour above mixture over 2 beaten egg whites. Continue beating until quite cool. Add vanilla. Pour in buttered 11 x 13 pan and store in frig until completely set then roll in toasted cocoanut and store in tupperware.

* * * *

He who has imagination without learning has wings but no feet.

The three most beautiful sights: a potato garden in bloom, a ship in sail, a woman after the birth of a child.
--Irish proverb

There is no better or more blessed bondage than to be a prisoner of hope.

Husband working on taxes, to wife: "Let me explain it this way, Doris. We have six apples. The IRS wants seven.

Saleswoman at perfume counter to customer: "If this stuff really worked, would I be standing here eight hours a day?"

Old bacteriologists never die--they just go out to Pasteur.

Old actors never die--they just lose their parts.

COCONUT DATE BALLS

1 c butter
1½ c sugar
2 c chopped dates
1 Tb milk
½ ts salt
2 beaten eggs
1 ts vanilla
6 c Rice Krispies
½ c finely chopped nuts
coconut

In 4 c glass bowl, micro-melt butter 50-60 secs. Add sugar, dates, milk and salt. Micro-cook 6 min. stirring 2-3 times. Gradually stir in eggs and vanilla, blending well. Fold in cereal and nuts. Chill. Form into balls and roll in coconut.

MICRO PEANUT BRITTLE

1 c raw peanuts
1 c sugar
½ c white karo
1/8 ts salt
1 Tb butter
1 ts baking soda
1 ts vanilla

In 1 qt glass bowl, mix peanuts, sugar, corn syrup and salt. Micro-cook 7-8 minutes, stirring well after 4 min. Add butter and stir well. Micro-cook 2-3 min. longer or until peanuts are golden brown. Watch carefully. Do not overcook! Quickly stir in baking soda and vanilla, mixing well. Pour onto greased cookie sheet. As soon as it begins to set, stretch out with forks and fingers until very thin. Stretch until it appears to be peanuts held together with spun sugar.

TIP: Candy thermometer <u>should not</u> be used in the Microwave oven. Testing of candy can be done by removing candy from the oven and using either the cold water test or thermometer. ALWAYS remove the thermometer before returning the candy to the oven.

HOT SPICED NUTS

1 c sugar
6 Tb milk
¼ ts vanilla
1 ts cinnamon
3 c mixed nuts

Combine thoroughly sugar, cinnamon and milk in saucepan; cook to soft ball stage. Remove from heat, add nuts and vanilla, and stir until creamy. Turn out at once onto waxed paper and separate. Serve warm or cold.

ALMOND BARK SUPREME

1½ lb white chocolate
1 c red cinnamon flavored candies
3/4 c whole almonds

Melt white cocolate and cinnamon candies in electric frypan or in microwave on "roast" setting. Stir in almonds. Pour immediately on wax paper and spread into thin layer. Cool, break into pieces. Makes about 1 lb.

DIPPED PRETZELS

1 lb white chocolate or confection coating
24 pretzels (small)

Cut coating in small pieces and place in double boiler over med. hot water. Stir constantly till it is melted. Do not let steam get in it or it will not melt. Cool to 105°. Set over water of same temp. Dip pretzels one at a time into coating to cover. Place on waxed paper to dry. Store in can with tight lid.

ALMOND CRUNCH

2 c white sugar
1 lb butter
½ c water
½ c chopped almonds

Mix sugar, water and butter. Cover and bring to boil. Remove cover and stir. Add almonds which have been slivered. Stir constantly and cook until mixture darkens and begins to smoke (290°). Should be about the color of brown paper. Pour onto cookie sheet all at once. When it begins to cool around edges cut in squares. Dip when completely cool.

POPCORN BALLS

1 c Karo syrup
½ c sugar
1 Tb vinegar
1 ts cream of tartar
Combine all ingredients in heavy saucepan and cook to soft ball. Then add:
2 Tb butter
¼ ts soda
½ ts coloring
Then mix with popcorn and make balls.

POPCORN

1 square butter
2 c brown sugar
1 c Karo (dark)
1 can sweetened condensed milk
Cook to medium soft ball butter, karo and sugar. Add sweetened condensed milk, stirring constantly until it forms soft ball again. Stir in vanilla. (The firmer the ball the less sticky the coating.) Pour over popcorn.

KARO CRAZY CRUNCH

2 qt popped corn
1 1/3 c sugar
1 1/3 c pecans
1 c margarine
2/3 c whole almonds
1 ts vanilla
½ c clear karo syrup
Mix popped corn and nuts on cookie sheet or in bowl. Combine sugar, margarine and karo in 1½ qt saucepan. Bring to boil over medium heat stirring occasionally for 10-15 min or till mixture turns light carmel color. Remove from heat. Stir in vanilla. Pour over popcorn and nuts. Mix and coat well. Spread out to dry then break apart. Store in tightly covered container. Nuts can be omitted and extra popcorn used.

POPCORN WITH JELLO

1 c corn syrup
1 c sugar
1 3-oz pkg raspberry jello
Stir together and bring to a boil--no longer. Pour over 6 qt popcorn.

CARAMEL APPLES

1 14-oz pkg caramels
2 tbs water
4 or 5 med. apples, washed and dried
4 or 5 wooden sticks
Combine caramels and water in top of double boiler or in saucepan. Place over hot water or low heat and cook until melted, stirring occasionally. Insert wooden sticks into stem end of each apple. Keep caramel mixture over hot water or low heat. Dip apples into caramel mixture turning to coat. Scrape off excess caramel mixture when removing apple from pan. Place on greased wax paper and chill until set. Makes 4-5 caramel apples.

GLAZED ALMONDS

1 c whole blanched almonds
2 Tb butter or margarine
½ c sugar
½ ts vanilla
In heavy skillet combine whole almonds, sugar and butter. Cook stirring constantly over med. low heat till almonds are well coated and the sugar is golden brown. (About 15 min.) Stir in vanilla. Spread nuts on a large sheet of aluminum foil. Separate almonds immediately. Sprinkle glazed nuts lightly with salt. Cool. Store in container with tight lid in dry cool place.

PEANUT BUTTER CUPS

Mix 1 c peanut butter and enough powdered sugar to make a consistency to roll in hand (3/4-1 c). Few chopped nuts if not using crunchy peanut butter. Roll in small balls for dipping or form in log.

* * * *

Man being congratulated by co-workers on his tan: "It was the only thing at the beach that was free, so I got a lot of it."

On a senior citizen's T-shirt: "Don't trust anyone under 68."

MIRACLE CARAMEL CORN

(Made in brown paper grocery bag)

2 gallons popped corn=(1 c unpopped)
1 lg double strength grocery bag (use 2 bags one inside the other)
1 sq butter ½ c white corn syrup
2 c brown sugar 1 Tb water
pinch soda

Place popped corn in bag. Bag should be about 1/3 full. Roll down edges of bag to the inside about 2 inches.

Melt butter in saucepan. Add brown sugar, corn syrup and water. Mix and place on med. heat. Stir constantly and bring to hard boil. Add pinch of soda, remove immediately from heat and pour syrup over popped corn in grocery bag. Close bag at top, carefully shake, then knead the bag with both hands, over and over, until the corn is well-coated with syrup. The bag will get soggy but if sturdy, should last. Like magic, the corn will be thoroughly coated. Form into balls or leave in clusters. Serve immediately or place in containers for storage. May be frozen for several weeks, if desired.

CARAMEL CRUNCH

1 1/3 c sugar
1 c butter or margarine
½ c light corn syrup
1 ts vanilla
8 c popped corn
2 c nuts

In saucepan, combine sugar, butter or margarine and corn syrup. Bring to boil over med. heat, stirring constantly. Continue boiling, stirring occasionally, till mixture turns caramel color. Remove from heat and stir in vanilla. Pour syrup over popcorn and nuts on shallow buttered baking pan. Separate into clusters with two forks. Store in plastic bag or container. Makes 2 lbs.

HIDDEN TREASURE POPCORN SURPRISE

Combine in saucepan:
1 lg pkg marshmallows (16 oz) ¼ c oil
½ c butter 1 ts vanilla
Cook over medium heat until marshmallows are melted and syrup is smooth. Pour syrup over:
3-4 qts popcorn, mixed with: 1 c cut-up gum drops
1 c roasted spanish peanuts
Mix together quickly and shape into popcorn balls, or shape into a pumpkin for Halloween or tree for Christmas. Excellent as a popcorn gift in any shape for any holiday.

CARMELIZED CORN PUFFS

2 c brown sugar 1 sq margarine
¼ c Karo 1 Tb water
1 ts vanilla
Bring to boil. Remove from heat and add pinch of soda. Stir and pour over two packages of Corn Puffs.

COCONUT BALLS

1 c sugar 1½ c chopped dates
1 cube butter 3 eggs, beaten
Melt butter and add rest of ingredients. Cook 10 min. stirring constantly. Add 1½ c Rice Krispies, 1 c nuts, 1 ts vanilla. Roll into small balls and roll in coconut.

OVEN POPCORN

Pop ½ lb popcorn and put in large kettle in a moderate oven. Mix 1½ c white sugar
1 c brown sugar
½ c and 2 Tb white Karo syrup
3/4 c water
Cook to 260° and then add:
1 c salted nuts and cook to 290°
Add: ½ cube butter, melted
1 ts soda
1 ts vanilla
Stir well. Scrape all syrup into corn and mix well together.

"CRACKER JACK"

6 qts popped corn
2 c brown sugar
1 ts salt
1 ts vanilla
1 c butter
½ - 2/3 c white corn syrup
½ ts soda

Melt butter and stir in sugar and syrup until sugar is dissolved. Bring to a boil for 5 minutes without stirring, removing from heat. Add vanilla, soda and salt. Pour over corn, coating well. Put in roaster pan, uncovered and put in 250° oven for 3/4 to 1 hr. Stir about every 10-15 minutes. Dark corn syrup may be used if you prefer the deep carmel flavor rather than the light.

YUM YUM BALLS

1 can sweetened condensed milk
1 lb graham crackers, crushed
2 c walnuts, chopped
1 c shredded cocoanut
1 c sugar
½ lb margarine, melted
½ c cocoa (mix in margarine)
2 ts almond extract (or vanilla)

Mix all dry ingredients in very large bowl. Pour butter and mix, then pour in milk and mix. Roll into balls and then in powdered sugar. Keeps well when stored covered, but hide well!

* * * *

Four year-old Tommy was fascinated with airplanes and rushed outside and watched every time he heard one. He gazed until the plane became a tiny speck in the distance.

When he had his first ride he was bug-eyed with excitement. About 10 minutes after they were airborne, he asked, "When do we start getting smaller?"

COTLETS

2 envelopes (2 Tb) unflavored gelatin
½ c cold water
2 c sugar
1 c chopped nuts
3/4 c pureed apricots
1 ts vanilla
powdered sugar

Combine unflavored gelatin with cold water; set aside to soften. Combine pureed apricots and sugar in medium saucepan and boil together 10 min. Add softened gelatin and stir until dissolved. Cook for 10 min more. Remove from heat; add vanilla and nuts. Pour hot gelatin mixture into buttered 4x8" loaf pan. Allow to stand several hours or overnight at room temperature. Do not refrigerate. Loosen gelatin, pull from pan and cut into squares, rolling powdered sugar. Makes about 32 1" pieces. Every bit as good as commercial cotlets.

Note: Applesauce, pureed cherries or grapes can be substituted for apricots.

FROSTED NUTS

1 c sugar
1 Tb light Karo syrup
3 c nuts
½ c water
1/8 ts peppermint (or less)
6 lg or 12-18 small marshmallows

Cook sugar, water, Karo and salt till forms soft ball stage (226°). Remove from heat and add marshmallows. Stir till melted. Add peppermint and nuts and stir to coat all nuts. Drop out on wax paper and separate and let cool.

* * * *

Doughnuts: dunk food.

Smorgasbord: eatcetera.

Church supper: sacred chow.

Whipped cream: plump pudding.

Rhubarb: celery with a sunburn.

CINNAMON CEREAL BALLS

½ c cinnamon candy red hots
1 c light corn syrup
½ ts salt
1½ c sugar
1/3 c water
¼ c butter or margarine
10 c assorted presweetened cereal (large and small size pieces, not flakes)

Crush cinnamon candies with rolling pin or in electric blender. Combine candy, sugar, syrup, water, salt, and butter or margarine in heavy saucepan.

Cook over low heat, stirring frequently, until syrup reaches the firm ball stage (238°). Syrup has reached the correct temperature when a small amount dropped into very cold water forms a firm ball which does not flatten on removal from water.

Combine a mixture of presweetened cereals in a large buttered mixing bowl.

Drizzle hot syrup over the cereals. Let stand to allow syrup to run down through cereals. Mix well. Form into 2" balls; place on waxed paper and twist paper to seal.

Serve as confection balls or push a small craft-stick into each ball for a holder. Cool at room temperature. Makes 24 to 27 balls.

* * * *

Woman complaining to marriage counselor about her husband: "When he won a trip for two to Hawaii, he went twice!"

Sign over teller's window: DEPOSITS WELCOMED, WITHDRAWALS . . . TOLERATED.

A great-grandmother explains how she managed to keep so young at 90: "It takes time to get old--and I've never had any."

Golfer Sam Snead: "The only reason I ever played golf in the first place was so I could afford to hunt and fish."

Notes

Notes

sauces

Notes

CHEESE SAUCE

1. Melt 1½ c butter or margarine
2. Blend in 1¼ c flour, 1 Tb and 2 ts dry mustard
3. Gradually add 11 c milk (2 3/4 qt)
4. Cook, stirring until thickened
5. Stir in 5 c shredded sharp cheddar cheese, 2½ ts salt, 1 ts pepper
6. Makes enough sauce to serve 50 two roll servings of ham and asparagus rolls, each with one Tb sauce.

TERIYAKI BASTING SAUCE

2/3 c soy sauce
2/3 c sugar
1 clove garlic, minced
1/8 ts Accent
2 Tb water
1 ts bouillon
dash powdered ginger

Combine all ingredients. Bring to a boil; lower heat and simmer 5 min. Use as basting sauce for steaks or hamburger patties. Makes 1 c.

SPAGHETTI SAUCE

1 lb hamburger, sauted in oil
1 lg onion, cut fine
1 ts salt and pepper
1 garlic clove, minced, or garlic salt
Add:
1 can mushroom soup
1 can water
2 cans tomato paste (8 oz)ea.
2 c water
½ ts oregano and 1 Tb cumin seed
Simmer until thick.

BAGNA CAUDA SAUCE

(Vegetable dip)

½ c butter ¼ c olive oil
4 small cloves garlic, mashed
1 can (2 oz) flat anchovy fillets, drained well

Choose a heatproof container that will be only about half filled by the quantity of sauce you make. Combine the butter, olive oil and garlic. Finely chop anchovy fillets and add to sauce. Stir over moderate heat until mixture bubbles.

To serve, set over candle or low alcohol flame. Mixture must not get hot enough to brown and burn. Makes 8-10 servings.

SHALLOT DRESSING

For those times when you would like to serve vegetables like a salad, this is delicious with both raw and lightly cooked vegetables. Try it on tomato slices, raw mushroom slices, or thinly sliced raw zucchini. It is also good with cooked and thinly sliced beets or carrots and French cut green beans cooked until just limp. Vegetables are best served at tepid temperatures.

1/3 c thinly sliced shallots, or green onions, including tops
¼ c white wine vinegar
4 ts prepared Dijon-style mustard
½ c salad oil or olive oil
¼ ts salt 1/8 ts pepper

Blend together the shallots or green onions, mustard, vinegar, oil, salt and pepper; stir or shake vigorously just before adding to vegetables. You can cover and keep dressing up to 2 days. Makes 1 c dressing.

GOURMET BASTING SAUCE

1½ c lemon juice
2 Tb ground marjoram
2 Tb salt
2 cloves garlic, pureed*
1½ c olive or salad oil
½ ts freshly ground peppercorns
1 c Worcestershire sauce

Blend together all ingredients for sauce. Let stand several hrs or overnight in frig. Brush steaks or chops frequently with sauce while broiling or frying. Remaining sauce may be stored in the frig. Makes 1 qt.

This is an excellent basting sauce for chops as well as steaks.

*If desired, use garlic salt, to taste, instead of the garlic cloves.

SPICY BARBECUE SAUCE

2 Tb flour
1½ ts salt
2 Tb brown sugar
½ c vinegar
1½ c catsup
1/3 c chopped onion
¼ ts ground cloves
1/8 ts pepper
1 Tb prepared mustard
3/4 c water
2 Tb Worcestershire sauce

Mix together flcur, cloves, salt, pepper and brown sugar. Add remaining ingredients. Mix well and simmer 15 min. Brush sauce on meat, as desired. Makes 3 c.

TOMATO BARBECUE SAUCE

1 can condensed tomato soup
¼ c chopped onion
1 Tb vinegar
2-4 Tb sweet pickle relish
1 Tb brown sugar
1 Tb Worcestershire sauce

Combine all ingredients. Cover; simmer until onion is cooked and flavors are blended. Brush on split franks on grill--or on whatever suits your fancy. Makes 1½ c.

SHELLFISH COCKTAIL SAUCE

½ c catsup
2 Tb lemon juice
1 Tb thinly sliced green onion with tops
2-3 drops liquid hot pepper seasoning
¼ c each tomato-based chili sauce & grapefruit juice
1 ts each prepared horseradish and Worcestershire
Thinly sliced green onions for garnish
1½ lb cold, cooked, shelled shellfish

Combine catsup, chili sauce, grapefruit juice, lemon juice, onion, horseradish, worstershire & hot pepper seasoning. Makes 1 c.

QUICK TARTAR SAUCE

½ c mayonnaise (or ¼ c each mayonnaise and sour cream)
¼ c sweet pickle relish, well drained
1 ts instant minced onion
¼ ts Worcestershire
4 drops liquid hot pepper seasoning
½ ts lemon juice

Combine mayonnaise, pickle relish, onion, Worcestershire, hot pepper seasoning, and lemon juice; mix well. Cover and chill for at least 30 min to blend flavors. Serve with hot or cold fish. Makes 3/4 c.

HOMEMADE MAYONNAISE

1 egg
½ ts each sugar & paprika
2 ts prepared Dijon style mustard
3 Tb tarragon-flavored white wine vinegar
1 c salad oil

Place in a blender the egg, sugar, paprika, mustard, and vinegar. Blend a few seconds and with motor running, gradually pour in salad oil, blending until smooth. Chill. Makes 1½ cups.

HAM SAUCE

1 lg can pineapple juice
1½ c brown sugar
1 ts dry mustard
¼ ts ground cloves
Cornstarch to thicken
Cook, stirring constantly, until thickened.

FRESH TOMATO SALSA

3 cans (30 oz each) tomatoes
3 bunches green onions, chopped tops and bottoms
3 Tb oil
3 Tb wine vinegar
3 ts oregano
salt and pepper to taste
1 can (4 oz) chopped green chilies

Drain tomatoes, saving juice. Take white core or stem out of each tomato and squeeze gently until juice is almost gone. Cut tomatoes into bowl. Add onions, oil, vinegar, oregano, salt, pepper and green chilies. Add juice to desired consistency.

Store sealed in jars in the refrigerator. Makes 3 qts. Use over omelets, as a dip, over steaks or as a meat sauce.

BIG MAC "SECRET" SAUCE

1 c Miracle Whip Salad Dressing
1/3 c creamy style French Dressing
¼ c sweet pickle relish
1 ts minced onion
1 Tb sugar
¼ ts pepper
Put sauce on, lettuce, cheese and bottom; two tops on outside toasted.

HOT SAUCES & VARIATIONS

Make 1 recipe MEDIUM WHITE SAUCE 2 Tb flour, 2 Tb butter, 1 c milk, ¼ ts salt and 1/8 ts pepper. Add any of the following for variation.

Mushroom Sauce: Saute 1 c sliced mushrooms in butter 5 min before adding flour.

Cheese sauce: Add ¼ ts dry mustard with seasonings and blend in ½ c grated cheese after the sauce has thickened.

Seafood Sauce: Stir in 1 c medium white sauce, ½ to 1 c cooked shrimp or pieces of other seafood.

Cucumber Sauce: Add to 1 c white sauce ½ c grated cucumbers and dash of cayenne. Simmer 10 min.

HORSERADISH SAUCE

½ c whipping cream
1 ts sugar
1 Tb prepared horseradish
½ ts lemon juice

Whip cream until stiff, and fold in horseradish, sugar and lemon juice. Chill for several hours. Serve with beef or tongue. Makes about 1 c.

TERIYAKI SAUCE

Makes an excellent marinade or baste for beef or chicken kebobs, a hot dip for batter-fried shrimp, or a sauce for broiled steak.

2 Tb cornstarch
¼ c sugar
1/3 c soy sauce
1 clove garlic, minced
2 ts minced fresh ginger (or ½ ts ground ginger)
¼ c dry white wine (optional)
2 c regular-strength beef broth (or 2¼ c, if wine is omitted)

In a pan, blend together the cornstarch, soy sauce, sugar, garlic and fresh or ground ginger. Stir in wine, if used, and the beef broth. Cook, stirring, until thickened. Makes about 2½ c.

MUSTARD SAUCE

2 Tb each dry mustard, sugar, water and white wine vinegar
1 Tb butter
1 egg, beaten
1 ts cornstarch
1/2 c whipping cream

Mix together in a small saucepan the dry mustard, sugar, water, and vinegar. Add the butter and cornstarch. Stirring constantly, cook until sauce comes to a full rolling boil and is thick and clear. Stir sauce into the beaten egg, return to pan, and cook, stirring constantly, 2 or 3 min longer, until thick--do not let boil. Chill.

Whip the cream until stiff and fold in just before serving. Makes 1½ c.

Red Sauce: Add 3 Tb tomato puree to 1 c medium white sauce.
Curry Sauce: Add ½ ts curry powder to the seasonings.
Dill Sauce: Add 1 ts minced fresh dill weed or use ½ ts dill weed and dash of nutmeg to 1 c medium white sauce. Combine all ingredients and heat until thickened. Simmer 2-3 min,

MARCHAND DE VIN SAUCE

3/4 c butter
1/3 c finely chopped mushrooms
½ c minced ham
1/3 c chopped shallots
½ c finely chopped onions
2 Tb minced garlic
2 Tb flour
½ ts salt
1/8 ts pepper
dash cayenne
3/4 c beef stock
½ c red wine

In a 9" skillet melt butter and lightly saute mushrooms, ham, shallots, onion and garlic. When the onion is golden brown, add flour, salt, pepper and cayenne. Brown well, about 7-10 min. Blend in the stock and the wine and simmer over low heat for 35-45 min. Makes 2 c.

HOLLANDAISE SAUCE

1. Place in blender 3-4 egg yolks
   1½ Tb lemon juice
2. Heat until melted and almost boiling 1 c butter
3. Turn blender on high speed and beat egg yolk mixture for a few seconds. Slowly pour butter into egg mixture and blend until thick and fluffy.
4. Place sauce over warm, not hot water until ready to use. Makes 1 c.

BEARNAISE SAUCE

3 Tb white wine vinegar
1 ts green onion, chopped
2 Tb fresh lemon juice
1 ts crushed tarragon
2 whole eggs
1 c butter, melted & hot

In small saucepan combine vinegar, tarragon and green onion. Remove from heat; set aside. Combine eggs and lemon juice in blender. Add vinegar mixture; blend. While still blending, slowly add hot butter. When blended, turn mixture into small saucepan. Cook over very low heat until slightly thickened, taking care not to boil as it will curdle. Serve with broiled steak.

SAVORY CHEESE SAUCE

Serve this as a topping for baked or broiled potatoes, over carrots, green beans, and Brussel sprouts. As an appetizer it makes a great dip for artichokes or other raw vegetables.

1 c cottage cheese
1 Tb lemon juice
1 slice of med-sized onion (about ¼" thick)
½ c unflavored yogurt
1 ts sugar
½ ts salt
dash pepper
½ ts dillweed
1-2 Tb finely chopped parsley
Put into blender container the cottage cheese, onion, lemon juice, and 3 Tb of the yogurt. Whirl until smooth and mounding like sour cream, stopping the motor and pushing cheese down into blades as needed. Turn into a bowl and stir in remaining 5 Tb yogurt, sugar, salt, pepper, dill weed or herbs and parsley. Cover and store in refrigerator. Makes 1½ c.

GREEN HERB SAUCE

This sauce goes particularly well with broccoli, artichokes, carrots, and baked potatoes.

1 c watercress leaves and small stems (or spinach leaves) pressed in cup
½ c parsley sprigs, pressed in cup
1 lg shallot, peeled and cut (or 1 lg green onion with top), sliced
½ ts each tarragon and thyme leaves (or 1 ts fines herbs)
½ ts salt
3/4 ts dry mustard
2 Tb white wine vinegar or tarragon vinegar
1 egg
1 c salad oil
Put into the blender container the watercress or spinach, parsley, shallot or onion, herbs, salt, mustard, vinegar, and egg. Whirl until liquified. With blender motor running, remove center of top and begin pouring oil in a thin stream; add oil very slowly in the beginning, then a little faster as it begins to thicken. Store in frig, tightly covered. Makes about 1 2/3 c.

SWEET & SOUR SAUCE

To be used with cooked shrimp, pieces of cooked chicken, turkey or roast pork, or crisp fried won ton to make a Chinese-style main dish. You can easily cut the recipe in half to make a smaller amount of sauce.

2 cans (14 oz ea) pineapple chunks, drained (reserve syrup)
1¼ c regular-strength chicken broth
¼ c brown sugar 3/4 c vinegar
1 Tb each soy sauce and catsup
¼ c cornstarch
1 c thinly sliced green onions
3 green peppers, seeded and cut in 1" squares

Combine pineapple syrup with chicken broth, brown sugar, vinegar, soy sauce, catsup and cornstarch. Cook, stirring until thickened. At this point, you can refrigerate the sauce as much as a day ahead.

Shortly before you want to use the sauce, heat slowly, stirring until bubbly. Add onions and green peppers. Cook 1 min longer. Remove from heat and add pineapple chunks. Makes about 2½ c liquid sauce (plus vegetables and fruit).

ITALIAN SEASONING

½ c leaf oregano ½ c leaf basil
2 Tb leaf sage 1 ts thyme
1 jar (3¼ oz) season salt 2 Tb lemon pepper
2 Tb garlic powder

Combine oregano, basil, sage, thyme, seasoned salt, lemon pepper and garlic powder in small bowl; stir to blend. Pack into small crocks, jars or plastic containers. Seal and label. Store in cool, dry place. Crumble in hand before using in salads, salad dressings, sauces, meat and vegetable casseroles. Makes 2 c.

RASPBERRY SAUCE

2 pkg (10 oz ea) frozen red raspberries
1 c water
dash salt
lemon juice
3 Tb cornstarch
sugar

Add water to frozen raspberries; bring to boil. Put through sieve, extracting all juice. (Use raspberry pulp in tapioca.) Add enough water to make 3 c juice. Combine a little cold water with cornstarch; stir into juice; cook until mixture is thick and clear. Add salt, sugar and lemon juice to taste. Chill. Serve over ice cream, plain cake or Norwegian Rice in Cream (or any rice pudding).

LEMON SAUCE OR FROSTING

grated rind of 1 lemon
½ c lemon juice
1 c whipping cream whipped
2 eggs
2/3 c sugar

Combine eggs, lemon rind and juice. Slowly add sugar & stir well. Pour into heavy saucepan and cook over low heat until thickened. Cool and fold into whipped cream. Frost cake on top, side and center.

BRANDY SAUCE

¼ c butter or margarine
2 egg yolks, well beaten
2 egg whites, beaten stiff
1 c powdered sugar
½ c light cream
¼ c brandy or 1 ts brandy flavoring

Cream butter or margarine with powdered sugar. Add egg yolks and light cream. Cook over hot water until thickened. Pour slowly over stiffly beaten egg whites. Add flavoring and serve hot.

* * * *

A jazz pianist in a San Francisco pub was banging away at the ivories when a heckler called out to him, "Say, where can a fella hear some live music in this area?" Without missing a note, the pianist replied, "Just wait till I finish typing this letter. Okay?"

CORDON BLEU SAUCE

411

1 can (10½ oz) cream of chicken soup
½ c sour cream
juice of 1 lemon (about 1/3 c)
Blend ingredients and heat. Serve over chicken rolls, if desired. Makes about 2 c, 8 servings of ¼ c each.

* * * *

Father: Isn't it wonderful how little chicks get out of their shells?
Son: What gets me is how they get in.

Summer picnics would be a great invention if they could only work the bugs out.

Tomorrow: a husband's greatest labor-saving device.

* * * *

Two men died and waited at the Pearly Gates for admission into heaven. "We've got room for only one more," Saint Peter declared. "Which one of you is more humble."

The newspaper where I worked had just announced that when its new building was completed, the old one would be donated to the United Way. A few days later, someone came into the office soliciting contributions to that charitable organization. "I'm sorry," one reporter quipped. "We gave the office."

* * * *

SEASONED SALT

½ c salt
1 Tb garlic salt
1 ts dry mustard
1 ts pepper
1 Tb celery salt
1 Tb paprika
1 ts onion powder

Place all ingredients in blender container; cover and blend on high speed for 20 seconds. Store in tightly covered container. Makes 3/4 c.

CARAMEL SAUCE

1½ c sugar
1 Tb butter
½ ts vanilla
1 c hot water
1/8 ts salt

Caramelize sugar by heating in a heavy skillet over low heat; stir constantly until sugar has melted and changed to a light brown syrup. Remove from heat and slowly stir in hot water. Return to heat and boil slowly while stirring until hard caramelized sugar completely dissolves and it reaches a temperature of 228° on candy thermometer (or until slightly thickened). Remove from heat and add butter, salt, and vanilla. Makes about 3/4 c or 4 servings of 3 Tb each.

SWEET CHERRY SAUCE

1 can (1 lb or 2 c) dark sweet cherries
1 c cherry juice and water
2 Tb cornstarch
1 Tb butter
¼ c sugar
dash of salt
3/4 ts vanilla or brandy extract

Drain and pit cherries, reserving juice. Measure reserved cherry syrup; add water to equal 1 c liquid. Combine sugar, cornstarch and salt in medium saucepan. Gradually stir in syrup; bring to boil over medium heat, stirring constantly. Add pitted cherries; boil 1 min. Remove from heat. Blend in butter and extract. Delicious over ice cream.

HARD SAUCE--PLAIN & FANCY

Hard sauces are spread in a dish to the thickness of about 3/4"; then thoroughly chilled. When firm they are cut into small shapes suitable for individual servings. To make about 1 cupful:

Sift 1 c confectioners' sugar; beat until soft 2-5 Tb butter; add sugar gradually. Beat these until well blended; add flavoring; teaspoon vanilla or fruit juice. When sauce is very smooth, chill.

FOAMY RUM SAUCE

2 egg yolks
½ c sifted confectioners' sugar
¼ c light cream
1 Tb rum or 1 ts rum flavoring

Beat egg yolks until thick; add sugar and cream. Pour in double boiler; beat constantly until mixture thickens. Stir in rum slowly. For a foamier sauce fold in 2 stiffly beaten egg whites.

EGGNOG SAUCE

1. In a small mixing bowl at lowest speed blend:
   - 1½ c light cream
   - ¼ c sugar
   - 1 c milk
   - 2 eggs
   - 1 ts vanilla or rum flavoring
   - 1 3 3/4-oz instant vanilla pudding
2. Blend until smooth (about 2 min.)
3. Cover and chill.
4. Serve over bread pudding or any other pudding.

Yields 2¼ c.

* * * *

Come to think of it, if it weren't for inflation a lot of people wouldn't know beans.

Now that they're showing X movies at the outdoor theaters, the birds and bees can learn a thing or two from us.--Jimmy Wong in <u>Chicago Tribune</u>

CHOCOLATE FUDGE SAUCE

1 c sugar
2 Tb cocoa
2 Tb butter
7/8 c evaporated milk

Mix together and heat over low heat until warm (2-3 min.) Blend in butter. Turn up heat and bring to boil, stirring constantly. Boil 2 min (more for thicker). Add 1 ts vanilla. Cool and refrigerate.

HOT FUDGE SAUCE

3 sq unsweetened chocolate
1 can sweetened condensed milk
½ c hot water
¼ ts salt
½ c sugar
1 ts vanilla

In the top of double boiler, melt chocolate over hot water. Stir in milk. Cook to thicken, stirring constantly. Stir in water, salt and sugar and condensed milk. Delicious either hot or cold over icecream.

BURNT SUGAR SAUCE

2 sq butter
3 c sugar
1 qt boiling water or more
3 heaping Tb flour

Mix flour with some cool water. Remove hot liquid from heat and stir in thickening. Put in double boiler and cook until thickened. Add more water if necessary. 4 Tb brandy or 1 ts brandy flavoring just before serving.

* * * *

The nice part about air-conditioning is, you finally know what to do with your winter clothes in July--wear them!

Freedom is worth whatever it costs.

Those who say you can't take it with you never saw a car packed for a vacation trip.

CHOCOLATE-CARMEL SAUCE

½ c (5.5 oz chocolate flavored sauce)
3 Tb milk
20 unwrapped carmels
Place ingredients in double boiler over hot, not boiling water. Stir until carmels are melted and mixture is smooth. Blend in 2 Tb butter. Keep warm until time to serve. *You'll find numerous uses for this recipe!

* * * *

Much as we enjoy the banks' generosity, is there some place we can turn in an electric toaster and get $5,000?

A few moments after his daughter announced her engagement, the father questioned, "Does he have any money?"

"Oh, you men are all alike," the girl replied. That's just what he asked about you."

The automobile did away with horses, Now it's working on the rest of us.

He who deliberates fully before taking a step will spend his entire life on one leg. --Chinese proverb.

No matter how I plan it, the tomatoes in my garden always ripen when I'm away on vacation.

Picnic: Meadow Lark.

Mohammed's wives: Prophet sharers.

Cucumber patch: Dillies of the field.

SUPER SPAGHETTI SAUCE

1 small can stewed tomatoes
1 48-oz can tomato juice
1 lg can tomato paste
2 cans tomato soup
4 med onions (chopped fine)
1 Tb chili powder
2 ts poultry seasoning (or less)
1 Tb celery seed
1 Tb salt
2 Tb sugar
1 ts oregano
1 ts garlic salt
½ ts pepper
½ ts crushed red peppers
1½ lb minced chuck
½ lb minced lean pork

Mix all ingredients together except the meats. Mix beef and pork with some salt, pepper and garlic salt or powder to taste. Then make small meat balls and mix into the sauce, and let simmer for 3-4 hrs, stirring occasionally.

Use spaghetti noodles, if possible, instead of spaghetti. Sprinkle with cheddar or parmesan cheese and hot peppers. Serve over rice or noodles.

* * * *

The big problem with airlines is seats--getting our into theirs.

Life is full of disappointments. Nothing ever comes off except buttons.

Frustration is trying to find your glasses without your glasses.

Social Security check: month-to-month resuscitation.

Electric bills: futility rates.

Food costs: vittle statistics.

Fund raising for charity: the alms race.

The note from King Tut started like this:
"Tomb It May Concern."

Notes

Notes

preserves

Since 1936 the Latter-day Saints (Mormons) have been counseled to put away a year's supply of food, clothing and resources, against the day when such may not be available. This counsel has proven a blessing to Mormons and non-Mormons alike throughout the world, where floods, earthquakes, and other natural "acts of God" have wracked destruction to normal living patterns. Hence, it is not surprising to learn that the greatest proportion of bottling and canning equipment in the United States is sold in the Intermountain West, evidence of their obedience to the counsel of their prophet. This Preserving and Canning Section is but a thumbnail sketch of an ongoing storage program in the modern LDS home, where an earnest endeavor is made to can, freeze, or dry the commodities needed to sustain a family in an emergency.

ORANGE SPICED PEACHES

1. Drain 1 No. 2½ can peach halves (6-8 halves)
2. Add to the peach syrup:
   - 1/3 c sugar
   - 8 whole cloves
   - a 3" stick cinnamon
   - 1 ts orange rind
   - ½ c orange juice
   - 2 Tb lemon juice
3. Boil the syrup 5 min. and pour over peach halves.
4. Cover and refrigerate overnight.
5. Drain. Serve chilled with ham, turkey or chicken.

CHILI SAUCE

30 med. tomatoes
4 Tb salt
½ Tb cloves
15 bell peppers (green)
½ Tb cinnamon
15 onions
12 apples
½ qt vinegar
½ qt water
½ Tb black pepper
4 c brown sugar
½ ts cayenne

Grind all vegetables and add spices. Boil gently for 2½ hrs. stirring frequently to prevent sticking. Bottle hot in sterilized bottles.

CHOPPED PICKLES

24 lg cucumbers
8 lg onions
8 green peppers
8 red peppers

Grind and cook in 2 qts water for 15 min. Drain.

Add:
8 ts mustard seed
8 ts celery seed
6 ts turmeric
9 c sugar
4 ts salt
1 ts cloves
2 scant qts vinegar
Green coloring

Boil 9 min. and bottle.

HOT DOG RELISH (4 pints)

2 c chopped onions
2 c chopped cabbage
2 c green tomatoes
6 green peppers
¼ c salt
2 c white vinegar
3 red peppers
3 c sugar
½ Tb celery seed
3/4 ts turmeric
1 c water

Grind vegetables using coarse blade. Sprinkle with salt and allow to stand overnight. Rinse well and drain. Combine remaining ingredients. Add to vegetables and heat to boiling point. Simmer 3 min. Seal in hot jars.

ZUCCHINI RELISH

10 c ground zucchini)
2 c ground onion) Let stand overnight
5 Tb salt)

Next morning, drain and wash in cold water. Drain and mix:

2½ c vinegar
4 c sugar
1 ts nutmeg
1 ts turmeric
1 ts cornstarch
2 ts celery seed
½ ts pepper

Cut up 1 green pepper and one red pepper. Combine all ingredients and cook 30 min. Bottle and seal.

TOMATO SALSA

¼ bushel tomatoes, skinned and diced (6 qts)
4 med. onions, chopped
2 green peppers chopped
2 lg. cans green chilies (4 oz. size)
½ can jallipieno peppers (use 2 to 5 according to taste)
dash garlic powder
2 Tb salt
2 Tb sugar
1/3 c vinegar

Boil hard for 20 min. Simmer 1 hour. Makes 12 pints.

REFRIGERATOR PICKLES

6 c unpeeled cucumbers, sliced
1 c chopped onion
1 Tb salt
Sprinkle salt over cukes and let stand for 1 hr.
Drain. Make marinade of:
2 c sugar
1 c vinegar
1 Tb celery seed
Stir and bring to boil. Pour over cucumber mixture and store in refrigerator.

DELICIOUS PICKLES

5 c cucumbers (dill size cubed, or if large, peel and seed before cubing)
2 c chopped onions
1¼ c vinegar
3/4 c water
1 c white sugar
3 Tb flour
1 ts celery seed
1/8 ts cayenne
1 ts turmeric
1 small can pimento if desired for color
Soak cucumbers and onions overnight in 3 Tb salt and cold water to cover. Drain cukes and onions. Add marinade and cook gently for 10-15 min. Seal hot.

EASY DILL PICKLES

2 qt water
1 qt vinegar
½ c salt
1 ts dill seed per qt
dill

Bring salt, vinegar and water to boil. Pour over cucumbers arranged in bottles to which dill seed and dill have been added. Seal.

SWEET DILL PICKLES

Slice 2 qts cucumbers and sprinkle with salt. Let stand 30 min. Rinse well.

Syrup: 1 c vinegar
1 c sugar
1 c water
¼ ts turmeric
¼ ts dill seed
¼ ts pickling spice
½ ts salt

Bring to boil and pour over cukes. Bring to boil again and put in jars and seal.

MUSTARD PICKLES

4 qt cauliflower
3 qts cucumbers
6 lg red peppers
2 qt cider vinegar
2 qt water
3 c white sugar
9 Tb mustard
2½ Tb curry powder
1 lg box pickling spice
3 qt sm. white onions
6 lg green peppers
3 hot red peppers
1 qt Terragon vinegar
2 pkg brown sugar
2½ c flour
2 Tb turmeric
8 stalks celery

Cook pickling spice, tied in cloth, in small amount of water for 1-2 hrs. Cut all vegetables and put in brine over night. Freshen in cold water for 2 hrs. Drain and let vegetables stand in liquor of ½ vinegar ½ water for 30 min. Scald in same liquor, drain. Grind peppers and celery in coarse food chopper and add to mustard dressing. Make mustard dressing by rubbing dry ingredients (mustard, sugar, flour, etc.) together and make paste with some vinegar and water. Add this paste to boiling vinegar and water. Add other vegetables and simmer 5-10 min.

FAMILY FAVORITE DILLS

100 cucumbers makes 20-22 qts
8 qts liquid
Pack bottles with cukes, 2 stocks dill
2 flowerets of dill (can use more if desired)
1 clove of garlic, one thin slice of onion
Bring to a boil 1 qt cider vinegar, 3 qts water
Add 1 c pickling salt and bring to boil again.
Pour liquid over cukes and process for 20 min.

NINE DAY SWEET PICKLES

22 cucumbers, med. to large
Each morning for 4 days, pour boiling water over.
5th day - cut in chunks
Heat 1 qt vinegar, 1/4 c salt (rock salt is best)
2 c sugar 1 Tb pickling spice (put in bag)
Pour mixture over cucumbers
7th & 8th day - add 1½ c sugar to brine. Heat and pour over cucumbers.
9th day - add 1 c sugar, 1 Tb alum and green coloring to vinegar. Heat to boiling. Pack cucumbers in jars. Pour boiling liquid over cucumbers and seal. Makes 12 pints.

PEPPER SAUCE

2 qts yellow peppers, sliced
1 qt sliced onions
1 pt grated carrots
2 qts tomatoes

Steam carrots and onion in ½ c oil until crisp. Add peppers and 2 qts skinned tomatoes. Then add:

½ ts pepper
1 ts salt
1/8 ts cayenne pepper
1/4 c sugar

Cook until it reaches desired thickness. Put in bottles while very hot so they seal properly.
(Once you try this old country recipe, you will make it again and again!)

CHUTNEY

1 qt cucumbers)
1 qt onions)
3 red peppers)
6 green peppers)
1 lg cauliflower)

Grind vegetables with coarse blade, nugget-size.

Mix well with ½ c salt. Cover with boiling water and let stand one hour. Drain, then add:
1 c sugar
½ gal weakened vinegar (half or 1/3 water)
1 oz celery seed
1½ Tb pickling spice
3/4 c flour
4 Tb mustard
½ oz turmeric
Mix together. Boil for 10 min stirring to keep from burning. Bottle in sterilized bottles. Makes 12 pts.

*This recipe is a two-time first place winner at the State Fair and was an old pioneer recipe.

APRICOT JAM

4 c pitted apricots
5 c sugar
½ can (6oz) lemonade or
2 Tb lemon juice
1 c crushed pineapple
2 whole oranges
1 3oz. package lemon
or orange jello

Blend apricots, oranges & pineapple in blender. Add sugar. Bring to a boil in large saucepan and cook, stirring for 10 min. Add jello and lemonade; boil 2 min. Pour into hot sterilized jars. Extra good!

* * * *

Message on the back of an Arizona taxi: "Don't drink and drive. My fee: $25 per hour. Your attorney's fee: $200 per hour.

Waiting for an elevator at our hospital, I stood next to a maintenance man holding a bicycle pump. Noticing my curious stares, he looked at me and remarked with a grin. "It's the new HMO oxygen program."

APRICOT LEATHER

For each 2 c apricot puree, use:
½ c crushed pineapple (optional)
1 Tb honey
⅓ ts cinnamon
dash of nutmeg
Wash fruit thoroughly. Drain, halve and pit. Put in large pot. Heat slightly. Puree warm fruit in electric blender (or food grinder). Measure puree. Add remaining ingredients in proportion. Mix well. Spread 1/8" layer of puree mixture on plastic wrap. Dry in direct sunlight for 8 hrs (dry center but not brittle). Place dried leather on a clean sheet of plastic wrap. Roll the fruit and plastic into a tight scroll. Wrap outside in more plastic wrap. Store in airtight container. Makes 3-4 rolls.

VARIATION:
For each 2 c cherry, plum or peach puree, use:
2 Tb honey
1 Tb lemon juice
The addition of pureed bananas gives a gloss and chewy texture, and it never dries out. Try grating the rind of an orange or lemon with your yellow fruits for another interesting flavor delight. Dried apple leather and bananas is one of our family favorites.

If the weather is inclement, may accomplish drying by turning oven on to 150° for 7-8 hrs. keeping the oven door slightly ajar with a folded hot pad.

* * * *

The world is not interested in the storms you encountered, but whether you brought in the ship.

There is a difference between blazing a trail and burning up the road.

TOMATO CATSUP

1 bushel tomatoes
2 stalks celery cut
5 lg onions
2 green peppers
Boil until tender and strain. Add:
6 c sugar
1½ c salt
1 level ts cayenne pepper
6 c vinegar
1 box pickling spice

Boil for 4-6 hours and bottle.

CANNED TOMATO SOUP

1 lug tomatoes (half bushel)
1 qt chopped onions
small bunch parsley
1 Tb celery seed
2 bay leaves
18-20 whole cloves

Tie bay leaves, cloves, celery seed and parsley in sack and boil with tomatoes and onions for 45 minutes. Strain through colander. Bring soup to boil. Combine 4 Tb salt, 8 Tb sugar, 14 Tb flour and 1 qt tomato juice. Add to soup and cook for 10 min. Put in sterilized jars and seal. (See No. 35 for another tasty tomato soup.)

PICKLED BEETS

3/4 c brown sugar
½ c white sugar
1 ts salt
1½ c beet juice
1½ c dark vinegar

Boil 5 min. with beets. Seal hot. Is sufficient to cover 5 pints of beets.

MOCK MINCE MEAT

3 lb tomatoes
3 lb apples
2 lb raisins
2 lb currants
1 c chopped suet
1 c vinegar
¼ c molasses
1½ Tb salt
2 Tb cinnamon
1 ts nutmeg
1 ts cloves
8 c brown sugar

Grind tomatoes, drain and measure juice. Then throw away and add as much water as juice. Cook until thick. Bottle. Do not have to seal.

PRUNE CONSERVE

7 c prunes (fresh Italian)
6 c sugar
2 oranges
1 lemon
1½ c walnuts
1-2 c pineapple
1 lb raisins
Grind prunes. Add sugar & raisins. Cook & stir for 45 min. Grind orange and lemon. Add pineapple to prunes. Cook 15 min. Add walnuts and cook 5 more minutes. Seal while hot.
*Everybody's Grandma had this recipe. It is a very old one and remains because it is so distinctively good.

STRAWBERRY JAM

4 c berries
3 Tb lemon juice
5 c sugar
Cook 9 min. Let stand overnight. Cook 9 more minutes. Let cool, seal.

MARASCHINO CHERRIES

4½ lb pitted white cherries
3½ lb sugar
1 oz red coloring
1 c water
Boil ½ hr. Add 2 Tb almond flavoring and seal.

RHUBARB STRAWBERRY SAUCE
(Topping for icecream)

4 c rhubarb
1 c sugar
1 small pkg strawberry jello
1 pkg frozen strawberries
Cook rhubarb until juicy. Add remaining ingredients and stir only until sugar and jello dissolve. Bottle or freeze.

RHUBARB GELATIN JAM

5 c finely cut rhubarb   4 c sugar
1 sm flat can crushed pineapple
1 pkg (3 oz) strawberry flavored gelatin
Few drops red food coloring optional
Combine rhubarb, sugar and pineapple and bring to boil. Cook 30 min. Remove from heat. Stir gelatin and add coloring if desired. Pour into sterilized jars and seal. To ensure sealing, process in hot water bath for 5 min.

TOMATO SOUP

½ bushel tomatoes, cut in small pieces
6 outside stalks celery, cut in pieces using leaves
6 onions, chopped
3 green peppers, cut up
3 red sweet peppers, cut up
½ ts cayenne pepper
6 bay leaves
Boil together about 1½ hrs. Put through colander. Then add:
½ c brown sugar
½ c white sugar
4 Tb salt
Bring to boil again and bottle. Makes 8 qts.

FROZEN CREAMED CORN

4 qts corn cut off cob
1 c cream (half & half)
1/3 c sugar
4 ts salt
Bake in oven at 350° in shallow pan approximately 45 min. or until slightly thick, stirring often. Let cool until slightly warm. Freeze in plastic containers.

* * * *

You can't have bread--and loaf.

Some cause happiness wherever they go; others whenever they go.

APPLE PIE IN-A-JAR

10 c water	)	berries
4½ c sugar	)	cherries
1 c corn starch	)	peaches
¼ ts nutmeg	)	
2 ts cinnamon	)	apples
3 ts lemon juice	)	

Put all ingredients in large pan. Bring to a boil stirring til clear and thick. Place slices of apples or fruit in jar and pour hot syrup over. Makes 6-8 qts. Process 6 min. in cold pack.

APRICOT NECTAR

(14 med. or 20 small apricots per pound)
1 lb apricots. Add 1 pt water
Cook until squishy. Put through colander. Measure 4 c sugar for every 5 qt juice. Heat to boiling and bottle.

FROZEN PEACH PIE FILLING

3½ c sugar 2 ts ascorbic acid
4 qts fresh peaches, sliced
½ c plus 2 Tb quick cooking tapioca
1/3 to ½ c lemon juice 1 ts salt
Blend together sugar and ascorbic acid. Stir in remaining ingredients. Line five 8" pie dishes with foil, leaving enough extra foil for each to wrap around frozen filling. Divide fruit mixture evenly among them. Wrap foil loosely around. Freeze immediately. When frozen, lift filling out of pie dishes; wrap foil securely around them so they are air-tight. Stack in freezer. To bake, remove frozen pie filling from foil; set into pastry-lined 9" pie plate. Dot with 2 Tb butter. Arrange top pastry over filling, sealing to lower crust and crimping. Slash top crust to vent. Bake for 1 hr at 425°. Makes 5 pies.

CANNED APRICOT PIE FILLING

10 lb apricots, washed and pitted (2½ to 2 3/4 c per lb)
2 c water 4 c sugar
1 c plus 2 Tb quick cooking tapioca
1½ c sugar 3/4 c lemon juice
In large heavy kettle combine apricots, water and 4 c sugar. Cook until mixture is just about ready to boil (190°). Add tapioca, remaining 1½ c sugar and lemon juice. Barely bring to boiling point again. Pour into sterilized jars. Adjust lids. Process ir boiling water bath for 25 min. For each pie, pour 1 qt filling into unbaked 9" pastry shell. Dot with 2 Tb butter. Adjust top pastry over pie. Trim, crimp and cut vent holes. Bake at 400° for 40 min. or until crust is golden brown. Makes 5 qts.

FROZEN FRUIT COCKTAIL

3 lb (12 medium) fresh peaches
2 c sugar 1 lb seedless grapes
1 can (15¼ oz) crushed pineapple, undrained
½ c lemon juice (2 lemons)
1½ c orange juice (3 oranges)
Peel peaches. Cut into bite-size pieces to make 6 c. Sprinkle with sugar; set aside while preparing remainder of fruit. Wash grapes, stem. Stir into peaches along with remaining ingredients. Spoon into plastic freezer containers and freeze. To serve while frosty (which is when it is best) allow to stand at room temperature about 3 hrs. Bananas may be added at serving time. Makes 4½ pts.

PEACH COMPOTE
(Topping)

1 c water
2-3 Tb tapioca
½ c sugar
2 Tb peach Quench powder
1 ts lemon juice
Bring to boil till clear and thick. Add 10-12 peaches. Bring back to boil and remove immediately. Serve over pudding or icecream.

CANTALOUPE PICKLES

1 qt cucumbers, cut fine
1 doz lg onions, chopped
1 lg cauliflower
3-4 green peppers
1 or 2 cantaloupe
1 doz small whole cukes
4 doz pickling onions
1 stalk celery
3-4 red peppers

Cut all in small chunks. Put together and cover with cold water and 1 c salt. Let stand overnight. Drain and rinse in the morning. Add:

2 c white vinegar
1 ts celery seed
8 c sugar
1 Tb mustard seed

Let come to a boil and add paste of 4 ts turmerick and 1 c flour. Moisten with 3/4 c water and ½ c vinegar. Stir and cook until it boils. Cook 20 min and seal in sterilized jars. Makes 8 pts.

Note: To sterilize jars, put clean jars in the oven on warm for 15-20 min. This sterilizes them and when lids are heated in boiling water, they seal readily.

FROZEN FRUIT PIES

#1 - Combine 4 qts fresh strawberries, 4 c sugar, 3/4 c quick tapioca ¼ c lemon juice and 1 ts salt Mix well.

#2 - Line four 8" pie pans with aluminum foil, let extend 5" beyond rims. Pour filling into pans. Fold foil loosely over filling. Freeze until firm. Put in shells and add top crust. Bake 1 hr at 425°.

Cherry Pies

Mix 6 c sugar, 3 ts ascorbic acid, and 4 qts pitted cherries. Add 3/4 c quick tapioca and 1 ts salt. Mix and freeze.

Rhubarb Pie

Mix 4 qts rhubarb (cut in ½" pieces), 6 c sugar, 2/3 c tapioca and 1 ts salt. Mix and freeze.

Raspberry Pie

Mix 4 c sugar and 4 qts raspberries, 2/3 c quick tapioca and 1 ts salt. Mix and freeze.

FROZEN PEACHES

3 lb peaches (5 large) diced
2 c sugar (less)
1 sm can crushed pineapple
juice of 2 lemons (½ c)
juice of 2 oranges (3/4 c)
seedless grapes if desired
Freeze and serve cold.

RASPBERRY JAM

8 c berries 8 c sugar
Measure berries and cook for 1 min. at rolling boil. Add sugar and cook 2 min. Take off stove and beat with egg beater for 2 min. Bottle in sterilized jars.

MOCK RASPBERRY JAM

8 c zucchini (peeled and seeded) (put in blender)
1 c lemon juice
Cook for 15 min. at full boil. Do not drain.
Add 2-6 oz. pkg raspberry jello
6 c sugar
1 pkg pectin
Cook 10 min at rolling boil. Pour into sterilized bottles and seal.

* * * *

The way some people drive you'd think they were late for their accident.

A man can fail many times, but he isn't a failure until he begins to blame somebody else.

BEEF-VEGETABLE SOUP

4 lb cross-cut beef shanks
1 46 oz can tomato juice
3 Tb salt
½ ts pepper
¼ ts thyme
¼ ts marjoram
1 c shell macaroni
2 Tb parsley flakes
4 beef bouillon cubes
4 c sliced carrots
2 c chopped onion
2 c chopped celery
3 qts water

Combine beef, tomato juice, spices and bouillon. Bring to boil, reduce heat and simmer 2 hrs. Remove beef, cut up meat and return to kettle. Simmer 15 minutes. Makes 3½ qts concentrate. Add 1 qt water per 1 qt concentrate. Freezes well or put in sterilized bottles and seal.

PUMPKIN-APRICOT BUTTER

1 qt pumpkin or banana squash puree
3 c sugar
1 c finely chopped dried apricots
1¼ c water
2 Tb grated lemon peel
3/4 c lemon juice
1 ts vanilla

In large kettle, set puree and sugar over medium heat. Cook, stirring, until sugar is dissolved. Add apricots, water, lemon peel, juice and vanilla. Continue cooking, stirring constantly, until mixture boils.

Reduce heat and simmer, stirring often, for 30-40 min, or until mixture thickens to desired consistency. To test consistency, drop a small amount of the butter onto a chilled saucer.

Ladle hot butter in sterilized jars to within ½" of top. Wipe rims with a clean, damp cloth and set lids in place; screw on ring bands. *A refreshing change any time of the year!

RASPBERRY-PEACH JAM

5 c chopped peaches
½ c lemon juice
1 pkg frozen raspberries
red coloring
2 pkg sure jell pectin
8½ c sugar
Mix all ingredients together except sugar. Bring to boil. Add sugar. Boil 4 min. Makes 6 pts.

APPLE MARMALADE

2 c oranges unpeeled
6 med. apples, pared, cored and coarsely cut (6 c)
3 Tb lemon juice
5 c sugar
Quarter oranges, remove seeds and slice thin. Combine orange, apples, 2 c water & lemon juice. Bring to boil. Boil gently 10 min. until apples are tender. Add sugar. Cook and stir till mixture comes to a full rolling boil and sugar is dissolved. Continue to cook until mixture is thickened and clear, stirring frequently. Pour into hot scalded jars and seal.

PEACH CONSERVE

7 pts ripe peaches
6 pts sugar
2 sm oranges and peeling
1 lemon peeled and cut up (no peeling)
1 sm can pineapple tidbits (chunks cut in half)
1 bottle maraschino cherries (no juice)
Cook oranges and lemon in enough water to cover for 1 hr. Add peeled sliced peaches and pineapple. Bring to good boil. Add sugar and bring to boil again. Cook 1 to 1½ hrs. Add cherries and bottle hot. Makes 6-8 pints. If you cook 1½ hrs it is thick. If you want a beautiful and light syrup, cook about 50 min. to an hour and remove fruit. Makes a couple of pints of hot cake syrup. Delicious!

Notes

Notes

Beverages

Sandwiches

Quantity Cooking

Substitutions

Cooking Terms

Equivalents

Child's Play

Household Hints

potpourri

Notes

PUNCH FOR THE BUNCH

1 3-oz pkg cherry jello)
1 c boiling water) Dissolve and add:
1 6-oz can frozen lemonade
1 6-oz can orange juice OR large can pineapple juice
3 c cold water)
1 qt cranberry juice) Mix altogether and enjoy!
1 bottle gingerale)

HOLLY BERRY WASSAIL

4 c bottle cranberry juice
2 6-oz frozen lemonade
6½ c water
9 whole cloves
2 sticks cinnamon
2/3 c sugar

Mix spices in cranberry juice and water. Bring to boil. Cover and remove from heat. Let stand 3 min. Lift out spices and discard. Add sugar and stir until dissolved. Add lemonade. Garnish with orange slices.

HOT FRUIT PUNCH

2 c water)
2 c sugar) Boil 5 min to make syrup

¼ c red hots)
¼ c water) Heat until red hots are melted

2 c orange juice
3/4 c lemon juice
red food color
2 qts water
1 ts vanilla

Simmer together; add few whole cloves; additional lemon juice may be added if desired.

ALMOND PUNCH

1 can (12-oz) frozen orange juice
1 can (6-oz) frozen lemonade
1½ c sugar
10 c water
1 ts vanilla
1 ts almond extract
1 qt gingerale

Combine all ingredients except gingerale and chill. Just before serving add gingerale.

QUICK ROOT BEER

1 gal water, warmer than lukewarm
1 ts yeast 3 c sugar
1/3 bottle root beer extract
Let set at room temperature all day and refrigerate over night. It's ready!

HONEY ROOT BEER

3/4 ts yeast
½ c warm water
1 2/3 c honey
1 qt hot water
3 Tb root beer extract
warm water

Combine yeast in the ½ c warm water. Dissolve honey in the 1 qt hot water. Mix together. Add root beer extract and blend well. Fill with warm water in gallon jug to one gallon mark. Let stand 8 hrs or overnight with loose lid at room temperature. Tighten lid and chill in refrigerator.

"MORMON CHAMPAGNE"

1. Place equal parts of chilled apple cider and gingerale in serving container.
2. Float an icering made from flat gingerale or apple cider with fruit slices.

CHOCOLATE BANANA BLITZ

1 c icecold milk
1 egg
1 fully ripe banana, cut in pieces
1/3 c cocoa mix
½ pt (1 c) vanilla or chocolate icecream, cut up
1 Tb malted milk powder, plain or chocolate
1 ts honey (optional)

Place all ingredients into blender. Whir on low speed until mixed. Blend on high until smooth. Makes 2 servings.

HOT GRAPE DRINK

4 c water
3/4 c sugar
6 cinnamon sticks
20 whole cloves
4 c grape juice
2 c orange juice
lemon slices

Combine water, sugar, cinnamon sticks and cloves. Bring to boil. Reduce heat and simmer 15 min. Remove cinnamon and cloves.

Add grape juice and orange juice. Simmer until very warm, but do not boil. Serve in cups with slice of lemon in each. Serves 12.

RASPBERRY FRAPPE

2 half gallons pineapple sherbert
2 boxes frozen raspberries thawed
4 bananas

Soften sherbert slightly. Fold in thawed raspberries and juice, then fold in 4 bananas cut up. Put in 9x13 dish and place in freezer. Take out of freezer 20 min before serving to let it thaw a bit. Scoop into dishes. Serves 16.

ORANGE JULIUS

1 c milk
1 c water
1 6-oz can frozen orange juice
2 Tb sugar
2 ts vanilla
2 eggs (optional)
12 ice cubes

Mix in blender.

FROSTY ORANGE NOG

3 c orange juice, chilled
¼ c lemon juice, chilled
6 eggs
¼ c sugar
¼ ts cinnamon
¼ ts cloves
¼ ts ginger

Blend the above ingredients with rotary beater. Then add: 5 c orange juice, chilled. Just before serving, spoon in 1 qt vanilla ice cream, softened and 1 qt gingerale. Garnish with nutmeg. Makes 1 gallon.

HOLIDAY WASSAIL

4 c water
2 c sugar

In large pan, combine and boil for 5 min. Tie together in small clean cloth:

3 sticks cinnamon
12 whole cloves
6 allsprice berries
½ ts ginger

Add:

1 can (6 oz) frozen lemonade and 2 cans frozen orange juice and 2 qts apple cider. Simmer to blend flavors. Serves 18, 6 oz. each.

OLD ENGLISH CITRUS NOG

1. Mix together in the top of a double boiler: 3/4 c sugar, 2 Tb flour, ½ ts nutmeg
2. Gradually stir in 4 c milk.
3. Beat until smooth and add slowly a spoonful at a time, 3 eggs
4. Cook over hot, not boiling water, stirring constantly, until slightly thickened.
5. Add and mix well 3/4 c orange, pineapple, apricot or apple juice.
6. Serve hot or cold, garnished with ground nutmeg.

Serves 16.

FRESH PEACH DRINK

Combine equal amounts of apricot nectar, gingerale and lemon lime pop. Freeze to slush. Chop peaches fine and add a little "fruit fresh." Put 2 Tb peaches in cup. Cover with slush. Serve with spoon. Good with crackers and cheeseball or blue cheese bites and lots of mixed nuts.

STRETCH-A-NOG

2 qts commercially prepared egg nog
1 lg pkg instant vanilla jello pudding
1 lg pkg instant lemon jello pudding
2 qts milk (half used to prepare pudding mix)
2 qts gingerale or sprite

In a large punch bowl or 2 gallon container, pour the commercial egg nog. In a blender, put 4 c milk and add two pkg instant pudding. Whip thoroughly and add to the egg nog. Add the other quart of milk and stir. If still too thick, add more milk. Just before serving, add gingerale. Stir occasionally if it is allowed to stand. If a punchier flavor is desired, add cinnamon and nutmeg to taste.

*This egg nog and date-bran muffins (see bread section) have long been holiday traditions at the Horman household.

HOT BUTTERED LEMONADE

"Anti-freeze for cold winter days"

4½ c boiling water	3/4 c lemon juice
3/4 c sugar	1½ ts grated lemon peel

Heat through, stirring occasionally. Pour into mugs and top with 1 ts butter. Serve with cinnamon stick stirrers.

* * * *

Naked and nude mean the same thing--except that naked sounds like a surprise while nude suggests it was done on purpose.

If you say what you think, don't expect to hear only what you like.

HOT 'N SNAPPY TOMATO COCKTAIL

4 c tomato juice
2 Tb sugar
1½ ts celery salt
1 bay leaf
1 c dairy sour cream
¼ c lemon juice
2 ts Worcestershire sauce
½ ts grated onion
4 drops Tabasco sauce

Combine tomato juice, lemon juice, sugar, worcestershire sauce, celery salt, grated onion, bay leaf and Tabasco sauce. Heat to boiling, stirring occasionally. Simmer, uncovered, five minutes. Remove bay leaf. Serve hot with sour cream dollop.

TOMATO REFRESHER

2½ c tomato juice
1 ts sugar
1 ts Worcestershire sauce
3 Tb lemon juice
¼ ts celery salt

Combine and chill. Stir before serving. Float lemon slices on top. Makes 5 4-oz servings.

CUCUMBER TOMATO FROST

4 c tomato juice
1 ts salt
1 med. cucumber chopped fine
1 ts prepared horseradish

Combine all ingredients. Chill an hour or more. Strain out cucumber. Serve in frosted glasses. Serve very, very cold. (No ice cubes). Dip glasses in lemon juice then in parsley (chopped) or salt. Have glasses very, very cold.

BREAKFAST PICK-UP

1 can (12 oz) spicy hot V-8 juice
1½ c plain yogurt
1 ts lemon juice
fresh ground pepper
4 drops Worcestershire
1 ts celery or seasoned salt

Combine all ingredients in blender container. Whip until thoroughly blended. Serve with broiled cheese sandwiches on wholewheat or rye bread. Makes 3 c. May be made with regular V-8 juice if desired.

TROPICAL WHEELIES

6 slices whole wheat bread
2 c low fat cottage cheese
cinnamon
6 slices pineapple, drain

Toast lightly the bread. Drain cottage cheese and spread to edges. Sprinkle with cinnamon. Top with pineapple and place under the broiler for 5 min until pineapple is golden brown.

SLOPPY JOES

3 lb ground beef
2 lg onions, chopped
2 8-oz cans tomato sauce
2 cans chicken gumbo soup
1 c catsup
6 ts dry mustard

Brown ground beef and onion together until onion is tender and meat loses color. Add remaining ingredients and simmer for 30 min, stirring occasionally. Serve on hamburger buns. Serves about 20 people.

CORNED BEEF LOG

1 14-16" long loaf Italian bread
1 12-oz can corned beef
½ c mayonnaise
¼ c chili sauce
2 Tb minced green onion
2 Tb minced celery
2 Tb hot dog relish
1/8 ts pepper

With sharp knife, slice off one end of loaf; set end aside. Hollow out loaf leaving a shell about ¼" thick; reserve bread crumbs. In medium bowl mix the remaining ingredients and blend in bread crumbs. With spatula press corned beef into hollow log. Replace end piece and refrigerate or freeze. This filling can also be used in sandwiches and wrapped and frozen.

MEXICAN MIX FOR TACOS

1½ c cooked wheat
2 cloves garlic, crushed
1 c dry lentils
2 ts dried, crushed parsley
1 qt tomatoes
1 ts salt
1 ts onion salt
1 ts oregano crushed
½ ts cumin
2 ts chili powder
1 c water as needed.

Mix together and simmer for several hours until wheat, lentils and tomatoes lose their identity. Serve with tortillas or tacos.

BIRD SEED

"Guaranteed to keep picnickers chirping!!"

4 c sugar-coated corn cereal
2 lb candy-coated chocolate candies, peanut & plain
2 c raisins
2 lbs salted peanuts
3 c caramel-covered popcorn
Mix all ingredients together and store in covered container. Nutritious, energy-giving snack.

CRUNCHY BAKED BANANAS

1. Peel and cut in half lengthwise, 4 large bananas
2. Place cut sides up in a lightly greased 8x8x2" dish.
3. Combine and spoon over bananas, 1 c miniature marshmallows, ¼ c brown sugar
4. Combine and top with 1 c corn flakes cereal and 1 Tb melted butter or margarine
5. Bake in a 350° oven for about 12 min or until bananas are tender. Serves 4.

YOGURT

Preheat oven to 275°.
½-1 ts plain gelatin softened in ¼ c water
Add 1 c boiling water and 1 Tb sugar. Put in large bowl and add 5 c warm water and 3 c powdered milk and 1 large can evaporated milk. Mix all in blender. Add 3 Tb plain yogurt and mix well. Pour in covered pyrex dishes or pint or quart jars. Turn off the oven and put yogurt in to bake for 8 hrs or until it is sufficiently set. The longer it is left in, the more sour it becomes. Can be used for most recipes calling for sour cream or mixed with mayonnaise to make a less rich dressing. If a fruity yogurt is desired, just add a ts or more of your favorite jam. You have already stretched the food budget enormously if you use yogurt in the kitchen the way we do!

HOT CHOCOLATE MIX

2 lbs Nestles Quick — 12 c dry instant milk
1 lg bottle Pream (16 oz) — 1¼ c powdered sugar

Mix and store in airtight container. Use 3 heaping teaspoons to a mug of hot water. Delicious and another money saver!

RICH FRENCH CHOCOLATE

Smooth and creamy, the perfect hot beverage that even the non-chocolate lovers will enjoy.

1. Melt over low heat in a small saucepan
   1 c semisweet chocolate pieces
   1 c light corn syrup — ¼ c water
2. Add — 1 ts vanilla
3. Refrigerate to cool.
4. In large bowl beat until soft peaks form
   2 c whipping cream
5. Gradually beat in cooled chocolate syrup. Continue beating until mixture mounds.
6. Refrigerate until serving time.
7. Before serving, scald, then pour into warm pitcher
   2 qts milk
8. Spoon some of the chocolate whipping cream into cup. Fill with warm milk to serve. Serves 12-16.

YORKSHIRE PUDDING

1. Sift in bowl 1 c minus 2 Tb flour and ½ ts salt
2. Make a well in center into which you pour ½ c milk
3. Beat in the milk
4. Beat until fluffy — 2 eggs
5. Beat eggs into the batter, then add ½ c water
6. Beat batter until large bubbles rise to the surface
7. Pour into a hot 10x10 or 8x12" ovenproof dish containing ¼" hot beef drippings (approx. ½ c)
8. Bake 20 min at 400°, then 10 min at 350°.
9. Cut in squares and serve at once. May also be baked in muffin tins for individual servings.

MEXICAN HERO SANDWICH

1 can (8¼ oz) crushed pineapple
2 med.-size firm ripe tomatoes
¼ c chopped green onion
2 Tb finely chopped green pepper
2 Tb finely chopped mixed sweet pickle
2 Tb canned diced green chile
3/4 ts salt (seasoned)
1 clove fresh garlic, minced or pressed (¼ ts)
1 unsliced loaf (16 oz) French, multi-grain or other bread (long and narrow loaf shape)
Mexican Spread
2 c shredded iceberg lettuce
1½ c sliced cooked chicken
1 c soft Monterey Jack cheese, sliced

Turn pineapple into wire strainer and drain well, pressing out syrup with back of spoon.

Seed and chop tomatoes to measure 1 c. Combine with drained pineapple, onion, green pepper, pickle, chile, seasoned salt and garlic; mix lightly.

Cut bread in halves lengthwise and spread each cut surface generously with HALF the Mexican spread.

On bottom half of loaf, layer in order the lettuce, HALF the pineapple-vegetable mixture (a scant cup), chicken (seasoned with additional salt and pepper, if desired), Jack cheese and remaining pineapple-vegetable mixture. Set the top half of loaf on the sandwich, press sandwich firmly together and wrap well. Refrigerate until serving time. Cut into thick slices to serve.

Mexican Spread

Combine 2 pkg (3 oz) cream cheese, 1/3 c (2/3 stick) softened butter, 1 ts chili powder, 1 ts Dijon mustard and ½ ts seasoned salt; beat until light and well blended. Makes about 1 c.

* * * *

Real charity doesn't care if it's tax deductible.

The fragrance always stays in the hand that gives the rose.

Anything will give up its secrets if you love it enough.

SALAMI FROM SCRATCH

4 lb ground beef (maximum fat content 25%)
¼ c curing salt
2 Tb liquid smoke
1½ ts garlic powder
1½ ts pepper OR
2 ts whole black peppercorns

In a large bowl, combine beef, curing salt, liquid smoke, garlic powder and pepper. Mix thoroughly. Cover and refrigerate overnight.

Divide mixture into 4 equal portions. Shape each portion into a compact 8" long log and place each on a 12x18" piece of nylon net. Roll up tightly in net and tie ends with string. Place logs, slightly apart, on a rack in a broiler pan. Bake, uncovered, in a 225° oven for 4 hrs.

Remove net and pat rolls well with paper towels. Let cool slightly, then wrap in foil. Refrigerate for up to 3 weeks or longer. Keeps 2 months in freezer. Makes about 3 lbs.

Variations

Herb Beef Salami. Follow recipe for Smoky Beef Salami (above), omitting liquid smoke; instead use 3 Tb dry red wine. Reduce garlic powder to 1 ts and omit pepper. Instead, add 2 Tb mustard seeds, 1 Tb each dry basil and oregano leaves, 1 ts onion powder, and 2/3 c Parmesan cheese.

Spicy Beef Salami. Follow recipe for Smoky Beef Salami, omitting liquid smoke; instead, use 3 Tb dry white wine. Reduce garlic powder to 1 ts and omit pepper. Instead, add 2 Tb chili powder, 2 ts crushed red pepper, and 1 ts ground cumin.

* * * *

A kind word is never lost. It keeps going on, from one person to another, until at last it comes back to you again.

Inspiration works best when you do.

If you can't remember a joke, don't dismember it.

LIVERWURST HERO LOAVES

6 small (6") French loaves — Prepared mustard
2 cans (4 3/4 oz each) liverwurst spread
6 scallions or green onions — cucumber slices
hard cooked egg slices — tomato slices
Swiss cheese — pickle slices
iceberg lettuce leaves

Slice loaves in half horizontally, not quite all the way through. Partially hollow out loaves to make room for filling. Spread bottom half with mustard, then with liverwurst spread. Place a scallion or green onion along uncut edge of loaf, then cover liverwurst spread with cucumber, egg, tomato, cheese, pickle and leaf of lettuce. Close loaves. Makes 6 hearty sandwiches.
Note: 2 cans deviled ham may be substituted for the liverwurst spread.

HOT LUNCHEON SANDWICH

1 can Spam — 1 lg onion
½ lb nippy cheese

Grind together above. Grease well a shallow pan. Decrust 1 loaf sandwich bread. Lay half of slices out flat. Spread mixture over. Put other slices on top. Butter outside bread.

Beat 4 eggs and 3 c milk until lemon colored. Pour over sandwiches. Let stand 4 hrs before baking. Turn before baking at 325-350° for 1 hr.
Make sauce of 1 can mushroom soup or celery soup. Add 1 Tb milk. Heat through and serve 1 Tb over sandwich.

* * * *

Do you know why mountain climbers rope themselves together? To prevent the sensible ones from going home.

It doesn't hurt to be optimistic. You can always cry later.

FALAFEL (For Pocket Bread Sandwich)

1 med potato
2 small onions
3 c cooked, ground garbanzo beans
¼ c sesame seed meal (tahini)
1 Tb yogurt
1 Tb salt
1/8 ts pepper
Juice of 1 lemon
1 lg bunch parsley
3 Tb oil
1/8 ts garlic powder
dash of cayenne
1 ts paprika

Cook and mash potato and set aside. Mince parsley leaves. Chop onions and saute in oil until soft. Add parsley and cook briefly. Add to ground beans. Mix well with remaining ingredients.

Form into balls or shape into patties, using about 2 Tbs of the mixture for each one. Place on greased cookie sheet and bake for 10 min on each side in a 350° oven. Or fry in hot oil until brown.

To serve, split the pocket bread, insert the cooked falafel, add chopped cucumber, tomatoes, lettuce, yogurt and if desired, garbonzo spread. Or simply make the spread, and add any of the other ingredients that suit your fancy.

PITA BREAD SANDWICHES

1 c cottage cheese
3 Tb sweet pickle relish
1 Tb minced green onion
dash of pepper
leaf lettuce
12 small tomato slices
6 lg thin turkey breast slices, rolled
1/3 c chili sauce
2 hard cooked eggs, chopped
½ ts salt
3 sesame pita breads
6 slices (6 oz) cheddar cheese cut into 4 small triangles
alfalfa sprouts

For dressing, beat cottage cheese in small mixing bowl on high speed of mixer until almost smooth, about 5 min. Stir in chili sauce, sweet pickle relish, chopped hard-cooked eggs, minced green onion, salt and pepper. Chill, covered, 2-3 hrs to allow flavors to blend.

For sandwiches, preheat oven to 350°. Bake breads on unbuttered baking sheet 8-10 min, or until crisp. Remove from oven; cut vertically in half. Gently press each half open. Fill with dressing, vegetables, turkey cheese and sprouts, then Tb dressing. Enjoy! Serves 6.

PUMPKIN SEEDS

(Tastes best if you boil seeds first in salt water)

2 c pumpkin seeds
1 ts worcestershire sauce
3 Tb butter or margarine
1 ts salt

Rinse pumpkin seeds until pulp and strings are washed off. Boil seeds in salt water for 10 min. Dry seeds on paper towel. In medium bowl, combine worcestershire sauce, melted butter and salt. Add seeds. Stir until seeds are coated with mixture. Spread on baking sheet. Bake 1-2 hrs at 225°. Stir occasionally. Seeds should be crisp. Makes 2 c.

DIDDLE DADDLE

2 qts popped corn
1 1/3 c pecan halves
2/3 c unblanched almonds
1 1/3 c brown sugar
2 squares butter or margarine
½ c white corn syrup
1 ts vanilla

Mix together corn, pecans and almonds and spread evenly over large baking sheet. Combine brown sugar, butter, and corn syrup in heavy saucepan and cook and stir until mixture boils. Reduce to simmer and cook 10 min. Stir in vanilla. Pour over popped corn mixture. Cool thoroughly and break into chunks.

SCRAMBLES

2 lb mixed salted nuts
1 10-oz pkg cheerios
2 pkg pretzel sticks
1 12-oz pkg corn chex
2 c salad oil
2 Tb salt
2 Tb worcestershire sauce
1 pkg cheese crackers

Mix in roaster pan. Bake in slow oven for 2 hrs, 250°. Stir every 20 min with wooden spoon. Do not crush. Can be frozen. Good in tomato soup or as a snack.

BUTTERCREAM

1 lb fresh creamery butter
¼ c non-instant milk
1 c safflower oil
1 ts salt

Soften butter to room temperature, then whip with rotary beater until smooth. Gradually add the dry milk and salt, followed by the safflower oil.

Buttercream has the delicious taste of butter, is rich in essential fatty acids, and does not contain the preservatives, colorings, and flavorings found in margarine which is listed as a "plastic" product. The safflower oil brings the polyunsaturated-saturated fat ratio in better balance than most margarine. For all recipes calling for butter, margarine, or vegetable shortening, this is a good substitute.

BUTTERCREAM BREAD SPREAD

To one recipe of Buttercream, gradually add 1½ c cold water, whipping it into a delightful bread spread. This buttercream has the delicious taste of butter, yet it is a light product which can be piled a little higher on toast without fear of too many calories or cholesterol.

HERB BREAD

3/4 c buttercream
½ ts thyme
dash of cayenne
¼ ts each of salt, paprika and savory

Soften buttercream; add seasonings. Butter thickly sliced bread. Bake uncovered at 375° for 15 min.

HONEY BUTTER SAUCE

Warm 1 c honey with ½ c Buttercream, ¼ ts cinnamon and dash of nutmeg.

HONEY BUTTER

As you are whipping water into Buttercream Bread Spread, substitute a few tablespoons honey (to taste) for equal parts of water.

ORANGE BUTTER

1 stick (½ c) butter or margarine
1 pkg (1 lb) confectioners' sugar
¼ c orange juice concentrate
Soften butter; thaw orange juice concentrate. Cream together. Add confectioners' sugar. Beat until smooth. You may need to use more confections' sugar for a thicker consistency.

LEMON SESAME BUTTER FOR VEGETABLES

¼ c butter or margarine
Grated peel and juice of ½ lemon
¼ ts onion or garlic salt
Cooked vegetables
1 Tb toasted sesame seeds
In small saucepan melt butter. Add lemon peel, juice, sesame seed and salt; heat. Serve over cooked asparagus, broccoli, cauliflower, beans, summer squash (zucchini, yellow pattypan), spinach, carrots.
Makes about 1/3 c sauce.

HONEY BUTTER

½ lb butter
2½ c honey
2 egg yolks
½ ts vanilla
Whip yolks and butter together and while still beating add honey and vanilla. Beat until stiff. Makes 2 c honey butter.

SWEETENED CONDENSED MILK

To 1 c hot water, add:
¼ c butter
4 c powdered milk
2 c sugar
Whip with mixer to make smooth. Use in any recipe that calls for sweetened condensed milk.

OVEN-DRIED JERKY

The following recipe is for lean cuts of beef (flank, brisket, or round steak), venison, and the white meat of turkey or chicken. Partially freezing the meat before cutting makes it easier to slice evenly. Cut with the grain of the meat if you like a chewy jerky; cut across the grain for a more tender, brittle product.

1½-2 lbs lean, boneless meat, partially frozen
¼ c soy sauce
¼ ts pepper
½ ts onion powder
1 Tb Worcestershire
¼ ts garlic powder
1 ts hickory smoke-flavored salt

Trim and discard all fat from meat (it becomes rancid quickly). Cut the meat in 1/8 to ¼" thick slices. If necessary, cut large slices to make strips about 1½" wide and as long as possible.

In a bowl combine all ingredients except meat and stir until seasonings are dissolved. Add meat strips and mix to thoroughly coat all surfaces. (Meat will absorb most of the liquid). Let stand 1 hr, or cover and refrigerate overnight.

Shaking off any excess liquid, arrange strips of meat close together, but not overlapping, directly on the oven racks or on cake racks set in shallow, rimmed baking pans.

Dry meat at the lowest possible oven temperature (150-200°) until it has turned brown, feels hard and is dry to the touch (about 5 hrs for chicken and turkey, 4-7 hrs for beef and venison). Pat off any beads of oil. Let cool, then remove from racks and store airtight in plastic bags or in a jar with a tight-fitting lid or in covered coffee or shortening cans.

Keep at cool room temperature or in the refrigerator until ready to use; it keeps indefinitely. Makes ½ lb. Note: To keep indefinitely, you'll have to hide it!

POTATOES au GRATIN

To serve 30 ½ c servings 2 9x13x2" pans	60 ½ c servings 4 9x13x2" pans
8 lb potatoes	15 lbs
4 qts cooked, diced	7½ qts
3/4 c butter	1½ c
7/8 c flour	1 3/4 c
1 Tb salt	2 Tb
3/4 ts pepper	1½ ts
2¼ qts hot milk	4½ qts
1¼ qts processed Cheddar, finely cut	2½ qts (2 lb 8 oz)
2 c shredded cheese	1 qt (1 lb)

Boil potatoes, either in jackets or peeled, until just tender. Remove skins; cube or slice potatoes. Combine butter, flour, salt, pepper. Add milk gradually, stirring constantly. Cook while stirring until thickened. Add finely cut cheese and stir until cheese is melted. Add potatoes and additional salt, if needed. Pour into buttered baking dish. Sprinkle with grated cheese. Bake 15 to 20 min, or until cheese is lightly browned.

CHILI FROM SCRATCH

8½ c dried chili beans
  or use 10 #1½ size cans
  chili beans
4 qts water
4 lb ground beef
1 c fat (if hamburger is used cut fat quantity)
2 qts finely chopped onion
10 #1½ size cans tomatoes
5½ Tb salt
5½ Tb chili powder
3 Tb cumin powder (or camino seeds)
4 bay leaves
dash of cayenne (if desired)

If using canned beans, drain and save liquid. Brown beef and add onions. Add rest of ingredients and enough water to make 1 qt of liquid with bean liquid. Cook 1 hr with pre-cooked beans.

Add bay leaves to dry beans if used, while they are cooking. When tender add rest of ingredients. Best when made a day ahead. Serves 50 3/4 c servings.

USING CORN MEAL

Breading

1. Sift together ½ c corn meal and ½ c sifted flour. Add salt and pepper as desired.
2. For thin coating: roll fish, seafood or pre-cooked chicken in corn meal mixture.
   For thicker coating: dip in slightly beaten egg to which 1 Tb water has been added, then in corn meal mixture.
3. Fry raw food in deep fat at 375°,cooked food at 390° until cooked and golden, or pan-fry in moderately hot fat.

Batter Dip

1. Sift together ½ c corn meal and ½ c sifted flour. Add salt and pepper as desired.
2. Add 1 beaten egg and ½ c milk; fold in 2 Tb melted fat
3. Dip fish, seafood or cooked chicken in batter ; fry raw food in deep fat at 375°, cooked food at 390°, until cooked and golden. (If batter gets too thick, add a little more milk.)

French Fried Onions

1. Peel medium-sized Bermuda onions and slice cross wise in ¼" slices. Separate rings.
2. For thin crisp french fried onions: soak rings in milk for 15 min, then dip in a mixture of 2/3 c corn meal and 1/3 c flour to which salt and pepper have been added.
   For thicker coated french fried onions: dip rings in batter made according to Batter Dip directions above.
3. Fry in hot deep fat (375°) for about 2 min.

The following recipes are "Quantity Cooking"; should a greater variety of food be desired, refer to Mountain Fuel Quantity Cooking, the "Meet Together Often" section of The Mormon Family Cook Book or similar publication by Utah Power and Light.

BEEF STEW

50 3/4 cup servings (2½ gallons)

2½ c chopped onions ½ c shortening or oil
10 lb stew beef, trimmed and cut in pieces
3 qts water salt & pepper
3-4 lbs potatoes (2½ qts diced in large pieces)
3-4 lbs carrots (2½ qts diced)
1¼ c flour
2½ c liquid water from potato and carrot cooking
Brown onions in shortening slowly until browned. Add meat, water, salt and pepper. Cook 1½ hrs or until meat is tender. Cook potatoes and carrots in salted water until tender. Drain and add to meat. Shake flour and 2½ c liquid in glass jar. Add to stew and cook to desired consistency. Correct seasoning, if needed.

POTATO SALAD

6½ quarts (about 50 servings)

15 lb potatoes 1½ Tb salt
2 c Italian-style dressing (seasoned oil & vinegar)
½ c vinegar 12 hard cooked eggs, chopped
4 c celery, chopped 1 large onion, chopped
2 c mayonnaise (or as desired) 3/4 c chopped parsley

Red or white potatoes are especially good for potato salad. Scrub, then cook with skins on until just tender. Cool slightly; remove skins. Cube or slice potatoes. Or use old potatoes from storage; pare, then cook until tender. Slice.

Combine dressing, salt and vinegar. Pour over warm potatoes. Mix gently, then let stand until cold. Add remaining ingredients; mix gently. Chill at least an hour (overnight is better), then serve.

MARINATED VEGETABLE MEDLEY

1. Combine together refrigerating until ready for use:
   3 c salad oil
   1 c white wine vinegar
   1 Tb salt
   1 Tb sugar
   1 ts black pepper
2. Drain and place in 2 pans 9 x 13"
   2 cans (16 oz) baby carrots
   1 can whole green beans
   2 cans (16 oz each) asparagus tips
3. Wash and cut into flowerets. Cook in boiling salted water until tender, 1 lg head cauliflower
4. Cut into wedges, 4 medium tomatoes
5. Quarter lengthwise and cut into 3" pieces; cook 1½ lb small zucchini
6. Cook according to package directions
   2 pkg broccoli spears
7. Place all vegetables in oblong pan when they have been cooked and drained.
8. Pour marinade over vegetables in oblong pan, cover and refrigerate over night.
9. Arrange drained vegetables on lettuce. Refrigerate until serving time.
10. Serve with Green Mayonnaise
    Serves 24.

GREEN MAYONNAISE

Combine and let set a day before using:

3 c mayonnaise
6 Tb lemon juice
6 Tb chopped parsley
3 Tb chopped chives
1 Tb dill weed

Serves 24.

CURRIED TURKEY

One-half of a 12 lb cooked turkey (meat is cut from the turkey and diced). Do a day ahead and make at least 6 c. Make a large bowl of gravy from drippings (approx. 6 c) In a deep skillet add enough salad oil to saute the following:

4 lg onions, chopped
3 green apples chopped (with skins)
1½ ts allspice
2 Tb chili powder

Add to gravy in saucepan
salt to taste

To this mixture add:
1 c tomato juice
3-4 Tb curry powder (or to taste)
1 Tb sugar

Let all simmer together in deep skillet or saucepan, 20 min. Then add 2 small cans mushrooms, drained. Heat until ready to serve. Serve in chafing dish over hot buttered rice surrounded by the following suggested garnishes in small bowls. (Pile all or some on top the curry on each individual plate.)

Ripe chopped olives
(2 cans already chopped)
chopped onions (1 lg)
chopped hard cooked eggs (8)
1-2 lb cooked bacon, cut in small pieces
coconut, slightly browned or toasted under broiler
chopped unsalted peanuts
chutney

Serves 20.

FRUIT PUNCH FOR 80

4 pkg cherry cool aid
4 pkg orange cool aid
8 c sugar
1 lg can pineapple juice
2 12-oz cans orange concentrate
6 bananas, mashed
Water and ice to make 4 gallons
Part may be made into slush the rest poured over it. Really refreshing!

* * * *

The mystery-month diet--you can only eat during those months containing the letter "w."

The garlic diet--you lose ten pounds and all your friends.

SERVINGS FOR 50 PEOPLE

Chicken (creamed)	-	20 lb
Chicken (roasted)	-	25 lb
Roast beef boned	-	20 lb
Baked ham	-	12 lb
Gravy	-	5 qts
Soup	-	2½ gal
Corn or green beans #2 cans		5 cans
Peas	-	7 cans
Baked beans	-	10 qts
Potatoes	-	16 to 18 lbs
Steamed puddings, 8 qt mold, 2 qt sauce		
Creamed peas or other vegetables		5 qts
Vegetables, 2½ qts white sauce		
Potato Salad	-	9 qts
Cabbage (for slaw)	-	10 lb
Mayonnaise	-	1¼ qts
Ice Cream (brick)	-	2½ gal
Cream (whipped)	-	1¼ qts
Butter	-	1½ lbs
Rolls	-	8 doz
Sweet Pickles	-	2 qts
Lemonade or punch	-	10 qts

* * * *

Cross a South American cowboy with German money, and you'd get Gaucho Marks.

Don't fight a good breakfast. Go with the grain.

World: a big ball that revolves on its taxes.

Debt: the first thing a person runs into when he buys a new car.

MAKE-AHEAD LAYERED MUSHROOMS & EGGS

1 can (10 3/4 oz) cream of mushroom soup undiluted
3 Tb dry sherry or milk
1½ c each shredded sharp Cheddar cheese and jack cheese
18 eggs
1 ts parsley flakes
1/8 ts pepper
¼ lb mushrooms, sliced
Paprika
2 Tb milk
½ ts dill weed
4 Tb butter or margarine
¼ c chopped green onions including tops

In a small pan over medium heat, combine soup and sherry and cook, stirring until smooth and heated through. Remove and heat and set aside. In a small bowl, lightly mix cheddar and jack cheeses; set aside. In another bowl, beat eggs with milk, parsley, dill weed, and pepper; set aside.

In a wide frying pan over medium-low heat, melt butter. Add mushrooms and onions and cook, stirring until onions are soft. Add egg mixture and cook, gently lifting cooked portion to let uncooked egg flow underneath, until eggs are softly set.

Spoon half the egg mixture into a 7x11" baking dish and cover with half the soup mixture; then sprinkle evenly with half the cheese mixture. Repeat layers; sprinkle top with paprika. (At this point, you may cool, cover and refrigerate until next day.)

Bake, uncovered, in a 300° oven for 30-35 min (1 hour if refrigerated) or until bubbly and heated through. Let stand for 10 minutes before cutting. Makes 8-10 servings.

LEMON CURRY SAUCE

1½ c fresh lemon juice
4 ts salt
4 ts dry mustard
2 c olive or salad oil
3 Tb curry powder
½ c brown sugar

Makes 1 quart, sufficient for 30-40 lamb chops. Keeps in the refrigerator indefinitely. Good also on lamb loaf, or lamb roast.

WAYS TO PERK UP MEALS

1. Use fennel and anice to cut the salty taste of smoked herring or salmon.
2. Add margarine to hashed brown potatoes.
3. Simmer savory with green peas.
4. Use sweet basil on tomatoes and zucchini.
5. Use oregano, rosemary, sage and thyme in meat dishes. (Never use more than 2 at once.)
6. Use nutmeg in creamed dishes and soups, with squash, oyster, and canned or cooked peaches.
7. Allspice in beef.
8. Ginger sprinkled over leg of lamb. Use fresh mint in a sauce for lamb.
9. Little nutmeg in whipped cream to use over chocolate pudding.
10. Chilled pear or orange slices in a dressing of honey and ginger.
11. Curry powder dissolved in lemon juice over buttered carrots.
12. Chili powder in beef gravy.
13. Worcestershire sauce on steaks and chops before broiling.
14. Dill in the sour cream dressing in new potato salad.
15. Dill on cooked beets or baked tomatoes.
16. Add sugar, cream and grated lemon peel to rice pudding.
17. Baste ham with marmalade thinned with orange juice.
18. Add juice and grated rind of orange to mashed or buttered sweet potatoes.
19. Add juice of a fresh orange to can of frozen orange juice.
20. Put toasted sesame seeds in soups and vegetable salads.
21. Put poppy seeds on toasted soda crackers to serve with salads.
22. Put poppy seeds over boiled potatoes and noodles.
23. Put mustard seeds in salads.
24. Cumin on string beans and in chili.
25. Use little vinegar in water to "set" poached eggs.
26. Serve vinegar in cruet to put on french fried potatoes.
27. Use parmesan or cheddar cheese grated over soups and salads; also grated cheese over cauliflower. Parmesan over spaghetti.

28. Use lemon juice and grated lemon peel mixed with cream and sugar in cottage cheese.
29. Serve fresh strawberries with lime halves to squeeze over them.
30. Try dark molasses in custards, maple syrup in apple desserts, and honey on tart fruits.
31. Use honey in fruit salad dressing and brown sugar on berries.
32. Add grated orange peel to fresh fruit compote; the juice and rind of lemon in any baked fruit dessert.
33. Use little vinegar in any meat gravy to cut the fatty taste and add its own touch of flavor.
34. Add a little sugar to peas just before serving; also mushrooms to peas.
35. Use horseradish with boiled tongue, boiled new England dinner, and in sauces for fish.
36. Add lemon juice, worcestershire sauce and onion juice to tomato juice.
37. Add a teaspoon of honey to whipped cream to keep cream light and fluffy.

EQUIVALENTS

3 teaspoons =	1 tablespoon =	½ fluid ounce
4 tablespoons =	¼ cup =	2 fluid ounces
8 tablespoons =	½ cup =	4 fluid ounces
12 tablespoons =	3/4 cup =	6 fluid ounces
16 tablespoons =	1 cup =	8 fluid ounces
2 cups =	16 fluid ounces =	1 pint
4 cups =	32 fluid ounces =	1 quart
4 quarts =	1 gallon	
8 quarts solid =	1 peck	
4 pecks =	1 bushel	
16 ounces =	1 pound	

SUBSTITUTIONS

1 c fresh sweet milk	1 c sour milk or buttermilk + ½ ts soda (decrease baking powder 2 ts.)
1 whole egg	2 egg yolks + 1 Tb water (in cookies, etc.) 2 egg yolks in custard
1 c sour milk or buttermilk	1 Tb lemon juice or vinegar + enough fresh sweet milk to make 1 cup
1 c honey	3/4 c sugar and ¼ c liquid
1 c canned tomatoes	1 1/3 c cut-up fresh tomatoes simmered 10 minutes
1 square chocolate	3 Tb cocoa + 1 Tb butter
1 cup butter	1 c vegetable shortening, ½ ts salt
1 c sour cream	1½ Tbs vinegar + sweet milk to fill 1 cup
1 c cake flour	1 c - 2 Tb all purpose flour
1 cup catsup	1 c tomato sauce + ½ c sugar and 2 Tb vinegar
Baking powder	1 ts baking soda + 2 ts cream of tartar and 1 ts cornstarch
Sour milk	1/3 c evaporated milk + 2/3 c water and 1 Tb vinegar
1 cup milk	¼ c powdered whole milk + 1 c water ½ c evaporated milk, ½ c water
wine or liquor	If the ingredient is used only for seasoning, simply omit it and taste to adjust seasonings, adding herbs, spices, or any other "pick up" desired. Seasonings can be potent, so add cautiously. A quantity of an alcoholic beverage will require replacement by an equal quantity of liquid. For a main dish, use clear soup; for a dessert, use fruit juice. Sometimes milk or water will work well. When the recipe calls for rum, use rum extract with juice, water, or milk. A syrup of butter, sugar, and water with rum extract serves very well as a sauce for mince pie.

SUBSTITUTIONS- cont'd.

1 Tb cornstarch	2 Tb flour (for thickening)
1 oz unsweetened chocolate	3 Tb cocoa plus 1 Tb butter or marg.
1 clove garlic	1 ts garlic salt or 1/8 ts garlic powder
2 ts minced onion	1 ts onion powder
1 Tb finely chopped fresh chives	1 ts freeze-dried chives
1 ts dry leaf herb	1 Tb chopped fresh herbs
1 ts dry mustard	1 Tb prepared mustard

* * * *

VINEGAR & LEMON

1. Home sewers like this time-tested method for pressing a sharp crease in clothing. Use ½ c white vinegar and ½ c water. Wring the press cloth out of this solution and press. It works especially well for wash-and-wear clothing.
2. The same white vinegar solution will help remove a permanent crease (hemline shows). Sponge the material liberally with the solution and press flat with warm iron.
3. Before you manicure, rub cuticles with lemon rind to help whiten them (especially after canning season).
4. Lemon rinds are good refrigerator deodorizers. Lay them on a shelf toward the back for a fresh clean scent.
5. Everything from furniture polish to shampoo has lemon these days. Save the rinds--one favorite trick helps the grubby elbow set. If you have this problem, put your elbows cupped in empty lemon rinds while you read a good book for a half hour. The lemon acts as a bleach.

COOKING TERMS

Au jus	With natural gravy.
Aspic	A savory jelly made from stock or from tomato juice with gelatin.
Au gratin	Covered with cheese or crumbs or both.
Baste	Moisten food while baking with juices from pan or other liquid or fat.
Bake 'til tender	Until a fork or skewer can easily be inserted.
Blanche	Pour boiling water over a food, or immerse in boiling water, followed by cold water.
Blend	To mix well.
Braise	Cook in a covered pan with a small amt. of liquid.
Broil	Subject a food to direct heat, as coals, flame or electric coils.
Bouillon	A clear soup stronger than broth, yet not so strong as consomme, which is clear soup
Chill	Place food in refrigerator until cold, not frozen.
Dredge	Sift a light coating over food, usually flour or powdered sugar.
Fricassee	A dish of any boiled meat served in rich milk sauce.
Glaze	Iced or glossed over. Meats are glazed by covering with concentrated stocks or jellies. Fruits may be frozen or covered with a shiny film of hardened sugar syrup.
Hors D'oeuvres	Appetizing side dishes such as olives, radishes, celery, pickles, etc.
Knead	To place dough on a flat surface and work it, pressing down with knuckles, then fold over, repeating several times.
Marinate	Allow fruits or vegetables to stand in dressing or syrup to improve flavor.
Mince	To cut with knife or scissors in very fine pieces.
Parboil	To boil food in water until partially cooked.
Puree	Food boiled to a pulp and put through a sieve.

COOKING TERMS (continued)

Saute	Cook gently in small amount of hot fat.
Scald	To bring to a temperature just below the boiling point. In milk, tiny bubbles appear around the edge.
Scallop	To bake a food, usually in a casserole with sauce or other liquid. Food and sauce may be mixed together or arranged in alternate layers. Crumbs are often sprinkled on top.
Score	To cut narrow grooves or gashes part way through the outer surface of food.
Simmer	To allow liquid to come to a heat where it barely moves; temperature about 185°.
Steam	Cook food in a covered steamer over boiling water.
Steep	To leave in a liquid just below boiling to extract color, flavor, or other qualities.
Stew	To cook slowly in a small amount of liquid for a long time.

* * * *

When melting only one or two chocolate squares use a deep soup ladle, which is easier to handle than a hot bowl and smaller to wash than the top of a double boiler.

A small pinch of salt makes cream whip faster and egg whites beat up in a jiffy.

If you are watching calories, add a sprinkle of salt to applesauce or rhubarb and you'll need less sugar.

Spinach fresh from the garden requires fewer washings if the first washing has 3 Tb of salt in water.

Use big sharp safety pins instead of skewers the next time you truss a turkey.

To bring out the flavor of chocolate dishes, add a tiny pinch of salt.

USING BAKING SODA

1. Vacuum bottles left in a child's lunchbox overnight present an odor problem. To clean, fill with warm water, stir in 2 ts soda, then tear a piece of newspaper into small bits and poke down into the soda water. Let the bottle stand 15 min. then rinse and dry. The newspaper absorbs the sour odor.
2. This once-a-week drain cleaner keeps drains running smoothly without harsh chemicals. Pour 2 Tb soda, ½ c vinegar, and 1 quart of warm water into the drain. Let stand one-half hour.
3. As an effective cleaner for painted woodwork, walls, tile, and glass surfaces, use 3 Tb soda to 1 qt of warm water.
4. Do you have a grease spot on the carpet? To prevent spot from setting permanently, remove it as soon as possible with dry baking soda. Brush the soda into the stain and let it set overnight. Vacuum the following morning.
5. Use dry baking soda on a damp cloth to clean countertops. It is gentle and will not scratch.
6. A little dry baking soda on a damp cloth will polish a toaster or coffee pot to a high gloss.

* * * *

Intricate molds and bundt pans (not teflon-lined) clean up quickly when scrubbed with a vegetable brush.

No more green eggs: rapid boiling cracks the shell and overcooks the yolk. To hard cook eggs, the water should simmer gently for about 15-20 min. Then douse the eggs under cold water to keep the yolks from turning greenish.

When stuffing a chicken or other poultry, insert a heel from a loaf of bread to close the pocket. This eliminates sewing the bird's cavity and dressing stays inside.

Use pastry brush to quickly butter corn on the cob.

When cutting plastic containers or styrofoam, use a heated knife blade. Cutting will be easy and smooth.

The following recipes are lovingly dedicated to the "small fry" in your family, who need a little special attention on those rainy days when they can't go out to play. Let them get involved in the following:

MAGIC CRYSTAL GARDEN

6 Tb water
1 Tb ammonia
6 Tb blueing
6 Tb salt
food coloring
5 pieces charcoal

Mix first four ingredients. Pour over charcoal and scatter the food coloring over. Set the dish for one day in a warm, dry place. It's truly magic!

PLAY DOUGH

3 c salt
6 c flour
3 Tb alum
1 Tb oil
6 c boiling water

Mix dry ingredients. Pour water and oil over and knead well, until smooth. Divide into piles and knead a different color (food coloring) into each one, if desired.

OCEAN WAVES

Mix equal parts of Turpentine, Rubbing alcohol and water tinted blue. Pour into a clear bottle. Glue the cap on. Watch the waves as you tilt the bottle back and forth. Try to describe how they look.

FINGERPAINT

½ c white flour
¼ c water
½ c liquid detergent or liquid laundry starch
food coloring or poster paint

Mix the flour, water, and detergent or starch. Divide into separate bowls and add coloring to each one. Use popsicle stick to spread. Paint!

APPETIZERS

Artichoke Frittata, 13
Avocado Tuna Spread, 8
Bacon & Mushrooms, 1
Bacon Wrapped Dates, 1
Barbequed Ham Bites, 11
Bleached Blond Radishes, 11
Blue Cheese Bites, 2
Cheese Board, 5
Cheese Crab Dip, 14
Cheese Filled Triangles, 15
Cheese & Ham Roll-ups, 7
Cheese Loaf, 8
Cheese Olive Snack, 1
Cheese Puffs, 2
Cheese Yummies, 5
Chili Con Questo, 3
Chinese Meat Balls, 6
Chinese Sweet & Sour Sauce, 12
Clam-Cheese Dip, 15
Crab Grapefruit, 6
Cream Puffs, 4
Corn Beef Roll, 7
Currant-Orange Sauce, 10
Deviled Cheese Filling, 2
Dilly Avocado Boats, 13
Elegant Last Minute Hors D'Oeuvre, 1
Elegant Spinach Dip, 8
Fruit Dip, 3, 14
Frozen Fruit Cocktail Slush, 9
Glazed Almonds, 3
Got-let Chicken Wings, 12
Honeydew Balls, 4
Hot Clam Dip, 9
Hot Stuff, 1
Italian Tuna Dip, 14
Magic Muffins, 5
Marinated Mushrooms, 6
Mexican Bean Dip, 16
Muffins Plus, 10
Onion-Cereal Nut Crunch, 3

Ruby Grapefruit, 9
Shrimp Cocktail, 2
Shrimp Cocktail Dip, 18
Sombrero Bread, 4
Spinach Stuffed Mushrooms, 16
Stuffed Dates, 18
Stuffed Dill Pickle, 8
Taco Chicken Wings, 4
Tex Mex Dip, 17
Toasted Mushroom Rolls, 7
Triscuits, 7
Tuna Cheese Spread, 8
Twin Cheese Mold, 16
Warm Crab Dip, 1
Vegetable Diamonds, 18
Vegetable Dip, 14
Zippy Pineapple Sauce, 10

BREADS

Anadama Bread, 30
Applesauce Pumpkin Bread, 31
Apricot Nut Bread, 31
Bacon Biscuit Balls, 40
Bake Day Surprises, 38
Banana Nut Bread, 33
Bran Bread Sticks, 42
Bread Sticks, 37
Cheese Pimento Biscuit Ring, 27
Cinnamon Rolls, 23
Coconut Pumpkin Bread, 34
Corn Meal Bread, 26
Cranberry Bread, 29
Crescent Layer Herb Bread, 42
Crescent Rolls, 22
Crown Ring Bread, 29
Danish Dumplings, 36
Date Nut Bread, 27
Date Nut Muffins, 36
Dilly Bread, 37
Dry Hotcake or Waffle Mix, 32

BREADS - continued

Easy White Bread, 44
Fabulous French Loaves, 39
Fruity Muffins, 38
Funnel Cakes, 38
German Apple Fritters, 35
German Pancakes, 34
Good Neighbor Loaf, 28
Homemade Pizza, 24
Lemon Loaf, 28
Lemon Nut Bread, 28
Mock Rye Bread, 37
Molasses Whole Wheat Rolls, 25
Mom's Refrigerator Rolls, 26
One Rise Wholewheat Bread, 44
Orange Bowknots, 20
Orange Rolls, 22
Peppy Apple-Cheese Bread, 24
Poppy Seed Rolls, 21
Quick Orange Loaf, 33
Quick Stollen Bread, 32
Rabanadas, 40
San Francisco Sour Dough Bread, 19
Scalidis, 35
Sesame Poppy Seed Loaf, 30
Spudnuts, 43
Star Lite Twists, 25
Supfa Swiss Bread, 26
Sweet Potato Fruit Loaves, 43
Two Hour Rolls, 20
Wheat Bread, 21
Whole Wheat Buns, 39
Whole Wheat Hotcakes, 35
Whole Wheat Rolls, 23
Vegetable Bread, 41
Zucchini Bread, 33

SALADS

Ambrosia, 68
Apple-Strawberry Salad, 55
Apricot Fruit Dressing, 62

Avocado Salad, 63
Beet Salad, 63
Birthday Luncheon Salad, 64
Blueberry Salad, 50
Candied Apple Salad, 52
Catalina Dressing, 65
Cauliflower with Black Olives, 46
Chart House, 1000 Island Dressing, 66
Chicken Iceberg Mexicali, 60
Chicken Mushroom Salad, 63
Chicken Vegetable Salad, 60
Christmas Apple-Cranberry Salad, 68
Christmas Ribbon Salad, 51
Cinnamon Apple Salad , 53
Cole Slaw, 63
Combination Salad, 48
Cranberry Rice Salad, 56
Cranberry Salad, 50
Cucumber Salad with Sour Cream, 48
Dilled Cottage Cheese Dressing, 67
Easy French Dressing, 65
Easy Roquefort Dressing, 67
Five Minute Osterizer Salad, 49
Fluffy Fruit Salad, 55
French Salad Dressing, 62
Frozen Cranberry Salad, 56
Frozen Fruit Salad, 53
Fruity Ham & Chicken Salad, 58
Fruit Pasta Salad, 57
German Salad Dressing, 67
Green Goddess Dressing, 67
Ham Avocado Salad, 60
Herbed Macaroni Salad, 59
Homespun Thousand Island Dressing, 65
Honey-Lime Dressing, 66
Hot Chicken Salad, 59
Italian Marinated Cauliflower, 48
Jello Salad, 49
Lentil Salad, 45
Lemonade Salad, 50
Lemon Salad, 52

Macaroni Shrimp Salad, 57
Marinated Vegetables, 68
Mexican Chef Salad, 61
Midnight Sun Dressing, 65
Orange Fruit Salad, 56
Orange Jello Salad, 49
Orange Sour Cream Salad, 53
Overnight Fruit Salad, 51
Overnight Layered Chicken Salad, 61
Pasta Salad, 57
Patio Salad, 54
Peachy Chicken Salad, 58
Pineapple Dressing, 66
Pineapple Mint Freeze, 49
Potato Salad, 45
Roquefort Dressing, 62
Savory Dressing, 62
Seven Layer Salad, 47
Shrimp Salad, 54
Shrimp Salad Supreme, 54
Special Green Salad, 47
Spinach & Mushroom Salad, 52
Superb Salad, 47
Tabboulah Salad (Lebanese), 46
Tomato Aspic Salad, 64
Tuna-Chicken Salad, 58
Vegetable Set Salad, 64
Waldorf Salad Deluxe, 51
Walking Salads, 55

SOUPS

Austrian Cream Soup, 99
Basic Chicken Stock, 71
Basic Raw Meat Stock, 71
Bavarian Cabbage Soup, 97
Bratten's Boston Clam Chowder, 80
Broccoli Bisque Soup, 87
Calorie Watcher'sMinestrone Soup, 85
Chicken Avocado Soup, 73
Chicken Cabbage Soup, 98

Chicken Velvet, 98
Cioppino, 81
Clam & Avocado Soup, 80
Classic Oyster Soup, 78
Cold Strawberry Soup, 75
Cold Tomato Soup, 70
Corn Cheese Chowder, 79
Corn Chowder, 77
Cream of Cauliflower Soup, 94
Cream of Corn Soup, 79
Cream of Mushroom Soup, 92
Cream of Pumpkin Soup, 98
Cream of Zucchini Soup, 96
Creamy Fresh Carrot Soup, 95
Delicious Stew, 76
Divine Ministrone Soup, 93
Fresh Asparagus Bisque, 100
Fresh Pea Soup, 95
Fresh Tomato Soup, 100
Fruit Soup, 73
Garnishes for Soup, 69
Gaspacho (Spanish), 99
German Bean Soup, 85
Gypsy Chowder, 91
Hamburger Soup, 86
Hearty Soup, 92
Hints on Making Soup Stock, 69
Hotel Utah Borscht, 96
Iced Carrot Soup, 72
Lentil Soup, 92
Manhattan Clam Chowder, 89
Master Beef Vegetable Soup, 88
Mexican Soup, 87
Ministrone Soup, 90
Mongolian Hot Pot, 88
Monterey Jack Cheese Soup, 83
Navy Bean or Lima Bean Soup, 84
Old Fashioned Beef Stew, 75
Orange Cantaloupe Soup, 70
Oxtail Stew, 74
Park City Oven Stew, 76
Pioneer Stew, 77

Potato Ham Chowder, 86
Potato Soup, 95
Print Shop Cheese Soup, 83
Pumpkin Soup, 90
Rocky Mountain Soup, 82
Round-up Stew, 74
Russian Borscht, 94
Scrap Stock, 71
Seafood Soup, 78
Soup Stock with Cooked Meat, 72
Spicy Lamb Meatball Soup, 91
Split Pea-Sausage Ball Soup, 82
Sweet Soup, 73
Summer Peach Soup, 70
Tortilla Cheese Soup, 85
Thrifty Lima Pot, 84
U. S. Senate Bean Soup, 82
Vichyssoise, 72
Warm-up Stew, 76
Yorkshire-Style French Onion Soup, 93
Zucchini Soup, 96

VEGETABLES

Artichokes with Mushrooms, 123
Baked Beans Supreme, 119
Baked Lentil Casserole, 133
Baked Sauerkraut, 106
Best Au Gratin Potatoes, 101
Best Scalloped Potatoes, 103
Broccoli Benedict, 107
Broccoli Lorraine, 118
Brussel Sprout Casserole, 105
Calico Beans, 108
Caramel Sweet Potatoes
Carrot Souffle, 134
Cauliflower & Carrot Medley, 120, 119
Cauliflower in Cheese Puff, 109
Cheese & Mushroom Filling for Crepes, 118
Cheezy Vegetable Platter, 132
Chick-Pea Chili, 110

VEGETABLES - continued

Chinese Vegetables, 130
Company Potato Casserole, 103
Copper Pennies, 115
Cranberry Sweet Potato, 122
Creamed Potatoes, 104
Eggplant Parmesan Frittata, 109
Extra Fancy String Beans, 111
Flemish Carrots, 116
French Pancakes, 117
French Peas, 105
Fresh Spinach Casserole, 134
Gateau De Crepes A La Florentine, 117
Green Beans with Water Chestnuts, 133
Holiday Spinach, 136
Indian Spiced Lentils, 102
Italian Zucchini Crescent Pie, 113
Layered Baked Vegetables, 135
Lemon Green Beans Bechamel, 121
Lima Bean Casserole, 126
Lima Curried Beans, 121
Marinated Mushrooms, 127
Mushrooms Stuffed with Brazil Nuts, 127
Noodles Romanoff, 108
Norwegian Red Cabbage, 107
Oven French Fries, 103
Posh Squash, 102
Potato Puff, 101
Pumpkin Succotash, 112
Ratatouille, 124
Red Cabbage, 108
Refried Beans, 119
Saucy Potatoes & Carrots, 114

Savory Green Beans, 104

Scrumptious Beans, 111
Sesame Broccoli, 112
Simple Squash Delight, 131
Simple Zucchini, 128
Sour Cream Zucchini, 128
Southern Hominy Casserole, 106
Steamed Cauliflower, 107

VEGETABLES - continued

Stir-Fry Beans, 135
Stir-Fry Bean Sprouts, 111
Stuffed Artichokes, 123
Stuffed Baked Sweet Potatoes, 136
Stuffed Cabbage Leaves, 106
Stuffed Mushrooms, 127
Stuffed Tomatoes, 112
Sunshine Carrots, 114
Sweet & Sour Carrots, 120
Three King Vegetables, 129
Tomatoes Oregano, 110
Vegetable Casserole, 135
Whipped Turnips, 130
Wild Rice, 136
Yam Cashew Casserole, 125
Yam Casserole, 122
Yam Souffle, 125
Yankee Roll-ups with Cheese Sauce, 110
Zesty Winter Vegetables, 131
Zucchini Casserole, 104, 128
Zucchini Flats, 113
Zucchini Pizza Pie, 115
Zucchini Tomato Quiche, 126

PASTA & GRAINS

Barley Casserole, 140
Basic Gluten Recipe, 140
Chinese Fried Rice, 137
Chinese Medley, 153
Cracked Wheat Cereal, 143
Creamy Clam Shells, 155
Easy Granola, 143
Fettucini, 151
Fruit-Nut Granola, 144
George Mardikian's Rice Pilaf, 141
Glorified Macaroni & Cheese, 142
Greek Style Manicotti, 154
Green Noodles with Zucchini, 145
Greens and Pasta, 158
Hawaiian Rice, 139
Homemade Egg Noodles, 146
Homemade Noodles, 148
How to Figure Pasta Quantities, 145

Japanese Fried Rice, 137
Jewish Noodles, 146
Kolliva, 143
Linguine with Clam Sauce, 151
Macaroni Beef Casserole, 142
Macaroni Casserole, 144
Micro-wave Rice, 138
Noodles with Cabbage, 147
One Pot Macaroni Supper, 144
One Pot Spaghetti Supper, 149
Old Fashioned Chicken & Noodles, 147
Pasta with Sauce Supreme, 149
Pasta Wheels with Sausage & Tomatoes, 148
Pearl Barley Casserole, 141
Savory Nut Cake, 154
Savory Rice, 138
Shrimp Tetrazzini, 152
Stuffed Manicotti, 146
Toasted Rice Stuffing, 139
Vegetable Lasagne, 150
Wheat & Cheese Casserole, 139
Wheat Stuffing, 138
Wheat Lentil Pilaf, 141

MEATS

Alston Meat Balls, 185
Barbecued Beef, 157
Barbecued Beef Short Ribs, 186
Barbecued Bologna, 173
Barbecued Spare Ribs, 162
Beef & Seven Vegetables, 193
Beef Kebob, 189
Beef Pot Pie, 190
Beef Pot Roast with Lima Beans, 199
Beef Tenderloin, 160
Buffalo Meatloaf, 175
Cherokee Casserole, 178
Chimichangas, 172
Chow Mein, 161
Corned Beef Casserole, 188
Corn Patch Supper Plate, 169
Curried Hamberger, 180

Curried Lamb Chops, 176
Cutlets Supreme, 169
Easy Casserole, 181
Easy Corned Beef & Cabbage, 188
Economy Cabbage Casserole, 181
Enchiladas, 195
Fancy Swiss Steak, 191
Favorite Meat Loaf, 183
Festive Beef Stir-Fry, 192
Fiesta Burgers, 194
Filet of Beef Madagascar, 157
Fruit Stuffed Pork Roast, 164
Ground Beef Stroganoff, 193
Gourmet Corned Beef, 188
Gourmet Stuffed Meat Loaf, 184
Hamburger Casserole, 178
Ham Casserole, 167
Ham in Sour Cream, 167
Ham Hocks with Lima Beans, 168
Ham Loaves, 168, 200
Hawaiian Beef Jerky, 186
Hearty Meal Filling, 170
Holiday Ham & Turkey Combo, 167
Korean Barbecued Short Ribs, 177
Kun Koki (Korean Broiled Steak), 191
Lamb Shanks, 176
Lamb Zucchini Casserole, 198
Lasagna, 181
Lemon Pork Chops, 158
Lentil & Sausage Goulash, 166
Marinated Beef & Vegetables, 177
Marinated Beef Pot Roast, 199
Meat Balls in Marinara Sauce, 187
Meatloaf Wellington, 182
Meatza Pie, 180
Mexican Skillet, 196
Ming's Beef, 189
Most Requested Chili, 197
Most Requested Liver, 171
Old Fashioned Kraut & Frank Stew, 173
Oven Kalua Pork, 164
Paella, 165

Pioneer Stew, 191
Porcupine Balls, 187
Pork Chops, Filipino Style, 158
Quebec Meat Loaf, 183
Quick & Easy Barbecued Spare Ribs, 162
Quick Rouladin, 160
Raised Meat Balls, 185
Rouladin, p. 190
Sauerbraten, 159
Sausage & Zucchini, 166
Sausage n' Apple Baked Stuffed Squash, 169
Savory Sausage Casserole, 171
Savory Spare Ribs & Sauerkraut, 166
Seven Layer Casserole, 178

Spaghetti Pie, 180
Spicy Pork Skillet, 174
Stuffed Pork Chops, 158
Sub Gum Chow Mein, 163
Sukiyaki, 179
Swedish Meat Balls, 184
Sweet & Sour Meatballs, 185
Sweet & Sour Pork, 161
Sweet & Sour Flank Steak, 179
Taco Pie, 196
Teriyaki Steak, 179

Tostada Grande, 195
Venison Pot Roast, 175
Winner Casserole, 192

FISH

Baked Crab Imperial, 203
Baked Fish Hawaiian, 218
Baked Red Snapper, 224
Broiled Fish Steaks or Fillets, 207
Chilled Salmon with Cucumber, 214
Coquilles St. Jacques Au Gratin, 217
Crab Casserole, 220
Creamed Scallops with Grapes, 219

Creamed Shrimp, 215
Creamy Baked Halibut Steaks, 207
Easy Salmon Thermidor, 221
Fancy Fish Dish, 220
Fish A La Canadienne, 204
Fish Fantastic, 204
Fish & Spinach Quiche, 203
Golden Haddock Fillet, 202
Halibut Au Gratin, 202
Halibut or Turbot Casserole, 204
Indian Shrimp Curry, 213
Orange Poached Fish, 214
Oven Fried Fish, 221
Oyster Crisp, 210
Oyster Stew, 210
Quick Salmon Platter, 223
Salmon Loaf, 216
Salmon Scallop Divan, 223
Seafood Fondue, 201
Seafood Newberg, 206
Seafood & Rice Casserole, 205
Seafood Stew, 216
Seven Seas Casserole, 220
Shrimp & Clam Sauce, 219
Shrimp Creole with Rice, 208
Shrimp Delights, 208
Shrimp Newberg, 213
Shrimp Parmesano, 215
Spiced Shrimp, 206
Tempura, 212
Trout Armandine, 211
Trout & Mushrooms in Cream, 211
Trout with Sugar Snaps, 209
Tuna Almond Crisp, 205
Tuna Corn Bake, 218
Wild Rice Casserole with Tuna, 205

POULTRY

Almond Chicken, 241
Almost Kentucky Fried Chicken, 225
Apricot Chicke n, 236
Baked Chicken, 230, 235, 236

POULTRY - continued

Baked Chicken Supreme, 236
Banana Curry Chicken, 240
Breast of Chicken Supreme, 239
Chicken & Cashews, 243
Chicken-Apricot Barbecue, 230
Chicken Aspargus Supreme, 237
Chicken Bean Sprouts & Oyster Sauce, 238
Chicken Broccoli Bake, 233, 237
Chicken Cacciatori, 229
Chicken Casserole, 232
Chicken Cordon Bleu, 239
Chicken Dumplings, 231
Chicken Royale, 234
Chicken Suey, 238
Chicken Montery with Pecan Pilaf, 241
Chicken Tacos with Avocado & Cheese, 226
Chicken & Vegetable Crepes, 228
Creamy Lemon Chicken, 235
Crunchy Chicken Casserole, 229
Crunch Turkey Casserole, 244
Delightful Chicken, 232
Easy Chicken Bake, 233
Hawaiian Chicken, 240
Mexi-Chicken, 229
Nested Chicken, 225
Old Fashioned Chicken & Vegetables, 227
One Pan Turkey & Stuffing, 233
Oriental Chicken Wings, 238
Parmesan Chicken Bake, 234
Quick Turkey or Chicken Pie, 244
Reuben Chicken, 231
Sour Cream Enchiladas, 226
Swiss Turkey Ham Bake, 242
Triple Divan, 227
Turkey Tetrazzini, 242

EGGS & CHEESE

Asparagus Souffle, 263
Basic Crepe, 264
Broccoli-Cheese Quiche, 247
Brazilian Omelet Con Carne, 260

EGGS & CHEESE - continued

Cheese Ball, 255
Cheese & Mushroom Filling for Crepees, 264
Cheese Fondue, 257
Chili Relleno Casserole, 253, 258
Country Omelet, 249
Cream Cheese Roll, 255
Danish Sandwich Puff, 248
Deviled Eggs, 245
Egg Foo Yung with Ham, 251
Eggs Sausage Casserole, 248
Eggs Hussarde, 246
Eggs Piquiant, 260
Fluffy Puffy Omelet, 254
Fresh Mushroom Quiche, 247
Garden Fresh Quiche, 261
Green Bean Scramble, 252
Ham & Cheese Casserole, 258
Heavenly Egg Casserole, 259
Mushroom Souffle, 263
Oven Omelet (Quiche), 252
Pecan Cheese Log, 253
Pizza Buns, 263
Quiche Salsalito Supreme, 245, 247, 252, 261
Rinkum Tiddy on Toast Snippets, 259
Scramble Egg Casserole, 246
Spanish Omelet, 256
South-of-the-Border Brunch Eggs, 251
Spiced Eggs, 258
Sweet Corn Omelet, 250
Taco Scrambled Eggs, 262
Veggie Cheese Ball, 255
Welsh Rarebit, 261

DESSERTS

Baklava, 283
Berry Dessert, 283
Best Ever Apple Pudding, 272
Best Ever Pudding Sauce, 272
Blintzes (Crepes) 281
Bread Pudding, 292
Brownie Pizza, 296

DESSERTS - continued

Burnt Almond Fudge Icecream, 266
Canadian Vanilla Icecream, 267
Caramel Fondue, 269
Cherry Chocolate Dessert, 270
Cheese Cake, 295
Chocolate Angel Dessert, 270
Chocolate Cinnamon Torte, 279
Chocolate Dessert, 270
Chocolate Eclairs, 276
Chocolate Fondue, 269
Chocolate Icecream, 273
Chocolate Mint Dessert, 275
Chocolate Refrigerator Dessert, 270, 273
Chocolate Sour Cream Dessert, 272
Coconut Torte, 275
Date Pudding, 289
Date Refrigerator Dessert, 284
Easy Apple Crisp, 271
Easy Mint Chocolate Chip Icecream. 267
Easy Sherbet, 266
Egg Nog Icecream, 265
English Trifle, 293
Fancy Summer Dessert, 287
Festive Christmas Icecream, 273
French Mint Dessert, 273
Fresh Apricot Icecream, 268
Fresh Fruit Pizza, 295
Frozen Pumpkin Squares, 294
Frozen Strawberry Dessert, 286
Fruit Cocktail Dessert, 271
Fudgesicles, 266
Hawaiian Five-O-Torte, 280
Heavenly Hash, 284
Holiday Meringue Torte, 277
Icecream, 265
Jello-Pineapple Fluff, 285
Lemon Angel Food Dessert, 282
Lemon Fluff, 282
Lemon Meringue Dessert, 282
Mexican Sweet, 281
Mini-Cheese Cakes, 269
Norwegian Rice in Cream, 292

DESSERTS - continued

Nut Brittle Icecream, 267
Old-Fashioned Apricot Cobbler, 290
Orange Dream Dessert, 285
Orange Raisin Rice, 292
Peach Cobbler, 290
Peppermint Candy Icecream, 267
Pineapple Sherbet, 268
Pineapple Snow Balls, 287
Pistachio Dessert, 284
Plum Pudding, 291
Popsicles, 266
Raspberry Angel Cake, 286
Raspberry Icebox Dessert, 288
Raspberry Icecream, 265
Refreshing Fruit Pizza, 293
Rhubarb Crisp, 271
Rhubarb Icecream, 268
Rice Custard Pudding, 278
Sachertorte, 274
Schaum Torte, 278
Strawberry Crepes, 288
Strawberry Icecream, 265
Steamed Gumdrop Pudding, 289
Steamed Holiday Pudding, 291
Vanilla Icecream, 265
Vanilla Refrigerator Pudding, 288

CAKES

Almond White Fruit Cake, 316
Angel Clouds, 313
Apple Cake, 312
Applesauce Wedding Cake, 311
Boiled Frosting, 320
Boiled Raisin Cake, 298
Bottoms-up Gingerbread, 305
Candy Carnival Frosting, 320
Caramel Icing, 319
Carrot Cake, 301
Cherry Cake, 300
Cherry Chocolate Roll-up, 323
Chocolate Chiffon Cake, 307
Chocolate Pound Cake, 302
Chocolate Roll, 321
Chocolate Sheet Cake, 302
Cinnamon Butter Bundt Cake, 313

Cranberry Puff Cake, 301
Devil's Food Cake, 308
Dream Cake, 297
Easy Chocolate Log, 307
Easy Choco-Almond Roll, 318
Easy Orange Cake, 298
Easy Penuche Frosting, 319
Fourteen Karat Cake, 303
French Banana Cake with Mix, 303
French Butter Icing, 319
Fruit Cocktail Cake, 309
German Chocolate Cake Frosting, 319
Italian Cream Cake, 303
Light Fruit Cake, 317
Little Fruit Cake, 314
Lunar Rhubarb Cake, 309
Mint Frosting, 320
Mantero's California Fruit Nut Loaf, 314
Oatmeal Cake, 308
Old Fashioned Jam Cake, 310
Orange Coconut Pound Cake, 299
Orange Pecan Cake, 300
Orange Cake Supreme, 306
Pennsylvania Dutch Apple Cake, 310
Poppy Seed Cake, 306
Pound Cake, 298
Prune Cake, 311
Pumpkin Roll Cake, 297
Quick Orange Refrigerator Cake, 304
Ready Frosted Chocolate Cake, 322
Rhubarb Cake, 324
Sea Foam Frosting, 319
Snow Peak Frosting, 317
Sponge Cake, 299
Spoof Raisin Cake, 308
Texas Pecan Cake, 304
Toasted Spice Cake, 312
Twinkie Cupcakes, 305
Unbaked Fruit Cake, 316
Walnut Raisin Spice Cake, 315
Whole Prune Cake, 311
Zucchini Chocolate Cake Deluxe, 324

COOKIES

Almond Brownies, 340
Best of All Chocolate Chip Cookies, 344
"Better Than Robert Redford" Squares, 345
Bishop's Squares, 339
Butterscotch Brownies, 340
Butterscotch Cookies, 327
Brownies, 338
Cashew Carmel Yummies, 336
Choco-Marshmallow Brownies, 338
Chocolate Drops, 347
Chocolate Macaroons, 347
Chocolate Mint Cookies, 326
Coconut Butter Chews, 326
Corn Flake Macaroons, 328
Dad's Cookies, 325
Date Cherry Squares, 334
Date Crumbles , 334
Double Chocolate Cookies, 347
Dream Bars, 330
English Toffee Cookies, 326
Finnish Almond Bars, 335
Fresh Orange Chewies, 336
Fruit Cocktail Cookies, 335
Fruit Nut Squares, 339
Fruit Pinwheel Cookies, 348
Fruit Refrigerator Cookies, 329
Ginger Snaps, 348
Great Pumpkin Squares, 329
Gum Drop Cookies, 341
Hello Dolly Cookies, 329
Honey Scotch Cookies, 328
Jim Dandy Cookies, 343
Lemonade Cookies, 343
Lemon Bars, 337
Marzipan Bars, 333
No Bake Skedattles, 329
Oatmeal Carmelitas, 338
Oatmeal Macaroons, 348
Old Fashioned Oatmeal Cookies, 345
Orange Date Bars, 331
Orange Frosted Carrot Drops, 342
Pargas Ginger Cookies, 346
Peanut Blossoms, 344
Peanut Butter Criss-Crosses, 342

COOKIES - continued

Peanut-butter Oatmeal Cookies, 332
Pineapple Bars, 333
Pineapple Cherry Squares, 332
Refrigerator Oatmeal Cookies, 332
Sesame Bars, 340
Sesame Seed Cookies, 327
Spicy Raisin Bars, 331
Soft Cookies, 328
Sugar Cookies, 328
Tea Time Tassies, 325
Terzel Tarts, 325
Thumb-print Cookies, 341

PIES

Angel Pie, 356
Apple Pie, 369
Banana or Coconut Cream Pie, 358
Baked Alaska Pie, 367
Black Bottom Crust, 349
Black Bottom Pie, 370
Canned Peach Pie, 368
Cider Custard Pie, 351
Cheese Cake, 350, 352
Cherry-Rhubarb Pie, 363
Cherry Pie Supreme, 364
Chess Pie, 354
Chocolate Cheese Cake, 352
Chocolate Cream Cheese Pie, 353
Coconut Custard Pie, 365
Crunchy Cookie Crust, 349
Dream Pie, 357
Easy Pineapple Pie, 361
Flaky Pie Crust, 350
French Silk Chocolate Pie, 358
Fresh Apricot Peach Pie, 362
Frozen Fruit Pies, 365
Graham Cracker Crust, 349
Heavenly Lemon Pie, 356
Huckleberry Pie, 364
Icecream Pie, 365
Impossible Pie, 367
Jello-Cheesecake Pie, 353

PIES - continued

Lemon Meringue Pie, 354
Lemony Mince Meringue Pie, 371
Libby's "Most Famous Pie of All", 359
Lip Smackin' Cherry Pie, 351
Marshmallow Pumpkin Pie, 357
Mince Chiffon Pie, 371
Never Fail Pie Crust, 349
Orange Chiffon Pie, 355
Orange-Marshmallow Cracker Pie, 355
Pineapple Pecan Pie, 370
Pumpkin Cheese Pie, 350
Pumpkin Chiffon Pie, 359
Pumpkin Icecream Pie, 360
Raspberry Pie, 368
Raisin Pie, 372
Rhubarb Cream Pie, 361
Rhubarb Strawberry Pie, 361
Ritz Cracker Pie, 356
Royal Coconut Pie, 360
Simple Fresh Peach or Strawberry Pie, 366
Soda Cracker Pie, 356
Sour Cream Lemon Pie, 366
Southern Pecan Pie, 392
Strawberry Mallow Pie, 362
Swiss Apple-Cherry Pie, 366
Three Minute Pie Shell, 351
Traditional Lemon-Lime Pie, 363

CANDY

Almond Bark Supreme, 393
Almond Brittle, 384
Almond Crunch, 393
Almond Toffee, 384
Basic Cream Fondant, 373
Bavarian Mints, 374
Brown Sugar Nut Roll, 374
Brown Sugar Fondant, 373
Buckeyes, 379
Buttermints, 389
Butterscotch Drops, 387
Candy Chews, 388
Caramels, 385, 387
Caramel Apples, 395

CANDY - continued

Caramel Crunch, 396
Carmelized Corn Puffs, 397
Chewey Licorice, 376
Chocolate Carmels, 378
Chocolate Fudge, 378,381, 383, 390
Cinnamon Cereal Balls, 400
Coconut Balls, 397
Coconut Date Balls, 392
Cotlets, 399
Cracker Jack, 398
Creamy White Fudge, 380
Creme De Menthe Squares, 387
Dipped Pretzels, 393
Divinity, 379
Elegant Chocolate Candy, 382
English Toffee, 377
Fondant, 373, 375
Frosted Nuts, 399
Fruit Chews, 386
Glazed Almonds, 395
Hidden Treasure Popcorn Surprise, 397
Honey Taffy, 377
Hot Spiced Nuts, 393
Karo Crazy Crunch, 394
Kraft Balls, 379
Little Angel Marshmallows, 388
Marshmallows, 391
Micro-Peanut Brittle, 392
Micro-Butterscotch Cashew Crunch, 390
Miracle Caramel Corn, 396
Olympian Cremes, 375
Oven Popcorn,397
Peanut Brittle, 382
Peanut Butter Cups, 389, 395
Pecan Roll, 377
Penuche, 376
Pineapple Fondant, 375
Popcorn, 394
Popcorn Balls, 394
Popcorn with Jello, 394
Rocky Road Candy, 385
Sea Foam, 374
Taffy, 377
Torrone Nougat, 386

CANDY - continued

Water Fondant, 373
White Christmas Fudge, 380
Yum Yum Balls, 398

SAUCES

Bagna Cauda Sauce, 402
Bearnaise Sauce, 407
Big Mac "Secret" Sauce, 405
Brandy Sauce, 410
Burnt Sugar Sauce, 414
Caramel Sauce, 412
Cheese Sauce, 401
Chocolate Carmel Sauce, 415
Chocolate Fudge Sauce, 414
Cordon Bleu Sauce, 411
Egg Nog Sauce, 413
Foamy Rum Sauce, 413
Fresh Tomato Salsa, 405
Green Herb Sauce, 408
Gourmet Basting Sauce, 403
Ham Sauce, 405
Hard Sauce, Plain & Fancy, 413
Hollandaise Sauce, 407
Homemade Mayonnaise, 404
Horseradish Sauce, 406
Hot Fudge Sauce, 415
Hot Sauces & Variations, 405-407
Italian Seasoning, 409
Lemon Sauce or Frosting, 410
Marchand De Vin Sauce, 407
Mustard Sauce, 406
Quick Tartar Sauce, 404
Raspberry Sauce, 410
Savory Cheese Sauce, 408
Seasoned Salt, 412
Shallot Dressing, 402
Shellfish Cocktail Sauce, 404
Spaghetti Sauce, 401
Spicy Barbecue Sauce, 403
Sweet Cherry Sauce, 412

SAUCES -continued

Sweet & Sour Sauce, 409
Super Spaghetti Sauce, 416
Teriyaki Basting Sauce, 401
Teriyaki Sauce, 406
Tomato Barbecue Sauce, 403

PRESERVES

Apple Marmalade, 432
Apple-Pie-In-A-Jar, 427
Apricot Jam, 422
Apricot Leather, 423
Apricot Nectar, 427
Beef Vegetable Soup, 431
Canned Apricot Filling, 428
Canned Tomato Soup, 424
Cantalope Pickeles, 429
Chili Sauce, 417
Chopped Pickles, 419
Chutney, 422
Delicious Pickles, 419

Easy Dill Pickles, 419
Family Favorite Dills, 421
Frozen Creamed Corn, 426
Frozen Fruit Cocktail, 428
Frozen Fruit Pies, 429
Frozen Peaches, 431
Frozen Peach Pie Filling, 427
Hot Dog Relish, 418
Maraschino Cherries, 425
Mock Mince Meat, 424
Mock Raspberry Jam, 430
Mustard Pickles, 420
Nine-Day Sweet Pickles, 421
Orance Spiced Peaches, 417
Peach Compote, 428
Peach Conserve, 432
Pepper Sauce, 421
Pickled Beets, 424

Prune Conserve, 425
Pumpkin Apricot Butter, 431
Raspberry Jam, 430
Raspberry Peach Jam, 432
Refrigerator Pickles, 419
Rhubarb Gelatin Jam, 426
Rhubarb Strawberry Sauce, 425
Strawberry Jam, 425
Sweet Dill Pickles, 420
Tomato Catsup, 424
Tomato Salsa, 418
Tomato Soup, 426
Zucchini Relish, 418

POT POURRI

Almond Punch, 433
Batter Dip (Cornmeal), 451
Beef Stew (Quantity), 452
Bird Seed, 440
Breading (Cornmeal), 451
Breakfast Pick-up, 438
Buttercream, 447
Buttercream Bread Spread, 447
Chili from Scratch, 450
Chocolate Banana Blitz, 434
Cooking Terms, 461, 462
Corned Beef Log, 439
Crunchy Baked Bananas, 440
Cucumber Tomato Frost, 438
Curried Turkey, 454
Diddle Daddle, 446
Equivalents, 458
Falafel, 445
Fingerpaint, 464
French Fried Onions (Cornmeal) 451
Fresh Peach Drink, 436
Fruit Punch for 80, 454
Frosty Orange Nog, 435
Green Mayonnaise, 453
Herb Bread, 447
Holiday Wassail, 436
Holly Berry Wassail, 433
Honey Butter, 447, 448, 449
Honey Root Beer, 434

Hot Buttered Lemonade, 437
Hot Chocolate Mix, 441
Hot Fruit Punch, 433
Hot Grape Drink, 435
Hot Luncheon Sandwich, 444
Hot 'n Snappy Tomato Cocktail, 438
Lemon Curry Sauce, 456
Lemon Sesame Butter for Veggies, 448
Liverwurst Hero Loaves,444
Magic Crystal Garden, 464
Make-Ahead Layered Mushrooms & Eggs, 456
Marinated Vegetable Medley, 453
Mexican Hero Sandwich, 442
Mexican Mix for Tacos, 439
Mormon Champagne, 434
Ocean Waves, 464
Old English Citrus Nog, 436
Orange Butter, 448
Orange Julius, 435
Oven Dried Jerky, 449
Pita Bread Sandwiches, 445
Play Dough, 464
Potatoes Au Gratin, 450
Potato Salad, 452
Pumpkin Seeds, 446
Punch-for-the-Bunch, 433
Quick Root Beer, 434
Raspberry Frappe, 435
Rich French Chocolate, 441
Salami from Scratch, 443
Scrambles, 446
Servings for 50 people
Sloppy Joes, 439
Stretch-a-Nog, 437
Substitutions, 459, 460
Sweetened Condensed Milk, 448
Tomato Refresher, 438
Tropical Wheelies, 439
Using Baking Soda, 463
Using Corn Meal, 451
Vinegar & Lemon, 460
Yogurt, 440
Ways to Perk Up Your Meals, 457
Yorkshire Pudding, 441

ıe ideal gift for birthdays, weddings, Christmas, or
ıy other time you want to say "You're Special".

CENTURY OF MORMON COOKERY
4 Sunwood Lane
andy, utah 84092

Phone (801) 576-1369
Fax (801) 576-1950

---

order form

A CENTURY OF MORMON COOKERY
14 Sunwood Lane
Sandy, Utah 84092

Please send _____ copies of A CENTURY OF MORMON COOKERY
cookbook at $16.95 plus $3.50 for handling and mailing.

Makes checks payable to A CENTURY OF MORMON COOKERY

Name ____

Address ____

City & State ______________________________ zip __________

---

order form

A CENTURY OF MORMON COOKERY
14 Sunwood Lane
Sandy, Utah 84092

Please send _____ copies of A CENTURY OF MORMON COOKERY
cookbook at $16.95 plus $3.50 for handling and mailing.

Makes checks payable to A CENTURY OF MORMON COOKERY

Name ____

Address ____

City & State ______________________________ zip __________

Notes

Notes

Notes

Notes